New Visions in Foreign and Second Language Education

New Visions in Foreign and Second Language Education

Edited by
Gerd Bräuer
Karen Sanders

LARC Press
San Diego
2004

Printed in the United States of America.

Text design by Maria Ortega
Cover Design by Maria Ortega

Published by LARC Press
5500 Campanile Drive, San Diego, California 92182-7703

Table of Contents

List of Contributors

Theresa Austin	University of Massachusetts Amherst, Massachusetts
Gerd Bräuer	Emory University Atlanta, Georgia
Adrian Butler	European Centre for Modern Languages Graz, Austria
Christine M. Campbell	Defense Language Institute Monterey, California
Svenja Dahlmanns	University of Education Freiburg, Germany
Rolf Dubs (emeritus)	University of St. Gallen St. Gallen, Switzerland
Rebecca K. Fox	George Mason University Fairfax, Virginia
Catherine C. Fraser	Indiana University Bloomington, Indiana
Marjorie Hall Haley	George Mason University Fairfax, Virginia
Dierk O. Hoffmann	Colgate University Hamilton, New York
Britta Hufeisen	Technical University of Darmstadt Darmstadt, Germany
David Jahner	Gwinnett County Public Schools Lawrenceville, Georgia
Michael Langner	University of Fribourg Fribourg, Switzerland
Betty Lou Leaver	Coalition of Distinguished Language Centers Monterey, California

Maria D. Lekic	University of Maryland College Park, Maryland
Peter Lenz	University of Fribourg Fribourg, Switzerland
Randall J. Lund	Brigham Young University Provo, Utah
Nicole Marx	Technical University of Darmstadt Darmstadt, Germany
Peter Merrill	Phillips Academy Andover, Massachusetts
Andreas Müller-Hartmann	University of Education Heidelberg, Germany
Terry A. Osborn	University of Connecticut Storrs, Connecticut
Manfred Prokop (emeritus)	University of Alberta Alberta, Canada
Karen Sanders	Adult Basic Skills Program Portland, Oregon
Marita Schocker-v. Ditfurth	University of Education Freiburg, Germany
Johanna Schwarz	Innsbruck High School Innsbruck, Austria
Joseph Sheils	Council of Europe Strasbourg, France
Amy Snyder Ohta	University of Washington Seattle, Washington
Lee Wilberschied	University of Cincinnati Cincinnati, Ohio
Sharon Wilkinson	West Virginia University Morgantown, West Virginia
Dieter Wolff	University of Wuppertal Wuppertal, Germany
Helene Zimmer-Loew	American Association of Teachers of German Cherryhill, New Jersey

Introduction: New Visions in Foreign and Second Language Education?

Gerd Bräuer

Focus of the Publication

This book has come a long way. Originally conceptualized as the fourth volume in the series *Advances in Foreign and Second Language Pedagogy* (Ablex Publishing), I envisioned this text as a continuation of the many discussions generated in the process of editing the second volume of the same series, *Pedagogy of Language Learning in Higher Education* (2001). At several points, colleagues expressed the need for an additional anthology on language instruction in primary and secondary schools. It seemed necessary to examine these areas, in order to better inform instruction in college foreign and second language classrooms. After all, college students bring unique language learning experiences from their grade school careers and, as teachers, administrators, parents, and citizens, many will eventually influence the next generation's attitude toward language learning.

In 2000, I learned of a movement with the ambitious goal of redefining the field of foreign language education. This movement, known as *New Visions,* is housed at the National K-12 Foreign Language Resource Center (Iowa State University) and run by the American Council on the Teaching of Foreign Languages (ACTFL). This initiative challenged me to reshape my original plan for the manuscript into a more complex discussion around the future of foreign language education, including the architecture of the profession, curriculum, instruction, articulation, assessment, research, and teacher development, recruitment, and retention. In the original *New Visions* initiative, each of these areas was assigned to a separate task force, yet all five groups had one unifying goal: to formulate a national agenda for foreign and second language education. As it states on the current homepage of what is now called the *New Visions in Action* initiative <www.educ.iastate.edu/newvisions>:

> New Visions is an innovative series of actions that both involves and impacts the entire academic foreign language community in the United States. It is broad in scope, ambitious in goals, and far-reaching in its long-term impact. Most importantly, it is structured to yield significant and achievable results: graduates of US schools who demonstrate foreign language competency. (12-12-02)

In order to reach this goal, between 1998 and 2000, a steering committee developed a set of questions to be answered in the coming years by members of the profession. These included:

> What would it take? By exploring: What could we do? (a compendium of possible action steps), What should we do? (identify priorities among the possible action steps), What will we do and who will do it? (deciding upon specific actions and taking responsibility for carrying them out). (12-12-02)

In 2001, after initially analyzing the current state of the profession and its major challenges, the *New Visions* initiative moved into a new phase. Four task forces developed national and regional schedules to put into practice what had been identified as the most pressing needs for change. The *New Visions in Action* website describes the goals of its task forces as follows:

Curriculum, Instruction, Assessment, and Articulation
(The goal of this task force is) to produce online and paper documents that synthesize information about available learning strategies, assessments, curriculum and program models to guide and inform local decision making.

Professional Development
(...) to identify and define the key components that might be included in a national foreign language teacher education program for pre-service teachers and a national agenda for professional development for in-service teachers.

Research
(...) to make research accessible to a broad constituency who influence and shape the teaching and learning of world languages and cultures.

Teacher Recruitment and Retention
(...) to assure a linguistically competent and culturally diverse American society by recruiting, supporting, and retaining a qualified world-language teaching force. (12-12-02)

Goals of the Publication

While reading *New Visions in Action,* some may wonder why this volume would focus on an initiative which, as Lee Wilberschied points out in her introduction to part five of this book, "provides focus, cohesion and effort at the national, or macro, level," rather than focusing on a discussion of changes in our daily classrooms. I made this choice because, as Wilberschied also points out, "participation at this level will help to engender efforts at other levels—national, regional, state, and local." I see the writing and reading of this book as a way to participate on the *macro level*, and to hopefully inspire changes across our profession.

For this very function—bridging the gap between a national initiative and individual classroom practice—the new home of this publication, LARC Press at the Language Acquisition Resource Center, San Diego State University, is ideal. Instead of reserving a lonely place for this book on the shelves of the few libraries that can still afford to buy hardcover editions from academic presses (which would have been the outcome of the original concept), I hope this anthology will be affordable and accessible. I hope it will find its way into the hands of student teachers, teaching assistants, and colleagues in grade schools, colleges and universities. Hopefully, while reading and writing in and with this book, we will enable ourselves to answer some of the questions raised by the *New Visions* initiative. At the same time, we will understand more about the importance and impact of our daily classroom efforts on the future of the profession.

International Scope

In order to initiate a more diverse dialogue around organizational strategies, theoretical concepts, and classroom practices, the contributors to this book take the discussion of *New Visions in Action* to an international level.

Looking at the state of current European foreign and second language education and research, three issues seem to be especially challenging for the *New Visions* task forces mentioned above:

- Early foreign language education.
- Multilingualism in primary and secondary schools.
- Reflective practice.

Let me provide one example that illustrates these three challenges. In times of vanishing borders in Europe (though Switzerland is not yet a member of the EU), the area of the Upper Rhine, between Basel (Switzerland), Mulhouse (France) and Freiburg (Germany), as one can imagine, is *breathing* multilingualism. For the residents, in order to be able to take advantage of this intersection of cultures and languages, it is essential to start learning the languages of one's neighbors as early as possible. As we all know, Switzerland alone carries four official languages! Yet, parents, kindergarten/pre-school and primary school teachers still have much to learn about what happens to a child who grows up surrounded by multiple languages. It is easy to imagine similar multilingual living situations in cities like Los Angeles, San Francisco, and New York, where many might never take advantage of the mingling of languages and cultures for personal growth or language learning, but rather only go to the *other* neighborhood to enjoy *exotic* foods and music.

For those with an interest in early language learning, whether it be on the Upper Rhine or in a multicultural US city, an MA Program on the Pedagogy of Early Language Learning has recently been conceptualized. The program is a collaborative effort between all Universities of Education in the state of Baden-Württemberg and the University of Gießen (situated in the state of Hessen). Their program will be tested, evaluated, and further developed during the coming years before being officially launched in 2006. The hope is to enable participants to improve their own foreign language competency, to understand theory and practice of language acquisition, to research aspects of classroom practice, and, finally, to successfully run both traditional and alternative early language education in a fruitful marriage. This program will also consider that learners in regions such as the Upper Rhine are introduced to more than one foreign language at a time. Students in a multilingual environment usually possess a wealth of skills and knowledge about the functioning of languages and language learning that is rarely tapped in traditional language education.

Finally, in order to maximize one's own learning potential, students must be aware of the resources available to them. Therefore, another important component of the MA Program on the Pedagogy of Early Language Learning is reflective practice. A version of the European Language Portfolio, specifically developed at the University of Gießen for early language learners, will help students and teachers to better understand learning processes and learner biographies.

As indicated above, topics such as the development of an early language learning methodology, the analysis of theoretical and pedagogical concepts for multilingualism in early education, and the European Language Portfolio are all inspirational models for the further improvement of language instruction in the US.

Furthermore, with the help of this book, the most recent insights of *New Visions in Action* on topics such as professional organization, learner diversity, technology, teacher development, recruitment, and retention, have the potential to significantly impact and benefit the quality of future language education in Europe.

Audience and Structure of the Book

This publication contains articles, statements, and conversations, from both the European and US perspectives, on many of the key topics of the *New Visions* initiative. This book also includes interviews of former and current task force members, as developed by student teachers of foreign/second language pedagogy in Germany and finally written and conducted by one of them, Svenja Dahlmanns. With this chosen format, which includes pre-reading, while-reading, and post-reading questions, I am hoping to foster an inspirational exchange of thoughts and ideas far beyond the dialog of those who created this publication. I believe that this imaginary conversation between the readers and writers in teacher training seminars, classroom research projects, reading logs, proposals for curriculum development, teaching portfolios. has the potential to be a springboard for future collaboration among scholars, classroom practitioners, and administrators. The intensive collegial exchange I witnessed and experienced myself while working on these manuscripts via the Internet, sometimes thousands of miles apart, seems a promising beginning for this transatlantic exchange.

This book is primarily directed at foreign language student teachers and in-service teacher training participants in the US. These groups represent the driving force behind any significant change in foreign language education as proposed by the *New Visions in Action* initiative. However, as the international scope of the book suggests, it also targets future and current language educators overseas. With this diverse audience in mind, I asked all contributors to introduce the theoretical, practical, and organizational frameworks of their projects in *global* terms that are easy to interpret across different educational systems.

The first part of the book, *Architecture of the Profession,* is introduced by Helene Zimmer-Loew, a long-time board member of the American Association of Teachers of German (AATG). This is followed by an interview with her about why it is so important to invest efforts in the organizational structure of a professional field. Maria Lekic, Betty Lou Leaver, and Peter Merrill deepen the insight into the topic by showing, based on the case of the American Council of Teachers of Russian (ACTR), the potential of a strong architecture for the further development of what is the core of our profession: classroom practice, research, and teacher training. In Europe, the architecture of the profession looks quite similar but yet is very different from that seen in the United States. A conversation with Joe Sheils, Language Policies Division at the Council of Europe (Strasbourg, France), and Adrian Butler, European Centre for Modern Languages (Graz, Austria), provides details on educational and institutional structures in Europe and should inspire future transatlantic collaboration.

The second part of the book, *Curriculum and Instruction,* is opened by Marjorie Hall Haley, whose introduction to learner diversity and technology covers two important aspects of the original *New Visions* task force. In addition, an interview with her includes the current *New Visions in Action* extension, *Articulation and Assessment* (see chapter three). The chapter by Catherine Fraser and Dierk Hoffmann expands the conversation toward technology in the foreign and second language classroom, by looking at collaborative learning in virtual space connecting projects of experiential learning in the US and in Europe. Dieter Wolff opens up another topic central to current curriculum development: bilingual instruction and autonomous learning. In his article, he shows how constructivism can provide a helpful theoretical framework for making bilingual instruction and autonomous learning happen successfully in Europe. Autonomous learning, seen this time from a more institutional point of view, is discussed in an already existing transatlantic collaboration between Michael Langner and Manfred Prokop on the inclusion of a self-access language facility in a language center.

In part three, Theresa Austin and Christine Campbell examine *Articulation and Assessment.* In their article, they respond directly to the increasing call for accountability in American language education. Randal Lund follows with a chapter on language portfolios in the US. He discusses the further development of the portfolio method for language instruction in light of its European counterpart. This European approach is presented by Peter Lenz, one of the key figures in the development of the European Language Portfolio, now administered by the Council of Europe. While the two previous chapters are more theoretical and conceptual in nature, this section closes with a dialog between Johanna Schwarz and Gerd Bräuer on the potential of portfolio work in the daily practice of teaching in the foreign and second language classroom on both sides of the Atlantic.

Part four of the book, *Research,* is introduced by Sharon Wilkinson, who focuses on how knowledge about language acquisition can be fostered through research. In her interview, Wilkinson describes ways of making research outcomes available to language practitioners, with the goal of raising the understanding of language learning and, through that, the overall quality of language education. An example for the mingling of theory and practice, languages, and academic disciplines within the field of foreign and second language education can be found in the transatlantic collaboration between Nicole Marx and Britta Hufeisen, who shed some light on the phenomenon of multilingualism and its main theoretical concepts, research methods and didactics. In a conversation with Amy Snyder Ohta, she provides an introduction to Lev Vygotsky's *zone of proximal development*. Her introduction helps teachers identify the skills required to push learners to their limits and make language education more effective. One important approach to shaping the profession on a long-term basis, is the understanding and use of action research, as promoted by Lee Wilberschied in her chapter on integrating research into daily classroom practice. The multifaceted collaboration between theory and practice, disciplines, languages, cultures, and nations is exemplified in the chapter written by Nicole Marx and Britta Hufeisen, who focus on the phenomenon of multilingualism and its main theoretical concepts, research methods and didactics.

The last part of the book, *Teacher Development and Recruitment,* brings together once again the main topics of the previous chapters, this time from the perspective of teacher training: What needs to be changed in the way we prepare our next generations of language educators in order to let our new visions on the architecture of the profession, curriculum and instruction, articulation, assessment, and research become reality? The final part of the book begins with an introduction by Lee Wilberschied and an interview with her on the potential of *New Visions in Action* for change with regard to teacher development and recruitment. It is followed by Andreas Müller-Hartmann and Marita Schocker-v. Ditfurth, who look at technology-enhanced project work and the autonomous student teacher in Germany. Marjorie Hall Haley and Rebecca Fox then discuss teacher candidates in the US and their role as continuing language learners. They examine issues related to the further development of language proficiency of teacher candidates. Terry Osborn provocatively asks *Corpus disciplinae?,* and critically reviews contemporary language teacher preparation in the US, of which an example is presented by David Jahner, who introduces a support system for new language teachers in Gwinnett County (Georgia) public schools.

At the conclusion of this volume, we come back to where we started: the architecture of the profession. This time, however, we do not look at the large organizational level, but rather at the level of the individual institutions. *Instead of an Afterword* contains a chapter by Rolf Dubs on institutional development. In his article, Dubs suggests the theoretical framework and practical implications of how to run quality management in school development. Through his definitions of the key terms of quality management in school development, he provides a language to teachers that is necessary in order to appropriately discuss the future of our schools.

Working with the Book

As you explore the pages of this book, you will notice very quickly that this collection is about *asking questions*. After all, even the title of this book could embody a question: *New Visions in Foreign Language Education*? The simple reason for this questioning lies in the topic of this publication: *New Visions*. New ideas may be obvious to their creators, but we as readers are always wise to question these ideas, in order to clearly understand their premise. Curiosity and doubts are other reasons to question what has been presented to us, afterall, not all ideas are really new and truly visionary. And please remember, the authors in this book come from different countries. Therefore, they not only represent different cultures and languages, but they also may have very different opinions on foreign language education. So, in some cases, you may think you understand, because what has been said makes sense to you. Nevertheless, you may experience a murky feeling of not being quite sure whether you understood the author's idea in its entirety. Therefore, keep asking yourself (in writing), your peers, teachers, and the authors of this book, on both sides of the Atlantic. Drop them a line via the Internet, tell them what you think about their stances on education, praise their ideas and courage in bringing them forth, but also question their ideas, share your own opinion, and ask for more *food for thought*.

To help you get involved with the topics in this book, three sets of questions were developed:

Pre-reading questions are for focusing your mind on the chapters to be read, and for connecting with your own knowledge and experience. What is this part of the book about? What do I already know about it? What experience do I have with it as a language student and/or (future) teacher?

While-reading questions foster understanding and an open mind for the immediate context of what has been read. What did the author just say? Do I really understand? What other ideas and opinions are being presented in this book related to the topic I am currently reading about?

Post-reading questions help to summarize what has been read, and to make sense of it again on a personal level. What does this all have to do with me? Did I read what I expected when I answered the pre-reading questions? How much do these new ideas influence my own knowledge and experience? Will there be consequences for my own learning and teaching?

In addition to these three sets of questions there are a number of interviews, conducted by Svenja Dahlmanns with representatives of the *New Visions* task forces and by Gerd Bräuer with foreign language researchers and administrators from both sides of the Atlantic. Read these interviews from your perspective. What would you have asked? What else would you like to ask these people? Any questions for Svenja and Gerd? Or to Karen Sanders who primarily wrote or edited the pre/while/post reading questions?

To develop true ownership of what you have been working on during the pre-, post- and while-reading questions, we would like to suggest the following special working modes:

Summarize what you read. What is the main information of a particular text?

Comment on the summaries of your peers and have your summaries regularly commented on by your peers. In this way you can make sure that you truly understand what you read. Take the clarity of your summaries as the most important sign of your own construction of knowledge.

Experiment with ideas presented in this book. Before each reading, brainstorm, cluster, or freewrite about the topic you are going to read about. After the reading, map out the concepts and ideas of the chapter you read. Brainstorm, cluster, or freewrite to explore the connections to your own practice as a foreign language learner and to your (future) career as an educator.

Reflect on your personal insight. Follow your intuition and the emotional relationship between what you have read and your own experience as a language learner and teacher. Take note of what the inspirations in this book *feel* like to you.

Dialogue with yourself and/or develop a conversation with members of your professional field. Let yourself be inspired by the interviews in this book, and ask your own questions about your future as a professional.

Contextualize what you have read. Collect other readings, teaching materials, and personal notes for each topic of the book you find personally challenging or interesting. Make this collection part of your seminar portfolio, teaching portfolio or start a special portfolio where you map out your personal view on our profession.

One last suggestion, writing, especially the kind of reflective writing mentioned above, is demanding and not always easy to accomplish if done alone. Get feedback on your writing as often as possible. Show it to your peers or colleagues and ask them if they understand your message. Go to the writing center at your institution and use the professional feedback offered by writing tutors. If you prefer to do that more anonymously, use the online tutoring services offered at <www.ph-freiburg.de/schreibzentrum>. This site gives you an opportunity to connect with student teachers from Germany who themselves experience foreign language education in all facets. Please do not get discouraged by the fact that the site is mainly written in German. Simply write your questions in English to <schreibzentrum@ph-freiburg.de> and well-trained writing tutors will respond in English. If you are a student of German, try out what you have learned. Good luck!

Acknowledgements

It is my pleasure to thank first and foremost Betty Lou Leaver who encouraged me to continue with this project after Greenwood Press decided to discontinue all academic series' inherited with the acquisition of Ablex Publishing. I would also like to thank Mary Ann Lyman-Hager, director of LARC, for providing a wonderful new home for this book. I would also like to thank Maria Ortega, editor of LARC Press, for the endless hours spent on copy-editing and layout. I also want to express my sincere gratitude to my long-time friend and colleague, Karen Sanders, who jumped in as a co-editor on short notice with enthusiasm at a time when I felt rather unsure about the outcome of this publication project. Collaborating with you was a great pleasure, Karen! Thanks also to all the students of my foreign and second language pedagogy classes during my DAAD professorship in Freiburg, Germany, who, with great enthusiasm read early drafts of book chapters about the *New Visions* task force and provided excellent feedback. I would especially like to thank Svenja Dahlmanns, still a student herself, who then drafted and conducted interviews with representatives of *New Visions in Action*. Last but not least, I thank all the authors of this volume for their creative work, patience, and collegiality.

Freiburg (Germany), July of 2003
Gerd Bräuer

Chapter 1
Architecture of the Profession

Chapter one of this publication will introduce you to the organizational structure of the field of foreign and second language education in the US and Europe. The authors show some of the current obstacles within the architecture of our profession on both sides of the Atlantic. Based on creative ideas from both sides, they discuss ways by which individuals can help to further develop foreign and second language teaching and learning.

Pre-Reading Questions

1. *What do you know about the organizational structure of your (future) profession? Brainstorm.*

2. *Draw a mind map of the profession showing the different areas you might have experienced as a language learner.*

3. *In another color, add to your mind map the areas of the profession you believe are necessary for language educators.*

4. *Mark all areas in which you are currently active.*

5. *Indicate the areas of your mind map of the profession in which you are (or might be in the future) interested in actively participating. Ask yourself how this additional involvement could influence your current work.*

6. *A profession that is truly alive encourages its members to continuously improve themselves as professionals and will support them in this endeavor. Looking at your mind map, locate possible resources for your current work, and ask yourself how extensively you have been using them. Choose one resource you think of as important for your work in the future and brainstorm how you could use it.*

Introduction to the New Visions Initiative: The Architecture of the Profession

Helene Zimmer-Loew

New Visions in Foreign Language Education is a process begun in 1998 by the National K-12 Foreign Language Resource Center (NFLRC) at Iowa State University and the American Council on the Teaching of Foreign Languages (ACTFL).

Its creators envisioned the project as an innovative series of actions that both involves and impacts the entire academic community of foreign language educators. Its original goal was to revamp and strengthen the teaching and learning of languages, as well as the language education structure, in order to produce a high level of foreign language competence in the graduates of US schools, colleges, and universities.

NOTE

Founded in 1967 by the Modern Language Association of America, ACTFL remains the only national organization representing teachers of all languages at all levels of education. Its vision is that all Americans should be proficient in at least one language and culture, in addition to English. Take action—search the ACTFL web site <www.actfl.org> for information that can help you in your development as a professional.

The New Visions Steering Committee divided the work of the participants at the project's two meetings (June 1999 and June 2000) into five categories: Architecture of the Profession; Curriculum, Instruction, Articulation, and Assessment; Teacher Development; Teacher Recruitment and Retention; and Research.

A number of participants began the development of a new *Architecture of the Profession* that would facilitate the creation of a national agenda for foreign languages. This agenda, based on a set of agreed-upon core principles, would result in a collaboratively developed vision, mission statement, and rationale. To accomplish this goal, four integrated strategies were identified:

- Development of processes that would support continued collaboration among a variety of foreign language organizations
- Establishment of a strong continuous public relations program for the field of foreign languages
- Development of a centralized electronic database for the profession
- Review and possible reconfiguration of the present structure of foreign language organizations

Since education in the United States is in the purview of the states, and there is no centralized or mandated national language policy or national agenda, professional language organizations have assumed the role of policy–makers through several collaborative structures.

The first of these is the *Joint National Committee for Languages* (JNCL) and the *National Council for Languages and International Studies* (NCLIS). Since 1976, JNCL has provided a forum for cooperation and discussion among language professionals. What began as an informal coalition of eight national language associations now brings together over sixty organizations encompassing virtually all areas of the language profession: the major and less-commonly taught languages (including English as a second language), bilingual education, the classics, linguistics, translation, interpretation, research, and American Sign Language. Most national, state, and regional organizations are active members. The mission of JNCL-NCLIS is to support the member organizations that are united in the belief that all Americans must have the opportunity to learn and use English and at least one other language. Over the years, an effective and successful strategy for shaping language policies has evolved in JNCL. This broad coalition serves as the forum where the associations can discuss, develop, and create unified public policy positions about professional issues affecting the schools, higher education, research, technology, teacher development, standards, multiculturalism, governmental programs, business use, exchanges, and a myriad of other professional concerns with public policy implications. NCLIS then seeks to mobilize the necessary support and influence policy makers to create the actual national (and, recently, state and local) laws, regulations, and administrative decisions that constitute public policies.

DISCUSS

Discuss the strategies used by the JNCL-NCLIS and other collaborative structures mentioned in this article to shape language policies. What is the role of the local language professional in the shaping of state and national policy?

Another coalition was begun by ACTFL with the AATF, AATG, and AATSP. In 1996 the four organizations published *Standards for Foreign Language Learning: Preparing for the 21st Century*. As this initial project was ending, the four associations expanded the group so there are now nine members in the *National Foreign Language Standards* Collaborative, together representing close to 40,000 foreign language educators: American Association of Teachers of French (AATF <www.aatf.org>), American Association of Teachers of German (AATG <www.aatg.org>), American Association of Teachers of Italian (AATI <www.italianstudies.org/aati>), American Association of Teachers of Spanish & Portuguese (AATSP <www.aatsp.org>), American Classical League (ACL <www.aclclassics.org>), American Council of Teachers of Russian (ACTR <www.americancouncils.org>), American Council on the Teaching of Foreign Languages (ACTFL <www.actfl.org>), Chinese Language Association of Secondary-Elementary Schools (CLASS <www.classk12.org>), Chinese Language Teachers Association (CLTA <http://clta.deall.ohio-state.edu>), National Council of Japanese Language Teachers (NCJLT <www.colorado.edu/ealld/atj/ncjlt>), and Association of Teachers of Japanese (ATJ <www.colorado.edu/ealld/atj>). The collaborating partners not only expanded their membership but also the original generic document to include K-16 students and language-specific (Chinese, Classical Languages, French, German, Italian, Japanese, Portuguese, Russian, and Spanish) standards in a volume called *Standards for Foreign Language Learning in the 21st Century* (1999).

CONSIDER

Consider joining a professional organization. These groups can *give you the support you need to fully realize the potential of your status as a professional*, as ACTFL states in its vision.

Additional examples of collaboration include ACTFL's annual meeting of its Delegate Assembly which consists of representatives of all fifty state organizations, the five regional language associations, most language-specific associations, the National Council of State Supervisors of Foreign Language, and the National Association of Directors and Supervisors of Foreign Language, among others. For several decades, the AATG, ATJ, AATI, and CLTA have met jointly with ACTFL at its annual meeting.

DISCUSS

Helene Zimmer-Loew describes several efforts at collaboration in the language teaching field over the past several years. Discuss why continued collaboration is important for the future of the profession.

CONSIDER

Watch for more information on the work of *New Visions in Action* in the following chapters. As you learn more about the work in each area, remember that together curriculum, instruction, assessment and articulation; research; teacher recruitment and retention; and professional development are the *architecture of the profession.*

Over the past three decades there have been several major efforts to reduce duplication and coordinate the work of the profession, beginning with the Modern Language Association's *A National Foreign Language Program for the 1970s*. The MLA proposed a seven point program that would unify and provide visibility for the entire profession. In 1980 ACTFL proposed the *Prolegomena to the Future of ACTFL and the Foreign Language Profession: ACTFL as a Unifying Force*. A press release in March 1990 for the Northeast Conference and ACTFL was entitled *Professional Unity Efforts Initiated*. In 1983 David Benseler writing in the Northeast Conference Reports proposed an American Language Association. In 1984 the National Executive Service Corps analyzed ACTFL's position among language associations with respect to possible areas of conflict, collaboration, and duplication with other organizations. The Report of the President's Commission *Strength Through Wisdom* in 1979, perhaps the most dramatic public document to influence foreign language teaching in that decade, called for a unified presence for foreign language organizations in Washington, DC and hence the establishment of JNCL-NCLIS.

CONSIDER

Will the current generation of leaders have the will to develop and implement the vision of a new professional structure or set of structures? This question, posed by the author of this article, is one to keep in mind as you read the other thoughts and visions expressed in the remainder of this volume.

Recently, the New Visions Steering Committee renamed the project *New Visions in Action*. The ACTFL logo no longer appears on the project's letterhead. Four Task Forces, each with a chair, have been formed to carry out the work of *New Visions in Action: Curriculum, Instruction, Assessment, and Articulation; Research; Teacher Recruitment and Retention; and Professional Development*. The *Architecture of the Profession* has been eliminated as a separate category, perhaps subsumed and implied in each of the four remaining task forces.

It is not for a lack of determination on the part of leaders in the profession over the years that the role of professional language associations has been reviewed and discussed. The question now is whether this generation of leaders will have the will to develop and implement the vision of a new professional structure or set of structures.

Interview with Helene Zimmer-Loew

Svenja Dahlmanns

Svenja Dahlmanns (SD)
What should a new member, let's say somebody like me, a graduate from a teachers' training program, know about the *architecture of the profession* in order to make the most out of it?

Helene Zimmer-Loew (HZ-L)
It is important to know the structure of one's profession to gain an understanding of where one is in the hierarchy and where one can eventually exert influence on the profession as a whole. It is particularly important to understand the structure in order to articulate from level to level. Often K-12 teachers don't know what goes on in higher education, and vice versa, to the students' detriment. We also learn from each other's organizations.

SD
Let's pretend someone starts her career as a teacher of German. What should she know about the AATG, the organization you worked for as Executive Director for many years? Where are the places this young teacher could bring herself actively into the work of AATG in order to add diversity?

HZ-L
The young teacher should know what services, publications, and programs the organization offers, many of which are inexpensive and unavailable elsewhere, and many created by other teachers of German. The chapter structure of AATG (60 in US and 1 in Europe) provides the teacher a place to meet other teachers and to involve themselves in the chapter programs and structure. This is where leaders for the most part are discovered and trained in the ways of an organization. There is a great need for new young blood, and AATG has implemented a program called *TraINDaF* (Transatlantisches interkulturelles Nachwuchsförderungsprogramm Deutsch als Fremdsprache) to find young potential leaders to get involved at the chapter, regional, and national level.

CONSIDER

Check out the material section in this volume for further information on *TraINDaF*. Ask yourself if you would be willing to commit yourself to working for a professional organization. To learn more about TraINDaF, visit: <http://www.mtholyoke.edu/acad/germ/aatg/zugdaf.html>

SD
What are the most important benefits in joining a regional chapter of the AATG as a beginning High School teacher of German?

HZ-L
The networking aspect is important, as are the organized activities for teachers and often for students. Many chapters hold immersion days, *Sprachfeste*, chapter compe-

titions, and the like for students. Other than our annual meetings, there is no event in most areas of the country at which a teacher of German can meet others. Most school districts have only one teacher of German, and many colleges have a small German faculty as well.

SD
What should this beginning German teacher know about ACTFL and the role of AATG within ACTFL? In what ways does ACTFL extend this teacher's professional opportunities beyond what she already gained through her membership in AATG?

HZ-L
ACTFL is an independent partner of AATG. We are in no way (nor is any other FL organization) beholden to ACTFL. AATG has cooperated with ACTFL in mounting their annual meeting since the late 1960s. ACTFL serves as the organization that gets the US federal funding for which we are either ineligible or too specific. We work with ACTFL collaboratively, e.g., in areas of proficiency, student standards, beginning teacher licensing, among others.

SD
The *Architecture of the Profession* seems to be a big organizational project with large expenses. What are the general principles for financing the expenditure?

HZ-L
Since there has not been any major movement in this direction, there have been no expenditures. If there were, none of us could afford such large amounts of money, at least at this time. Ironically, we could all save money by collaborating more, but to date there has been no willingness or discussion to do so.

SD
In your introduction to this chapter, you list national organizations such as the JNCL (Joint National Committee for Languages) and the NCLIS (National Council for Languages and International Studies), that existed since 1976. What are the fields of action in which the *New Visions Initiative* works that are not covered by these organizations? Or, in other words, what made it necessary, in your opinion, to initiate *New Visions*?

HZ-L
JNCL-NCLIS, particularly the latter (which is an advocacy coalition), is not a policy-making organization. It concentrates mainly on listening to what the field needs at a given time and on going to Congress to develop and push through legislation which will meet those needs. *New Visions* was created to fill that policy-making gap and to focus on major themes. Also, the US does not have a national language policy or any group structure (governmental or non-governmental) to develop such a policy.

SD
In your introduction, you stated that reconfiguration and the avoiding of duplication in organizing the professional field is necessary. Restructuring also means eliminat-

ing parts of the old structure. Sometimes people are not easily willing to give up or even share the responsibility for what they created. I was wondering if you anticipate any resistance, especially on the local level, when organizational structures are being more centralized, as planned by *New Visions*?

HZ-L

There is no doubt that a restructuring of the profession will be difficult and may never happen. Instead, we have formed a FL Collaborative which has moved ahead in publishing K-16 student standards in 9 languages and has developed standards for teacher education programs through NCATE on behalf of ACTFL (a good example of where ACTFL is recognized as the *lead organization*). The Collaborative has also been active behind the scenes in supporting the development of the National Board of Professional Teaching Standards and the standards for beginning teacher licensure (INTASC).

CONSIDER

Read the interview with Lee Wilberschied in chapter five of this volume and summarize what she has to say about professional teaching standards. Also, check out the material section in this volume for additional information on NCATE.

SD

It seems difficult to lead the different foreign language associations toward an intensified cooperation. How can negative competition concerning funding, number of students, ideas, and political influence be avoided within the professional field of foreign language teaching?

HZ-L

We compete with each other as organizations for members-teachers at all levels who are not willing to join/attend ACTFL, their state association, a regional conference, their AAT, or other specifically-focused organizations. They simply do not have the time or funds and therefore choose whichever organization(s) serves them best. We also compete for students at the school/institutional level, and students choose where they want to study, depending on what has influenced them. I don't sense as much competition for funding since AATG would rarely go to a US agency for support, since we have the governments of German-speaking countries as a resource. Political influence is JNCLs task, and all the member organizations compromise on legislation for the greater good, e.g., support of less commonly taught languages vs. Spanish, French, and German.

SD

How does a language organization measure the accomplishments of its work? Do you regard increasing numbers of enrollments and of teaching positions as a sign of success?

HZ-L

We at AATG receive many compliments on the high quality of our services, publications, and programs. We believe we are doing a great job supporting those who teach German out there. If we depended on the number of students and members at this point in time, we'd be disappointed since the number of students and positions are stable or decreasing. I think the other organizations have a similar attitude about their work. The feedback from their members is the most important criterion. There is nothing we can do that we haven't already tried to get more students in German classrooms!

CONSIDER

Brainstorm ideas to recruit and keep students interested in learning a foreign language. Also, remember how you became a foreign language student yourself.

SD
In your introduction, you listed the most commonly taught foreign languages. Obviously, the focus of what has been taught has shifted in the past decade. Before then, the emphasis was on European languages, whereas presently there is a clear tendency in North America towards Asian languages and Latin American Spanish. What does this shift mean in regard to the teaching of European languages and cultures? Even though US liberal arts college education still seems to focus greatly on European traditions, the teaching happens more and more often in English, and not in the language of the target culture. How should we interpret this trend?

HZ-L
Despite an overt interest in teaching/learning languages other than the European languages, students learn very quickly how difficult many of the less commonly taught languages (LCTLs) are and how long one has to stay with them in order to develop a minimum level of proficiency. There is always a substantial number of students at all levels who want to learn the European languages, and until we have a large cohort of teachers who are proficient enough to teach those LCTLs, institutions will stay with the European languages.

NOTE

FTE means full-time equivalency. FTE represents the percentage of a full-time teaching load.

Needless to say, none of us is pleased to hear that classes on German topics are being taught only in English. There are just so many protests that one can lodge about this failure on the part of colleges and universities. Many faculty are trying to keep a decent FTE in their departments and have therefore compromised the language, perhaps in hopes of attracting some of those students to a German language class.

SD
Once, when I was watching TV in the US, I was surprised by a commercial that advertised the importance of becoming a member of the teaching profession by strikingly demonstrating the great influence of good teachers on society. Something similar seems unimaginable for German TV for various reasons. I am wondering: *What are the specific goals for getting the media involved in the work of Public Relations Programs?*

CONSIDER

Read the chapters about early language learning and bilingual education by Wolff, Oomen-Welke/Karagiannakis, Legutke, and Marx/Hufeisen.

HZ-L
The Foreign Language Collaborative has pledged $40,000 toward the development of a public relations campaign for foreign language instruction, another good example of how we do cooperate for the common cause. At the present time, only 44% of grade 7-12 students and 8% of college students are involved in foreign language study. We also want to push for beginning language instruction in kindergarten and studying languages until 12th grade and beyond.

It will be interesting to see what the public relations firm and those of us who have been giving them ideas will come up with as far as themes that we believe the general public will find alluring for promoting language study! I'm assuming that meeting other people through learning languages, travel to other countries, good career opportunities, knowing your heritage, fun, economic competition, and national security, will be on the list of reasons.

SD
In Germany, we encounter a major problem with the integration of non-academic immigrants (from Russia or African countries, for example), because they often do not gain the needed language skills in German. What is the role of foreign language organizations in reaching the goal of ensuring that everybody is able to communicate in English?

HZ-L
Of course, TESOL is heavily involved in teaching English as a Second Language, and does belong to JNCL-NCLIS. Also the AATSP and ACTFL have developed publications and materials to assist teachers in teaching the mother tongue (Spanish, mainly) to heritage learners. In general, professional foreign language organizations do not get directly involved in teaching English to immigrants.

SD
Many people nowadays think that it is important to communicate with your enemies and understand the cultural contexts of political and religious tensions. What has changed after 9-11 for foreign language organizations in the promotion of cross-cultural learning?

HZ-L
Other than a large infusion of funds and efforts into government programs for the languages we all know are critical (examples: Defense Language Institute and Foreign Service Institute), I don't see any increased involvement in cross-cultural learning. Most teachers were infusing that element into their courses before 9-11 and will continue to do so.

The Role of Language-Specific Professional Organizations in Teacher Education and Support: The Case of the American Council of Teachers of Russian (ACTR)

Maria D. Lekic
Betty Lou Leaver
Peter Merrill

Language-specific professional organizations can play a substantial role in teacher education and support, and the *American Council of Teachers of Russian* (ACTR) provides an exemplary case in point. ACTR brings together primary, secondary, and university-level teachers in order to improve the teaching of Russian language and culture, foster professional growth, and assist teachers and institutions in dealing with the pressing issue of rapidly changing enrollments at both the secondary and post-secondary levels. The programs and activities of ACTR extend well beyond those of most similar professional organizations and may therefore serve as a developmental model for other language-specific professional associations for less commonly taught foreign languages.

The relatively small size of the Russian teaching field in the US creates both opportunities and challenges for the profession. With approximately 2,500 full- and part-time specialists and practitioners at public schools, universities, and private language schools at all levels, the Russian language teaching profession in the United States is small enough to facilitate easy communication among its members. ACTR seeks to take advantage of these demographics to encourage cooperation among school teachers and higher education professionals through joint projects, training programs, conferences, and publications addressing the interests and professional needs of both groups. Recent ACTR conferences, newsletter articles, and projects have focused, for example, on the uses of technology for teacher development at all levels; the significant changes in the norms of spoken and written Russian since the collapse of the Soviet Union; and the elaboration of an effective school-to-university transition curriculum for use by students and teachers of Russian at upper-secondary through early tertiary levels of education.

DISCUSS

The authors mention that the size of the Russian language teaching profession in the US is small enough to facilitate easy communication among its members. Discuss any challenges faced by professional associations for less commonly taught foreign languages such as Russian.

The series of ACTR projects focused on school-to-college articulation over the past ten years serves as an example of what is understood in this context as an *action-oriented professional organization*. Among American professional associations for teachers, one may distinguish between traditional organizations with membership responsibilities such as conducting an annual convention, publishing a journal and/or professional newsletter, and distributing a portion of annual dues to local or regional chapters of the national association, and the *action-oriented* professional associations, groups which work in cooperation with the traditional associations to implement specific projects required by the profession, such as the development of standards, curriculum, organization of teacher development workshops and seminars, design and implementation of exchange programs, collaboration with colleagues abroad, and advocacy efforts at the national level in support of the professional field.[1] In the case of the Russian language professions in the US, many professionals elect to belong to both the traditional membership organization and ACTR.

NOTE

This paragraph provides an excellent example of the advantages that emerge from collaboration, as described in the article by Helene Zimmer-Loew.

The interests of the student and of the profession are best served when the student succeeds in navigating the critical juncture between secondary school and university study of Russian. *Success* for the student (and the high school program) is usually defined as placement at the university level into a course in which the student's previous accomplishments and demonstrated competencies in the field are acknowledged. *Success* for the university program means placing the student among a group of learners more or less at the same level of competence in Russian. ACTR has addressed the widely recognized articulation issue in US education by developing and promulgating language-specific standards for learners and for teachers, as well as assessment instruments for use in the placement process, through extensive organizational cooperation with the National Foreign Language Standards Collaborative.

The ongoing collaboration between ACTR and the National Foreign Language Standards Collaborative has had two major outcomes to date: first, it has ensured the inclusion of Russian among those modern foreign languages for which national standards are available; second, it has guaranteed alignment of the Russian-specific standards with those of the eight other major world languages, which were published together in a single volume in 1999. As a result, a new generation of standards-based curricular materials and assessment instruments for teacher training, as well as teacher and program evaluation, has begun to emerge, including the National Board for Professional Teaching Standards (NBPTS), World Languages Other than English Standards (2001), and the ACTFL Program Standards for the Preparation of Foreign Language Teachers: Initial Level (2002). The future of Russian in the US depends on its inclusion as a specific subject area in the nationwide effort for standards development in American education in general.

The elaboration of the Russian-specific K-12 standards and the current ACTR program to expand those standards to K-16 are examples of approaches to field development undertaken by ACTR which may be of use to other foreign language fields, including the commonly taught languages with their larger learner bases. The Russian Language Advanced Placement Curriculum and School-to-College Articulation Test, now being field-tested by ACTR and the College Board, will be the first standards-based national placement examination in a modern foreign language in the US. The leaders of the other national foreign language associations are in regular contact with ACTR and the College Board to explore the possibility of extending the Russian model to both smaller and larger language groups in the US. That collaboration is now formalized through the workings of the National Standards Collaborative, of which ACTR is a charter member, and a newly created Foreign Language Advisory Committee of the College Entrance Examination Board in New York, the organization responsible for the Advanced Placement testing in all fields.

History and Description

Founded in 1974 as an association for area and language professionals, the American Councils for International Education and its daughter organization, the American Council of Teachers of Russian (ACTR), have focused their expertise on the design and implementation of academic exchange, professional training, distance learning, curriculum and test development, delivery of technical assistance and consulting services, research and evaluation, and institution building.

NOTE

New Visions in Action is a project involving a wide range of educators in a collaborative effort to improve their profession. Through professional organizations such as ACTR, foreign language professionals have the strong and stable support necessary to improve service delivery throughout the country.

Originally incorporated as ACTR, American Councils has worked to advance research, training, and materials development in the fields of Russian and English, as well as strengthen communication within and among the communities of scholars and educators in language, literature, and area studies of the United States and the former Soviet Union. In 1987, the ACTR Board of Directors created the American Council for Collaboration in Education and Language Study (ACCELS), which quickly became a leader in the design and administration of US-Eurasian exchange and training programs funded by the US government.

In its four decades, American Councils has developed into one of the premier American education and international training organizations, administering more than 30 exchange and training programs, including US government programs and non-US national fellowship programs. The organization develops collaborative and partnership programs between individuals and institutions in the United States and the countries of Eurasia, Eastern Europe, Southeast Europe, consults on project design and education innovation programs, and actively contributes to the development of Eurasian language and area studies in the United States. The organization maintains its commitment to the teaching of the Russian language, with over 100,000 textbooks and educational materials sold, and 6,500 Russian-language learners registered online through its RussNet web resource.

Since the early 1980s, ACTR has been an active institutional member of the Joint National Committee for Languages (JNCL) and the National Council for Languages and International Studies (NCLIS). ACTR officers have been elected to positions on the Board of Directors of JNCL and to the organization's executive committee. JNCL-NCLIS has helped to provide a consistent and strong voice for the foreign language profession as a whole in Washington DC, functioning as an instrument for raising public awareness about foreign language issues.

In its in-service education programs, ACTR provides support for school in-service and university faculty in six areas. These include:

- Teacher instruction and professional growth
- Publication of textbooks and support materials
- Development of classroom and independent study resources
- Development of standards and instrumentation
- Research
- Advocacy

Teacher Instruction and Professional Growth

One of the most popular and long-lasting ACTR programs is the seven-week Summer Teachers' Institute in Moscow and St. Petersburg. The Summer Teachers' Institute has been the principle vehicle for K-12 teacher development since 1986. For the past sixteen years, ACTR has sent 15-25 teachers abroad annually, in the early years to the Herzen State Pedagogical Institute (now Russian State Pedagogical University)[2] and to Moscow State University since 1998. The program places teacher-participants in small groups, based on each participant's Russian language proficiency, and focuses on development of linguistic skills, cultural knowledge, and methodological expertise. The programs are intensive and demanding. Formal classroom work occupies six hours per day and is conducted by leading specialists in Russian as a foreign language; excursions to various points of cultural and historical interest are exclusively in Russian; and most participants elect to reside for the duration of the program with a Russian family. The Summer Teachers Institute is funded by the US Department of Education (Fulbright-Hays Group Projects Program) and open to qualified American teachers on a competitive basis. The summer program complements other summer, semester, and academic year programs administered by ACTR on site in Russia and the other Russophone states of the former Soviet Union for undergraduate students, graduate students, and researchers.

DISCUSS

As you read the section on teacher instruction and professional growth, compare your personal priorities/expectations in this area with those of the authors. Discuss both similarities and differences with others.

For teachers who cannot travel to Russia, annual stateside summer institutes for teacher training are offered at the Russian Language Institute of Bryn Mawr College, a major institutional partner of ACTR, since 1976. These summer programs have received funding from the Dodge Foundation, the Ford Foundation and other private funds, as well as from public moneys provided by the National Endowment for the Humanities (NEH), and are co-administered by the Center of Russian Language and Culture (CORLAC) at Friends School in Baltimore. Unlike most stateside summer institutes which are four weeks in duration, the Russian Language Institute lasts 8-weeks. Like their counterpart programs in Russia, the Bryn Mawr summer institutes for teachers are taught exclusively or primarily in Russian and feature a strong language development or language maintenance component, with formal class work in small groups and daily language skills enhancement seminars. Other seminars include materials development and methodology, both of which are large-group formats and are conducted in Russian. Visiting specialists from the US, Europe, and Russia are invited to lecture or lead seminars at the Bryn Mawr Institute on a regular basis, where cultural immersion activities ranging from screenings of films, miniature theatricals and musicals, field trips, and explorations of Russian cooking and cuisine are a regular part of the programming. The institutes offer a total immersion

ACTION

Interview someone who has participated in an institute similar to that described in this chapter. What positive and negative experiences did that person have? In your opinion *who* benefits from such programs? How?

experience with native-speaker tutors and faculty in a specially designated *Russian* residential facility, although no *language pledge* is required. Teachers improved their language skills at the institutes and returned to their home schools with materials specifically developed and tested for their own students, as well as a network of colleagues available for consultation.

For the past 20 years, ACTR has also invited exchange teachers from Russia to the United States to work as classroom partners with US teachers of Russian as part of its Curriculum Consultants Program. Curriculum Consultants are visiting appointments normally lasting one semester or academic year. Based on the requirements of the US host school or university department of Russian, ACTR draws on a network of institutional partners in the Russian Federation with experience in teaching Russian as a foreign language to identify candidates for short- or long-term placements at US programs. Selection of candidates includes observation of classes and evaluations provided by US students who have attended courses in Russia taught by the candidate. American teachers benefit from the professional expertise of the visiting teacher-specialists, as do the American students and colleagues, who frequently praise the energy, intellect, and *insider view* of Russian culture brought to their institutions. Visiting consultants, in turn, benefit from the experience of teaching in a different academic environment, and typically return to their home university or school programs with a better understanding of US teaching practices and of the psychology of the American learner of Russian.

The ACTR Curriculum Consultant Program has been in operation since 1984 and is provided under the terms of a formal agreement with the Russian Ministry of Education. Beyond the obvious direct benefit to programs and individual teachers and students, the ACTR Curriculum Consultant Exchange has led to larger-scale collaborations between US and Russian teachers, such as the development of new curricula or new partnerships between American and Russian institutions. For example, the respected collaborative series, *Russian Faces and Voices* (Dabars, Lutskaya, and Morris, 1997) was the result of a Curriculum Consultants collaboration between high-school teachers from the United States and authors and illustrators from Russia.[3]

ACTR-sponsored professional development programs are also made available to teachers through conferences and grant-funded projects. For example, in the summer of 1999, teachers using the newly developed business Russian textbook, *Russkii jazyk v delovom obshchenii "Russian for Business Communication"* (Klobukova et al., 1997) and the accompanying set of online modules[4] attended an ACTR-sponsored teacher conference led by the authors of the project. ACTR conducts a number of trainer conferences each year for Russian teachers, primarily to support head teachers and other professionals charged with teacher training in their respective school districts or university departments. These programs are typically supported by grants to ACTR from the US Department of Education.

Another venue for direct professional outreach is provided through the several annual foreign language teacher conferences with which ACTR and the Russian language are associated, such as AAASS, ACTFL, AATSEEL, and the National Council of Less Commonly Taught Languages. For example, ACTR sponsors several panels at the annual meeting of the American Council on the Teaching of Foreign Languages (ACTFL), in which high school teachers may participate both as panelists and as participants.

Still another form of Russian teacher support was provided by ACTR through the Partners in Education Program (PiE), a US Department of State Bureau of Educational and Cultural Affairs-funded bilateral exchange with Russia and Eurasia, one of several governmental exchange programs administered in both countries by ACTR. This project paired individual schools, one in the United States and one in Russia. For one month, educators from the Russian school visited the American school, and the following year, the US educators visited the Russian counterpart. The American students (and their teacher) attended classes in the Russian school and lived with Russian host families. Both the hosting and the visiting experiences brought American teachers into close professional contact with Russian counterparts on a wide range of educational issues, such as integrating language study into other academic disciplines, democratic institution building, civic education, and using information technology in the classroom. Teachers reported positive benefits for their language skills, knowledge of Russian culture, and awareness of contemporary culture. Some schools and teachers chose to continue the relationship on an informal, self-funded basis after the period of federal funding for the partnership had ended.

RussNet, the Russian language network established by ACTR, is a Russian language field resource center. The site <http://www.russnet.org> provides Russian language learning services and products—information, language learning modules, courses, materials, in-service teacher training, databases, discussion forums, and gateways to other Russian language resources. RussNet has teacher guidelines online. ACTR employs two specialists in technology-based language learning, exclusively assigned to RussNet to provide direct assistance (by telephone or E-mail at <RussNet@actr.org>) to any teacher using Russnet.

ACTION

Explore the *russnet.org* web site. Is it clearly organized and easy to use? Do you have any suggestions for changes or additions? How would you use such a resource in your own teaching?

RusTeach is a listserv maintained and moderated by ACTR for teachers of the Russian language. The listserv allows them to share expertise and answer questions about teaching issues, both for the benefit of new teachers just learning the ropes as well as experienced instructors.[5]

ACTR represents the United States in the work and activities of the International Association of Teachers of Russian Language and Literature (MAPRIAL), a non-profit, non-governmental international organization of Russian teaching organizations and programs around the world. Headquartered in Moscow at the renowned Pushkin Institute, MAPRIAL publishes an international professional journal (*Russkij jazyk za rubezom*) and a newsletter, organizes the International Congress of Russian Teachers and Scholars every four years, and conducts a popular international contest for high school learners of Russian, the High School Russian Language Olympiada, held in Moscow every third year. MAPRIAL activities are open to university and school teachers of Russian and provide opportunities to present work, share experiences, and network with counterparts from the more than 60 nations around the world where Russian is taught.[6]

ACTR is the primary vehicle in the United States for study abroad programs for school and university students, teachers, graduate students, and researchers in Russia and the successor states of the former Soviet Union, as well as central and southeastern Europe. Each year more than 500 Americans travel to the region under ACTR sponsorship for language study, research, or teaching assignments for periods ranging from two to twelve months, on programs funded privately or by the US government. Given the inherent complexities in administering programs for US citizens in the region, ACTR maintains a network of field offices throughout Russia, eastern and southeastern Europe, and Eurasia to oversee programs, both logistically and for purposes of guaranteeing participant safety and academic integrity. In Russia, ACTR offices can be found in Moscow, St. Petersburg, Ekaterinburg, Novosibirsk, Nizhny Novgorod, Samara, Volgograd, and Vladivostok. In all, the organization operates 47 offices in 17 countries, with a multilingual local and expatriate staff of 330 in the field offices and 100 in Washington DC. Institutional partner relationships include more than 800 US and NIS schools, academies, universities, governmental, and non-governmental partners.

The *ACTR Letter*, the quarterly newsletter of ACTR, edited by George Morris, a prominent and now-retired high school Russian teacher from St. Louis, is also used as a means of indirect instruction. Each newsletter contains a 4-12 page section, called *Classroom Potpourri*, in which teachers share lesson plans and classroom activities that have been successful. Each issue begins with a debate column, *Front Page Dialogue*. Every 2-3 years a direction for discussion is introduced, and teachers debate various aspects of the topic. The *Front Page Dialogue*, a refereed column, serves to bring to the attention of the field new ideas that are yet to be published elsewhere. Professional colleagues from other language fields and related academic disciplines, such as cognitive psychology, have frequently contributed. Contributions have included theoretical and practical articles concerning the teaching and acquisition of Russian, case studies, classroom-based research, and longitudinal investigations.

In 1999, ACTR compiled and updated the *Front Page Dialogues* of the last twelve years in a collection of articles with supporting commentary and reference material on each topic (Leaver 1999). Most contributors from earlier years updated their contributions in light of the responses published in the ACTR Letter to their earlier work as well as new research findings pertinent to their topics. Secondary school teachers have participated in the *Front Page Dialogue* since its inception, and the edited volume contains contributions from a number of high school teachers.

Twelve Years of Dialogue on Teaching Russian (1999) and the Russian-specific standards component of the *National Standards for Modern Foreign Languages* (1999) join a distinguished list of prior ACTR publications, including the Soviet-American

Conference series on the study and teaching of Russian, to form the core materials which support student-teacher education in the nation's colleges and universities in the field of Russian.

Publications

ACTR textbooks range from high school readers to specialized textbooks to reference volumes to materials for the development of teachers' own skills and knowledge. ACTR produces handbooks, dictionaries, grammars, and materials on Russian culture, as well as specialized readings for those preparing to study abroad in Russia. A number of ACTR books have been written specifically for high school teachers, for example, a reference grammar (John L. Watzke and James W. Sweigert, Jr. *The Russian Reference Grammar: Core Grammar in Functional Context*. Dubuque: Kendall/Hunt, 1997); the high school textbook series *Russian: Face to Face*, described below; and video support materials for many textbooks. (A bibliography is included below; see app., A.)

In collaboration with the National Textbook Company (now McGraw-Hill Publishing), Kendall/Hunt Publishing, and CORLAC, ACTR developed and published the *Russian: Face to Face* high school textbook series (Level 1, Morris, Vyatunyev, and Vokhmina 1993; Level 2, Dabars, Morris, and Smirnova 1995; Level 3, Dabars, Morris, Sosenko, and Vokhmina 1995; Level 4, Dabars, Morris, and Stramnova 1997). These texts constitute the only four-year basal series for American high school learners of Russian and were made possible, in part, by grants to ACTR from the Geraldine R. Dodge Foundation and the US Department of Education. The extensive series includes textbooks for all four years of high school, workbooks, annotated teachers' editions, video materials, a grammar reference volume, and testing masters, and was developed and written by American high school teachers in collaboration with specialists in teacher education in Russian as a Foreign Language from the Pushkin Institute in Moscow. The series was field-tested at a number of high schools across the United States, and consultation was provided by an advisory board consisting of high school teachers and university-based specialists. The support of a national professional organization allowed for a much more extensive series and in-depth collaboration for foreign and US consultants than would have been possible financially or logistically for an individual author.

In addition to basic textbooks, ACTR has published a number of supplementary and special topic textbooks. One of these, *Russkij yazyk v delevom obshchenii*, has been used at the high school, collegiate, and corporate levels. A video series, *Rovesniki/Peers* (Lekic et al. 1994), is aimed at the secondary-school Russian heritage learner as well as students at any level who are planning to study abroad.

For education professionals and researchers, ACTR has produced a series of published reports on the impact of study abroad on student language proficiency gains in Russian. With financial assistance from the Ford Foundation and in working cooperation with the National Foreign Language Center, ACTR prepared *A Russian Language*

Learning Framework for Secondary and Postsecondary Education (Merrill et al. 1996) to guide teachers in developing and implementing Russian language programs and courses.

ACTR also publishes books and support materials for use in college programs, some of which are used in advanced-level high school programs and in intensive/immersion programs for high school learners.[7]

Development of Classroom and Independent Study Resources

Through external grants and the use of the organization's own funds, ACTR and American Councils have made a number of cutting-edge resources available to teachers at no cost to the user. These include RussNet, the online web site that provides a wide range of learning modules in Russian language and culture, and CenAsiaNet, which provides learning modules at beginning and intermediate levels in Azeri, Kazakh, Turkmen, and Uzbek.

ACTION

There is a wealth of online resources and materials available to language teaching professionals (see material section of this volume). This article gives several examples for teachers of Russian. Choose a language other than Russian and search the web for resources in the areas of grammar, writing, reading comprehension, and vocabulary instruction. Keep a list of the best sites to share with your colleagues.

RussNet modules include interactive video that can be used in high school and college classrooms, materials which are regularly updated, expanded, and enhanced. The special needs of Russian heritage speakers are also addressed by RussNet, which provides a video-based course for heritage students; business Russian at the beginning, intermediate, and advanced levels; and a set of modules on Russian culture, ethnography, and geography. A new set of modules on the geography of the Russian Federation makes extensive use of audio, video, and film archive sources to support the study and teaching of the minority cultures of Russia. Another module permits the learner to explore the vast geographical regions of Russia which until very recently had been inaccessible to most Westerners. Materials on western Siberia are currently available on RussNet, and a new module on the northwestern districts of Russia are forthcoming.

Modules designed to bridge the high school-to-college articulation gap have been prepared by both high school and college teachers. Currently, fifteen modules have been written, and that number continues to grow monthly. Based on surveys of student interests, topics include Russian history, contemporary events, and aspects of Russian culture ranging from the *matryoshki* "nested wooden dolls" to women to Stalin to Peter the Great to holidays to the *New Russians*, with new themes constantly under development. These online materials can be used in class, as homework, or for independent study. High school teachers have played a key role in the development and test-teaching of all of these modules, as well as in the preparation of supplementary materials that reflect the needs and learning attributes of their own students and programs. The purpose of the AP modules is to support programs for students who plan to continue their study of Russian in college with the learning and teaching resources necessary to undertake advanced placement course work during the final year of high school.

Available online is the *ACTR Learning Styles Assessment Tool*, a widely used learning style diagnostic test for adult learners of any foreign language. The ALSAT assesses cognitive and perceptual styles, including visual-auditory-kinesthetic differences, as well as differences between leveling and sharpening, concreteness and abstraction, randomness and sequentiality, holistic and atomistic approaches, impulsivity and reflectivity, analysis-synthesis, and right-brain and left-brain differences. Originally produced by the American Global Studies Institute, the ALSAT was used extensively by ACTR in the 1990s. In 2000, ACTR acquired the rights to use and administer the ALSAT test online via RussNet after improving the module's self-scoring device and revising its content parameters. The new version was revalidated and is now available online to anyone who wishes to access it at <http://www.russnet.org/alsat/alsat.html>. The ALSAT is used widely at US schools and universities, as well as at government training institutions (e.g., NASA), and abroad.

Feedback on ACTRs online resources is sought from teachers and students, as well as outside evaluators. For grant-funded projects, an external evaluator provides formal feedback. Surveys among educators are collected regularly to assist formal evaluation. A formally constituted advisory board of high school and college faculty members regularly provide written and verbal (group meeting) feedback. The online modules also have a mechanism that allows users to provide electronic feedback. The feedback contributes to minor or major revisions of the various products.

A further step in module development is the design and programming of online activities that are *learning style sensitive*, that is, programming that will allow students to proceed through modules in different tracks depending on their learning styles. This attribute is rarely found in online learning programs and is still in the development and testing phase.

The graphics and interactive features of RussNet have been praised by a number of government organizations, teachers, and students at universities and high schools (Sample comments are included below; see app. B.) The National Foreign Language Center in Washington views RussNet as a prototype for its LangNet project and other language web sites that aim to provide teacher support.

Development of Standards and Instrumentation

ACTR developed the K-12 Russian-specific standards as part of a broad inter-association initiative of the nine major foreign language professional organizations in the US to establish the Foreign Language Standards Collaborative, which went on to produce *the National Standards in Foreign Languages* in 1999. ACTR also represents the Russian field on the Foreign Language Committee of the National Board for Professional Teaching Standards (NBPTS).

ACTR also has contributed to the development of proficiency tests in areas of specific, not global, proficiency: financial language proficiency for the International Monetary Fund and aerospace language proficiency for NASA (Leaver and Bilstein, 2000). These tests follow ILR/ACTFL guidelines for the definition of proficiency level but are task-based assessments of the examinees' ability to use specific linguistic and cultural information to perform work in intrinsic domains (in these cases, finance and space). To the best of our knowledge, these tests are the first attempts at assessing linguistic performance in specific content domains in any language.

Most recently, ACTR has undertaken the task of developing a new AP (Advanced Placement) curriculum for Russian, one that the College Entrance Examination Board expects to serve as a model for the revision of most other foreign-language AP curricula and tests. The AP project concept is to assess students' competencies in Russian for the purpose of awarding college credit or establishing the appropriate college level placement, using an online, interactive, self-scoring test that will test proficiency, not just knowledge, and be sensitive to learner differences. In addition to developing the test, ACTR has undertaken the development of supportive online learning modules, described above, as resources to assist high school teachers with content, especially cultural history, in conducting AP courses and preparing students for the AP test. The ACTR AP Advisory Council consists of an equal number of high school teachers and university faculty members.

Research

ACTR has maintained the largest and longest-running database of study-abroad statistics in the country. As such, ACTR has been able to develop predictors of student success (Brecht, Davidson, and Ginsberg 1993), develop requirements for the ways in which courses are taught, develop criteria for selecting programs for placement, and contribute to the larger question of how students acquire languages in second-language environments (Brecht and Robinson 1993). A number of additional studies have been conducted and published on the basis of this database, and the database has served as an especially rich source of empirical data for a range of doctoral dissertations. No other foreign-language teaching field has this kind of data, yet all language fields would benefit from emulating this ACTR project. Funding for some statistical analyses and data collection projects have come from outside sources, but throughout the project's history, data have been collected and analyzed nearly cost-free through the use of the database as a primary source for graduate student research projects.

CONSIDER

What role do you imagine research playing in foreign language teaching? For additional information and opinions on this topic review the articles in chapter four of this volume.

Another useful piece of research conducted by ACTR has been its word association study, *A Bilingual Dictionary of Word Associations,* which currently encompasses 169 semantic domains and is scheduled for electronic publication in 2003 (Davidson and Szalay).[8] The dictionary is expected to be of use to K-12 teachers, teacher trainers, and materials developers in addressing important aspects of Russian culture, as well as bringing home to students the notion that different cultures view the world in different ways.

ACTR has conducted an alumni survey to determine how former students of Russian have used the language in their careers. There are now more than 700 entries in this database. It can provide information to help teachers attract and retain students. Many former students have found positions requiring or taking advantage of their Russian language proficiency and in-country experience. Even those who are not employed in specifically Russia- or Russian-related fields have found their language-learning experiences significantly benefit their personal and professional lives.

Advocacy

To help teachers with enrollment issues, ACTR has created a viewbook called *Why Study Russian?*[9] on RussNet[10] and an accompanying videotape for classroom use. The American Association of Teachers of Slavic and East European Languages (AATSEEL) maintains a link to it from its web site, making the viewbook easily available to members of the profession. The viewbook is similar to one produced by the Modern Language Association (MLA) to help teachers *sell* enrollment in language classes to potential students and their parents, however ACTRs viewbook is language-specific.

ACTR also supports a language proficiency competition for high school students, the *Olympiada*. Held every other year, the competition is international in scope. In years when the competition is held, the International Association of Teachers of Russian Language and Literature pays in-country expenses for the *Olympiada* winners who are sent to Russia, along with 2-3 teachers, as their reward for their *Olympiada* performance, and ACTR pays the transportation costs. In the other years, ACTR pays all expenses. Over the years, ACTR has created and revised curriculum for teachers to use in preparing their students for the *Olympiada*, as well as materials to assist *Olympiada* judges in the evaluation process. There is also an essay contest for the *Olympiada*.

Funding

ACTR is funded in part by association dues. These dues, however, cover only a small portion of ACTRs activities. Additional support comes from many sources, including the US Department of State, Bureau of Educational and Cultural Affairs; the US Department of Education, Center for International Studies and Research; the US Department of Education's Fund for the Improvement of Post-Secondary Education; the National Endowment for the Humanities; the Library of Congress; the governments of Kazakhstan, Kyrgyzstan, Russia, and Uzbekistan; the Carnegie Corporation, Open Society Institute; the Ford Foundation; and other public and private organizations. ACTR maintains a small grant-writing staff to assist in the location of support funds for its projects. Some small revenues are also generated from sales of ACTR publications and fee-for-service programs.

Management

ACTR is governed by a Board of Directors, which convenes biannually to discuss and set policy, and an Executive Director, who manages the operations of ACTR on a daily basis. There is a general membership meeting held in conjunction with the annual convention of the American Association of Teachers of Slavic and East European Languages. Issues prompted by the bylaws or recommended by the Board of Directors are discussed at the annual meeting, as are member-initiated topics, and, where appropriate, resolutions are adopted. At the Annual Meeting, ACTR members are provided with financial and programmatic details for the previous year.

Summary

Among professional associations ACTR is, to some extent, unique in that it combines high school and college teacher interests. This combination bridges the gap between secondary and postsecondary programs and finds resolutions to articulation and placement issues.

ACTRs success at the active support of high school teachers can be emulated by the professional associations of other foreign-language fields. Although little mention has been made in this article about elementary school programs – these being nearly non-existent in Russian—many of the programs conducted by ACTR would also have value at that level of study. For that reason, ACTR has joined forces with other foreign language associations and JNCL/NCLIS in supporting legislation that provides resources for early learning.

ACTRs success has come about as the result of 25 years of intensive effort by its Executive Director, staff, members, and governing boards. Its successes are the result in large part of the willingness of members of the Russian field at all levels of education to work together for common goals. The same can be said for achievements accomplished by any group of equally dedicated teachers in any other language field. Many of the organizational models and activities are, in fact, directly transferable—and activities abroad will be easier to establish than was the case for ACTR programs during the Cold War period.

Professional teachers' organizations can generate unlimited opportunities for faculty development. They can also provide teachers with resources and tools to make their classrooms more successful. Most important, they can serve as a highly supportive resource—and safety net—for both new and experienced teachers, one where new ideas, materials, and resources can be developed and shared.

NOTE

As Leaver et al. clearly show, professional organizations can play a substantial role in teacher development and support. For additional information and opinions on teacher development and support, read chapter five of this volume.

Notes

1. For an example of this collaboration in action see Brecht, Caemmerer, and Walton, *Russian in the United States: A Case Study of America's Language Needs and Capacities* (Washington DC: National Foreign Language Center, 1995).
2. ACTR continues to maintain a program at Herzen/Russian State Pedagogical University for American exchange students participating in semester and year-long programs.
3. A college textbook series was also developed through a similar collaborative effort, as was the video-based supplementary text for heritage learners, *Rovesniki/Peers* (Lekic et al., 1995).
4. Development of the book and modules was supported by ACTR.
5. To join the RusTeach listserv, visit <http://www.russnet.org/connect.html>.
6. See <http://www.mapryal.org>.
7. These materials are not listed here, but they can be found on the ACTR website <http:

//www.actr.org>.

8. For example, do the factually identical words "dom" to a Russian and "house" to an American bring forth the same image? The answer in many cases is *no.*
9. The first edition of this booklet was prepared by Zita Dabars, Center of Russian Language and Culture, Friends School, Baltimore, Maryland. The second edition was in the format of a videotape, prepared by ACTR and distributed by Middlebury College. The third, written by Andrew Wachtel of Northwestern University, was a joint effort with ACTR and AATSEEL.
10. It is available at <http://www.russnet.org/why/index.html>.

References

American Council on the Teaching of Foreign Languages. *Standards for Foreign Language Learning in the 21st Century*. Lawrence: Allen Press, 1999.

American Council on the Teaching of Foreign Languages. *Program Standards for the Preparation of Foreign Language Teachers: Initial Level.* Yonkers: ACTFL, 2002.

Brecht, Richard D. and Dan E. Davidson. *Soviet-American Russian Language Contributions.* Urbana: AATSEEL, 1977.

Brecht, Richard D., Dan E. Davidson, and Ralph B. Ginsberg. *Predictors of Foreign Language Gain During Study Abroad*. Washington DC: NFLC Occasional Papers, 1994.

Brecht, Richard D. and Jennifer Robinson. *Qualitative Analysis of Second Language Acquisition in Study Abroad: The ACTR/NFLC Project*. Washington DC: NFLC Occasional Papers, 1993.

Dabars, Zita D., George W. Morris, and Nadezhda I. Smirnova. *Russian Face to Face: Level Two*. Lincolnwood: National Textbook Company, 1995.

Dabars, Zita D., George W. Morris, Ellina Yu. Sosenko, and Lilia L. Vokhmina. *Russian Faces and Voices*. Dubuque: Kendall/Hunt; Baltimore: CORLAC, 1995.

Davidson, Dan E., ed. *Soviet–American Contributions to the Study and Teaching of Russian: Theory, Strategies, and Tools*. Washington DC: ACTR/Russian Language Journal Publishers, December 1983. Also appeared as Russian Language Journal, Volume 36, no. 125, Fall 1982.

Davidson, Dan E., ed. *American Contributions to the Seventh International Congress*. Moscow/Washington DC: International Association of Teachers of Russian Language and Literature, 1990.

Davidson, Dan E. *The Professional Association as Field Infrastructure and Agent of Change*. Summit Conference on the Future of Language Learning, American Councils and FIPSE, US Department of Education, Washington DC, 27 APR. 2001.

Huber, Robert T. *A History of the American Councils for International Education: ACTR/ ACCELS*. Pittsburgh: Karl Beck Papers in Russian and East European Studies, University of Pittsburgh, forthcoming in 2003.

Leaver, Betty Lou and Paula M. Bilstein. "Content, Language, and Task in Content-Based Programs," *Languages Across the Curriculum: Interdisciplinary Structures and Internationalized Education*, eds. Regina-Maaia Kecht and Katharina von Hammerstein. Columbus: Ohio State University Press, 2000, pp. 79-118.

Leaver, Echo and Betty Lou Leaver. *ACTR Learning Styles Assessment Tool [ALSAT]*, 2002 <http://www.russnet.org/alsat/alsat.html>.

Leaver, Echo and Betty Lou Leaver. *American Global Studies Institute Learning Styles Assessment Tool (ALSAT)*. Salinas: AGSI Press, 1993.

Merrill, Peter, Maria Lekic and James Levine. *Russian Language Programs in the United*

States: A Russian Language Learning Framework for Secondary and Postsecondary Education. Washington DC: ACTR, 1996 <http://www.russnet.org>.

Morris, George W., Mark N. Vyatyutnev, Lilia L. Vokhmina. *Russian Face to Face: Level One.* Lincolnwood: National Textbook Company, 1993.

National Board for Professional Teaching Standards. *World Languages Other Than English Standards*. Southfield; Arlington: NBPTS, 2001.

Wachtel, Andrew. *Why Study Russian?* Washington DC: ACTR, 2000; electronic <http://www.russnet.org>, ACTR, 2000.

Appendix A
ACTR/ACCELS Publications

Business Russian

Klobukova, L., I. Mikhalkina, T. Soltanovskaya, and S. Khavronina. *Russkij yazyk v delevom obshchenii*. Washington DC: ACTR, 1997.

Milman, Nyusya. *Business Russian: A Cultural Approach*. Dubuque: Kendall/Hunt, 1997.

Nisula, Dasha C. *English-Russian and Russian-English Glossary of Marketing Terms*. Washington DC: ACTR, 1999.

Textbook Series for High School

Dabars, Zita D., Natalia M. Lutskaya, and George W. Morris. *Mir russkikh: Exercise Book*. (1995; Dubuque: Kendall/Hunt; Baltimore: CORLAC, 1995).

Dabars, Zita D., George W. Morris, Ellina Yu. Sosenko, and Lilia L. Vokhmina. *Russian Faces and Voices*. (1995; Dubuque: Kendall/Hunt; Baltimore: CORLAC, 1995).

Dabars, Zita D., George W. Morris, and Nadezhda I. Smirnova. *Russian Face to Face: Level Two*. Lincolnwood: National Textbook Company, 1995.

Dabars, Zita D., George W. Morris, and Nadezhda I. Smirnova. *Russian Face to Face Workbook: Level Two*. Lincolnwood: National Textbook Company, 1995.

Davidson, Dan E., Kira S. Gor, and Masha D. Lekic. *Russian Stage 1: Live from Moscow*. Dubuque: Kendall/Hunt, 1996.

Morris, George W., Mark N. Vyatyutnev, Lilia L. Vokhmina. *Russian Face to Face: Level One*. Lincolnwood: National Textbook Company, 1993.

Morris, George W., Mark N. Vyatyutnev, Lilia L. Vokhmina. *Russian Face to Face Assessment Package Including Blackline Masters: Level One*. Lincolnwood: National Textbook Company, 1993.

Watzke, John L. and James W. Sweigert, Jr. *The Russian Reference Grammar: Core Grammar in Functional Context*. Dubuque: Kendall/Hunt, 1997.

Textbook Training, Teacher Reference/Informational Texts, and Other Supplements

Akishina, Alla A. *Minirus: A Starter Course in Russian*. Dubuque: Kendall/Hunt, 1996.

Choate, Lisa A. and Dan E. Davidson. *Cultural Handbook for the New Independent States*. Washington DC: ACTR, 2000.

Chomym, Valentin. *Art and Spirituality: The Russian Icon* (English- and Russian-language editions). Washington DC: ACTR, 2000.

Davidson, Dan E., Kira S. Gor, and Masha D. Lekic. *Russian Stage 1: Live from Moscow*. 1996; 2000; Dubuque: Kendall/Hunt, 2002.

Garza, Thomas. *Fundamentals of Russian Verbal Conjugation for Students and Teachers*. Dubuque: Kendall/Hunt Publishing, 1994.

Leaver, Betty Lou, ed. *Twelve Years of Dialogue on Teaching Russian: From the Front Page of the ACTR Letter: 1987-1999*. Washington DC: ACTR, 1999.

Lekic, Maria, Nadezhda Nitkina, and Tatiana Kirsh. *Rovesniki/Peers*. Washington DC: ACTR, 1994. *(For heritage learners)*

Lekic, Masha, Olga Rassudova, and Tatiana Kirsh. *Chto vy ob etom dumaete? What Do You Think About That?* Washington DC: ACTR, 1994. *(Teacher proficiency improvement)*
Martin, Cynthia, and Andrei Zaitsev. *Russian Stage 2: Welcome Back!* Dubuque: Kendall/Hunt, 2000.
Shamshin, Leonid B., Zita D. Dabars, and Ellina Yu. Sosenko. *In Search of Orlovsky: A Video Mystery*. (1997; Dubuque: Kendall/Hunt; Baltimore: CORLAC, 1997).
Shamshin, Leonid B., Zita D. Dabars, Ellina Yu. Sosenko. *Russkie temy (Russian Themes): Video Resource Manual*. (1997; Dubuque: Kendall/Hunt; Baltimore: CORLAC, 1997).
Simes, Natasha, and Richard Robin. *Political Russian*. (1992; 1996; Dubuque: Kendall/Hunt, 2000).
Simes, Natasha. *Years of Change: Reading the Soviet Press*. (1992; 1996; Dubuque: Kendall/Hunt, 2000).
Simes-Timofeeva, Natasha and Marina Rappoport. *Scientific Russian: Readings in Russian Science and Technology*. Dubuque: Kendall/Hunt, 1993.
Townsend, Charles and Yuri Belchikov. *Russian Readings for Close Analysis*. Dubuque: Kendall/Hunt, 1993.

Appendix B
Selected Comments on RussNet and CenAsiaNet Modules

"I found your online modules for learning (business) Russian extremely good. It is the best material I have found on the Internet so far."

"I can't wait 'til my little first-years go into the lab tomorrow."

"I studied Russian as an undergraduate several years ago, but unfortunately have not had the opportunity to keep it up. While I was once quite proficient in the language, it has been sad to see my ability atrophy. Your site provides high quality material for those who are familiar with Russian and want to refresh their skills. For that, I would like to thank you for such a wonderful content-full site."

"I just love the new format of the russnet site! It is much easier to read and the extensive links are great...Thanks so much! And, once, again, the new design of the russnet site is wonderful!"

"Now that I've got on to these materials again, I can't stop looking at them! My husband keeps having to get up from his football game to see the next amazing thing. Since I'm locked out of my classroom, I'm going to be trying to farm kids out to various computers around the school to work online this week, but then I will definitely be using the materials regularly in both my first-year and second-third-fourth-year classes....this makes up for all the lack of other worthwhile materials out there. Wow...am I glad I went to the session at ACTFL on Business Russian. The last time I used these modules, they were all really way too hard for anyone but my heritage speakers, and they were not the most exciting things in the world. I REALLY like how you've inserted meaningful grammar and real reading, and I like how interesting they are for my kids!"

In Conversation with Joe Sheils and Adrian Butler About the *Architecture of the Profession*

Gerd Bräuer

The Council of Europe, a political organization founded in 1949, brings together the Committee of Ministers and the Foreign Affairs Ministers of 45 member countries. The mission of this organization is "to achieve a greater unity between its members for the purpose of safeguarding and realizing the ideals and principles, which are their common heritage, and facilitating their economic and social progress."

The Council of Europe has been active in the area of language education for almost forty years. It aims for linguistic and cultural diversity of its member states in order "to fight against intolerance and xenophobia by improving skills of communication and cultural understanding between individuals."

Its work in this field is carried out by two administrative structures, the Language Policy Division in Strasbourg (France) and the European Centre for Modern Languages in Graz (Austria).

Gerd Bräuer (GB)
Joe Sheils (Language Policy Division, Strasbourg) and Adrian Butler (European Centre for Modern Languages, Graz), could you please further explain the main goals of each council?

Joe Sheils & Adrian Butler (JS & AB)
The missions and programs of each of these two Council of Europe instances are complementary and they are organized for administrative and coordination purposes in a single Department of Language Education and Policy. In summary, the Language Policy Division is concerned mainly with the development of policy, while the ECML concentrates on matters related to practical implementation. This means that the Division in Strasbourg is concerned in particular with policy analysis and development related to multilingualism in societies and the development of plurilingualism among citizens. Its main activities include assistance to states in reviewing and planning national language education policy (all languages), developing instruments for policy making, as well as for setting common European standards, and focusing on language education policies for minorities. The ECMLs mission is to assist the member states in the implementation of their language policies and to promote innovative approaches to the learning and teaching of modern languages. Its specific strategic objectives are, therefore, to focus on the teaching and learning of languages, to promote dialogue and exchange among the various actors in the field, and to train

multipliers. It collects and disseminates examples of good practice, organizes central and regional workshops, and supports program-related networks and projects. The ECML is an Enlarged Partial Agreement with 33 member states while the Language Policy Division facilitates cooperation between the 45 member States of the Council of Europe and three additional non-member countries which have ratified the European Cultural Convention.

GB
Please describe the character of cooperation between the Language Policy Division in Strasbourg (France) and the European Centre for Modern Languages in Graz (Austria). To let the description become more concrete, could you please refer to the development of the Common European Framework of References for Languages (CEF) as an example?

JS & AB
The CEF was developed through the program in Strasbourg to respond to the demand for greater transparency and coherence in language programs and certification. The Framework has been widely adopted and has become the basis for national curricula and examinations and for international certification. The European Union has recommended that states set up systems of validation of language competence based on the CEF levels, taking account of non-formal learning, and the Association of Language Testers in Europe (ALTE) has adopted its six level scale. The Language Policy Division is now completing a manual to offer guidance to all those involved in relating their examinations in a reliable manner to the CEF levels. Essentially the manual will offer guidance to users on how to:

- Describe the examination coverage, administration and analysis procedures.
- Align results reported from the examination to the CEF levels.
- Provide supporting evidence to illustrate the procedures followed in order to achieve this.

The draft manual will be available in autumn 2003 and will be supported by illustrative videos and scripts for each level (2004). The ECML has organized workshops to assist in the implementation of the CEF in curriculum development and classroom practice (learning strategies), and it is proposed that, in its new medium-term program (2004-07), the Centre could assist its members in the application of the manual by organizing training workshops for those responsible for national examinations and certification.

ACTION

Use the Internet and other sources to gather additional information on the Common European Framework of References for Languages (CEF). Find out if there is a similar framework of references benefiting language education policy in the US.

GB
The European Language Portfolio (ELP) was developed by the Language Policy Division between 1998 and 2000. What were the main steps in this process that brought together foreign language research and instruction in a rather unique way?

JS

The Ruschlikon symposium (Switzerland 1991), which launched the framework development process, recommended the development of the portfolio once the CEF was available. After piloting and preliminary revision of the CEF, work began on developing and piloting portfolio models appropriate to young, adolescent, and adult learners. The three core elements (Language Passport, Language Biography, and Dossier) were developed taking into account the needs of different education sectors and target groups, with a common Language Passport recommended for older learners (school learners and adults).

CONSIDER

To learn more about the European Language Portfolio, see the chapter by Peter Lenz in this volume.

The Language Policy Division organized European seminars throughout the piloting in order to develop a consensus on the ELP content and form. Seminars now focus on new developments and dissemination. While there is a welcome diversity in portfolios depending on context of use, all respect the agreed common criteria. A number of optional common elements or templates are currently being developed so as to facilitate the work of portfolio developers and the validation process, mainly concerning descriptors for specific target groups, and the *learning to learn* and intercultural dimensions which will be under consideration by member States at the Division's European seminar in Turkey in October 2003.

GB

What were the most important political decisions which had to be made before it was finally possible to launch the ELP across Europe?

JS

The European Year of Languages provided the platform to initiate the more widespread introduction of the portfolio concept in Europe. As early as 1998, the Committee of Ministers had recommended the development and use by learners of a personal document (European Language Portfolio) to record their qualifications and other significant linguistic and cultural experiences in an internationally transparent manner as part of an effort to extend and diversify language learning at all levels in a lifelong perspective. Further political support was provided by the Resolution of the Standing Conference of European Ministers of Education in 2000, and by the Recommendations of the Parliamentary Assembly of the Council of Europe in 1997 on Linguistic Diversity, and in 2001 on the European Year of Languages.

ACTION

Go to <http://culture.coe.int/portfolio> and choose one case study to present and discuss with a colleague.

Members States responded most positively, and the 15 countries in the pilot scheme were soon joined by many others. After piloting, portfolios are submitted to the European Validation Committee which meets in Strasbourg and if they are considered to conform to the basic Principles and Guidelines established by the Steering Committee for Education, they receive formal Council of Europe approval which means the right to use the title *European Language Portfolio*. These accredited portfolios bear a specific accreditation number and logo. There are now 40 validated *European Language Portfolios* covering primary, secondary, vocational, higher, and adult education, and many others are in a pilot stage. Guides for portfolio developers and for teachers/teacher trainers, as well as case studies of the ELPs in use, have been developed by the Division. Further information is available on the ELP website <http://culture.coe.int/portfolio>.

GB
What role will the ECML play in the future promotion of the ELP?

AB
Now that the ELP is starting to *come on stream* in the member States, the resources of the ECML can come into play. ELP implementation is a priority for our members, and we expect that there will be a number of projects linked to it in our second medium-term program (2004–2007), for which the selection procedure takes place this autumn. These projects are likely to include activities such as awareness raising, training of multipliers, teacher-training or materials development, involving workshops and regional meetings, networks of experts, and so on.

GB
Has there been any contact established between the European Centre for Modern Languages in Graz and any of the National Foreign Language Resource Centers in the US? If so, what kind, and what else could be possible in the near future?

AB
So far there has been practically no contact between the Graz Centre and any US institutions. However, the ECML is open to countries that are not members of the Council of Europe and so it would be possible for the US to join. In the meantime, we have the possibility to accept a limited number of observers from non-member states at our activities, and so anyone interested should consult our next program when it is published in December. In any case, all of the Centre's work and publications can be accessed through our website <http://www.ecml.at/>.

CONSIDER

In your opinion, why has there been up to this point so little contact between the Graz centre and US institutions? At which level (local, state, or federal) should US language educators pursue a connection with the ECML? Brainstorm two or three strategies for facilitating this connection.

GB
How does the Council of Europe respond to the competing demands of national (and regional) languages in its activities, and are there languages favored over others, due to their influence in Europe, or due to current political circumstances?

JS & AB
The Council of Europe policy on language education is guided by Article 2 of the European Cultural Convention whereby contracting states commit themselves to facilitating the teaching of the languages of other member States and to supporting the teaching of its own language(s) in other states.

The most recent and comprehensive description of the Council of Europe language education policy is contained in the *Guide for Language Education Policies in Europe* elaborated by the Language Policy Division (for a current draft, April 2003, see <http://www.int/lang>). The Guide, in keeping with the CEF, stresses that it is a question not only of protecting languages but equally of enabling Europeans to develop their linguistic abilities. This is seen as the development of a unique individual linguistic competence (*knowing* languages whatever they may be), and this competence is developed not just for utilitarian or professional reasons, but also as education for linguistic tolerance. Language education policies should, therefore, promote the learning of several languages for all individuals in the course of their lives, so that Europeans become plurilingual and intercultural citizens, able to interact with other Europeans in all aspects of their lives. Policies to promote linguistic diversity in societies and plurilingualism for citizens should be coherent with the promotion of social inclusion and the development of democratic citizenship in Europe.

Consequently, the programs in Strasbourg and Graz are concerned with plurilingualism in the broad sense. Policy for individual countries is of course the prerogative of their governments. The Council of Europe's task is to facilitate European cooperation in developing a consensus on guiding principles and good practice in the development and implementation of policy. More detail on the policy issues involved can be found in the proceedings of the conference organized in Strasbourg (November 2002) on *Languages, Diversity, Citizenship: Policies for plurilingualism in Europe*.

GB

Looking at the major focuses of the training provided by the European Centre for Modern Languages, they are quite similar to the task-force groups of the *New Visions* initiative in the US. The only major difference is your focus on *organization and set-up of language education*, where workshops look at the organization of language education in different states, neighboring language teaching in border regions, and the set-up of multilingual education. What is the purpose of giving these aspects in Europe specific care?

AB

The focus on the organization and the set-up of language education in our first medium-term plan was designed to underline the fact that, however much you improve teaching methodology and materials, if you still concentrate on formal language teaching in the academic context, you will not radically improve things. Language education is essentially about communicating, and we learn far more effectively when we face the real need to communicate. We wanted to show the potential that exists for radically new approaches to language education taking advantage of different contexts and applying diversified models: border regions or town-twinning arrangements are examples where intercultural communication should be encouraged and where situations for creative language learning can easily be created; multilingual education brings richness and diversity to children's education; language learning should be seen in a lifelong context. One of the major questions we are asking is: is it not better to offer pupils and students a **partial knowledge** of several languages, but which they can actually use (and from which, with luck, they will retain a lifelong thirst to learn and discover more) than academic **mastery** of one language, which is never *activated*?

DISCUSS

Do you agree with this argument? Discuss with a partner the pros and cons of offering partial knowledge of several languages, rather than mastery of one to language learners.

GB
Another permanent entity of the Council of Europe is the Day of Languages. Could you please explain how this works and what it was founded for?

JS & AB
Following on the success of the European Year of Languages (2001), its aims are sustained by the European Day of Languages which is celebrated each year on September 26th by the 45 member States. The day is coordinated at the European level by the Language Policy Division and the ECML, and a flexible approach is adopted in member States in keeping with the Recommendation of the Committee of Ministers. The day generated considerable interest in 2001 and 2002. More information is available at the website <http://www.coe.int/EDL>.

GB
How, in reverse, is the expertise of individual language educators being used by the Council of Europe to further shape the foreign teaching profession in Europe?

AB
The Centre is not a teaching institution—its activities are run by teams composed of precisely the sort of individual language educators you refer to. And, we don't believe in one-way communication! Our workshops are highly interactive and designed to give participants maximum opportunity to present their own experience and personal best practice. Thus, the results of the projects run in the framework of the ECML, in the form of the publications, materials, or web sites that we publish and make available to other language educators throughout Europe (and, via our website, throughout the world) are the sum of a wide range of individual contributions.

GB
Are there any Internet resources within the network of your institutions which you can suggest that foreign language educators and teacher students visit, in order to better understand how language learning and teaching works in Europe?

JS & AB
We suggest that readers visit our web sites for further information:

ACTION

Take the authors' suggestion and explore these web sites!

Language Policy Division
<www.coe.int/langculture.coe.int/portfolio>

European Centre for Modern Languages
<www.ecml.at>

European Day of Languages
<www.coe.int/EDL>

Post-Reading Questions

1. *In part one of this book you were introduced to the role of language-specific professional organizations in teacher education and support. Make a list of the key points you learned. Compare this information with what you are familiar with from your own language-specific professional field. What is different? What, in your opinion, could be improved, and what can you do to help make these improvements happen? Use the ideas you have sketched out as a springboard for working on the following questions.*

2. *If you don't yet belong to a language-specific professional organization, in what areas would you like to participate based on your readings of chapter one? Write your ideas down and compare them with your pre-reading material. Has your opinion changed? What might be the reasons for any differences?*

3. *Using a mind map, draw the organizational structure Leaver et al. introduced you to, and compare it with a language-specific professional organization you are familiar with (or imagine for your professional field). Within the organizational structure of your working environment, what areas do you, or could you, influence with your expertise? Again, write your ideas down and compare them with your pre-reading material. Has your opinion changed, and if so, why?*

4. *Think about how you could use the resources of the Council of Europe for your work as outlined above.*

5. *What kind of transatlantic collaboration have you experienced so far as a learner and/or teacher and what do you imagine for your future? Write down the names of possible supporters of your ideas.*

Chapter 2

Curriculum and Instruction

The authors featured in chapter two of this book critically analyze the current state of curriculum and instruction in foreign and second language education in the US and Europe. Around the main topics in this international discussion—learner diversity, classroom technology, bilingual education, and autonomous learning—the authors suggest new ideas, methods and concepts. In addition, through their own collaborative projects, they demonstrate how to make use of the wealth of professional experience on both sides of the Atlantic.

Pre-Reading Questions

1. *Think back to when you started learning your first foreign language. Would you have benefited from an earlier start? What support or additional opportunities would have been necessary for an earlier beginning of your foreign language education?*

2. *What will have to change in foreign language education in your country, in order to make early language learning possible for the majority of students?*

3. *Describe one or two of the main teaching methods you have experienced as a foreign/second language learner. What advantages and disadvantages did these approaches have on your learning?*

4. *As a language learner, what experiences did you make with the countries and cultures of your target language(s)? What effect did these experiences have on your learning?*

5. *How much did new technology, especially computers and the Internet, influence your approach to language learning? In what way did the Internet foster your contact with countries of your target language(s)?*

6. *What is your opinion on bilingual instruction in primary and/or secondary schools? What, from your point of view, are advantages and disadvantages of it? Do you have any experience with it yourself?*

7. *All groups of learners are diverse in any number of ways. What aspects of learner diversity do you think influence language learning? Give examples of how your teachers used diversity to enhance the learning environment.*

8. *Independent learning can be a challenge, autonomous learning even more so. In your understanding, what is the difference between these two methods, and how have you experienced the differences in your role as a language learner?*

Introduction to the New Visions Initiative: Curriculum and Instruction

Marjorie Hall Haley

Curriculum and Instruction in foreign language education will certainly require *new visions* during the current millennium. While there are numerous challenges, there also are scores of opportunities to re-shape curricula and think differently about pedagogical approaches to language instruction. Changes in our teaching and learning models will continue to impact classroom practices. A myriad of questions must be raised which shape the debate over educational design: What is to be taught? How is it to be taught? To whom? For whom? By whom? For what purpose(s)? With what outcome(s)?

CONSIDER

Think about the student population you will be/are working with. Describe the ways this group is diverse. What challenges might (or does) this pose for your teaching practices and philosophy? How could technology support your effort to meet the needs of your culturally, linguistically, and cognitively diverse class?

Two areas are defined as being highly influential in providing opportunities as well as challenges in foreign language education in the new millennium. They will be discussed briefly in this introduction:

- Curriculum and instruction designed to address the needs of culturally, linguistically, and cognitively diverse learners.
- The role and impact of technology in foreign language classes of the new millennium.

Curriculum and Instruction for Culturally, Linguistically, and Cognitively Diverse Learners

The demographic characteristics of today's classrooms are very different than they were just twenty years ago and according to Banks (1997) by the year 2020 "Whites will make up only 54.5% of the nation's population," (5) and students of color will comprise 45.5% of that population. This change in population brings new opportunities and challenges for teachers. Today's teachers, as never before, work in school populations largely comprised of culturally, linguistically, and cognitively diverse students.

One way curriculum and instruction may address the needs of culturally, linguistically, and cognitively diverse students is to incorporate instructional strategies and assessment practices that are learner-centered, shifting the pedagogical paradigm away from teacher-centeredness. Howard Gardner's theory of Multiple Intelligences (MI) provides such a shift. According to Gardner's theory, there are eight intelligences: Bodily/Kinesthetic, Interpersonal/Social, Intrapersonal/Introspective, Logical/Mathematical, Musical/Rhythmic, Naturalist, Verbal/Linguistic, and Visual/Spatial.

Every learner has the capacity to exhibit all of these intelligences, but some are more highly developed than others in certain individuals. Based on the MI theory, the challenge in education is for teachers to create learning environments that foster the development of *all* eight intelligences. Balanced instructional presentations that encourage addressing the multiple intelligences benefit all learners, (culturally, linguistically, and cognitively) and expose students to the appropriate means by which they can strengthen their under-utilized intelligences. Providing opportunities for students to learn in ways in which they are most receptive maximizes their potential for success in the academic setting and in real life (Armstrong 1994; Beckman 1998).

CONSIDER

What kind of learner are you? Where do you locate yourself within Gardner's multiple intelligences? How does this influence your preferred teaching approach? What do you do to foster the other intelligences that are usually not your favorite?

The literature on multiple intelligences provides a sound theoretical foundation for an integrated, multidimensional style of education across learning styles and cultures. Hall Haley (2001) conducted a study involving culturally, linguistically, and culturally diverse students which showed that the theory of multiple intelligences may have significant implications for instruction in foreign and second language classrooms. Although it is not a quick fix, the MI theory has the potential to make a positive impact on both teachers and students. Practitioners who thoughtfully apply the theory to support educational goals may find multiple intelligences contribute to their overall effectiveness as educators. Teachers who plan and organize instruction around the learning preferences of individual learners, emphasizing special strengths and shoring up under utilized gifts and talents, may unlock the full learning potential of their students.

ACTION

Design a lesson plan (balanced instructional presentation) around the topic of your choice addressing as many different intelligences as possible. Don't forget to prescribe to each intelligence, use a concrete function for reaching the main goal of your lesson. In addition, how could you integrate technology into your lesson plan?

The MI theory suggests that there is a plurality of intellect. From birth, individuals may differ in particular intelligence profiles, that is to say, "all human intelligences are a function of genes and environment interacting in different ways and in different proportions for each group and for each individual" (Kagan & Kagan 1998). Life experiences may alter these profiles over time. Intelligences are biological potentials which are seen in *raw* (unchanged) form in individuals. According to Gardner (1983), one of the most important purposes of schools is to develop multiple intelligences, helping people reach vocational goals that are appropriate to their particular spectrum of intelligences. This theory is a pluralistic view that recognizes different cognitive strengths and contrasting cognitive styles.

In foreign language teaching; thematic, content-based, and contextualized teaching, go hand in hand with the use of alternative performance assessments where student evaluation goes beyond traditional pencil and paper testing. Such practices provide optimal achievement opportunities for culturally, linguistically, and cognitively diverse students. Classrooms implementing the principles of Gardner's MI theory use authentic assessment, giving students opportunities to demonstrate higher order thinking skills, and providing examples of content learned and its application in new situations (Campbell 1997).

The Role and Impact of Technology

In 1998, President Clinton introduced the Educational Technology Initiative in which he outlined the *Technology Literacy Challenge*. Included in this were four areas of emphasis:

- Modern computers and learning devices will be accessible to every student.
- Classrooms will be connected to one another and to the world
- Educational software will be an integral part of the curriculum and as engaging as the best video game.
- Teachers will be ready to use and teach with technology (USDOE 1998).

Educational research has shown that self-learning and interactive multimedia are particularly effective in facilitating the teaching of English skills (Cates 1992; Hill 1988; Laurillard 1995; Meskill 1996; Squires & Preece 1996). As foreign language teachers we will want to provide a classroom environment which involves students in authentic, culturally-appropriate, and meaningful experiences that stimulate their language proficiency. Technology can provide both a teaching and learning tool which will support and enhance schools' curricula.

Instructors and researchers agree that the use of any technology in the classroom must be integrated into the curriculum as a tool to support and enhance the learning experience rather than serve as the driving curricular force (Armstrong & Yetter-Vassot 1994; Bedford 1991; Garrett 1992; Hughes & Hewson 1998; Kearsley 1998; LeLoup & Ponterio 1996; Patrikis 1995; Phillips 1998). Kearsley (1998) and Hedderick (1997) warn against the seductiveness of integrating technology as a quick fix to more serious problems.

In the recent past foreign/second language teachers have utilized such technologies as audio and video tapes, radio, television programs, language labs, films, filmstrips, slides and the overhead projector. More recently there has been an explosion of newer technologies for classroom adaptability: computers, CD-ROMs, distance learning, satellite broadcasts, videoconferencing, electronic mail. Now, as never before, students can have access to multiple resources and communicate both orally and in writing with innumerable speakers of other languages.

CONSIDER

Explain in concrete terms what Byrnes (1996) means when she says that through technology the emphasis shifts from teaching to student learning. To illustrate your explanation, use examples from your own work as a student or teacher.

What impact will technology have on the role of the teacher? Byrnes (1996) notes that technology such as the Internet "inherently shifts the emphasis from teaching to student learning" thus creating new roles for both learners and teachers, and forcing us to rethink the process of learning.

Patrikis (1995) points out that computer-based learning individualizes the learning process and gives students more control over both what and how they learn.

Will the computer replace the teacher? Probably not. Will teachers change the way they teach because of computers? Probably. Because of the growing use and popularity of new technologies, teachers find themselves being urged to keep up. More and more states and school districts are implementing a technology competence requirement as part of students' standards of learning. Similarly, schools of education are requiring educational technology courses in teacher licensure programs. Thus, the role of the teacher has been and will continue to be redefined in part by new technology.

One direct influence of technology has been seen in teachers moving from whole class to small group instruction, as well as a shift from students all learning the same things to learning different things. This affords teachers the opportunity to move from verbal thinking, to the integration of visual and verbal thinking. According to Cummins (2000), "...our task as educators in general, and as language educators in particular, should be to assess the potential of Information Technology (IT) to improve the human condition. As educators, we are committed to drawing out the potential of the students we teach; as language educators, we strive to increase students' capacity to use language to fulfill their personal goals and contribute to their societies."

DISCUSS

In your opinion, what impact will technology have on the role of the classroom teacher? Address the fears of some teachers that they may be *replaced* by technology.

Pedagogical Implications for Using Technology

Integrating technology successfully begins with an explicitly defining the pedagogical role for that technology (Ragan 1999). Every individual teacher must choose why, how, and when to use technology. This choice is often influenced by access, ease of comfort in using technology and knowledge of *how* to use existing resources. Access to information technology (IT) differs among and within countries, states, and school districts. The digital divide is clearly visible. According to Cummins (2000), "I believe that IT also has considerable potential to promote language learning in a transformative way when it is aligned with a pedagogy oriented towards promoting collaborative relations of power in the classroom and beyond."

Garrett (1991) cautions us that using the computer does not replace methodology, since the computer is nothing more than a tool. According to Garrett (1991), the more critical issue is the quality of the software material available, and the ways teachers use the material to achieve the desired learning outcomes. "...Teachers must learn to use the new technology to allow students to interact more effectively with the same *old* material. The change must be carefully and thoughtfully crafted, for we cannot continue to ask teachers to use the *newest* devices if we continue using pedagogical practices that are no different from those previously used" (Moore 1999).

DISCUSS

According to Haley, "every individual teacher must choose why, how, and when to use technology." Discuss your specific location/situation. What resources are available to you in order to make the best use of technology, and how can you best utilize them?

A myriad of questions must be raised which shape the debate over educational design: What is to be taught? How is it to be taught? To whom? For whom? By whom? For what purpose(s)? With what outcome(s)? This second part of the book will address these questions and pose answers and implications.

References

Armstrong, T. *Multiple Intelligences in the Classroom*. Virginia: Association For Supervision and Curriculum Development, 1994.

Armstrong, K. and C. Yetter-Vassot. "Transforming Teaching Through Technology." *Foreign Language Annals* 27.4 (1994): 475-486.

Banks, J. *Teaching Strategies for Ethnic Studies*. 6th ed. Needham Heights: Allyn and Bacon, 1997.

Beckman, M. *Multiple Ways of Knowing: Howard Gardner's Theory of Multiple Intelligences Extend and Enhance Student Learning*. 1998 <http://www.earlychildhood.com/articles/artmi.html>.

Campbell, L. "Variations on a Theme: How Teachers Interpret MI Theory." *Educational Leadership* 55.1 Sep. 1997 <http://www.ascd.org/pubs/el/sept97/campbell.html>.

Cates, W. Fifteen Principles for Designing More Effective Instructional Hypermedia/Multimedia Products." *Educational Technology* 32.12 (1992).

Cummins, J. "Academic Language Learning, Transformative Pedagogy, and Information Technology: Towards a Critical Balance." *TESOL Quarterly* 34.3 (2000): 537-548.

Gardner, H. *Frames of Mind: The Theory of Multiple Intelligences*. New York: Basic Books, 1983.

Garrett, N. "Technology in the Service of Language Learning: Trends and Issues." *Modern Language Journal* 75 (1992): 74-96.

Hall Haley, M. "Understanding Learner-Centered Instruction from the Perspective of Multiple Intelligences." *Foreign Language Annals* 34.4 (2001): 355-367.

Hedderich, N. "Peer Tutoring via Electronic Mail." *Die Unterrichtspraxis Teaching German*. 2 (1997): 141-147.

Hill, B. "Developments in Interactive Video." *Die Neueren Sprachen*. 87.6 (1988).

Hughes, C. and L. Hewson. "Online Interactions: Developing a Neglected Aspect of the Virtual Classroom." *Educational Technology* 38.4 (1998): 48-55.

Kagan, S. and M. Kagan. *Multiple Intelligences – The Complete MI book*. San Clemente: Kagan Cooperative Learning, 1998.

Kearsley, G. "Educational Technology: A Critique." *Educational Technology* 38.2 (1998): 47-51.

Laurillard, D. "Multimedia and the Changing Experience of the Learner." *British Journal of Educational Technology* 26.3 (1995).

LeLoup, J. & R. Ponteiro. "Choosing and Using Materials for a *Net* Gain in FL Learning and Instruction." *Reaching Out to the Communities We Serve. NYSAFLT Annual Meeting Series 13*. Ed. V.B. 1996.

Meskill, C. "Listening Skills Development Through Multimedia." *Journal of Educational Multimedia and Hupermedia* 5.2 (1996).

Moore, Z. "Technology and Teaching Culture in the L2 Classroom: An Introduction." *Journal of Educational Computing Research* 20.1.1-9 (1999): 1-9.

Patrikis, P. "Where is Computer Technology Taking Us". *ADFL Bulletin* 26 (1995): 2:36-39.

Phillips, J. "Media for the Message: Technology's Role in the Standards." *CALICO Journal* 16.1 (1998): 25-35.

Ragan, L. "Good Teaching is Good Teaching: An Emerging Set of Guiding Principles for the Design and Development of Distance Education." *Cause/Effect* 2.1 (1999) <http://www.educause.edu/ir/library/html/cem9915.html>.

Squirres, D. and J. Preece. "Usability and Learning: Evaluating the Potential of Educational Software." *Computers and Education* 27.1 (1996).

Interview with Marjorie Hall Haley

Svenja Dahlmanns

Svenja Dahlmanns (SD)
What topics in language education do you see as currently potential for international exchange and collaboration?

Marjorie Hall Haley (MHH)
Languages for special purposes—business, medicine, the arts, international affairs, information technology (IT), conflict analysis and resolution. There will continue to be a need for international exchange programs. Perhaps this may become more widespread in K-12 schools and not just at post-secondary institutions in the same way that international teacher/professor exchanges enhance language instruction in our global community. Courses can be taught on various topics in multiple languages. Thanks to technology, someone wanting to learn about the pyramids will be able to (via distance learning) using Arabic as the language of instruction. In other words, not only are there opportunities to now study in the global community but one can also be taught in the language of choice.

CONSIDER

What forms of international exchange and collaboration have you yourself (as a language teacher and learner) experienced so far? How did this experience shape you as a language learner/teacher?

SD
What areas should pre and in-service teachers be prepared for in order to join the global dialogue successfully?

MHH
Pre and in-service teachers need to have the commitment to teaching. Teachers should go into the classroom because that is where they truly want to be. It is critically important for teachers to have a high degree of proficiency in the target language(s) as well as knowledge of theory, pedagogy, second language acquisition, and working with diverse learners. These are truly the ties that bind us all. The challenges and opportunities faced today in education are often mirrored in many parts of the world.

ACTION

In the process of working with this book, collect in a separate reading log instructional strategies that are new to you. Define them briefly, reflect on their specific nature, and ask yourself how you could incorporate these instructional strategies into your teaching/learning practice.

SD
What needs to take place to reshape curricula and approaches to language instruction?

MHH
Curricula will need to reflect the new learners of the 21st century. This means that texts, and resources. must encompass a truly pluralistic population. Students will enter our classrooms expecting to be taught in ways that are meaningful and relevant to their lives. Because of that, language instruction must include an eclectic pedagogy.

Teachers will be required to draw from a wide repertoire of instructional strategies—these include from teaching the gifted student to teaching the disabled student.

SD
What role can/should an ordinary school teacher play in these changes?

MHH
Teachers can be proactive and participate in curricula writing, staff development, and action research. Included in this is professional development and reflective practice and inquiry. These will inform teaching and then teachers become teacher leaders and take roles in their schools/districts where they work in conjunction with post-secondary scholars/researchers and textbook companies. Right now in some places these groups work in isolation and there is very little articulation. Classroom teachers are for the most part very willing participants when asked and encouraged to take part in this kind of articulation.

CONSIDER

Read both introductions and interviews in chapters 4 and 5 to get a better understanding of how you could participate in curriculum development.

SD
What are the advantages of the involvement of parents?

MHH
Parents are the best advocates for their children. The literature is very rich on the benefits of getting parents involved in the entire schooling process. Parents have an enormous influence especially with regard to policy and decision-making in political arenas.

CONSIDER

Develop specific ideas of how to include parents in the further enhancement of your classroom work. Find one or two current publications on this topic that may foster your own search for ideas.

SD
Why is it important for teachers to regard texts as resources and not primary modes of instruction?

MHH
The text is *not the* center of the teacher's universe. The text must be regarded as an ancillary material. There is no perfect text. We must accept that. Every class is comprised of no two learners who are exactly alike. Every student deserves to be taught and regarded as an individual. One size doesn't fit all and we must admit that and stop trying to superimpose a cookie-cutter textbook. The use of authentic materials is much more readily available today than ever before in our teaching profession. This is further enhanced through the use of the worldwide web.

SD
How can technology be used to enhance learner-centered instruction?

MHH
One of the greatest advantages of using technology is that it allows the learner to interact completely one on one with the computer and that provides self-paced instruction. The learner can work independently, in pairs, or in groups. Teachers can

CONSIDER

Read the chapters by Fraser/Hoffmann and Müller-Hartmann/Schocker-v. Ditfurth in this volume to get a better understanding about the influence of technology in both student learning and teacher training.

tailor fit instruction to meet the needs and interests of their students. Furthermore, technology allows students to work at their level of proficiency, thereby ensuring differentiated instruction.

ACTION

Identify all chapters in this book that deal with portfolios as an alternative means of assessment.

SD

What changes need to take place to improve assessment practices in language education?

MHH

Assessment practices need to move from one-dimensional to multidimensional. As educators, it is incumbent upon us to be clear about the purpose of an assessment philosophy. Why do we assess? When? For what purpose? How? Do we assess what we've taught or what we think we've taught? The shift in the paradigm has already taken place. We are witnessing today a trend toward performance-based assessment in which students are asked to *show* what they can do with the language. Since not all students learn in the same manner, a premise that has become more widely accepted, we must also acknowledge the need for alternative forms of assessment.

SD

What efforts can be made to help teachers actualize theory to practice?

ACTION

Find out about the opinion of two other authors in this book, Sharon Wilkinson and Lee Wilberschied, on the teacher-researcher issue and summarize their different views.

MHH

I am a big proponent of teachers engaging in action research and reflective inquiry. In my experiences I have discovered that this is a very empowering activity for teachers. First, it allows teachers to tackle a *puzzlement* that is of concern to them on a very real and personal level. Second, teachers will avail themselves of the current literature to discover what has already been written on the topic and this helps them formulate a strategic plan as to how they will investigate a particular phenomenon. Teachers quickly realize that their research is often *generalizable* and that it is of interest to other educators.

Collaboration in Virtual Space (CiVS): Technology in the Language Classroom

Catherine C. Fraser
Dierk O. Hoffmann

Introduction

Observation A

It is a truism that motivation—with all its various subcategories—is one of the prime factors contributing to educational success (Schmidt et al. 11). Unfortunately, a major factor for Foreign Language (FL) learning—societal expectations—is almost nonexistent in the US. This lack, certainly, is one of the main reasons underlying the FL crisis which, for years, has been discussed but not resolved (Schneider 2001). Knowing a FL is seen by most, even in academia, as unnecessary. FL requirements often are regarded as obsolete and superfluous. The world speaks English. Therefore, the study of FLs is taken care of with a minimum of time investment (standard requirement: three college semesters of one FL) and FLs do not play a major role in one's later career. It is not only Don DeLillo's Jack Gladney who is deficient (1984)—there are many like him. The view that every translation is a commentary (an axiom is part of the philosophy of language most distinctly seen in the Muslim approach to the Qur'án) is often expounded. In reality, however, it is a belief not truly shared by most US academics.

ACTION

Convince a partner that learning a foreign language is a worthwhile endeavor.

Observation B

Bob was on the wanted list of every football coach looking for a strong defensive line, but he was not a favorite of FL teachers. "I learn by experience, not by books," he remarked later. "I know something by feeling it. So unless I experience something and can relate a certain feeling to it, I have trouble retaining or understanding it" (personal E-mail). What he needed—as do all FL learners—was a suitable environment to maximize his learning potential. He found this type of environment in a German butchers' shop and a master class for butchers at a leading vocational school; Chris, the viola enthusiast, found it in orchestras; and Darcy, the future actress, in the theater as an assistant to the director.[1]

DISCUSS

How do you learn? Complete the following statement: *I learn by* ______ *not by* ______. Discuss your reasons with a classmate.

Experiential learning (Kolb 1984) combined with formal training is an old concept, addressing the needs for the different skills and intelligences of individuals (Gardner 1983). Yet it is not favored in the typical academic curriculum which stresses a cognitive approach to learning. Although most second language acquisition theorists will agree that there is no one learner type and that there is no one method which fits all, "language learning in the classroom tends to be mainly objective and analytical" and usually excludes learners who require the "subjective, participatory, and non-

CONSIDER

Review Howard Gardner's *Theory of Multiple Intelligences*, as summarized in Marjorie Hall Haley's article and *The Role and Impact of Learner Diversity and Technology*, in this volume.

analytical" (Stern 506). Even the movement towards more individualized instruction, which began in the early 1970s (Stern 447) and was often linked to the progress of self-paced computer learning programs, was not able to bring about a real paradigm shift. In the late 1990s M. D. Bush was still able to remark that there "is little evidence that technology is having any significant impact on the way most students learn languages in today's classroom" (288).

Consequence

Whereas it is almost impossible to find a solution to the motivational problems mentioned in observation A, technology may yet be of help in regard to observation B. "The reason for the widespread failure of learners to learn FLs in school settings (Selinker [1972] doubts that more than a small percentage of learners in school settings learn the L2 well) is very likely systemic in nature and built into the relationship between the task and the setting" (Hopkins 46). Technology may be able to bring about change and even strengthen the learners' motivation—at least the *instrumental* and *integrative* motives underlying their FL learning efforts (Gardner & Lambert 132)—because the current technology-mediated learning focuses less on FL as a skill but more on FL as a means for social interaction. Its ability to establish links to the multifaceted world outside the classroom "can play an important role in fostering second language acquisition by electronically increasing learners' contact with a wide array of authentic materials" (Blake 210) and with native speakers of the target language.[2] By creating new environments which allow for different learning strategies and which provide a multitude of opportunities for students to better match their personal interests with language learning goals, one can expand the group of potential FL learners, increase course offerings in traditional curricula through inter-institutional collaboration, and introduce cross-cultural programs which link students with the *real* world and lead them to a realization of the culturally biased approaches in their field of specialization and to a genuine cultural literacy, the "ongoing dynamic process of negotiating meaning and understanding differences of perspective" (Furstenberg et al. 56). As Tenzin Gyatso, the 14th Dalai Lama of Tibet, remarked in the foreword to *A World's Fair for the Global Village*, "The technology that lets us span the world, to communicate instantly across oceans, is a tool that we can use to preserve diversity, to enrich our understanding of each other, and enhance our sense of community" (Malamud xi).

ACTION

After reading the following two examples of the use of technology in the classroom, choose one type of technology (video conferencing or the Internet), and brainstorm two to three different project possibilities. Choose one, write it up, try it, and reflect on progression and results.

The *Smart Classroom* Tools

Example A: Video and Videoconferencing (VC)

"Slow, Woyzeck, slow," remarked the captain standing slightly above Woyzeck on a ramp of an abstract stage-design and pushed Woyzeck's head from under his coat: felatio as a symbol of absolute suppression instead of the shaving scene of the original text. The students stared in shock at the screen.

As part of a joint theater project between a city theater and various educational institutions,[3] real contemporary theater had entered the classroom and transformed the conventional academic discussion with the Socratic leading questions by the teacher into a heated conversation. Although it was only a video, the students felt as if they were in the audience in the Freiburg theater because the live performance of Georg Büchner's *Woyzeck,* a theatrical highlight of the season, had been especially taped for them. How did their peers in Germany view this production by the young and controversial but respected director Cihan Inan? How did the press react? What did the audience think? What caused the director to emphasize sexuality here in such a way and—perhaps worse—at the end where Woyzeck slowly penetrates the corpse of the just murdered Marie? Why did he combine different characters into one—the captain, the doctor, and the Charlatan; the Drum Major and Andres—and add a new character: Woyzeck's *soul* who also played the role of the son, the horse, and who ended the play with the anti-fairy tale of the grandmother? Did the actors feel comfortable presenting this version on stage? Were they influenced in their own interpretations by older productions? Why did the costume designer choose straitjackets as the underlying and unifying theme for the costumes of the characters? What inspired the stage designer to an abstract conception of the stage? With its ramps surrounding a square center, was the stage thought of as a form of cage for Woyzeck in which he was trapped by society? Why change the sequence of the scenes completely and have the action appear as memory?

As expected, the following meetings with the students' German peers in virtual space via VC and later with the actors, director and production staff raised only more questions. The German students and the audience which they had surveyed in the meantime seemed as puzzled and divided as the US undergraduates and even the professionals were not speaking in one voice. Yet, the director who sat in a third studio because he had left Freiburg for a new production in Berne, Switzerland, was convincing in presenting his case. The arguments went back and forth, faces appeared and disappeared on a large screen showing the distant site. Soon all participants understood how to manipulate the camera by pushing a button to have the camera zoom in on them to guarantee eye contact with their conversation partners in the other studios; they learned how to avoid the blurring of speech caused by simultaneously speaking at the different sites; and they knew when to mute their microphone to prevent confusion of the audio sensitive transmission bridge linking the participating studios. With time, the VC became ever more lively and intimate. Laughter and humor removed inhibitions and made the screen disappear: the distant partners seemed to be actually sitting in the room. The only missing element was the possibility of sharing the same bottle of wine.

DISCUSS

What can be the impact of using video conferencing on language learning? Discuss the advantages and disadvantages of using this kind of technology.

During the meeting between the US and the Freiburg students, both studios were even transformed into a stage. Individual scenes which were part of a class project were acted out, segments of a radio show based on *Woyzeck* presented, video clips and pictures discussed which documented school visits by the Freiburg students who studied pedagogy and were interested in the outreach efforts of the city theater to schools and other pedagogical institutions. The US students presented excerpts from a film project interspersed with live music recitals performed in the classroom studio.

And all ended with a joint dance led by a Freiburg student who demonstrated how she had worked with elementary school children when she tried to introduce them to dramatic forms and the theater.

Example B: Internet-Collaboration Facilities

The next day, the collaborative routine between the different student groups continued across the Atlantic, using the various tools their virtual learning environment *Blackboard* offers:[4] an announcement page for official messages; a bulletin board for posting notes and for organizing asynchronous threaded discussions (which can be archived); a *mail-room* for sending messages to selected individuals or groups; and a station for up- and downloading of word, sound, and picture files; a roster of all participants with access to their homepages, i.e., their personal introductions; a virtual classroom which features a white board for the display of pictures, web pages, and the possibility of working jointly on graphic designs; it can also be utilized for informal chats (with the possibility of having them saved for later scrutiny); working spaces for groups inside the larger class framework with the same built-in functionality; access to a special collaborative writing space (*Wiki*) and *NetMeeting* which allows application sharing across the ocean, chats, and web-based VC; links to a unique collection of material for the *Woyzeck*-production, the virtual project-library, as well as a special exhibition space, the *Virtual Museum*.

The aim of the *Virtual Museum*[5] is to bring "teachers and learners together in new and dynamic ways. As in a traditional museum, creations of permanent value can be presented digitally and interpreted in a variety of educational contexts. The added value of the virtual museum is its potential for engaging teachers and learners as they create or respond to *exhibits*. Whether the exhibit is an instructor-constructed learning environment, or a portfolio of student learning experiences, museum visitors have the opportunity to create, question, explore, and critique as part of a learning community online" (official welcome page).

Exhibitions can be public, i.e., the viewing open to anyone, or restricted to a specified group. In any case, visitors will enter a lobby with a pleasing view into the museum hallways with benches to rest on above which is the information board with the list of exhibitions available in this particular museum. Entering an exhibition room, they see well-lit walls with pictures and/or texts and/or loudspeakers depending on the exhibition. They can walk around the room (using simple navigation tools), glance at each wall separately besides getting an overview of the exhibition space. They can then select an exhibited piece (click on a picture or text icon) to get more information. The picture will be displayed in a large format in a new window with its accompanying text next to it. The text may have further links to more pictures and more text, to sound or video. But it is not a purely passive experience. Visitors have the opportunity to leave their comments and thereby give direct input to an exhibition.

Similarly to the *Virtual Museum*, the project-library is not an abstract space but a very concrete room. When its door opens—one does not yet feel the draft of the cold air emanating from the inside (that will be implemented in the next version)—one looks at a shelf with books and a poster of *Woyzeck* and a digital screen on the wall. While standard materials are available in the home libraries of the participating institutions, a very special online collection of authentic material has been assembled here for the *Woyzeck*-project: (1) dictionaries, grammars, and reference works; (2) information on Georg Büchner's life, the historical background, and his works (with special emphasis on his play *Woyzeck*) which the production staff of the theater of Freiburg had prepared for the actors; (3) access to examples of Georg Büchner's manuscripts; (4) the text with alterations and cuts by the director (Freiburg text version); (5) a video of and a report by the dramaturg of the first meeting of the actors and the production staff to discuss the concept of the production; (6) photographs of the "Bauprobe" (the very first improvised version of the stage design); (7) the figurines (sketches of the planned costumes); (8) the official information sheets about the play distributed by the theater (a short summary of the plot, historical background of the play, intentions of playwright and director); (9) the program notes; (10) photos from rehearsals and live performances; (11) digitized videos from various productions (historic ones and the newest staging by the Freiburg City Theater); (12) press releases about the performance; (13) links to other web sites on *Woyzeck* and Georg Büchner.

DISCUSS

What is your reaction to these creative uses of the Internet? As a student, would access to such resources increase your motivation to learn another language? Why or why not?

One just needs to click on a book in the bookshelf to have it open up, click on the poster on the wall to have other pictures of the performance displayed, or click on the TV screen to choose the viewing of a production from the list presented. Manuscripts are part of an electronic scholarly archive (Hoffmann, Jörgensen, & Fölsche 1993) and offer transcriptions and annotations. All texts allow for fast recall of dictionaries: highlighting a German word and a click on a button in the margin called *Mr. Check* displays a German-German definition from the *Duden*; placing an online dictionary next to a text page makes it possible to look up German-English and English-German translations on the spur of the moment.[6]

Pedagogical Evaluation of the Tools

Computer-Mediated Communication (CMC)

CMC has been thoroughly researched (Tschirner 1999) and the general consensus has been positive. It reduces stress and classroom anxiety (Fraser 1999; Tschirner 1999; Warschauer 1996; Pinto 1996; Beauvois 1992; Smith 1990) which has a clearly negative impact on language performance and affects the communicative strategies employed as Horwitz and Young (1991) explain in Language Anxiety referring to various studies. "That is, the more anxious student tends to avoid attempting difficult or personal messages in the target language" (Horwitz & Young 28). Kleinman found in an ESL study, "students with high levels of debilitating anxiety attempted different types of grammatical constructions than did less anxious ESL students" (28); and Steinberg and Horwitz concurred "that students experiencing an anxiety-producing condition attempted less interpretive (more concrete) messages than those experiencing a relaxed condition" (28). Using the various computer-communication tools, asynchronous as well as synchronous ones, shows, on the other hand, that there is increased participation from all members of the group, that more language is generated than in a normal classroom, that the contributions are more evenly spread over the class population, that they are less dominated by a few, that there is more genuine negotiations of meaning, more complex grammatical and lexical forms are generated, (Fraser 1999; Tschirner 1999) and discussions are extended "beyond the time frame of the class" (Kagel et al. 2002). As Kelm states, "the honesty and openness of the comments, the frequent tags and questions, the aside comments, the turn taking strategies, and the willingness to express opinions all supersede traditional language games and conversation activities" (Kelm 26). In addition, the archiving function is good for remedial learning because it allows exchanges to be assessed again at a later time when more thorough error analysis can take place. Especially the dual nature of chats (a written modality joined with an oral communicative attitude) seems to be good for development of speech production skills, for internalizing the cognitive knowledge (Tschirner 56).

ACTION

Try out Computer Mediated Communication (CMC). Work with a partner to locate a bulletin board or chat room of interest. Participate in the ongoing *discussion* and reflect on your experience. Share your experience with others.

The flexibility and user-friendliness of the new generation of computer technology, with visual, *humane* interfaces which mirror the real world in mock seriousness, can clearly contribute much in setting the right tone for learning. In this vein of thought, the distribution of joint projects among participants, of matching up teams across the ocean can become a *project*-market which can be as lively as the stockmarket on Wall Street after the bell has rung. Everyone hurries to the common bulletin board to *sell* ideas, to advertise her/his topic and to persuade others to participate—a flurry of genuine communication. Students can post their ideas, can add links to other web pages, including their personal home page on which the individuals can describe their hobbies and preferences to give a vivid picture of themselves in order to find the right partner—not for life but for the project (although experience shows, match making is often the result of lively pedagogical interaction). Interest in a topic proposal can be expressed by responding directly to the announcement by clicking a reply button or by going to the *post office* where a list of all participants is available and where one can select with a click the addressee or addressees one would like to contact. Now one can arrange a meeting in the common lounge (chat room) at a specified time for a quick exchange of ideas, or—if one is really daring—one arranges a face-to-face meeting via Webcam. This initial flurry of activity is a warm-up exercise in regard to content, language use, and mastery of the communication tools which are so important in the actual work later on in the semester.

Two-Way Simultaneous Videoconferencing (VC)

VC events, in contrast to CMC, add "several entirely new dimensions to the problem of classroom anxiety" (Kinginger 1998). Negative as well as positive features of a classroom are magnified. Paradoxically, the conversation partner in a VC appears to be closer than in a traditional classroom conversation because the camera is able to offer a front seat even to the person in the back row while presenting a point of view. Yet, this may also be a cause for stress. The learner cannot hide, is publicly exposed, perhaps even recorded on tape, the situation is face-threatening, the result may be a mental block, frustration, perhaps a total break-down. VC clearly favors the self-assured extrovert and the observations in regard to CMC can be reversed: there is no increased participation from all members of the group, the contributions are not more evenly spread over the class population. Even people who are used to public speaking, such as well-known writers, can experience the cold sweat breaking out and the feeling of abandonment and helplessness. "The experience with the teleconference was for me a nightmare," remarked one established author (personal E-mail). And it is easy to put oneself in the position of such a participant sitting alone in a studio in front of two monitors, one with one's own picture "(Why? Why does he have to watch death at work while he is talking to his audience?)" The second monitor displays—that's the way it seems at least—people with voices who ask a question or give an answer. But this *meeting* can be viewed as a dream of technology freaks, not reality. It is fake. At least, it used to be that way when the *perceptual latency* caused by the slight time lapse in satellite transmission (Kinginger 5) was more than 1/10 of a second and could turn conversation for sensitive participants into a farce. Each immediate reaction of the listener (shaking of the head, smile, frown, nodding) arrived when the person speaking had already moved on. But these physical (physiognomic) exchanges are part of the essence of communication and interaction. Under these conditions, one may stop functioning and the instinct to run away may become greater than the inbred sense of politeness and the joy of the adventure. Desperation may increase and depression sets in.

CONSIDER

Refer to your earlier discussion of the advantages and disadvantages of using video conferencing. Did you consider the difficulties listed here by the authors? What, if any, are the advantages of video conferencing? Read on to see the authors' view on how to effectively use this form of technology.

Besides negative psychological factors, the VC technology may cause severe problems. Whereas in computer use, the speed of the Internet may be slow because of the electronic traffic jams, or a server may be down, in VC the range of types of technical failure multiplies: the connection may fail; the picture may be snowy; the movement jerky; the sound disappear; the picture suddenly freeze while the sound still functions—not to mention the less than optimal set-ups of VC rooms where people are crowded in corners, the microphones are handed around, heads block the view of the people farther back, cameras with a sound sensitive setting zoom in on a person's coughing spell instead of the speaker or zoom in on the speaker after he or she has uttered a short remark; in multi-point videoconferences, participants may forget to mute their microphones when it is not their turn causing the satellite bridge to show the wrong pictures to the participating sites. The list could go on.

The above presented positive view (see Example A) in describing elements drawn from several collaborative projects should therefore not be misunderstood as representing unreflected euphoria with technology and is not intended to detract from the fact of stress and the possibility of technical failure. On the contrary, one must be very aware of the inherent restricting nature of VC in order to utilize its creative elements. But these difficulties can be overcome and VC does not need to be equated with dull question-and-answer sessions and stony faces marked by stage fright. Certainly, VC "poses a particular challenge because its visual element tends to encourage recidivism into lecturing modes" (Burge 12)—and this is probably the primary mode of interaction in VC: the talking head of the lecturer on the screen and a PowerPoint presentation on a second screen next to it—but it is up to the participants to alter this perception.

If real interaction is the goal, *ice-breakers* are fine for one time events (Jones & Sorenson 2001) and the fear of slight embarrassment and insecurity during a VC may actually be pedagogically productive and lead to more self-discipline and a greater learning effort afterwards (Kinginger 1998). But if one plans to integrate VC into a cross-cultural course as a more permanent feature, one needs to be very much aware of the *affective filter* in learning (Krashen 1981) and it is advisable to give the design of a remote collaboration facility (RCF) the same kind of attention and pedagogical scrutiny one gives to a classroom and its technical equipment. The overarching concern is the creation of a stress-free learning climate. This is as true for the general classroom atmosphere in which errors are not frowned upon but seen as natural as it is for working with technology.

The basic tenets of suggestopedia, a positive expectancy and motivation by creating a relaxed learning environment, (Daniels & Mehn 1985; Prichard & Taylor 1980) apply in VC more so than in the traditional classroom. Only if all aspects are optimal, one is really able to harness or overcome classroom anxiety and turn VC into a productive instrument for learning in the same way as CMC.

Fortunately, the fact that most learners today grew up in a media world and are used to talk shows and TV soap operas allows the instructor to employ these genres as a pedagogical aid. As theater productions (Maley & Duff 1982; Smith 1984) are an effective FL teaching tool, the studio set-up of a VC can be utilized to have the basic course structure revolve around the concept of talk shows and broadcasts. Depending on the nature of the upcoming conference, with peers or a distinguished guest, the preparations can take different forms but never lose their playfulness. Practice interviews and conversations in which students assume the roles of the future guests are one method among many. Students also learn coping strategies—which are always important and effective in live situations—and they can internalize much language by imitating news anchors, disk jockeys, faking free speech by reading from teleprompters or carefully placed notes. Mock sessions in the studio, getting used to cameras and microphones and all the technical paraphernalia alleviate stress even more. The studio has to be a workshop in which students feel at home and are familiar with all its features. It has to become a tool which actually empowers them to improve their self-image.

For this development to occur, a studio has to be set up optimally and the VC should not be a one time event but an integrated component of a course. Whereas this was seldom possible a few years ago due to the burden on the budget (Sanders 138), today VCs can be run via IP instead of ISDN connections.[7] Yet, the other aspects have not changed over the years and are as important today as they were years ago: The lighting should not distort faces; the microphone should be centrally located to evenly pick up the sound independently from the speaker's location; the camera should be mounted correctly over the monitor in which the image of the distant site appears to guarantee natural eye contact; it has to react instantly to the instructor's pre-sets or to call buttons or voice activation; the seat arrangement has to guarantee unobstructed views of all participants and has to fit the occasion—lecture, interview, casual conversation. The display of (a) computer screens, (b) documents and transparencies via document camera, (c) images via a slide projector, (d) sound via radio, CD, or cassette player, (e) video via VCR or DVD should be easy. Ideally, the conference should proceed—if texts and images are displayed via the computer—in a two-channel set-up, i.e., one screen/monitor should be devoted to the speaker(s), a second one to file sharing for the text and images. In addition, the classroom should allow for traditional use of a blackboard and have a white board which makes it possible to save the notes written on it on a computer (e.g., *Mimio Board*). Summarized briefly, the VC studio has to be a real learning space and not a closet into which many people are crammed.

ACTION

Interview someone who has experienced videoconferencing in language teaching. How specifically was the technology anchored in the overall lesson plan? What was the outcome of it in the classroom?

The Goal: Individualized Learning in a Global Environment

If a multi-cultural outlook is genuinely embraced by an institution of higher learning and FL outreach is part of the official policies, the pleas of second language acquisition theorists of the seventies who demanded of teachers that they "sharpen their skills as diagnosticians" (Altman 15) will gain new relevance because the focus has to be genuinely on individual learners and their needs (Allwright 1982; Altman & James 1980; Nunan 1988). Language courses as part of a traditional literature program—as is usually the case in US colleges—have only a limited usefulness in such a framework because they have to cater to different constituencies. They may be very successful in individual cases due to excellent instructors who understand well how to work with a pluralistic group of students, but they cannot be seriously considered a solution for bringing FLs to students who are far removed in their interests from the world of the Humanities. The same is true for FL courses whose content is not predetermined by a program but rather based on the biases and preferences of the instructor (Rosellini 1997).

Instead, courses are structured around the interests of the students, for example: 1) in a collaborative course setting between an intermediate German class in the US and a seminar for future teachers of German as a FL in Germany, the US students expressed their interests to the German students who then prepared individualized Web-based exercises incorporating the immediate feedback of the learners; the final results were presented to their US partners in a VC (Rössler 1997; see also Schneider et al. 2000); 2) on a larger scale, the University of Rhode Island's (URI) International Engineering Program (IEP) (Reinhard 2001) can serve as a model which does not need to be limited to engineering or business schools but which can be adapted by other institutions in accordance with their local situation. At the core of the approach is the linking of language use with one's academic field (an experiential aspect) as expressed in the mission statement by the Consortium of Languages Across the Curriculum (CLAC) (Straight 1998): "Languages Across the Curriculum (LAC) refers to the practice through which the study and use of languages take place throughout the curriculum. Its purpose is to prepare students for the cross-cultural and multilingual demands and opportunities of a global society. LAC is appropriate at all levels of education" (CLAC 1996). Primarily, St. Olaf College was and is a champion of the movement. They offer three different kinds of foreign language components:

- In the *paired instructor* model—known as the *St. Olaf Model* because of the pioneering efforts of the St. Olaf FLAC Program, you'll meet with two professors. The foreign language professor is responsible for the foreign language component; the professor of the core course attends as a participant.
- In the *single instructor* model, the professor of the core course is also responsible for the foreign language component.
- In the *readings enriched* model, the professor of the core course leads the discussion in English of materials you'll read in the foreign language.

ACTION

In your own words summarize the meaning of *languages across the curriculum (LAC)*, and the implications it has for curriculum development. To learn more about St. Olaf's FLAC Program, visit them online at: <www.stolaf.edu/depts/flac/>

A fourth type can be based on the concept of tandem learning (Brammerts 1996; Kötter 2002). Learners in different cultures with the same interest can be linked. To facilitate and structure their interaction, an online instructor supervises their joint projects and is available as a language resource person. Organizationally, such a course can be implemented in various ways. Clustering of tandems, i.e., several tandem groups are observed by one instructor; outsourcing of learner groups, i.e., individual pairs are supported by free-lance online instructors; creation of a Virtual FL Collaborative (VFLC).

The VFLC is a group of instructors in different small institutions who are interested in sharing expertise and resources. In its ultimate form, it is a virtual FL department consisting of a consortium of small autonomous departments which agreed to a set of common goals, to design a joint curriculum, and to synchronize their annual course offerings in order to be able to collaborate more easily and to offer their students a wider range of courses going far beyond the capacity of any single program (Morrell 2000). The same is true for the Virtual German Collaborative (VGC) supported by the Mellon-funded National Institute for Technology and Liberal Education (NITLE).

> It seeks to extend and enrich the resources and expertise available to students of small departments through inter-institutional collaboration. Designed to strengthen the instruction of German language and culture, this project endeavors to use technology to bring individuals and resources together in new ways <www.nitle.org/german>.

The scenarios for such collaborative efforts (Comeaux 2002; Palloff & Pratt 1999)—which can be extended to a Global Learning Environment (GLEn, see Barson & Debski 1996)—are numerous, especially if these courses are also supported by online Writing Across the Curriculum Centers (WAC) which are today a common feature at most US campuses to help an interdisciplinary clientele with their compositions in English and which are also making inroads at European institutions (Bräuer 2002).

Although it is impossible in all learning situations to accommodate the learners' *functional* expectations fully, electronic communication tools such as MOOs (Pinto 1996; Sanchez 1996) are predestined for a constructivist pedagogical approach and—as Von der Emde, Schneider, and Kötter remark in regard to one of their exemplary MOO-based collaboration courses—almost automatically restructure "language learning dynamics away from drill-like exercises or an exclusive attention to grammatical accuracy to content-based activities and meaningful communication between students" (213). Being placed in charge, being given autonomy, learners identify much more with their own learning process in general and their individual class projects in particular, invest more time and energy in revisions, and develop a new pride in their final products (Schaumann 2001). Greater self-reliability and independence means greater self-responsibility. A basis for this task-based approach is Bloomfield's age-old recognition that "our fundamental mistake has been to regard language teaching as a set of facts [...] Language is not a process of logical reference to a conscious set of rules; the process of understanding, speaking, and writing is everywhere an associative one. Real language teaching consists, therefore, of building up in the pupil those associative habits which constitute the language to be learned" (294; quoted in Prabhu 6-7).

Because of this shift from an *object-regulated* and *other-regulated* to a *self-regulated* approach, the learners' "interactive experience of the ontogenesis of <their> first language" is not contradicted but is instead reconfirmed (Foley 68). The once experienced psychological framework is the same and therefore alters the perception of the present learning task. FL learning becomes an interactive and social event in which the role of the instructor changes to one of facilitator, resource person, and interactor. They are only one part of the newly established community of autonomous learners. "We are no longer talking of teachers teaching and learners learning, but everyone contributing to the management of everyone's learning (including their own, and including the teacher's, of course)" (Allwright 166). Learning and teaching merge in this decentralized workshop atmosphere which is characterized by empathy and authenticity because it is not only the material which is authentic—see the content of the special library for *Woyzeck*—and the communication between the partners but the relationship and responsibility for each other and the projects.

DISCUSS

Discuss your strategies for integrating technology into the foreign language classroom. How can you use videoconferencing or a virtual classroom to motivate your students and positively impact the quality of the learning that takes place?

In contrast with the acquisition of their first language, the learners can now draw from much more experience and they can gradually construct their own world—experiencing the process as an intellectually as well as emotionally rewarding experience—which may meander in unforeseen and uncharted territory putting into practice the research by cognitive scientists who "have found that by matching new language input with old bits of knowledge—what linguists call *schemata*—students constantly *negotiate* between what they already know and what they hear and see in new communicative situations" (Hunt 1982; Rüschoff 1993, both quoted in Von der Emde, et al. 213).

Conclusion

It is self-evident that "the computer"—and one can also include VC—"is rather a medium or an environment in which a wide variety of methods, approaches, or pedagogical philosophies may be implemented" (Garrett 75). Technology is not the alpha and omega for successful FL teaching, but whereas early computer-assisted FL learning (CALL) was primarily oriented towards the syntagmatic aspect of FL learning (Barson & Debski 49)—even in its *communicative* form—the technology referred to in these remarks has as its focus the pragmatic aspect. The special rewards it can offer are a new excitement and additional pedagogical avenues (e.g., easy access to authentic material and language, including contemporary spoken language[8]) to optimize the FL learning environment (Tschirner et al. 2000) and to realize basic strategies which proved to be effective in achieving the traditional fundamental communication goals: autonomous learning and peer teaching in a student-centered classroom, individualized learning, experimentation, and play (Von der Emde, et al. 2001; Tschirner 1999; Underwood 1984). In this context, not only the role of the instructor will change from teacher to "designer, guide, mentor, facilitator" (Kelm 27) but the concept of class may take new forms: learning groups of two or three or four which may only be organizationally tied together through the presence of the former instructor (Tella 11).

"If being human is all about talking, it's the tittle-tattle of life that makes the world go round" (Dunbar 4), the emphasis even for FL instruction should be to place "purpose" (Wells 16) before form. And as paradoxical as it may seem at first glance, such a shift of emphasis can be better achieved in a virtual than in a traditional classroom because the traditional classroom is characterized by the concept of the one expert and the many *ignoramuses*, the virtual classroom can be much more of a mixture. In such a situation in which personal tutoring is the norm, *purpose* instead of practice of form can become the prime mover of generating language. In this way, computer-communication and videoconferencing are excellent aids to create real interactive learning groups which will, in addition, lead also to the recognition of subtle distinctions between cultures, uncovering prejudices, and engendering an understanding and respect for differences. It is a training in the art of searching for patterns of meaning in the target as well as one's own language by comparing, discussing, and analyzing parallel concepts, being aware of the investigators' own biases and historical horizon. This open-ended hermeneutical process—which brings self-awareness as well as awareness of the foreign (Krumm 1995)—comes close to an intellectual as well as emotional understanding of the elusive feature called culture (Furstenberg et al. 2001).

Not as elusive but, on the contrary, sometimes painfully obvious—and often posing serious problems—are the mundane organizational and structural questions on which such subtle investigations rest: semesters in Europe and the US do not run parallel and overlap only partially, access to *smart* classroom/RCFs vary, academic expectations, evaluations, and self image (Scollon & Scollon 166) are different in the various cultures and will influence students' attitudes towards collaborative projects which may result in frustration and tension (Belz & Müller-Hartmann 2002)—but can become themselves a topic of scrutiny.

Adding up the pros and cons, it becomes clear that there is still a large untapped pedagogical potential. One can also come to the conclusion that technology is able to bring about a transformation in language learning and not just an expansion of new playgrounds for creativity because the major change caused by the inclusion of Web technology and/or videoconferencing will lead to a new understanding of language learning as described by Von der Emde, Schneider and Kötter, the representatives of a young generation of language, culture and literature teachers who show the future in FL instruction. "Rather than seeing language learning as the successful application of grammatical and lexical rules or even, as Turbee (1997) suggests, the internalization of 'language structures within the broader contexts of dialogue and culture,' we would provisionally suggest a broader definition that emphasizes language as a developing and changing practice that not only reflects cultural differences but shapes the very constitution of humanistic knowledge" (Von der Emde et al. 221-222). And as the new approach, the conscious application of autonomous learning principles recognizes that each learner is motivated in different ways, one has also to accept that "what constitutes success may vary greatly from one student to another. Measuring all students against the same proficiency goals may not provide an accurate picture of language learning successes, many of which are more intellectual and cultural than practical. This logic does not mean that practical goals should be devalued in favor of intellectual awareness but rather only that instructors should help our students make informed decisions for themselves—and that means opening up, rather than narrowing down, their options in the language classroom" (Von der Emde et al. 222).

Notes

1. In a study on learning achievements during a study group abroad experience, the experiential learners were clearly ahead, see Fraser 2002.
2. Warschauer, ed., 1996. Collaboration can be achieved on different levels, see Hedderich 1997, Wienroeder-Skinner & Maass 1997, Sanders 1997, Brammerts 1996, Johnson 1996, Kern 1996. For authentic material see the various link trails on the ATTG and Goethe-Institute Home pages; Moehle-Vieregge, Brid, & Manteghi 1996; Di Bella 1997, Tschirner 1997.
3. The performance was one of the focal points of a cross-cultural theater project "Drama -Theater-School" in which four groups from three countries participated in conjunction with the *Stadttheater Freiburg* (organization: Angelika Weiß, TheaterKontakt): students from (1) the *Collegio Papio*, Ascona, Switzerland; (2) the *Angell Gymnasium*, Freiburg, Germany; (3) the *Pädagogische Hochschule*, Freiburg; and (4) *Colgate University*, New York. Although the institutional situations were not comparable, the class schedules different, even the pedagogical goals not the same, learning was enhanced for all groups by a new excitement, by the experience of an international learning community, by sharing resources as well as ideas.
4. Similar programs are FirstClass,WebCT, Topclass, and Learning Space. (See Kearsey 2000).
5. Hosted by: Center for Educational Technology, Middlebury College. Design by: J. Scott Payne, Bret Olsen, and Aaron Coburn. Part of the National Institute for Technology and Liberal Education (NITLE) in Middlebury, formerly, Mellon Project 2001.
6. *Mr. Check* is now only commercially available by Tanto Xipolis GmbH. The dictionary by Informatik der Technischen Universität München, on the other hand, is still publicly accessible.

NOTE

As Leaver et al. clearly show, professional organizations can play a substantial role in teacher development and support. For additional information and opinions on teacher development and support, read chapter 5.

7. IP stands for Internet Protocol. It uses the standard network connection. ISDN stands for Integrated Services Digital Network. ISDNs are like modems, but 5 times faster. They require special telephone lines, which have a higher cost than normal phone lines.
8. For French, see Kinginger. As Carter and McCarthy (1995) suggest, some features of the spoken language may not be suitable for models for productive use by students, but might instead become the focus of activities designed to help learners become keen and critical observers of language use, aware of the complex relationship between language and context.

References

Allwright, R. L. "Perceiving and Pursuing Learners' Needs." *Individualisation*. Ed. M. Geddes and G. Sturtridge. Oxford: Modern English Publications, 1982.

Allwright, R. L. "The Importance of Interaction in Classroom Language Learning." *Applied Linguistics* 5.2 (1984): 156-171.

Altman, H. B., and C. V. James, ed. *Foreign Language Teaching: Focus on the Learner*. Altman and James 1-16.

——. *Foreign Language Teaching: Meeting Individual Needs*. Oxford: Pergamon, 1980.

Barson, J., and R. Debski. "Calling Back CALL: Technology in the Service of Foreign Language Learning Based on Creativity, Contingency, and Goal-Oriented Activity." Warschauer 49-68.

Beauvois, M. H. "E-Talk: Attitudes and Motivation in Computer-Assisted Classroom Discussion." *Computers in the Humanities* 28 (1992): 177-190.

Belz, J. A., and A. Müller-Hartmann. "Deutsch-amerikanische Telekollaboration im Fremdsprachenunterricht—Lernende im Kreuzfeuer der institutionellen Zwänge." *Die Unterrichtspraxis* 35.1 (2002): 68-78.

Bennett, M. *Basic Concepts of Intercultural Communication*. Yarmouth: Intercultural Press, 1998.

Blake, R. J. "The Role of Technology in Second Language Learning." *Learning Foreign and Second Languages. Perspectives in Research and Scholarship*. Ed. H. Byrnes. New York: MLA, 1998. 209-237.

Bloomfield, L. *An Introduction to the Study of Language*. London: G. Bell and Sons, 1914.

Brammerts, H. "Language Learning in Tandem Using the Internet." Warschauer 121-130.

Bräuer, G. "Drawing Connections Across Education: The Freiburg Writing Center Model." *Language and Learning Across the Disciplines* 5.3 (2002): 61-80.

Burge, E. J. "Electronic Highway or Weaving Loom? Thinking about Conferencing Technologies for Learning." *Educational Resources Information Center (ERIC)*, 1994.

Bush, M. D. "Implementing Technology for Language Learning." Bush & Terry 287-349.

Bush, M. D., and R. M. Terry, ed. *Technology-Enhanced Language Learning*. Lincolnwood: National Textbook Company, 1997.

Carter, R., and M. McCarthy. "Grammar and the Spoken Language." *Applied Linguistics* 16 (1995): 141-158.

Comeaux, P., ed. *Communication and Collaboration in the Online Classroom. Examples and Applications*. Bolton: Anker Publishing Company, 2002.

Consortium for Languages across the Curiculum (CLAC). "Declaration of Principles and Practices." Nov. 1996 <http://www.language.brown.edu/LAC/endorsements.html>.

Crookes, G., and R. Schmidt. "Motivation. Reopening the Research Agenda." *Language Learning* 41 (1991): 469-512.

Daniels, K., and I. Mehn. *Konzepte emotionellen Lernens in der Deutsch-Didaktik*. Bonn-Bad Godesberg: Verlag Dürrsche Buchhandlung, 1985.

DeLillo, D. *White Noise*. Harmondsworth: Penguin, 1984.

DiBella, I. A. "German in Cyberspace: Tips and Strategies for Beginners." *Die Unterrichtspraxis* 30.2 (1997): 206-209.

Dunbar, R. *Grooming, Gossip, and the Evolution of Language*. Cambridge: Harvard UP, 1996.

Foley, J. "A Psycholinguistic Framework for Task-based Approaches to Language Teaching." *Applied Linguistics* 12 (1991): 62-75.

Fraser, C. "Goethe Gossips with Grass: Using Computer Chatting Software in an Introductory Literature Course." *Die Unterrichtspraxis* 32.1 (1999): 66-74.

Fraser, C. "Study Abroad. An Attempt to Measure the Gains." *German as a Foreign Language: Teaching and Learning German in an Intercultural Context* 1 (2002): 45-65.

Furstenberg, G. "Teaching with Technology: What is at Stake?" *ADFL Bulletin* 28.3 (1997): 21-25.

Furstenberg, G., S. Levet, K. English, and K. Maillet. "Giving a Virtual Voice to the Silent Language of Culture." *The Cultura Project. Language Learning and Technology* 5.1 (2001): 55-102.

Gardner, H. *Frames of Mind: The Theory of Multiple Intelligences*. New York: Basic Books, 1983.

Gardner, R. C., and W. E. Lambert. *Attitudes and Motivation in Second Language Learning*. Rowley: Newbury House, 1972.

Garrett, N. "Technology in the Service of Language Learning. Trends and Issues." *Modern Language Journal* 75 (1991): 74-101.

Hedderich, N. "Peer Tutoring via Electronic Mail." *Die Unterrichtspraxis*. 30.2 (1997): 141-147.

Herrington, TyAnna. *Global Classroom Development Project*. 1999 <http://www.cies.org/stories/s_therr.htm>.

Hoffmann, D., P. Jörgensen, and O. Foelsche. "Computer-Edition statt Buch-Edition. Notizen zu einer historisch-kritischen Edition - basierend auf dem Konzept von *hypertext* und *hypermedia*" *Editio* 7 (1993): 211-220.

Hopkins, E. A. "Contrastive Analysis, Interlanguage, and the Learner." *The Contrastive Grammar of English and German*. Ed. W. F. W. Lohnes and E. A. Hopkins. Ann Arbor: Karoma Publishers, 1982. 32-48.

Horwitz, E. K., and D. J. Young. *Language Anxiety. From Theory and Research to Classroom Implications*. Englewood Cliffs: Prentice Hall, 1991.

Hunt, M. M. *The Universe Within: A New Science Explores the Mind*. New York: Simon and Schuster, 1982.

Johnson, L. C. "The Keypal Connection." Warschauer 131-142.

Jones, T. C., and K. Sorenson. "Combining Studio Videoconferencing and the Internet to Promote Intercultural Understanding." *Proceedings of the Annual Mid-South Instructional Technology Conference. ERIC*. 2001.

Kagel, M., A. Krüger, A. Luca, and H. Schwandt Carriger. "Break on through to the Other Side: Web-Based Teaching Technology in International Collaboration." *Teaching German in America: Past Progress and Future Promise. A Handbook for Teaching and Research*. Ed. G. F. Peters. Cherry Hill: AATG, 2002. 285-298.

Kearsey, K. *Online Education: Learning and Teaching in Cyberspace*. Belmont: Wadsworth/Thompson Learning, 2000.

Kelm, O. R. "The Application of Computer Networking in Foreign Language Education: Focusing on Principles of Second Language Acquisition." Warschauer 19-28.

Kern, R. "Computer-Mediated Communication: Using E-mail Exchanges to Explore Personal Histories in Two Cultures." Warschauer 105-119.

Kinginger, C. "Videoconferencing as Access to Spoken French." *The Modern Language Journal* 82.4 (1998): 502-513.

Kolb, D. A. *Experiential Learning: Experience as the source of learning and development.* Englewood Cliffs: Prentice Hall, 1984.

Kötter, M. *Tandem Learning on the Internet:Learner Interactions in Virtual Online Environments(MOOs).* Frankfurt and New York: P. Lang, 2002.

Kramsch, C. *Context and Culture in Language Teaching*. Oxford: Oxford UP, 1993.

Krashen, S. *Second-Language Acquisition and Second-Language Learning*. Oxford: Pergamon Press, 1981.

Krumm, H. J. "Interkulturelles Lernen und interkulturelle Kommunikation." *Handbuch Fremdsprachenunterricht 3. Aufl.* Ed. K. R. Bausch, H. Christ, and H. J. Krumm. Tübingen: Francke, 1995. 156-161.

Macnamara, J. "Nurseries, Streets and Classrooms: Some Comparisons and Deductions." *Modern Language Journal* 57 (1973): 250-254.

Malamud, M., ed. *A World's Fair for the Global Village*. Cambridge: MIT Press, 1997.

Maley, A., and A. Duff. *Drama Techniques in Language Learning*. 2nd ed. Cambridge: University of Cambridge Press, 1982.

Moehle-Vieregge, L., S. R. Bird, and C. Manteghi. *Surf's Up! Website Workbook for Basic German*. Guilford: Audio-Forum, 1996.

Morrell, K. *Sunoikisis Initiative*. 2000 <http://www.sunoikisis.org>.

Neuner, G. "Lernerorientierung und ihre Folgen für Forschung und Lehre in DaF: Zur Entwicklung der Fremdsprachendidaktik seit den 70er Jahren." (Unpublished article mentioned in Tschirner, 1997): 1996.

Nunan, D. *The Learner-centered Curriculum*. Sydney: Cambridge UP, 1988.

Oxford, R. L., ed. *Language Learning Motivation: Pathways to the New Century.* Honolulu: University of Hawai'i Press, 1996.

Oxford, R. L., and J. Shearin. "Language Learning Motivation in a New Key." Oxford 121-144.

Palloff, R. M., and K. Pratt. *Building Learning Communities in Cyberspace: Effective Strategies for the Online Classroom.* San Francisco: Jossey-Bass, 1999.

Pinto, D. "What Does *schMOOze* Mean? Non-native Speaker Interaction on the Internet." Warschauer 165-184.

Prabhu, N. S. *Second Language Pedagogy.* Oxford: Oxford UP, 1987.

Prichard, A., and J. Taylor. *Accelerating Learning: The Use of Suggestion in the Classroom.* Novato: Academic Therapy Publications, 1980.

Reinhart, W. von "German for Science and Technology: Teaching Strategies for Beginning Students." *Unterrichtspraxis* 34.2 (2001): 119-132.

Rosellini, J. J. "Untimely Observations on Using the World Wide Web in Teaching German Composition and Conversation." *Unterrichtspraxis* 30.2 (1997): 200-205.

Rössler, H. "Learning across the Ocean." Unpublished, summarized in C. Fraser, D., Hoffmann, H. Rössler, and H. Zils. (1998). "Joint Learning across the Ocean." *Ed-Media & Ed-Telecom 98. Proceedings of the Tenth World Conference on Educational Multimedia and Hypermedia & World Conference on Educational Telecommunications, Freiburg, Germany.* 2 Charlottesville: AACE, 1997. 1635-6.

Rüschoff, B. "Language Learning and Information Technology: State of the Art." *CALICO* 10.3 (1993): 5-17.

Rüschoff, B., and D. Wolff. *Fremdsprachenlernen in der Wissensgesellschaft. Zum Einsatz der neuen Technologien in Schule und Unterricht*. Ismaning: Hueber, 1999.

Sanchez, B. "MOOving to a New Frontier in Language Learning." Warschauer 145-163.

Sanders, R. H. "Distance Learning Transatlantic Style: How Videoconferencing Widened the Focus in a Culture Course." *Die Unterrichtspraxis* 30.2 (1995): 135-140.

Schaumann, C. "Erzählraum im virtuellen Raum: Rewriting Bernhard Schlink's *Der Vorleser* on the Web." *Die Unterrichtspraxis* 34.2 (2001): 150-157.

Schmidt, R., D. Boraie, and O. Kassabgy. "Foreign Language Motivation: Internal Structure and External Connections." Oxford 9-70.

Schneider, A. "A University Plans to Promote Languages by Killing Its Languages Department." *Chronicle of Higher Education* 9 Mar. 2001.

Schneider, J., and S. von der Emde. "Brave New (Virtual) World: Transforming Language Learning into Cultural Studies through Online Learning Environments (MOOs)." *ADFL Bulletin* 32.1 (2000): 19-26.

Scollon, R., and S. W. Scollon. *Intercultural Communication. A Discourse Approach.* 2nd ed. Malden: Blackwell Publishers, 2001.

Selinker, L. "Interlanguage." *International Review of Applied Linguistics* 10 (1977): 209-231.

Smith, K. "Collaborative and Interactive Writing for Increasing Communication Skills." *Hispania* 73 (1990): 77-87.

Smith, S. M. *The Theater Arts and the Teaching of Second Languages.* Reading: Addison-Wesley Publishing Company, 1984.

Stern, H. H. *Fundamental Concepts of Language Teaching.* Oxford: Oxford UP, 1983.

Straight, H. S. *Languages Across the Curriculum [microform].* Washington DC: ERIC Clearinghouse on Languages and Linguistics/Center for Applied Linguistics, 1998.

Tella, S. "Foreign Languages and Modern Technology: Harmony or Hell?" Warschauer 3-17.

Tschirner, E. "Neue Perspektiven für DaF durch die neuen Medien." *Die Unterrichtspraxis* 30.2 (1997): 121-129.

Tschirner, E. "Kommunikation und Spracherwerb per Computernetz. Blick auf einige Forschungsergebnisse." *Fremdsprache Deutsch: Zeitschrift für die Praxis des Deutschunterrichts* 21.2 (1999): 54-58.

Tschirner, E., H. Funk, and M. Koenig, eds. *Schnittstellen: Lehrwerke zwischen alten und neuen Medien.* Berlin: Cornelsen Verlag, 2000.

Turbee, L. "Educational MOO. Text-based Virtual Reality for Learning in Community." *ERIC Digest* Mar. 1997. Retrieved 25 May 2000 <http://ericit.syr.edu/ithome/digests/turbee.html>. Quoted in Von der Emde et al., 2001.

Underwood, J. H. *Linguistics, Computers, and the Language Teacher. A Communicative Approach.* Rowley: Newbury House Publishers, 1984.

Von der Emde, S., J. Schneider, and M. Kötter. "Technically Speaking: Transforming Language Learning through Virtual Learning Environments (MOOs)." *The Modern Language Journal* 85.2 (2001): 210-225.

Warschauer, M., ed. *Telecollaboration in Foreign Language Learning.* Honolulu: University of Hawaii Press, 1996.

Warschauer, M. "Motivational Aspects of Using Computers for Writing and Communication." Warschauer 229-246.

Wells, G. *Learning Through Interaction. The Study of Language Development.* Cambridge: Cambridge UP, 1981.

Wienroeder-Skinner, D. A., and S. G. Maass. "Telefonkonferenz -- mehr als ein Direktgespräch! Praktische Tips für ein erfolgreiches, interkulturelles Kommunikationsprojekt." *Die Unterrichtspraxis* 30.2 (1997): 130-134.

Content and Language Integrated Instruction and Autonomous Learning: A Successful Alliance?

Dieter Wolff
(summarized in English by Karen Sanders)

Editor's Note: Gerd Bräuer
This article about content and language integrated learning and autonomous learning is written in German. If you are not able to read German at all, you will obviously rely on information from people who understand the language. If you have some knowledge about German, you can guide yourself through the chapter with help of the extended summary and additional material about bilingual education and autonomous learning listed above. Please share your insights with peers who are not able to read German at all.

Think about what specific information you want to provide to your peers. Obviously, it would be too time-consuming to provide a full translation. What are the key information of the article? Try to extract the provided summary even further. Come up with examples to illustrate your comprised summary. What aspects from other articles of this volume would you suggest to your peers in order to get a sense of the larger context of Dieter Wolff's ideas?

Material on Content and Language Integrated Learning (CLIL <www.cec.jyu.fi/clil_compendium/index.htm>), including:

- Compendium (key terms, milestones of development, future steps)
- Expertise (participating partners and their specializations)
- CLIL types (in progress)
- Products (films, development programs, books)
- Links

Material on autonomous learning in English:

- Chapter by Langner/Prokop in this volume
- ERIC/CLL Resource Guides Online <www.cal.org/ericcll/faqs/RGOs/selfdirected.html>

CONSIDER

The ERIC/CLL Resource Guides Online web site provides a wealth of material on autonomous learning.

Introduction

In the mid 1990s, the foreign language teaching profession began looking at autonomous learning in their classrooms. Out of these inquiries came an agreement that certain characteristics are necessary to form the foundation of a learning environment that will contribute to independent learning. These characteristics are: authenticity, learning as a social process, self-reflection, process-orientation and evaluation. Unfortunately, in today's school systems true autonomous learning is rare, and often quite difficult to implement within the existing structure. One framework that could facilitate the introduction of autonomous learning and other modern pedagogical ideas into today's classrooms, is that of content-based bilingual instruction. The following article will outline the potential of this type of instruction to further autonomous learning in the classroom.

Autonomous Learning: An International Educational Objective

In recent years, research in both cognitive psychology and constructivist paradigms has increasingly influenced both pedagogical thought and practice. In looking at the constructivist paradigm in the context of language teaching and learning, the following six concepts should be further examined:

- Educational Content
- Educational Objectives
- Educational Context
- Learning as a Social Process
- Learning Strategies
- Self-Assessment

Educational Content

Through research, we know that students learn best when they are able to build on existing knowledge. In order to offer this opportunity, it is best to provide educational content that is both diverse and wide-ranging. With a variety of content to choose from, students are more likely to make the connection between their personal knowledge and the new information, thus ensuring their success.

Educational Objectives

Inherent in the constructivist paradigm is the fact that students must be able to recognize and define their own learning objectives. To make this possible, the content of the class should be relevant and meaningful to the students' lives.

Educational Context

Under the constructivist paradigm educational context is developed collaboratively. The teacher and learner work together to make decisions and to form the context for the class. In fact, learners and teachers take equal responsibility in the success or failure of a project or assignment.

The Social Process

Looking at learning as a social process has implications for classroom practice. Traditional forms of teaching, such as teacher-fronted instruction, have no role in the constructivist paradigm. Rather, other models of instruction, such as small group and pair work, need to be included.

Learning Strategies

Procedural knowledge, or learning strategies, is a key concept in constructivist theory. The ability of a learner to recognize, develop and implement his own learning strategies must be central to any classroom in which autonomous learning is desired.

Self-Assessment

Another key concept is that of self-assessment. This is perhaps the most important aspect of a constructivist oriented learning culture. At the same time, however, it is also the most difficult to achieve within today's institutionalized systems. Currently, assessment is an external process, one in which the learner is not accustomed to evaluate his own learning process. This is in direct contradiction to the idea the learners should be responsible for evaluating their own progress.

Content and Language Integrated Learning (CLIL): Definition and Methodology

Definition

Content Language and Integrated Learning (CLIL) is a general concept that refers to the use of an additional language (i.e. not the learners' primary language) to teach information in one or more content areas. More specifically CLIL:

- Focuses on both language and content, rather than solely on language, as in a foreign language classroom. Research shows that learners learn more, and are more motivated in this type of instruction than in traditional content-area classes.
- Teaches content and language together. The two subjects, for example the language and a content area such as history or geography, are integrated and viewed as one.
- Differs from full immersion programs in that only some, not all, of the content areas are taught in a second language. In this model some subjects continue to be taught in the primary language so that the students will also improve their skills in their first language.
- Uses the second language as both the medium of instruction as well as part of the classroom content. In other words, the students will learn about the language at the same time they are using it to master a content area.

Organization and Structure of CLIL

Despite developing in multiple European countries, there are many similarities in CLIL instruction across the continent. In general, European schools offer one or more content areas that are given, for a minimum of four years, in the second language. The most common subjects are history, geography and social science. These subjects are most commonly taught in English, French or German. Most CLIL is offered at the secondary level, although some primary and vocational schools also offer programs. Statistics show that the age of students enrolled in various CLIL programs throughout Europe range from 3-21 years.

In most countries the students must pass either a written or oral test to be accepted into the program. The number of schools that offer preparatory classes remains small—around 15%—with the exception of Germany where pre-requisite classes are a requirement for any CLIL program.

Also with the exception of Germany, the teachers in these programs are usually *either* language teachers *or* content area experts. The content area instructors are often native speakers of the target language, and in many countries the language teachers will get additional qualifications in the chosen content area.

In general, instructors use both authentic and commercially produced materials, and often develop their own as well. With the exception of Germany, there is no officially developed CLIL curriculum, but rather in most places the schools or the CLIL instructors have developed their own. Often instructors will modify the content area course curricula to include more information on the culture underlying the target language.

Methodology

Up until recently, most CLIL classrooms have closely resembled the traditional teacher-centered model. Over the past few years, however, both theorists and practitioners have recognized that a specific approach to CLIL must be developed in order to fully realize the potential of this approach to teaching and learning. Currently, the discussion is focused in three areas: reading comprehension, writing, and the development of a *language sensitive* process, in which teaching *and* learning play the central role.

Reading is a key skill for successful CLIL instruction. Although reading strategies play an important role in all learning contexts, learners who cannot read well, or who have low comprehension skills, will not be able to acquire the content information necessary to succeed in a CLIL classroom. For this reason, reading strategies have played a central role in the methodology discussion. Indeed, learners read texts not to acquire language, but rather to gain context specific information—and it is this reality that needs to drive the future development of CLIL methodology.

The same is true for writing. From the beginning, learners must be able to use the second language to express what they have learned. They need to be able to write reports, give definitions and summarize. As a result, CLIL methodology must also focus on writing competence.

Nevertheless, the most important aspect of the current discussion is focusing on the integration of language and content. It is the content of the chosen course that is at the center of the teaching and learning process, *but* in order for the learner to really be able to work with the content, it is absolutely necessary that he/she also acquires knowledge and competence in the second language. Related to this idea of language and content integration is that of classroom discourse. Because of the emphasis placed on content in a CLIL classroom, communication in the classroom plays a much larger role than in traditional second language instruction.

Content and Language Integrated Learning: An Environment that Promotes Autonomous Learning

Bilingual instruction can provide the foundation for an environment that promotes autonomous learning. To illustrate this potential the author looks again at the six concepts that characterize current institutionalized learning environments: educational content, educational objectives, educational context, learning as a social process, learning strategies, and assessment.

Educational Content

In traditional language learning classrooms the materials available to most teachers is limited. It is here that the integration of content-area information can help. For example, subjects such as geography or history contain classroom ready information that is both rich in content and *real*. Using information from the real world, rather than the contrived content found in most foreign language classrooms, has been found to increase both student motivation and success. In fact, most language teachers would agree that the benefits of using the richer and more complex *real-life* materials are many.

Educational Objectives

In an autonomous learning situation, the learner is expected to be able to define both general and specific learning objectives. Working within a content-based context facilitates this process, because it allows the learner to draw from personal experience, much more so than in a traditional language learning context.

Educational Context

In an autonomous learning context students and teachers develop a collaborative relationship. Together, they experience the content of both the language and the target culture, and work cooperatively to motivate and discover.

The Social Process

In a classroom characterized by autonomous learning, the possibilities for group work are endless. Through the integration of the subject-area content, and the potential this brings for research and experimentation, instructors in CLIL classrooms have multiple opportunities to engage the students in meaningful social interaction.

Learning Strategies

In order to be truly independent in ones learning, it is necessary to master specific learning techniques. Such techniques, both for language learning and content mastery, are highly complex, yet essential to a successful autonomous learning environment.

Assessment

In the field of education, assessment is one of the most challenging areas in which to initiate change. For CLIL the issue is especially complex, because one must decide if the learner should be assessed on language, *and/or* content-area achievements. Perhaps the concept of self-evaluation, which plays such an important role in autonomous learning, could provide a starting point for this discussion.

Conclusion

Much more than with traditional instructional models, CLIL offers an educational environment in which language and content are of equal value, and in which students are motivated to become independent learners.

Bilingualer Sachfachunterricht und Lernerautonomie: eine glückliche Verbindung?

Einleitung

Die typischen Merkmale eines autonomen fremdsprachlichen Klassenzimmers sind bereits Mitte der neunziger Jahre von unterschiedlichen Autoren herausgearbeitet worden (vgl. z.B. Dam 1994). Im Vordergrund standen dabei die folgenden Merkmale: Authentizität, Lernen als sozial vermittelter Prozess, Lernerreflexion, Prozessorientierung und Evaluation. Vertreter der Lernerautonomie empfehlen die Konstruktion von Lernumgebungen auf der Grundlage solcher pädagogischer und lerntheoretischer Konzepte, um die Lernenden selbstständiger und selbstverantwortlicher zu machen. Die genannten Kategorien sind aus pädagogischer Sicht von einzelnen Schulfächern unabhängige, neutrale Kategorien, die als übergeordnete allgemeine Kategorien moderner Erziehung gelten können (vgl. hierzu Holec 1981; Little 1992; Wolff 1994).

Die Implementierung von Lernerautonomie erweist sich im Kontext des heutigen Schulsystems als ein sehr schwieriges Unterfangen. Fast alle Parameter unseres gegenwärtigen Erziehungssystems widersetzen sich der Einführung der genannten

Konzepte. Nur wenn wir unsere Schulen mit innovativen Rahmenbedingungen ausstatten, wird es möglich sein, Lernumgebungen zu schaffen, innerhalb derer moderne pädagogische Ideen verwirklicht werden können. Ein solches innovatives Konzept von Rahmenbedingungen, das meines Wissens bisher noch nicht im Hinblick auf seine Eignung als Plattform für die Einbringung von Lernerautonomie und anderen modernen pädagogischer Ideen in das schulische Klassenzimmer erprobt worden ist, ist der bilinguale Sachfachunterricht. Er stellt meiner Meinung nach einen sehr interessanten Rahmen für die Herausbildung einer Lernumgebung bereit, in der Selbstverantwortung und Selbstbestimmung des Lerners gefördert werden können. Das Hauptziel dieses Beitrags ist es deshalb, das Potenzial des bilingualen Sachfachunterrichts für die Entwicklung von Lernerautonomie herauszuarbeiten.

Lernerautonomie: ein globales Erziehungsziel

Die Forschungen, die in der kognitiven Psychologie und im Rahmen des konstruktivistischen Paradigmas betrieben wurden, üben einen immer stärker werdenden Einfluss auf unser pädagogisches Denken aus. Obwohl das Schlagwort „Konstruktion statt Instruktion", das heutzutage überall in der Pädagogik zu hören ist, eine unangemessene Vereinfachung ist, scheint mir kein Zweifel daran zu bestehen, dass der Grundgedanke des Konstruktivismus—dass die menschliche Kognition und das menschliche Lernen konstruktive Operationen sind, die der Lernende autonom plant und durchführt—unsere Lehr—und Lernkonzepte für institutionalisierte Kontexte dramatisch verändern muss. Dieser Wandel im lerntheoretischen Paradigma, der auch der Lernerautonomie als einem pädagogischen Konzept innewohnt—eigentlich könnte man Lernerautonomie auch als die Fähigkeit bezeichnen, Konstruktionsprozesse selbstständig zu planen und durchzuführen—beeinflusst sowohl unser theoretisches pädagogisches Denken als auch unser praktisches pädagogisches Handeln im Klassenzimmer. Es sind wenigstens sechs theoretische didaktische Konzepte, die auf der Grundlage des konstruktivistischen Paradigmas neu diskutiert werden müssen: Lerninhalte, Lernziele, Lernkontexte, soziale Formen des Lernens, Lernstrategien und Leistungsbewertung.

Lerninhalte müssen aus einer neuen Perspektive gesehen werden, wenn man sich auf das konstruktivistische Paradigma bezieht. Aus der lerntheoretischen Forschung wissen wir, dass Lerner neues Wissen auf der Grundlage ihres bisherigen subjektiven Erfahrungswissens konstruieren. Lerninhalte müssen daher eher in ihrer ganzen Komplexität eingebracht werden, um dem individuellen Lerner die Möglichkeit zu geben, sein eigenes Wissen mit dem zu erwerbenden Wissen zu verknüpfen. Als Konsequenz daraus ergibt sich, dass es sinnvoller ist, eine große Menge authentischer Materialien, die sich auf einen spezifischen Lerninhalt beziehen, für den Lerner bereitzustellen als ein Lehrwerk mit eingeschränkten Inhalten.

Innerhalb des konstruktivistischen Paradigmas müssen die Lerner in die Lage versetzt werden, ihre eigenen *Lernziele* definieren zu können. Dies ist nur möglich, wenn die Lerninhalte, die vom Lehrer in das Klassenzimmer eingebracht werden, für den

Lerner glaubhaft sind. Ein glaubhafter Lerninhalt ist einer, mit dem sich der Lerner identifizieren kann, d.h. dessen Bedeutung für sein eigenes Lernen und sein eigenes Leben er erkennen kann.

Der *Lernkontext* spielt in traditionellen pädagogischen Überlegungen keine wirkliche Rolle. Ein konstruktivistisch orientierter Lernkontext muss so organisiert sein, dass der Lerninhalt überzeugend eingebettet werden kann und dass das, was gelernt wurde, auch gebraucht werden kann. Dies bedeutet, dass sowohl der Lehrer als auch der Lerner an der Gestaltung und Organisation eines solchen Klassenzimmers teilhaben müssen. Entscheidungen müssen gemeinsam getroffen werden und die Lerner müssen verstehen, dass auch sie verantwortlich sind, wenn ein Projekt oder eine Aufgabe nicht erfolgreich abgeschlossen wurde.

Wenn das *Lernen ein sozial vermittelter Prozess* ist, dann ist es notwendig, über die Konsequenzen nachzudenken, die eine solche Annahme für das konkrete Klassenzimmergeschehen hat. Traditionelle Formen der Arbeit im Klassenzimmer (wie z.B. der Frontalunterricht) passen in ein solches Konzept nicht hinein. Stattdessen müssen andere Formen sozialer Zusammenarbeit eingesetzt werden, und dazu gehört in erster Linie die Gruppenarbeit.

Ein sehr wichtiges Konzept im Kontext konstruktivistischer Theorien ist das des *strategischen* oder prozeduralen *Wissens*. Die Fähigkeit, die eigenen Konstruktionsprozesse gestalten zu können, schließt strategisches Wissen ein. Konstruktionsprozesse sind strategiegeleitet, und um unabhängiger zu werden, müssen Lerner solche Strategien entwickeln. Die Förderung von Verarbeitungs- und Lernstrategien, die im traditionellen Klassenzimmer bisher nur von marginaler Bedeutung war, muss zu einem zentralen Ziel in einer Lernumgebung werden, in der mehr Lernerautonomie angestrebt wird.

Das letzte Konzept, das hier angesprochen werden soll, ist das der *Eigenbewertung*. Dies ist wahrscheinlich der wichtigste Aspekt einer konstruktivistisch orientierten Lernkultur, gleichzeitig aber auch von der Realisierung in einem institutionalisierten Lernkontext her die am schwierigsten zu realisierende Aufgabe. Unsere derzeitigen Schulsysteme werden überwiegend durch Bewertungsprozesse charakterisiert, die von anderen durchgeführt werden, und die Lerner sind nicht daran gewöhnt, ihre eigenen Lernprozesse zu bewerten. Das Portfolio-Konzept des Europarates könnte eine mögliche Lösung zur Förderung von Selbstbewertung sein; es ist allerdings notwendig, es in eine tragfähige Lernumgebung einzubetten.

Der bilinguale Sachfachunterricht: Definition und methodische Ansätze

Eine Definition des bilingualen Sachfachunterrichts

Bilingualer Sachfachunterricht (engl. *Content and language integrated learning* oder CLIL) ist ein generischer Begriff, der sich auf jede Situation institutionalisierten Lernens bezieht, in der eine zusätzliche Sprache, d.h. nicht die in der Umgebung am häufigsten gebrauchte Sprache für das Lehren und Lernen von Sachfächern genutzt wird (Marsh & Langé 2000).

Es gibt eine Reihe von Aspekten, die im Kontext dieser Definition von Bedeutung sind: 1) CLIL darf nicht als ein fremdsprachendidaktischer Ansatz betrachtet werden, sondern er bezieht sich sowohl auf Sprache wie auf Inhalt und impliziert damit eine neue Didaktik. Was wir heute über das Lernen von Sachfächern in einer fremden Sprache wissen, deutet darauf hin, dass Lerner mehr lernen und motivierter sind als im traditionellen Sachfachunterricht. Lerner lernen den Inhalt des Sachfachs aus einer anderen und breiteren Perspektive, wenn er in einer anderen Sprache vermittelt wird. Beim Lerner bilden sich präzisere Sachfach-Konzepte heraus, wenn eine andere Sprache in die Wissensvermittlung einbezogen ist. 2) Im Rahmen des bilingualen Sachfachunterrichts werden Inhalt und Sprache integriert gelernt. Die beiden Fächer—d.h. die Sprache und ein Sachfach wie Geschichte oder Geographie—werden aufeinander bezogen und als etwas Ganzes behandelt. 3) Der bilinguale Sachfachunterricht greift anders als die kanadischen Immersionsansätze, nur eine begrenzte Zahl von Sachfächern auf. Wenn alle Sachfächer in einer anderen als der Mutersprache der Lernenden unterrichtet würden, dann wäre es unmöglich, ihre muttersprachliche Kompetenz zu verbessern. 4) In unserer Definition wird festgehalten, dass andere Sprachen benutzt werden, um Sachfächer zu vermitteln, d.h dass die Fremdsprache das Medium der Instruktion ist. Dies bedeutet jedoch nicht, dass die Sprache als solche nicht im Klassenzimmer thematisiert wird. Die Sprache ist im bilingualen Sachfachunterricht sowohl Inhalt wie Medium des Unterrichts (vgl. auch Wolff 1997a).

Organisation und Struktur des bilingualen Sachfachunterrichts

Aus einem erst vor kurzem erstellten Überblick (Marsh, Maljers & Hartiala 2001) lassen sich interessante Informationen über organisatorische und strukturelle Aspekte des bilingualen Sachfachunterrichts in Europa ableiten. Obwohl CLIL sich in verschiedenen europäischen Schulsystemen unterschiedlich entwickelt hat, gibt es eine Reihe von Ähnlichkeiten, die hier erwähnt werden sollten, um den Ansatz in seiner didaktischen Variabilität und Komplexität deutlicher zu machen.

Im Allgemeinen ist der bilinguale Sachfachunterricht in den Schulen Europas so organisiert, dass ein oder mehr Sachfächer (im Allgemeinen aus den Geistes- oder Sozialwissenschaften) wenigstens vier Jahre in einer Fremdsprache unterrichtet werden. Die Sachfächer, die am häufigsten gewählt werden, sind Geschichte, Geographie und Sozialwissenschaften. Die am häufigsten verwendeten Sprachen sind Englisch und Französisch; Deutsch steht an dritter Stelle.

Die meisten Schulen, in welchen bilingualer Sachfachunterricht angeboten wird, sind die Sekundarschulen. Aber es gibt CLIL-Schulen auch für die Primarstufe, und in einigen Ländern haben sich sogar Berufsschulen dafür entschieden, berufsbezogene Fächer in einer fremden Sprache zu unterrichten. In diesen Schulen sind es natürlich andere Sachfächer, die unterrichtet werden; sie reichen von Informatik über das Hotelwesen bis hin zu Wirtschaft und Gestaltung. Die Statistik zeigt, dass das Alter der Lernenden in den CLIL-Schulen von drei bis einundzwanzig Jahren reicht.

In den meisten Ländern werden die Lerner, die in CLIL-Klassen aufgenommen werden, mit Hilfe schriftlicher Tests oder mündlicher Interviews ausgewählt. Die Zahl der Schulen, die vorbereitende Sprachkurse für den bilingualen Sachfachunterricht anbieten, ist noch recht klein; wenn man Deutschland ausnimmt, wo vorbereitende Kurse verpflichtend sind, machen weniger als fünfzehn Prozent ein solches Angebot.

Mit Ausnahme der deutschsprachigen Länder, in welchen die Lehrerausbildung zwei Fächer einschließt, sind die Lehrer entweder Sachfach- oder Sprachlehrer. Die Sachfachlehrer sind oft Muttersprachler der CLIL-Sprache; in vielen Ländern erwerben Sprachlehrer eine zusätzliche Qualifikation in einem Sachfach.

Die Materialien für den bilingualen Sachfachunterricht kommen oft aus Ländern, in welchen die Sprache, die für das Sachfach genutzt wird, die offizielle Sprache ist. Im Allgemeinen benutzen die Lehrer sowohl authentische als auch Lehrwerkmaterialien (letzere stammen häufig aus den Lehrwerken, die in den Zielsprachenländern gebraucht werden). Die Lehrer passen auch authentische oder andere Materialien dem sprachlichen Niveau ihrer Lerner an oder schreiben ihre eigenen Materialien.

Mit Ausnahme Deutschlands gibt es bisher keine von den Erziehungsbehörden entwickelten Curricula. In den meisten Ländern entwickeln die Schulen oder die CLIL-Lehrer ihre eigenen Curricula. In fast allen Ländern unterliegt der Curriculum-Entwicklung als allgemeines Prinzip, dass Lerner, die Sachfächer in einer anderen Sprache gelernt haben, das Sachfach genauso gut kennen müssen wie Lerner eines muttersprachlichen Kurses. Häufig werden die Curricula der Sachfächer jedoch im Vergleich zu muttersprachlichen Curricula modifiziert; und insbesondere in Geschichte und Geographie werden mehr Inhalte einbezogen, die sich auf die Kultur beziehen, die der Zielsprache unterliegt.

Einige methodologische Überlegungen

In der Zeit, in der der bilinguale Unterricht nur eine untergeordnete Rolle in schulischen Kontexten spielte, wurden methodologische Aspekte vernachlässigt. Im Allgemeinen unterrichteten Lehrer das Sachfach in der Fremdsprache, so wie sie es in der Muttersprache unterrichteten. Ähnlich fand das Fremdsprachenlernen im bilingualen Klassenzimmer im Rahmen traditioneller Sprachlernverfahren statt. In gewisser Weise ersetzte der Inhalt des Sachfachs die traditionellen Inhalte des sprachlichen Klassenzimmers; das bedeutet also, dass das CLIL-Klassenzimmer dem traditionellen lehrerzentrierten fremdsprachlichen oder Sachfachklassenzimmer sehr ähnlich war.

Nicht nur der oben erwähnte Überblick zeigt, dass die Situation sich in den letzten Jahren verändert hat. Theoretiker und Praktiker haben erkannt, dass das pädagogische Potential des bilingualen Sachfachunterrichts höher ist als ursprünglich angenommen, und innovative Vertreter von CLIL bestehen darauf, dass eine spezifische Didaktik des bilingualen Sachfachunterrichts entwickelt werden muss. Zur Zeit kreist die methodologische Diskussion um drei allgemeine Themen: Förderung des Leseverstehens, Förderung des Schreibens, und Entwicklung von Verfahren, in welchen sprachsensitives Lehren und Lernen eine zentrale Rolle spielt. Es kann kein Zweifel daran bestehen, dass diese Themen weit über das hinausgehen, was im Fremdsprachen- aber auch im Sachfachunterricht diskutiert wird.

Das Lesen und die Entwicklung der Lesefertigkeiten werden im bilingualen Sachfachunterricht als sehr wichtig angesehen. Die meisten Erwerbsprozesse sind aufs engste mit dem Leseverstehen verbunden: die Lernenden arbeiten mit Dokumenten und anderen Quellen, um Wissen im Sachfach zu erwerben. Obwohl Lesestrategien eine wichtige Rolle in allen Lernkontexten spielen (man denke nur an die PISA-Studie), entscheiden sie im bilingualen Sachfachunterricht über den Erfolg oder Mißerfolg des Lernenden. Eine Didaktik des bilingualen Sachfachunterrichts muss dies berücksichtigen: deshalb spielt auch die Förderung von Lesestrategien eine zentrale Rolle in der methodischen Diskussion. Dabei muss auch berücksichtigt werden, dass die Sachfacharbeit spezifische Lesestrategien mit einschließt: die Arbeit mit graphischen Darstellungen, mit Karten, mit Tabellen erfordert ein anderes Lesevermögen als die Verarbeitung der einfacheren Texte des Fremdsprachenunterrichts. Besondere Verarbeitungsstrategien müssen erworben werden, die den Lernenden helfen, die Information, die sich in solchen Materialien findet, zu verarbeiten. In gewisser Weise ist der Fokus auf solche Verarbeitungsstrategien im bilingualen Klassenzimmer ein charakteristisches Merkmal eines neuen methodischen Ansatzes, der sich nicht nur auf Sprache sondern auch auf Inhalt bezieht. Lerner lesen Texte nicht, um Sprache zu lernen sondern um Wissen im Sachfach zu erwerben. Dies macht den gesamten Lernprozess stärker fertigkeitsorientiert sowohl im Hinblick auf die Sprache als auch den Inhalt.

Dies gilt auch für die produktiven Fähigkeiten. Während im kommunikativen Klassenzimmer die Förderung mündlicher Fertigkeiten von großer Bedeutung ist, spielen im bilingualen Unterricht die schriftlichen Fähigkeiten eine besonders große Rolle. Von Anfang an müssen die Lerner die Fremdsprache benutzen, um die Ergebnisse dessen aufzuschreiben, was sie erarbeitet haben: sie müssen Berichte erstellen, Definitionen festlegen, Ergebnisse von Beobachtungen zusammenfassen. Sprachkompetenz im Sachfach ist in hohem Maße Textkompetenz, und eine CLIL-Didaktik muss sich auf Schreibkompetenz in der fremden Sprache beziehen.

Der wichtigste Aspekt in der Diskussion ist jedoch die Integration von Inhalt und Sprache im bilingualen Sachfachunterricht. Aus den Erfahrungen mit dem kommunikativen Unterricht und anderen ähilichen Ansätzen ist deutlich geworden, dass ein rein auf Bedeutung fokussiertes Fremdsprachenlernen nicht sehr erfolgreich ist; der Fokus auf die Form der fremden Sprache ist gerade in institutionalisierten Lernumgebungen von ebenso großer Bedeutung. Aus diesem Grunde plädieren CLIL-Lehrer für einen Ansatz, der inhaltsorientiert und zur gleichen Zeit sprachsensibel ist. Es ist der Inhalt des Sachfachs, der im Mittelpunkt des Lern-Lehrprozesses steht, aber um den Inhalt der fremden Sprache verarbeiten zu können, müssen die Lerner Sprachwissen und Sprachfertigkeiten erwerben. Im Klassenzimmer funktioniert dies nach dem Prinzip *language across the curriculum*, d.h. auf die Sprache wird abgehoben, wenn immer es notwendig ist.

Zwei Aspekte der Spracharbeit sind in den letzten Jahren detaillierter behandelt worden. Ein Aspekt ist die Terminologie, die ihren überragenden Einfluss im Klassenzimmer verloren hat. Besonders in den frühen Jahren des bilingualen Unterrichts glaubten die Lehrer, dass dieser Unterricht nur funktionieren könne, wenn die Lernenden über die präzise Sachfachterminologie in der Fremdsprache verfügten. Spracharbeit bestand in dieser Zeit vor allem aus dem Lernen von Listen terminologischer Begriffe. Heute wird betont, dass das terminologische Inventar eines Sachfachs in allgemeinere und spezifischere Termini aufgeteilt werden kann. Wie eine Reihe von CLIL Spezialisten formuliert hat, sollte man im bilingualen Unterricht damit beginnen, die allgemeinere Sachfachterminologie bereitzustellen und sollte dann langsam die spezifischere Terminologie aufbereiten.

Der andere Aspekt ist stärker fertigkeitsorientiert und bezieht auf den sogenannten *classroom discourse*. Aufgrund der hohen Inhaltsorientierung des Unterrichts spielt das Klassenzimmergespräch eine sehr viel wichtigere Rolle im bilingualen Unterricht als im traditionellen Klassenzimmer. Ausserdem liegen sie auf einem weit höheren diskursiven Niveau. Nach Thürmann (2000) können Diskursfertigkeiten in einem CLIL-Klassenzimmer als aus zwei Mengen bestehend analysiert werden: eine allgemeinere funktionale Menge, die aus Sprechakten wie identifizieren—klassifizieren/definieren—beschreiben—erklären—schlußfolgern/argumentieren—bewerten besteht; und eine spezifischere Menge, die nach den Sachfächern oder Gruppen von Sachfächern definiert werden kann, z.B. Naturgesetze formulieren—Induktionen durchführen—Stadien und Prozesse beschreiben—mit Graphiken/Diagrammen arbeiten—interpretieren—Berichte schreiben.

Der bilinguale Sachfachunterricht als Lernumgebung, in der Lernerautonomie gefördert werden kann

Meine Grundthese lautet: Der bilinguale Unterricht stellt einen didaktischen Rahmen bereit, der zur Grundlage einer Lernumgebung gemacht werden kann, die besser dazu geeignet ist, Lernerautonomie zu fördern als die meisten der Ansätze, die derzeit im Vordergrund stehen.

Das Potential des bilingualen Unterrichts für das Sprach- und das Inhaltslernen kann nicht auf den Faktor *exposure time* reduziert werden, wie einige Theoretiker behauptet haben (vgl. hierzu Wolff 1997b). Das länger einer anderen Sprache Ausgesetztsein führt nicht automatisch zu einer höheren Sprachfähigkeit, obwohl es zweifellos zum Erfolg des traditionellen und konventionellen CLIL-Unterrichts beigetragen hat. Ich bin überzeugt davon, dass CLIL mehr Potenzial besitzt und möchte darlegen, auf welche Weise dieser Ansatz in der Lage ist, Lernerautonomie zu fördern. Dabei möchte ich erneut auf die sechs Konzepte zurückkommen, die institutionelle Lernumgebungen charakterisieren—also Lerninhalte, Lernziele, Lernkontexte, soziale Formen des Lernen, Lernstrategien und Bewertung

Lerninhalte: Ansätze, die dem pädagogischen Ziel der Lernerautonomie verpflichtet sind, heben eher auf weniger strukturierten, reichen Lernumgebungen ab, um auf diese Weise den Lernenden zu helfen, ihr bisheriges Wissen mit dem neu zu erwerbenden Wissen zu verknüpfen. Solche Lerninhalte sind für das fremdsprachliche Klassenzimmer jedoch recht schwer bereitzustellen, und sowohl Lehrer wie auch Lerner begnügen sich oft mit den stereotypen Inhalten des traditionellen Klassenzimmers: *England and the English, Black Americans, Youngsters in England, school uniforms in Britai*n gehören für den Englischunterricht zu den populärsten.

Die Integration von Sachfachinhalten kann hier von großer Hilfe sein. Die Fächer Geographie oder Geschichte stellen reiche Lerninhalte für das Klassenzimmer bereit, Inhalte, die nicht fiktiv sondern real sind und deshalb motivierender als die Inhalte, mit welchen gewöhnlich im fremdsprachlichen Klassenzimmer gearbeitet wird; und zwar auch dann, wenn Lerner die Freiheit haben, die Inhalte auszuwählen, mit welchen sie arbeiten wollen. Die Lerninhalte der meisten Sachfächer können als Realien bezeichnet werden, d.h. Fakten und Prozesse der realen Welt; sie erscheinen deshalb auch sehr viel relevanter als die pseudorealen Inhalte des fremdsprachlichen Klassenzimmers. In gewisser Weise begrenzt ein Sachfach wie Geschichte oder Geographie die Auswahlmöglichkeiten des Lerners in positiver Weise und reduziert sie auf bestimmte Themen und Projekte innerhalb der vordefinierten Bereiche des Sachfachs. Dabei ist von ebenso großer Bedeutung, dass die Sprache aller Sachfächer durch einen hohen Grad an Präzision definiert ist—Fachsprachen haben genaue Register—und sich deshalb von der Gemeinsprache, die vage und ungenau und deshalb vielleicht schwieriger zu lernen ist, unterscheidet. Ein letzter Aspekt, der für sachfachorientierte Lerninhalte spricht, ist der, dass diese durch eine wissenschaftliche Orientierung charakterisiert und deshalb reicher und komplexer sind als die meisten Lerninhalte, die im traditionellen fremdsprachlichen Klassenimmer behandelt werden.

Lernziele: Es wird vom autonomen Lerner erwartet, dass er sowohl die globalen wie auch die spezifischen Ziele seines Lernens definieren kann. Es erscheint mir sehr hilfreich zu sein, wenn der Lerner seine Entscheidungsprozesse im Rahmen eines sachfachlichen Kontextes durchführt. Ein solcher Kontext bezieht sich in stärkerem Maße auf die individuellen Erfahrungen des Lerners als ein reiner fremdsprachlicher Lernkontext.

Lernkontext: In einem Klassenzimmer, das sich der Förderung von Lernerautonomie verpfichtet hat, wird der Lernkontext durch die Kooperation zwischen Lernenden und Lehrenden geschaffen. Zusammen gestalten sie eine Art von Lernlabor, in welchem sie experimentieren und forschen und auf diese Weise mit dem Lerninhalt (der Zielsprache und der Zielsprachenkultur) in einer motivierenden Weise umgehen. Aber auch hier stellt sich die Frage, ob das Experimentieren und das Forschen nicht realistischer und motivierender für den Lernenden ist, wenn er mit konkreten Themen aus der Geographie oder der Geschichte arbeitet, z.B. mit Temperaturtabellen oder historischen Landkarten.

Gruppenarbeit als Sozialform des Lernens: In einem autonomen Klassenzimmer, das als Forschungslabor verstanden wird, sind die Möglichkeiten für Gruppenarbeit größer. Eine neue Dimension ist darüberhinaus natürlich durch die Integration mit dem Sachfach gegeben, das meist ein reiches Potenzial für Forschen und Experimentieren aufweist. Sachfächer verleihen der Gruppenarbeit Authentizität; man könnte sogar soweit gehen zu sagen, dass Sachfächer Gruppenarbeit im Klassenzimmer erzwingen.

Lernstrategien: Nur Lerner, die gelernt haben mit spezifischen Lern- und Arbeitstechniken umzugehen, werden in ihrem eigenen Lernen unabhängiger werden. Lern- und Arbeitstechniken sind sowohl für das fremdsprachliche wie für das Sachfachlernen hoch komplexe Fähigkeiten.

Das Konzept der *Leistungsbewertung* ist wahrscheinlich das Konzept, das in allen Lernumgebungen nur unter größten Schwierigkeiten umgesetzt werden kann. Im bilingualen Sachfachunterricht wird die Leistungsbewertung noch schwieriger als in einem traditionellen Kontext. Hier stellt sich nämlich in noch stärkerem Maße die Frage, ob die Lernenden im Hinblick auf ihre sprachlichen oder ihre inhaltlichen Leistungen bewertet werden sollen. Im Allgemeinen wird gefordert, dass das Sachfachwissen über die Bewertung des Lernenden im Sachfach, und die sprachliche Kompetenz über die Bewertung in der Fremdsprache entscheiden solle. Vielleicht kann vor allem im CLIL-Klassenzimmer der Gedanke der Selbstevaluation, der in der Lernerautonomie so wichtig ist, zu einer Lösung werden.

Abschließende Überlegungen

Alle Argumente für den bilingualen Sachfachunterricht lassen sich in einem Punkt zusammenfassen: mehr als andere eher fachisolierende Ansätze stellt der bilinguale Sachfachunterricht eine Lernumgebung bereit, in der Sprache und Inhalt von gleicher Bedeutung sind und in der die Lernenden mit Inhalt in motivierender Weise arbeiten und dabei auf Sprache—ihre Form und Struktur—fokussieren können, wenn immer es notwendig ist.

Literaturangaben

Dam, L. "How Do We Recognize an Autonomous Classroom." *Die Neueren Sprachen* 93 (1994): 503-527.

Holec, H. *Autonomy in Foreign Language Learning*. Oxford: Pergamon, 1981.

Little, D. *Learner Autonomy: Definitions, Issues and Problems*. Dublin: Authentik, 1992.

Marsh, D., and G. Langè. eds. *Using Languages to Learn and Learning to Use Languages*. Jyväskylä: University of Jyväskylä, 2000.

Marsh, D., A. Maljers, and J. Haartinla. *The CLIL Compendium*. Jyväskylä: University of Jyväskylä, 2001.

Thürmann, E. "Eine eigenständige Methodik für den bilingualen Sachfachunterricht?" *Bilingualer Unterricht: Grundlagen, Methoden, Praxis, Perspektiven*. Ed. G. Bach & S. Niemeier. Franfurt: Lang, 2000. 75-93.

Wolff, D. "Der Konstruktivismus: Ein neues Paradigma in der Fremdsprachendidaktik." *Die Neueren Sprachen* 93 (1994): 407-429.

Wolff, D. "Content-Based Bilingual Education or Using Foreign Languages as Working Languages in the Classroom." *Aspects of Implementing Plurilingual Education: Seminar and Field Notes*. Ed. D. Marsh, B. Marsland, and T. Nikula. Jyväskylä: University of Jyväskylä, 1997a. 51-64.

Wolff, D. "Bilingualer Sachfachunterricht: Versuch einer lernpsychologischen und fachdidaktischen Begründung." *Initiativen für den Fremdsprachenunterricht an Hamburger Gymnasien*. Hamburg: Amt für Schule, 1997b. 45-53.

Autonomous Students in Language Learning Centres

Michael Langner
Manfred Prokop

The following is based on discussions held in Section 27 ("Learning Centres—Learning Advising—Media") of the 12th International Conference of German Language Teachers in Lucerne, Switzerland in 2001. The section was moderated by the two authors. The establishment of a self-access learning facility (media library) and its integration into a language centre at the bilingual Swiss University of Freiburg/Fribourg have led to a further development of the views expressed at the conference. Current thinking on issues related to the integration of a media library into a language centre is the focus of this article.

Constructivism and Language Learning

In recent years, the discussion of approaches to and theories of teaching second/foreign languages has been strongly influenced by a debate of the merits of several constructivist approaches. What they have in common is the view that all learning (and therefore also second foreign language learning) may be conceptualized as a process in which *learners acquire knowledge autonomously by means of distinctively individual cognitive constructions*. Every language learner constructs his or her learning context by developing strategies that enable him "to process a language, to interact in a language, and to learn a language" (Wolff 367).

Disregarding the sometimes esoteric attempts to draw boundary lines between *transition from cognitivism to constructivism*, *constructivism*, and *radical constructivism*, reference has repeatedly been made in this discussion to the usefulness of the so-called New Media in constructivist approaches to second/foreign language learning. Let us examine this claim in more detail.

From a constructivist perspective, *learning* is defined as follows:

> Learning involves acquiring information and processing experiences. During this process, the learner selects and constructs knowledge that is useful and appropriate for him, and therefore he continuously manages and controls his learning process. In other words, from the point of view of constructivism, learning is a person's highly individualized process of interaction with his environment. (Dichanz & Ernst 50)

Unlike various other approaches and theories of second/foreign language learning of the last 120 years, the emergence of constructivist approaches has not been the consequence of changes in the theoretical underpinnings of the *lead sciences* (linguistics, pedagogy and psychology). Rather, it must be seen as the theoretical founding and corroboration of changes, which have occurred in the practice of second/foreign language teaching. The communicative approach that has dominated second language teaching since the 1970s has been increasingly influenced by ideas promoting learner autonomy in the last 20 years. However, this process of re-definition has not taken place at the same time and the same speed in all European countries: in this regard, Scandinavia, Great Britain, and Ireland have been the pioneers.

ACTION

Search for a definition of the *communicative approach* in foreign and second language education. Identify aspects within this approach that support learner autonomy and, therefore, may have contributed to the development of a constructivist perspective on language learning.

The Council of Europe has also played a leading role in re-thinking approaches to second and foreign language learning by initiating several publications on this topic (e.g., Holec 1980). Constructivist approaches, therefore, do not represent abrupt changes in the paradigm, but are the results of a developmental process.

The following features characterize a constructivist approach:

- Learner Autonomy: the learners set their objectives, choose appropriate materials and, in part, evaluate their progress.
- Recognition of the importance of learning strategies and techniques.
- In addition to individual study, socially anchored learning situations (such as partner work and small- and large-group work) become increasingly important.
- A dynamic, rich learning context facilitates problem-oriented, autonomous learning.
- Partner and self-evaluation become as important as evaluation by others.

Learner Autonomy at the University

The implementation of approaches fostering learner autonomy in second/foreign language learning has taken place at different rates in the various European countries and their national educational systems. In countries such as Finland, autonomous learning activities have been a common occurrence for a long time even in the public schools, while in other countries the introduction of such forms of learning is still only being discussed. In institutions of teacher education and professional development, however, the theoretical examination of learner autonomy, self-directed learning and project work has become an integral part of the curriculum. Yet, in spite of these developments, autonomous second/foreign language learning has not become a fundamental concept characterizing language courses offered at the post-secondary level.

CONSIDER

Think about your experiences in the educational system of your home country. Did you experience autonomous learning ONLY at the university level, or did you have some experience with it earlier? Give some specific examples and explain what has changed in the process of your education.

Because most of our students have not had the chance to experience such approaches to second/foreign language teaching and learning in their own education, it is only at the university that our student clientele has the opportunity to become familiar with autonomous forms of learning. No doubt, there is a certain incongruity between the ideal of a constructivist learning background and every-day reality; accordingly, the following remarks must be read against this background.

Integrated Language Learning Centres

Wherever there are university-level language centres in Europe (and this is by no means the case everywhere), they are frequently service departments where students may take courses in a variety of languages (groups of learners with one instructor and general language courses at various levels). Occasionally, other learning opportunities are offered (self-access learning activities utilizing audio, video and print materials, increasingly also the New Media). At a few universities, language learning partnerships with students of other languages at universities abroad (tandems) are available.

The term *Integrated Language Learning Centre* connotes the availability of traditional second/foreign language learning opportunities (general language courses and language courses for special purposes taught by one instructor, i.e., attendance courses) and self-access learning facilities (e.g., self-access learning centres), and *their integration into a single instructional concept*. Learning *scenarios* may include, for example, CD-ROMs for the development of a single skill (e.g., a vocabulary trainer), but also classroom instruction with an instructor, or a language learning tandem. Each of these types of learning scenarios can be tentatively situated along three dimensions in such an instructional concept: a) the type of *learning activity*, ranging from traditional classroom work to virtual learning; b) the *function of the media* in the learning process, ranging from learning materials which constitute or support a course, to stand-alone materials for independent learning; and c) *social contexts of learning*, ranging from instructor-centred classes to independently working groups of learners. Such a visualization of learning scenarios may well assist in the re-definition of traditional instructional programs; it may also help determine the meaningful use of different kinds of learning scenarios (e.g., is the CD-ROM an appropriate medium for the development of communicative skills?).

CONSIDER

Some instructors may feel threatened by the idea of shifting class content to an environment outside of their classrooms. Address this fear by naming two to three benefits to the students of this instructional model. How could classroom work and the work in *integrated learning centres* be tied together in a useful way?

Table 1. Types of Learning Scenarios

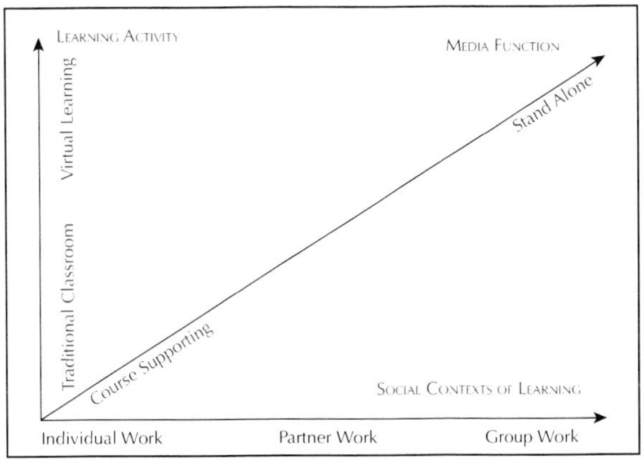

Of course, other parameters such as the learners' personality, their background in a specific type of learning culture, and learner type or motivation to learn, also play a significant role in the specification of learning scenarios at the university level. (Here we often come to the realization that our conception of learner autonomy is strongly Eurocentric!)

Learning scenarios characteristic of second/foreign language learning at the university level may also be arranged on this three-dimensional grid: basic courses (involving all skills) on the levels A1-C2 (the description of proficiency levels in the Common European Framework of Reference for Languages), learning opportunities for individual skills (reading comprehension, grammar, etc.), opportunities for the development of interconnected skills (e.g., reading and written summarizing), language learning tandems, etc.

In the ideal case, the learners will take advantage of several learning opportunities from the entire range offered (e.g., a small-group conversation course with an instructor plus grammar training with a CD-ROM plus a language learning tandem for interactive communication). In order to do so, however, they a) must know and be able to evaluate the learning opportunities offered; b) must be familiar with a variety of approaches to autonomous learning; and, c) must have access to personalized learning advising.

The Issue of Learning Materials

The constructivist re-orientation in the methodology and didactics of teaching second/foreign languages has made it clear that a rich learning environment is a prerequisite for successful (language) learning. For this reason, the issue of suitable learning materials is of the utmost importance for integrated learning centres: Commercial products abound in print, audio and video media, and currently very much so as well in New Media (off-line learning opportunities). However, these materials are frequently ill-suited for the specific requirements at universities and technical colleges and are often of questionable quality. This is especially true for the New Media. Classification grids (e.g., at <www.elias-nc.org>)—which increasingly take into account criteria for successful second language instruction)—facilitate the evaluation of such commercial products (CD-ROMs) and commercial and non-commercial Internet resources.

ACTION

Are there currently individuals at your institution who are working on the development of *new media* learning materials? If so, what materials have they developed, and what process is being used to evaluate them?

Consequently, we face the need at the post-secondary level to develop our own teaching/learning materials—a practice which has been a way of life for the more *traditional* materials for a long time. However, the expense of developing New Media learning materials locally is significantly greater. Therefore, colleges and universities are well advised to network and collaborate in the development of such learning resources.

Two Variants of an Approach which Fosters Learner Autonomy

A Concept for a Learning Advisement Scenario

The establishment of a media library (self-access learning centre) as part of a language centre was our starting point for conceptualizing a learning advisement scenario with a view to promoting learner autonomy and ensuring quality control over materials. We realized very quickly that simply making commercial materials available to the students did not promote learning. Even when there is a great deal of initial motivation, the danger may arise that the students get lost in the wealth of materials available to them. It was important for us, therefore, to offer the learners guidance and assistance—while assuring all possible learner autonomy—to give them a realistic chance to achieve their learning objectives.

Users of the self-access centre can be classified into two groups: a) students who are registered in courses at the Language Centre; and b) non-registered students who either may participate in traditional classes and simply *drop-in*, or who do not (or may not be able to) take advantage of traditional-type instruction. This distinction is relevant because drop-in users usually come to the self-access centre without having had personalized advising, while students registered in language courses will generally have received appropriate information from the course coordinators or in the course itself. Accordingly, two different versions of *learning advisement* are required.

We also needed to keep in mind that the two groups of users may have fundamentally different kinds of motivation for learning a second/foreign language. At our bilingual university, we must assume that language students may either want to, or have to, work on their proficiency in German or French, resp., in order to be able to succeed in their program of studies or to function more effectively in everyday life. Among those students who take German or French (sometimes English) language courses as part of their program requirements, there are those who plan to obtain a qualitatively and quantitatively defined bilingual exit qualification, and those who take classes in French or German below that level.

Which Information do Students Need to Become Autonomous Learners?

- Information about their language proficiency at the beginning of the learning process.
- Clarity about their objectives and their motivation.
- Familiarity with autonomy-promoting learning activities.
- Familiarity with the learning resources available.
- Skills in working autonomously.
- Reliable and valid information about their progress and the increase in their proficiency.

The following themes apply to learning advisement in general and must be addressed in the planning of the learning process:

Table 2. Planning of the Learning Process

Advisement Issues	Users Registered at the Language Centre	Drop-in Users
placement	-	mandatory
planning for learning	mandatory	mandatory
learning strategies	optional	optional
evaluation	optional	optional
learning difficulties	optional	optional

Students already registered in courses offered by the Language Centre usually do not need to take another placement test. First of all, placement tests are administered in each area at the beginning of each semester on the basis of which the students are assigned to courses at the appropriate level; furthermore, we use the Swiss version of the European Language Portfolio <www.sprachenportfolio.ch> in all courses, and the students have ample experience with the self-evaluation sheets. The results of the placement test and the self-evaluations form the basis on which we can proceed in advising the students on their learning process.

Drop-in users, however, do need placement. Because this group usually has no experience with the Language Portfolio either, we have to administer such a test at the beginning of the advising process. If we are dealing with one of the three main languages at the University of Freiburg/Fribourg, a computer-adaptive test (CAT) is currently available which selects items from a test bank for appropriate placement in certain types of skill courses. We are also convinced that the DIALANG project <www.dialang.org>—which has made available an Internet-based test in 14 European languages—will be very useful for proficiency assessment. For the remaining languages which students may be interested in taking, we will have to work with the self-evaluation materials provided in the Language Portfolio.

CONSIDER

If you speak one of the languages offered at <www.dialang.org>, find out about your own language proficiency level. Reflect on the difference between the test results and your self-evaluation prior to the test.

Autonomy-Promoting Learning and Teaching Materials

Planning the learning process and *designing a learning contract* are central features of the advising process for both target groups. On the basis of placement results, information about the foreign language to be studied, the students' motivation, the skills selected as learning objectives as well as the amount of time for which they can or want to commit themselves, we make suggestions for learning materials. We discuss these suggestions with the students and integrate them in a proposed learning plan. The development of a learning contract concludes this first phase.

> They [the learning contracts, ML/MP] contain details about the task to be completed, the materials to be used, scheduling, criteria for evaluation, and the manner in which self- or other-evaluation is to be conducted. (Edelhoff & Weskamp 246)

The two partners in the learning contract commit themselves to implementing the learning plan; changes are possible but only by mutual consent. This feature is intended to strengthen the learners' responsibility for themselves, among other things by the fact that a contract "creates a binding set of obligations for action and at the same time defines the instructor's role as one of learning adviser and assessor" (Edelhoff & Weskamp, ibid.).

The other three advisement issues listed above are not a mandatory part of the advisement process, but they are likely to gain importance, in particular the area of *evaluation*. In our view, however, much remains to be done in this area. On the one hand, a credit-granting process (explicit recognition of work done) is suggested by the reform of programs of studies in accordance with the *Bologna Model* and the introduction of the *ECTS (European Credit Transfer System*; see <http://europa.eu.int/comm/education/socrates/ects.html>), but this is only possible if an increase in learning can be ascertained (evaluation). On the other hand, the evaluation process involved in assessing progress for various skills and different languages is extremely work-intensive. While this may be possible in general language courses, it will not do to simply administer tests at the end of the learning segment which assess general skills in the target language, although the students had worked on specific objectives and skills. New and innovative ways to deal with this issue will have to be found.

CONSIDER

Reflect on your experience using a language lab or learning center. To what extent were the criteria (as represented in this article) available for you to become a successful autonomous learner? Was your experience a positive one? Why or why not?

Support Course for Autonomous Language Learning

The same considerations, which brought us to a conceptualization of learning advisement were also the point of departure for a new *course* concept. In this *course*, we combine the respective advantages of traditional second/foreign language instruction and of self-access learning facilities and, therefore, attempt to minimize the disadvantages of both approaches.

Among the advantages of traditional language instruction are, for example, a) frequent personal contact with a competent instructor, b) a structured learning path, and c) an evaluation of progress made by the learner. Benefits attributed to self-directed learning are d) increased self-responsibility and autonomy, e) an increase in the learners' motivation arising from their self-constructed learning scenario, and f) greater scheduling flexibility.

However, the conditions of study in such a setting may also turn advantages into disadvantages, e.g., a mutual dislike between learners and instructor, or excessive control of the learning process by the instructor.

The course description in the Appendix may serve to illuminate the concept underlying such a *course*.

Course Dossier

At the beginning of the term, the students receive a handout containing the following components:

- A questionnaire intended to produce data on the students' own and their target language, their motivation, and the priorities which they assign to the various skills.
- An information sheet about the computer-based placement test.
- The grid for self-assessment, taken from the European Language Portfolio.
- The sheet *Personal Learning Biography,* also from the ELP.
- A form for planning the learning process, and the learning contract.
- The form *Learning Journal.*
- The user regulations for the media library.
- Evaluation sheets for self-access learning materials.

Reference has been made in the section on *learning advisement* to several of the points listed above, but not to the learning journal. Students are expected to use it in regular intervals to reflect on their learning process so that they may become aware of the way in which they approach the learning task, the resources available for reaching their objectives, and their study habits and learning strategies.

On the basis of this information, we put together a sheet containing individualized suggestions for materials, which the students may use to attain their skill objectives. These may be the four basic skills, grammar, and vocabulary. (For the development of communicative skills, we try to find tandem partners when possible). Using our materials databank—which is indexed by departure language, target language, language level and language skills—we select suggestions which form the basis for the first intensive advising session. The students discuss these suggestions with the adviser, choose materials for a weekly schedule, and subsequently devise a learning plan for the time period selected. After the first experiences with the materials chosen—possibly after a change in the selection—the students sign the learning contract.

In order to intensify the personal contact between student and adviser as a *motivational tool and resource for learning,* the students as a rule commit themselves to another two (usually shorter) advising sessions during the term.

Anticipating Students' Information Requirements and Advisement Sessions

Following four semesters of experience with this type of course offering, we have come to the conclusion that the students' needs for information must be anticipated in order to make best use of the actual face time with them for the essential components of the advising session—motivation and support. This goal can be achieved by, for example,

- Online/off-line information with worksheets containing learning and study suggestions.
- A user-friendly arrangement of materials employing colour coding and catalogue numbering.
- Search opportunities in a data bank with learner-oriented keywords.
- Introductory information sessions focussing on available resources, technical assistance, and suggestions on how to increase one's autonomy as a learner.

A project currently undertaken will soon make browsing the media library more user-friendly: a web-based version of the data bank is being developed which will make the many different learning resources even more accessible. Using a few, but intuitively meaningful search terms, the learners will be able to launch computer-based materials (pre-installed CD-ROMs and web pages) or find the locations of other resources, including their catalogue numbers. Furthermore, they will be able to devise their own learning plan in the manner of a shopping basket where individual materials can be marked, put into the basket, and printed out as a single document.

Anticipating the students' needs in this manner makes it possible for the adviser and the learners to focus on themes which are important for extended periods of learning, viz. assistance in the selection of appropriate *learning strategies*, assistance in the process of *formative self-evaluation* (if necessary, facilitating partner evaluation as well), and advisement when students encounter *difficulties in their learning*.

Initial Experiences

The results of the first—admittedly quite unsystematic—assessment of experiences made in the four semesters since the project's inception have demonstrated that the emphasis on the learners' self-responsibility (planning the learning process, the learning contract, and learning journal) has resulted in a significant improvement of the learning product as well as in an increase in the subjectively experienced satisfaction with what was achieved. Clearly, the efficiency of such learning scenarios will need to be examined empirically.

A gratifying consequence of the success of this four-semester-long experiment is the fact that selected parts have already been implemented in similar *courses*—in French, for example, in a module for foreign students who are taking courses at our bilingual university.

Concerning the integration of the *learning journal* into the advisement process, we are planning to make its useful function for the learning process even more apparent and, if necessary, to take it into consideration as one of the relevant criteria in the assessment process.

It is envisaged to continue to develop the concept of the learning journal by giving more consideration to:

- The introduction of required attendance phases in addition to, or as substitutes for, advising sessions (possibly for clearly defined subgroups of students) in which small projects can be explored.
- The appropriate use of a course forum and an electronic chatroom.
- The deliberate formation of learner partnerships and groups for specific objectives.
- Plans for the use of locally developed self-access learning materials on the intranet or the internet.

Conclusions

The following points may serve as departure points for further consideration:

- Current trends in adult education—particularly at the college and university level—point to an increased demand for developing and fostering learner autonomy and to the need for a redefinition of the function of teaching staff (advisement, assistance, learning resource).
- Commercially available language learning software is largely unsatisfactory. For this reason, colleges and universities should collaborate in the development of appropriate learning materials.
- The commitment of teaching staff to learning advisement and the development of new self-access materials require much time and effort and must be rewarded, for example, by giving credit in the form of reduced teaching loads.
- We need to examine very carefully certain issues in the currently booming interest in media didactics and pedagogy, especially regarding the application of this research to second and foreign language learning and teaching.
- Although the Nintendo generation may have arrived at the university, our students are still far from having acquired real media competence. Accordingly, we will need learning opportunities for fostering and developing this competence in introductory training sessions and courses, clearly written information sheets and brochures.

DISCUSS

Review each of the points made by the authors in their conclusions. Choose one to discuss in more depth. Think about the pros and cons of your chosen statement and evaluate the impact this idea would have at your local institution.

References

Council of Europe. *Common European Framework of Reference for Languages: Learning, Teaching, Assessment*. Cambridge: University of Cambridge Press, 2001.

Dichanz, H., and A. Ernst. "E-Learning—begriffliche, psychologische und didaktische Überlegungen." *E-Learning. Die Revolution des Lernens gewinnbringend einsetzen*. Klett-Cotta: Stuttgart, 2002. 43-66.

Edelhoff, Ch., and R. Weskamp. "Leistungsbeurteilung im Fremdsprachenunterricht. Von der internationalen Perspektive zu den Entscheidungsprozesses vor Ort." *Fremdsprachenunterricht—Zeitschrift für das Lehren und Lernen fremder Sprachen* 4 (2002): 242-248.

Frischherz, B., and M. Langner, u.a. "Raster zur Evaluation von Software für das Sprachenlernen." *Zeitschrift für Interkulturellen Fremdsprachenunterricht. Didaktik und*

Methodik im Bereich Deutsch als Fremdsprache. 3 (1999): 2000 <http://www.ualberta.ca/~german/ejournal/langner1.htm>.

Holec, H. *Autonomy and Foreign Language Learning (Education et Culture)*. Strasbourg: Conseil de l'Europe, 1980.

Langner, M. "… und wo bleibt die Qualität? Lernsoftware und Internetangebote DaF evaluieren." *Mitteilungen des 'Österreichischen Lehrerverbands Deutsch als Fremdsprache (ÖDaF-Mitteilungen)'* 1 (2000): 24-31.

Langner, M. "Lernzentren – Lernberatung – Medien." *Mehrsprachigkeit und Deutschunterricht. Thesen, Beiträge und Berichte aus der Sektionsarbeit an der XII. Internationalen Tagung der Deutschlehrerinnen und Deutschlehrer IDT-2001 in Luzern. (bulletin vals-asla, Sonderheft)* (2002): 141-150.

Langner, M. "Autonomes Lernen—Lernberatung—Selbstevaluation: Zum Konzept eines Selbstlernzentrums." *Das Beispiel der Universität Freiburg/CH*. AKS Fremdsprachen und Hochschule, in print.

Overmann, M. *Multimediale Fremdsprachendidaktik: Theorie und Praxis einer multimedialen, prozeduralen Didaktik im Kontext eines aufgaben—und handlungsorientierten Fremdsprachenunterrichts (Internet communication, Bd. 4)*. Frankfurt/Main u.a.: Lang, 2002.

Rüschoff, B., and D. Wolff. *Fremdsprachenlernen in der Wissensgesellschaft: zum Einsatz der Neuen Technologien in Schule und Unterricht*. Ismaning: Hueber, 1999.

Scheffer, U. and Fr. W. Hesse. *E-Learning. Die Revolution des Lernens gewinnbringend einsetzen*. Stuttgart: Klett-Cotta, 2002.

Siebert, H. *Selbstgesteuertes Lernen und Lernberatung. Neue Lernkulturen in Zeiten der Postmoderne*. Neuwied: Luchterhand, 2001.

Tulodziecki, G., and B. Herzig, B. *Computer und Internet im Unterricht: medienpädagogische Grundlagen und Beispiele*. Berlin: Cornelsen Scriptor, 2002.

Wolff, D. *Fremdsprachenlernen als Konstruktion. Grundlagen für eine konstruktivistische Fremdsprachendidaktik*. Frankfurt/Main u.a.: Lang, 2002.

Appendix

INTERMEDIATE/UPPER-INTERMEDIATE	
Title	Support programme for guided autonomous language learning
Target Group	Students with a good knowledge of basic English
Dates	2 blocks at the beginning and end of the semester (Tuesday, Oct 29th & Thursday, Oct 31st 2002; from 5 to 7 p.m.) 2nd Block Negotiable
Place	Room No. 1101
Starting On	Tuesday, Oct 29th, 2002
Teacher	Michael Langner
Aim	Consolidation and development of all aspects of the language. The aim is level B2 of the European Framework.
Contents	The training is divided into three phases: 1) introduction; 2) the autonomous learning bases on a multifacted approach; and 3) review and consolidation. Learning will be drawn from a variety of media and students will be encouraged to broaden their communicative range. The introductory phase will include: • Information on the wide range of the learning media for the target-languages (audio-, video-cassettes, CDROM, Internet, printed material). • Opportunities for auto-evaluation. • Training in how to use the different media. • Information onthe infra-structures and opportunities for language-learning (mediatheque, UNI*Tandem*, work-groups). This first block ends with an examination which is part of a *self-learning contract* and shows the steps and paths to be used in oder to reach the aim. During the period between the two blocks, the students use their self-learning contract with the various tools and media. Support will be provided through the regular meeting with the course tutor. Two main areas will be reviewed in the final stage including the evaluation of: • The levels of achievement in relation to individual aims. • The tools, the paths and the infrastructure proposed in the course.
Prerequisites	• Level B1 in the target language. • Regular use of E-mail. • Willingness to work with the European Language Portfolio (possibility to buy it at the beginning of the course).

Post-Reading Questions

1. *If you had a chance to design a syllabus for one year with a class, what would it look like? Make a table including time-frame, main goals, content and methodology, then compare it to what and how you teach now. Finally, make a list of the main obstacles to changing your current way of teaching.*

2. *How much priority do you, or will you give technology in your teaching? Provide specific examples in order to clarify how you use technology in everyday practice.*

3. *What specifically could you do to foster bilingual education at your school? Make a list of ideas, and include the names of people who may be willing to support you in putting them into practice.*

4. *Think creatively about projects you could do in collaboration with countries of your target language. In listing your ideas, be as specific as possible, and move beyond the traditional E-mail exchange project.*

5. *Is autonomous learning possible in your class/school without having to significantly change the current organizational framework? What other forms of learning are desirable, and what would have to be changed to implement them? Finally, what support is available to make this change happen?*

6. *Brainstorm ideas for your personal curriculum in order to continue your own language learning. Include projects, short and long term goals.*

Chapter 3
Articulation and Assessment

Chapter three of this book looks at what happens in the individual foreign and second language classroom and at the negotiation of what will or should be happening in the future. Assessment is often misunderstood as *only* directed at students' learning. The authors in this section will introduce you to another form of assessment that, in addition to showing how students learn, also articulates the quality of classroom practice, and the processes and results of teaching. In this vein, the main focus will be on portfolios as a mode of documentation, reflection, and assessment of the dialogue going on between students, teachers, and institutions. Portfolios effectively communicate expectations, abilities, limitations, and the various reasons for these characteristics. They also often indicate the need for change within the triad of mutual development of students, teachers, and the institution. Finally, portfolios embody a lively part of an ongoing transatlantic dialogue between educators and researchers. The Concept of portfolio work began in the US during the 1980s in field of college composition. It was adapted to foreign language education during the 1990s in Europe and has now come back to the US to strongly influence foreign and second language instruction.

Pre-Reading Questions

1. *Draw a table for better comparison: What forms of assessment and evaluation have you experienced as a student? In what way were they similar or different in secondary and post-secondary settings? When in your learning process have these different assessment approaches happened? What detailed procedure did they follow?*

2. *What impact do/did these different forms of assessment and evaluation have on your learning motivation?*

3. *Which forms of assessment that you have experienced so far would you use in your own (future) teaching practice? Why?*

4. *Can you imagine alternative forms of assessment? Describe them briefly and address any obstacles you may face during implementation. How could you deal with these difficulties creatively?*

5. *Brainstorm or cluster around the term "portfolio": What does it mean?*

6. *What have you experienced, heard, or read about portfolio work, especially related to foreign and second language education?*

7. *Based on the above, what procedural differences do you see between portfolios and other forms of assessment? Also, what difference can you imagine with regard to learner motivation?*

Introduction to the New Visions Initiative: Articulation and Assessment

Theresa Austin
Christine Campbell

Introduction

For the language educator in K-12 settings, issues of assessment have taken on a larger social and political significance than ever before. Currently in the United States, the education reform movement has generated increased national calls for accountability in learning in the nation's public schools. Under the Bush administration's education policy, the *No Child Left Behind Act*, in order to receive federal funding, all states must establish standards for content and performance for all subject matter. Furthermore, assessment procedures to assure student progress towards the standards is required. With this increased monitoring, there is a greater push toward alignment of curriculum, assessment procedures, and scrutiny of decisions using these results.

> NOTE
>
> This push towards increased accountability can also be seen in adult education programs connected to the *Workforce Investment Act*. As in the K-12 system, programs designed to meet the language needs of adult immigrants and refugees seem to include a call for assessment procedures that assure student progress towards national standards.

For this reason, the issues surrounding assessment affect us all and require a new vision for our field. In the following sections we will present how these assessment issues raise concerns for pre-service teachers, in-service teachers, and teacher educators. We will then report on how language testing affects and is affected by theories of second language education, we conclude with a discussion of the rights and responsibilities of all language educators.

Teachers and Assessments

Most second language learning (L2) professionals would agree that assessment,[1] whether quantitative, qualitative, or a mixture of both, is a complicated subject. Freeman points out that its "technical and sometimes political dimensions...can often put teachers off" (1998 viii). The complex nature of assessment and a general aversion to test taking and, in some cases, to test *making* or development, may explain why the words *assessment, testing*, or *tests and measurements* conjure up negative associations for a number of K-16 teachers, undergraduate Foreign Language Education (FLED)/Second Language Acquisition (SLA) majors, and even some FLED/SLA graduate students.[2]

> ACTION
>
> Make word clusters. What associations do the terms assessment, testing, tests, and measurements, conjure up for you?

For example, a considerable number of L2 professionals, most of whom have liberal arts backgrounds, feel somewhat uncomfortable dealing with the numerical tasks connected with the process of establishing an assessment program. Additionally, the criticism of standardized testing in the press over the past fifteen years has raised serious questions about the merits of standardized testing given the profession's awareness of the impact of individual differences in learning, the limitations of using the multiple-choice test design to test complex communicative and cognitive performances, and the cultural biases of some standardized tests (Valdes & Figueroa 1999).

Despite these and other concerns about assessment, the majority of L2 administrators and teachers acknowledge that conventional educational systems cannot function effectively without an assessment program that provides information on which to base decisions about people and courses. For the in-service teacher, assessment is often included as a topic in methodology courses where techniques of assessment are provided. As apprentices to cooperating teachers, the in-service teacher may correct exams, write feedback to students on their essays, and even create chapter tests or quizzes. However, a wider perspective of how students are placed into the curriculum, how progress is assessed throughout the curriculum, and how students are impacted by these decisions is often missing from their preparation. There is a great need to include placement and progress issues as part of the pre-service teacher's responsibility. When students are placed at the wrong level of instruction or are not promoted into the next level, the validity of placement instruments and progress indicators needs to be examined. Without evidence from the teacher of an instructional mismatch for placement or without appropriate evidence validating rubrics for students' performances, faulty assessments can continue to mis-measure students' learning. These students may later be problematic in terms of discipline because they are not challenged or because instruction is far above their abilities. In this manner, the attention focused on disruptive behavior itself masks the reasons that the behavior occurs in the first place—incorrect placement or inappropriate instructional level. Similarly, the focus on chapter quizzes and achievement is important but not sufficient to examine if alignment exists between the chapter quiz and the measurement of achievement in curriculum, or if decisions to promote or retain students are based on sound interpretations of students' performances.

CONSIDER

What strategies can new teachers, who have little practical experience, use to best judge student performance? How can teachers balance years of experience with the need to envision new approaches to assessment?

Many in-service teachers have developed a sense of assessment in their own curriculum through their experience in their particular schools. The wisdom gained through professionalism and years working with a particular set of materials and types of students provide many of these teachers with valuable insights to judge student performances. Often the challenge for these teachers is to envision alternative ways to assess communications and learning.

Typically, language programs require learners to take tests or to submit work products such as portfolios. Tests have been the traditional source of information about a particular learner's ability, attributes, or progress in a course. For example, Scholastic Achievement Test (SAT) scores are often cited as a key indicator of the learner's academic progress in high school and potential for success in college. The members of the federal commission tasked with evaluating the state of the American educational system at the end of the 1970s highlighted the decrease in SAT scores at a national level in their report entitled *A Nation at Risk: The Imperative for Educational Reform* (US Department of Education 1983). Since the publication of this document and others like it focusing on deficiencies in US schools, federal and state governments have placed pressure on school districts and, most recently, on post-secondary institutions, to raise educational standards and revamp assessment programs in accordance with the revised standards. States have responded to the call in a variety of ways, some more effectively and efficiently than others. Specifically, in the L2 arena, advocates in states like New Jersey have worked tirelessly to promote language instruction in elementary schools. In 1996, New Jersey adopted state standards—the *Core Curriculum Content Standards for World Languages*—that require all K-12 students to study a world language. Since then, the state has delineated several key initiatives to address issues related to the implementation of the standards. One new program is the New Jersey Gaining Achievement in the New Standards Project, a three-year comprehensive statewide advocacy project aimed at involving parents fully in the standards process and recruiting qualified teachers.

DISCUSS

In your opinion, what is the relationship between quantitative and qualitative assessment? What role does each play in the foreign language classroom?

The question, then, is not whether to assess language ability or proficiency, interpreted within or outside the context of the national standards, and language program effectiveness, the two constructs of most concern to L2 professionals. Rather, it is how to assess them fairly and accurately using assessments that reflect current L2 theory and are appropriate to the educational setting.[3] Designing and developing an assessment program is no simple matter, whether at the macro-level, through a team from a learning institution such as a college or university, a consortia of learning institutions, a school district, etc., or at the micro-level, i.e., an individual teacher for his or her students. When implementing the national standards of foreign language learning (*Standards for Foreign Language Learning: Preparing for the 21st Century* [SFLL], 1996; *Standards for Foreign Language Learning in the 21st Century* [SFLL], 1999), what type of performance assessment is best suited to a particular standard of instructional content within one of the five goals of Communication, Cultures, Connections, Comparisons, and Communities? Should the assessment be quantitative, e.g., a test, or should it be qualitative, e.g., a work product like a portfolio? Or, should it be a combination of the two?

If the decision is made to use a test, then the concerns of validity, reliability, and the practicality of the test design and implementation must be addressed. Does the assessment program of the learning institution or school district in question provide for timely review and revision of features of the program by a team of knowledgeable professionals, to include assessment specialists from within the L2 field and outside of it? Do administrators responsible for making and implementing policy solicit input about assessment from classroom teachers and students before making decisions? These are among the questions that administrators and teachers interested in improving the assessment program within their sphere of influence must ask themselves.

The purpose of this article is to explore, in general terms, how L2 theory informs practice and how practice influences L2 theory within the area of assessment. Because assessment and curriculum are so intimately connected in most educational settings, the authors will examine the relationship as part of the discussion on the interaction between theory and practice in assessment, whether or not that assessment is based on the national standards.

Theory as a Catalyst for Change in Curriculum and Assessment: Communicative Frameworks and Their Effect on Assessment

Generally, changes in theory lead to changes in curriculum and the assessment program associated with the curriculum. Unfortunately, although changes in theory are essential for progress in any discipline, they usually do not affect the teaching and assessment practices of the vast majority of classroom teachers until years after their authors first present them in articles and/or at conferences. Such has been the case with the theoretical perspectives associated with communicative language teaching in the United States, often referred to as proficiency-based or proficiency-oriented instruction.

The term *proficiency* has been interpreted in a variety of ways in the literature, e.g., as a synonym of or as a narrower variant of *communicative competence*, the expression first introduced by Hymes (1972) in the mid-60s (Cf. Canale 1983). Bachman (1990) prefers the term *language ability* to *proficiency* given the many interpretations of the latter (16). Liskin-Gasparro has provided perhaps the most succinct definition of proficiency as "the ability to function effectively in the target language in real-life contexts" (12). According to Bachman and Savignon (1986), existing definitions of *proficiency* and *communicative competence* are more similar than dissimilar.

According to Hymes, communicative competence is comprised of grammatical competence, sociolinguistic competence, and contextual competence. Munby (1978), Canale and Swain (1980), Sauvignon (1972, 1983, 1997) and others did further research on communicative competence, Canale (1983) and Swain eventually producing a theoretical framework for communicative competence comprised of four elements: grammatical competence, sociolinguistic competence, discourse competence, and strategic competence. Bachman (1990) has posited a theoretical framework of *communicative language ability* consisting of three principal components: language competence (incorporating two main abilities—organizational competence and pragmatic competence), strategic competence, and psychophysiological mechanisms.

Omaggio-Hadley (2001) rightly points out that proficiency is "not a theory of language acquisition[,] ... a method of language teaching[, or] ... a curricular outline or syllabus..." rather, it is language ability as described and measured by the *American Council on the Teaching of Foreign Languages (ACTFL) Proficiency Guidelines* or some other framework (32-33).

Bachman (1990), when describing the uses of language tests, introduces the term *theory of proficiency*, presumably a reference to the theory associated with a particular theoretical framework such as Canale (1983) and Swain's for *communicative competence* and Bachman's own for *communicative language ability*. He states:

> [T]he *content* of language tests can be based on either a theory of language proficiency or a specific domain of content, generally as provided in a course syllabus. We can refer to theory-based tests as *proficiency tests*, while syllabus-based tests are generally referred to as *achievement tests*. (Bachman's emphasis; 71)

ACTION

Observe several teachers in a variety of classroom settings. What types of assessment are being done? Are they assessing proficiency or discreet skills? Does it appear to be effective?

In the 1970s, researchers and teachers in the United States, influenced by work in the area of communicative syllabus design in Europe and in ESL/EFL, began to explore and/or apply principles of communicative language teaching. The movement, however, did not gain momentum until the publication of two germinal documents—the *ACTFL Provisional Proficiency Guidelines* (1982) and *Teaching for Proficiency, the Organizing Principle* (Higgs 1984), the tome within the American Foreign Language Education Series. For many L2 professionals, these books heralded the end of one era and the beginning of another. The process of transforming the audio-lingual classroom into a communicative one has taken approximately fifteen years. Nevertheless, most assessment specialists acknowledge that while most of the profession now is teaching for proficiency, a considerable number of teachers recognize that they are not yet assessing for proficiency in all four language skills.

CONSIDER

Thinking specifically of your institution, how can program administrators and instructors work together to keep assessment and instructional practices up to date and aligned?

Assessing for Proficiency in the Four Language Skills

A sizeable number of teachers have not updated their assessment practices over time because of the pressures inherent in the teaching environment today such as lack of time due to additional duties and lack of professional development opportunities due to reduced funding. Teachers are often unfamiliar with basic information about assessment in general, and testing, specifically, the major uses of language tests—selection, placement, diagnosis, and assessment of student progress, the similarities and differences among achievement tests, proficiency-based achievement tests, prochievement tests, and proficiency tests.[4]

There is a prevailing opinion that proficiency testing is somehow restricted to the assessment of the speaking skill, as measured in the ACTFL or government Oral Proficiency Interview and the Center for Applied Linguistics' Simulated Oral Proficiency Interview.

The four skills have traditionally been assessed separately in high-stakes standardized language tests. They have generally been assessed separately so as to maximize test validity and reliability by restricting the number of examinee attributes or abilities (characteristics, in measurement terminology) to be measured. (It is interesting to note here that the interactive nature of the ACTFL and government OPI, which explicitly test the speaking skill, implicitly test the listening comprehension skill as well.) The Defense Language Proficiency Tests (DLPTs), the standardized exit tests at the Defense Language Institute (DLI), are currently developed in two skills—listening comprehension and reading comprehension. The new generation of DLPTs, the DLPTs V, will assess a wider variety of the sub-skills associated with the four skills.

Whereas assessing the four skills separately has been the norm in standardized testing, it has not always been the case in classroom assessment. At the K-16 levels, classroom tests have been the most common tools for evaluating language ability.[5] Except for the speaking skill, a considerable number of teachers do not organize their tests around the language skills, preferring instead to assess knowledge of discrete features of the language such as grammar and vocabulary in sections designed for that purpose. Omaggio Hadley's (1986) *hybrid approach to test design,* as viable today as when it was first introduced, is a needed alternative to the discrete-point, decontextualized achievement test (313). This approach produces a type of test she terms a *proficiency-based achievement test* (1993, 418). It "requires students both to show how well they can use specified features of the language [i.e., the grammar and vocabulary], and to demonstrate that they understand how such features function within naturalistic discourse [i.e., real-life contexts]" (Omaggio-Hadley 417-418).

In all three editions of Omaggio-Hadley's *Teaching Language in Context* (1986; 1993; 2001), she includes examples of item types and test items that could be included in a proficiency-based achievement test. She also provides a variety of formats to test listening and reading separately or in combination with another skill. Those teachers who might find developing proficiency-based achievement tests (i.e., hybrid tests or prochievement tests) daunting should be encouraged by the fact that graduate students at a major university had no trouble learning to do so when given models. Buck (2001) asserts that if teachers spent a reasonable amount of time validating the items they develop for their classroom tests, they could vastly improve test quality.

A growing number of teachers are experimenting with more creative ways of assessing the four skills, using either proficiency-based achievement tests such as those described earlier, or alternative assessments such as portfolios, exhibitions, presentations. A particularly innovative variety of proficiency-based achievement tests—the *Korean in Context Tests* that form a battery of course tests in the four skills to assess student progress throughout the 63-week Korean Basic Course at DLI—contain new and different variations on item types. (See the section entitled *Practice as a Catalyst for Change in Assessment: The Case of Alternative Assessment* for more details on alternative assessment.)

The Theory-Based National Standards as a Catalyst for Change in Curriculum and Assessment

Assessing for Proficiency in the Four Language Skills within the Context of the National Standards: A Broader Perspective

Until the advent of the national standards that clearly articulate what K-12 learners should know and be able to do as a result of their language study,[6] L2 instructional content was traditionally limited to the four skills and, in some cases, to culture as well. The standards have widened the content ranges to include Connections, Comparisons, and Communities, in addition to the original Communication and Cultures. These five *Cs* constitute the five goal areas; two or more content standards are attached to each goal area. As Phillips (1999) insists, "Content standards must become the basis for the new assessments that will judge student competencies in terms of quality and progress toward high and challenging performance standards" (2).

Regarding the L2 theory that informed the standards, members of the original National Standards Task Force (NSTF) were ever-attentive to the need to ensure their work was firmly grounded on current theoretical perspectives, e.g., language acquisition theory, theoretical frameworks of communicative competence and communicative language ability, research on individual learning differences, etc. Throughout the standards project, many recognized authorities in the field were consulted in their capacity as representatives of national and international language-specific associations such as the American Association of the Teachers of Spanish & Portuguese (AATSP), or as private parties. The participation of these authorities and the adoption of the standards as guidelines for K-12 by all the associations alluded to above are indicators of the legitimacy of the standards. The chapter authors in *Foreign Language Standards: Linking Research, Theories, and Practice* (Phillips & Terry 1999), as the title suggests, focus on the theoretical bases of the standards.

Concerning the impact of the standards in the ESL/EFL field, in government circles in the United States, and in academic environments abroad, the authors are unaware of any recent literature that addresses the issue. It remains to be seen whether the standards will have any effect in other countries. Just as developments in communicative language teaching in Europe in the 1970s shaped language teaching in the United States, so other nations may find aspects of the standards pertinent to their reality.

ACTION

Become familiar with the national content standards in order to better meet your responsibility of establishing comprehensive and effective local assessment procedures.

The existence of nationally-accepted goals and content standards for language learning could potentially contribute to a gradual improvement in assessment practices. Use of a common language across different educational settings has already enhanced communication in the profession about such topics as assessment needs and concerns. However, it is important to note here that although the standards describe the content of instruction, they do not a) specify performance standards for each of the eleven content standards, or b) provide tools such as tests to assess to what degree learners are mastering the content. Educational institutions and school districts are to take responsibility for establishing their own assessment programs.

Taking responsibility for outlining performance standards and identifying or designing a variety of tests or alternative assessment options such as portfolios to evaluate performance is no small task. Several complications surface that pose special challenges for the authors of assessments:

- The interconnectedness of the five goals, with the resulting conceptual overlap among the content standards, makes fair and accurate assessment of one particular performance standard more difficult.
- The introduction of the *Framework of Communicative Modes* that

describes learning performances as Interpersonal, Interpretive, and Presentational, requires assessment teams to broaden their view of communication.

- The curricular weave among content, processes, and technology[7] that characterizes the standards must be taken into account when performance standards are being drafted.

Professional assessment teams composed of both assessment specialists and classroom teachers will undoubtedly tackle and work out these complications. Phillips (1999) acknowledges that the process of developing new assessment tools within the framework of the standards is lengthy: "These new assessments will have to be designed, piloted, reviewed, and revised many times, given the changing psychometrics that must be adapted. Assessments will not be primarily of the forced-choice design that lends itself so readily to statistical analysis and traditional measures of reliability and validity" (10).

Learning institutions, school districts and individual teachers are currently exploring ways to create the new assessments. The program of the 2001 American Council on the Teaching of Foreign Languages (ACTFL) Conference in Washington DC had several sessions focusing on the topic. ACTFL has established a taskforce—*Beyond the OPI*—to research ways of assessing the standards. It is a crucial that those engaged in these assessment efforts investigate ongoing developments such as *alternative assessment* and *educative assessment* (Wiggins 1998). (See the following section for more details on alternative and educative assessment.)

Practice as a Catalyst for Change in Assessment: The Case of Alternative Assessment

From where does the expression *alternative assessment* come? These authors have not been able to identify the source. Bachman does not reference it or *portfolios*, perhaps the most widely recognized form of alternative assessment in L2 today, in his highly acclaimed *Fundamental Considerations in Language Testing*, published in 1990. Cohen (1994) does not mention it, although he does discuss portfolios for assessing speaking and writing. Neither does Wiggins (1993; 1998a; 1998b), the assessment expert who has worked with the National Standards Task Force on the subject of performance standards design. Lynch (2001) uses the expression *non-measurement (qualitative) techniques* in contrast to measurement techniques such as tests, when outlining the research priorities in the area of language assessment and program evaluation for the TESOL International Research Foundation (604). The first of five research questions he asks is of particular interest here given the confusion surrounding the use of the term *alternative assessment*, "What is the range of non-measurement assessment techniques that can be used for language assessment and program evaluation?" (604). He later asserts that research into the five questions will include "a combination of measurement and non-measurement techniques for language assessment and program evaluation" (604). It appears, then, that although assessment specialists are not using the expression *alternative assessment*, teachers will continue to do so.

How, then, do teachers define alternative assessment? In the language learning context, it is classroom assessment of learner language ability using a variety of tools other than tests. In the teacher education/faculty assessment context, it is assessment of ability to teach, knowledge of L2 theoretical trends, etc. using a variety of tools other than tests. The list below is a sampling of the more popular existing classroom assessments for use in language instruction. They can be used separately or in combination:

- Portfolio: A compilation of the student's work over time that reflects his or her progress in an organized and systematic way. Teacher and/or student determine the kinds of materials to be included. The teacher typically develops the assessment criteria, but s/he may include the student in the process.
- Teacher Observation: Observation of the student's work in the classroom, both individual and group. The teacher collects data on the student's work using checklists and rating scales.
- Peer Assessment: Student evaluates another student's/other students' performance using set assessment criteria. The teacher and/or students develop the criteria.
- Self-Assessment: Student evaluates his or her own performance using set assessment criteria. The teacher and/or students develop the criteria.
- Shorter-Term Work Products, Shorter-Term Projects: To be distinguished from the long-term work products or projects typical of the portfolio. One example would be a 15-day journal written in the target language. These tools are often included in the portfolio as evidence of student work. The teacher usually develops the assessment criteria, but s/he may include the student in the process.
- Presentations, Exhibitions, Skits: These tools can be included in the portfolio as evidence of student work. The teacher typically develops the assessment criteria, but s/he may include the student in the process.
- Conferencing: One or more dialogues between teacher and student in which the teacher evaluates the student's progress using set assessment criteria.

There are several possible reasons for the growing interest in alternative assessment:

- At the macro- and micro-levels, there is a genuine concern to improve both curriculum and assessment practices in American education. This concern is rooted in a new awareness of the flaws in conventional assessment, specifically tests. A test, for example, assesses performance at one moment in time and so may not be an accurate, representative sampling of performance.
- Alternative assessment empowers teachers because it provides them with more freedom to shape classroom assessment to suit the needs of their particular students.

- Alternative assessment empowers students because it requires them to take more responsibility for their own progress and for the assessment of that progress.
- Teacher reports indicate that alternative assessment positively affects learning.

Educative Assessment and the Standards

When members of the National Standards Task Force began to examine assessment of the standards, they brought in Grant Wiggins, a nationally-recognized assessment expert, to share his insights. According to Wiggins (1998), creator of the term *educative assessment*, assessment should be *educative* in two basic senses:

> First, assessment should be deliberately designed to teach (not just measure) by revealing to students what worthy adult work looks like (offering them authentic tasks). Second, assessment should provide rich and useful feedback to all students and to their teachers, and it should indeed be designed to assess the use of feedback by both students and teachers. (12)

CONSIDER

Do you agree with these four reasons for the growing interest in alternative assessment? Do you have other ideas as to why interest in this field continues to climb?

Most teachers would recognize that conventional L2 assessment that consists of discrete-point decontextualized achievement tests has neglected to teach students through real-life language tasks that promote student-centered learning through pair and group work, use of authentic materials, personalization, and the target language as the main medium of instruction. The feedback alluded to in the definition above is rarely fully exploited for the benefit of both students and teacher. More often than not, a feedback session after a test, if done with the whole class, is perfunctory. Individualized feedback from teacher to student is usually done in writing. Because of time constraints, many teachers are unable to follow up with students to determine whether they assimilated the feedback and were able to incorporate it into their work. Also because of the press of business, teachers generally do not use assessment as the powerful diagnostic tool it is. Whether the assessment is quantitative, qualitative, or a combination of both, it can provide valuable information on student strengths and weaknesses. Teachers must somehow find the time to annotate this type of information about each student after each assessment. This data can serve as the basis of individualized homework and class assignments that are particularly suited to the student's need.

Wiggins (1998) asserts that both teaching and assessment should continually encourage the student to construct meaning, and use knowledge and skill, in important contexts. He specifies 14 guidelines for improved assessment. They constitute the essence of his assessment philosophy. They are presented here because his ideas are informing current work by assessment teams and groups that are writing the performance standards associated with the national standards.

- Design interactive assessments.
- Use reiterative performance tasks to assess whether understanding is becoming more sophisticated.
- In light of the inevitability of misconception, use assessment tasks that will best evoke such misunderstandings.
- Require students to self-assess their previous and their present work.
- Conduct assessment along a novice-expert continuum, using longitudinal rubrics (scoring standards that remain the same over time), not merely task-specific rubrics.
- Design curricula and build tests around recurring essential questions that give rise to important theories and stories.
- Use assessments that routinely ask whether or not the student sees the big picture.
- Use tasks and rubrics that determine whether students have mastered the purpose of skills, knowledge, and performance, not just mastered techniques or formats.
- Use simulations or real applications that require students to use knowledge with a purpose and a context in mind.
- Assess student self-adjustment in response to human or situational feedback.
- Use rubrics that measure degree of sufficiency and power of answers, not simply their correctness.
- Assess students' ability to be spontaneously self-critical and flexible in perspective taking.
- Assess breadth and accuracy of knowledge independently of depth of understanding.
- Assess for self-knowledge (91-99).

Principles such as those above that are gleaned from educative and alternative assessment are influencing the work of assessment teams tasked with drafting performance standards, whether or not they are based on the national standards. These teams have the arduous task of choosing from among the plethora of competing concepts those that are especially applicable to L2 in the United States today.

Assessment as a Catalyst for Curricular Change

Although theory usually drives changes in curriculum, there are instances in which assessment, rather than theory, motivates changes in curriculum. In such instances, washback, defined by Bailey (1998) as "the effect a test or battery of tests has on teaching and learning" (249), is the catalyst. Whether overt or covert, it is a reality in education. The authors suggest the interpretation of the term can be broadened to include assessments other than tests.

Depending on the educational setting, washback can be either positive or negative. On the positive side, it can be a key force in bringing about needed curricular change. In one government language institute, for example, the introduction of a psychometrically- and pedagogically-sound battery of standardized exit tests in a particular language necessitated the development of a new curriculum. From a negative perspective, washback, if extreme, can lead to a teacher-centered learning environment in which the teacher creates activities and exercises in a testing rather than teaching mode. Here, learning can be reduced to memorization on the spot and/or through homework of information provided by the teacher in a lecture versus interactive delivery format.

Conclusion

As alluded to earlier, administrators and teachers alike face a difficult, but not impossible, challenge: To work towards ensuring, within their institutional context, that language ability or proficiency, as defined within or outside the context of the standards, and language program effectiveness are fairly and accurately evaluated using assessments that reflect current L2 theory. Practical stumbling blocks exist, such as lack of available time to devote to revamping an institutional or individual assessment program. Likewise, lack of funding can prevent initiatives from being taken. Finally, there are a number of views about which theoretical construct to adopt as the cornerstone of an assessment program. Given the number of existing L2 theories and/or theoretical perspectives, it may be difficult for an assessment task force to reach consensus on which theories should influence test design and test development efforts. The question *How do adults become proficient in a second language?* continues to generate answers in the form of models and principles. Ellis (1985) suggests Schouten may be correct in his observation that "too many models have been built and taken for granted too soon, and this has stifled relevant research" (Ellis 248). Spolksy (1989) calls for the development of a unified macro L2 theory. McLaughlin (1987) and Larsen-Freeman and Long (1991) caution against wholesale adoption of one theory over another, positing that more research in SLA is needed before arguing for the superiority of one specific theory (8).

NOTE

The current focus on accountability at all policy levels has pushed assessment issues, and the challenges associated with it for administrators and teachers alike, into the spotlight.

L2 professionals are challenged by these and other practical and theoretical concerns. Despite these concerns, we must proceed energetically to improve our assessment practices. If the collegial collaboration that characterized the crafting of the goals and content standards can extend into the area of design and development of assessment programs, there can be no doubt we will succeed in our endeavor.

Notes

1. *Webster's Unabridged Dictionary* (1997) defines assessment as "the act of assessing; appraisal; evaluation" (5). According to Bachman (1990), the term *assessment* has been used in the measurement literature in conjunction with impressionistic approaches to measurement and large-scale programs that measure a wide range of characteristics. Cohen (1994), however, uses the term to refer to the act of evaluating language ability through a variety of means which include, but are not limited to, quizzes and tests. Hence, the title of his book *Assessing Language Ability in the Classroom*. Cambridge University Press has recently published the Cambridge Language Assessment

Series edited by Alderson and Bachman. In this article, the plural form, *assessments*, which appears in the L2 literature (e.g., Phillips 1999; Omaggio-Hadley 2001), will refer to instruments, tools, and techniques for assessing performance that are either quantitative (e.g., tests), qualitative (e.g., work products such as portfolios), or a combination of both.

2. Bachman defines *measurement*, *test*, and *evaluation* as follows: "*Measurement* and *test* involve the quantification of observations, and are thus distinct from qualitative descriptions. Tests are a type of measurement designed to elicit a specific sample of behavior. *Evaluation* involves decision making, and is thus distinct from measurement, which essentially provides information. Thus, neither measures nor tests are in and of themselves evaluative, and evaluation need not involve measurement or testing" (49).
3. L2 *theory* here is interpreted to mean the collective array of theoretical perspectives in second language acquisition (SLA). It is not limited to a theory of second language acquisition.
4. Campbell (1998) compares and contrasts the four test types in "Proficiency Testing for Business and the Professions," in *Spanish and Portuguese for Business and the Professions* (Ed. T. Bruce Fryer and Gail Guntermann), a tome published under the auspices of the American Association of the Teachers of Spanish and Portuguese. To summarize: An achievement or attainment test, also called a progress test, is based on course content, typically provided in a course syllabus, and is designed to determine a given student's progress in a course or part of a course. A proficiency test is based on a theory of proficiency and is designed to determine a given learner's level of language proficiency. Bachman (1990) offers the following simple comparison: "We can refer to theory-based tests as proficiency tests, while syllabus-based tests are generally referred to as achievement tests" (71). See the sub-section *Assessing for Proficiency in the Four Skills* for Omaggio-Hadley's definition of proficiency-based achievement test, a term synonymous with prochievement test.
5. The term *classroom tests* is used by testing specialists to refer to unvalidated tests developed either by an individual teacher for use in his or her class or by a team of teachers for use within the context of a language program. Tests that have undergone a simple, as opposed to a thorough, piloting, or validation, are still classified as classroom tests. (Cf. Bachman, 1990, for details about what a thorough validation entails.)
6. While the standards were initially developed for K-12, the majority of the language-specific collaborating organizations have adopted them for K-16.
7. These three areas, as described in the *SFLL* (1996), are:
   - Content areas include the language system, cultural knowledge, and content from other school disciplines.
   - Processes include communication strategies, learning strategies, and critical thinking skills.
   - Technology includes a system for direct communication with language users, a source of materials, and an instructional delivery system. (29)
8. Omaggio-Hadley (2001) provides a succinct overview of the competing theories in Chapter 2 of the third edition of *Teaching Language in Context* (3rd ed.).

References

American Council on the Teaching of Foreign Languages (ACTFL). *Oral Proficiency Interview*. Hastings-on-Hudson: ACTFL, 1982.

American Council on the Teaching of Foreign Languages (ACTFL). *ACTFL Proficiency Guidelines*. Hastings-on-Hudson: ACTFL, 1986.

American Council on the Teaching of Foreign Languages (ACTFL). *ACTFL Provisional Proficiency Guidelines*. Hastings-on-Hudson: ACTFL, 1982.
Bachman, L. *Fundamental Considerations in Language Testing*. Oxford: Oxford UP, 1990.
Bachman, L. & S. Savignon. "The Evaluation of Communicative Language Proficiency: A Critique of the ACTFL Oral Interview." *The Modern Language Journal* 70(4) (1986): 380-390.
Bailey, K. *Learning about Language Assessment: Dilemmas, Decisions, and Directions*. Boston: Heinle & Heinle Publishers, 1998.
Buck, G. "Teaching and Testing Listening Comprehension." Paper Presentation Defense Language Institute, Monterey, 2001.
——. *Assessing Listening*. Cambridge: Cambridge UP, 2001.
Campbell, C. "Proficiency Testing for Business and the Professions." *Spanish and Portuguese for Business and the Professions*. Ed. T. Bruce Fryer & G. Guntermann. Lincolnwood (Chicago): National Textbook Company, 1998.
Canale, M. "From Communicative Competence to Communicative Language Pedagogy." *Language and Communication*. Ed. J. Richards and R. Schmidt. London: Longman, 1983.
—— & M. Swain. "Theoretical Bases of Communicative Approaches to Second Language Teaching and Testing." *Applied Linguistics* 1 (1980): 1-47.
Center for Applied Linguistics. *Simulated Oral Proficiency Interview*. Washington DC: CAL, 1995.
Cohen, A. *Assessing Language Ability in the Classroom*. 2nd Ed. Boston: Heinle & Heinle Publishers, 1994.
State Department of Education. *Core Curriculum Content Standards for World Languages*. Trenton: State Department of Education, 1996.
Defense Language Institute (DLI). *Defense Language Proficiency Tests IV*. Presidio of Monterey: DLI, 1988-2000.
Defense Language Institute (DLI). *Korean in Context Tests*. Presidio of Monterey: DLI, 1997.
Higgs, T, ed. *Teaching for Proficiency, the Organizing Principle: The ACTFL Foreign Language Education Series*. Vol. 15. Lincolnwood (Chicago): National Textbook Company, 1984.
Hymes, D. "On Communicative Competence." *Sociolinguistics*. Ed. J. Pride and J. Holmes. Harmondsworth: Penguin Books, 1972.
Ellis, R. *Understanding Second Language Acquisition*. Oxford: Oxford UP, 1985.
Larsen-Freeman, D. and M. Long. *An Introduction to Second Language Acquisition Research*. White Plains: Longman, 1991.
Liskin-Gasparro, J. "The ACTFL Proficiency Guidelines: A Historical Perspective." *Teaching for Proficiency, the Organizing Principle: The ACTFL Foreign Language Education Series*. Ed. T. Higgs. Vol. 15. Lincolnwood (Chicago): National Textbook Company, 1984.
Lynch, B. "Language Assessment and Program Evaluation." *TESOL Quarterly* 35(4) (2001): 603-605.
McLaughlin, B. *Theories of Second-Language Learning*. London: Edward Arnold, 1987.
Munby, J. *Communicative Syllabus Design*. Cambridge: Cambridge UP, 1978.
National Standards in Foreign Language Education Project. *Standards for Foreign Language Learning in the 21st Century*. Yonkers: National Standards in Foreign Language Education Project, 1999.
National Standards in Foreign Language Education Project. *Standards for Foreign Language Learning: Preparing for the 21st Century*. Yonkers: National Standards in Foreign Language Education Project, 1996.
Omaggio, A. *Teaching Language in Context: Proficiency-Oriented Instruction*. Boston: Heinle & Heinle Publishers, 1986.

——Hadley, A. *Teaching Language in Context*. 2nd ed. Boston: Heinle & Heinle Publishers, 1993.

——. *Teaching Language in Context*. 3rd ed. Boston: Heinle & Heinle Publishers, 2001.

Phillips, J. "Introduction: Standards for World Languages—On a Firm Foundation." *Foreign Language Standards: Linking Research, Theories, and Practices*. Ed. J. Phillips and R. Terry. Chicago: National Textbook Company, 1999.

Sauvignon, S. *Communicative Competence: An Experiment in Foreign Language Teaching*. Philadelphia: Center for Curriculum Development, 1972.

——. *Comunicative Competence: Theory and Practice*. Reading: Addison-Wesley Publishing Company, 1983.

——. *Comunicative Competence: Theory and Practice*. 2nd ed. New York: McGraw Hill, 1997.

Spolksy, B. *Conditions for Second Language Learning*. Oxford: Oxford UP, 1989.

Unites States Dept. of Education. A Nation at Risk: The Imperative for Educational Reform. Washington: GPO, 1983.

Webster's Unabridged Dictionary. 1997 ed.

Wiggins, G. *Educative Assessment: Designing Assessments to Inform and Improve Student Performance*. San Francisco: Jossey-Bass Publishers, 1998.

Portfolios in the United States—With a View Toward Europe

Randall J. Lund

Introduction

The portfolio movement in education in the United States has origins in various contexts, like the streams in a watershed, and those contexts are now merging into a current of considerable force. Portfolio use early on often was motivated by the search for alternative forms of learning, teaching, or testing in reaction to traditional, institutionalized forms of education and evaluation. Yet the portfolio is now on the verge of being institutionalized at the highest levels. Some wonder whether or not the portfolio can survive such prosperity.

The purpose of this chapter is threefold: a) to identify the main origins and uses of the portfolio in American (United States) education and to show how those currents all converge on second language education as a prime context for portfolio use; b) to identify the tensions and paradoxes that seem to be inherent in the nature of the portfolio and for which healthy solutions must be found; and c) to recommend learning from European portfolio developments as the American experience moves through some critical stages.

Definitions and Descriptions

There are many kinds of portfolios, and most definitions are too specific to reveal their essential qualities. Jordan and Purves (1996) capture the portfolio's essence before it became specialized: "a collection of representative pieces of an individual's work" (180).

More important than definitions are the attributes that are essential for a good portfolio. Hamp-Lyons and Condon (2000) offer nine characteristics—collection, range, context richness, delayed evaluation, selection, student-centered control, reflection and self-assessment, growth along specific parameters, and development over time—of which three are most essential, subsuming the others: collection, reflection, and selection.

A learner, for example, collects documents (artifacts) in a selective way according to the purpose and potential audiences of the portfolio. The documents may represent one's best work, the process by which the work came about, or other forms of documentation of one's ability, including self-assessment and external evidence (attestations). Reflection is necessary to make the collection more than a scrapbook or file box. Reflection gives context and meaning to artifacts individually and as a whole. In many portfolios, reflection is also linked with the whole point of the project, which is to stimulate awareness of the learning process and the effective use of goals, processes, and strategies.

How these nine portfolio attributes are realized depends largely on the purpose of the portfolio and the context in which it is used. Hammadou (1997) names four general types—showcase or best work, documentation, evaluation, and process—that often exist in combination.

The showcase portfolio is the type that has always been used in creative vocations such as art, architecture, music, and writing by both professionals and learners. The dossier presented by academics for tenure and promotion has many showcase qualities. Selection is the chief characteristic.

A documentation portfolio emphasizes the attribute of collection. It may capture the history of a major project, track activity over time, or demonstrate the completeness of one's achievement in various categories.

The evaluation portfolio is characterized by evaluator, rather than producer, control. Tasks are specified and standardized as much as possible.

By contrast, the process portfolio is largely under the learner/owner's control, because its purpose is to engage the learner in reflective and autonomous learning and to give the teacher insight regarding the learner's processes and progress. A process portfolio typically includes drafts, activity logs, diary entries, reflections on the artifacts themselves, group work, and feedback such as peer review or teacher consultation.

ACTION

Practice *writing to learn* and see if you can articulate yourself clearly about the key term of this chapter. Write an E-mail message to a friend describing the term *portfolio.* Start with something like, "Can you believe, this time we will finish the seminar with a portfolio, not with an exam! Oh, just in case you don't know, a portfolio is..."

Contexts and Concepts

Writing Process

Aside from the traditional showcase portfolio in the creative disciplines, the most influential discipline in portfolio development has been that of writing/language arts. The portfolio filled a need that was created by a paradigm shift in the theory of writing and writing instruction. Observers have identified various origins for these developments, such as the Dartmouth Conference in 1966, the work of Janet Emig (1971), and the Bay Area Writing Project in 1972 (Bräuer 2000; Calfee & Freedman 1996; Hamp-Lyons & Condon 2000). The result of the new views was that attention shifted from writing as product to writing as process—how good writers write—and to whole language—the immersion of learners in real communication through the natural interplay of all language modalities. Metacognition, reflection, personal voice, and awareness of audience are essential to these processes (Calfee & Freedman 1996).

CONSIDER

Think about why the portfolio concept did not get more recognition in schools until it became a topic in assessment.

In these approaches to writing and reading, the whole process—source texts, plans, drafts, peer feedback, revision, publication, and reflection on learning—is naturally facilitated by a writing portfolio, ideally a *process* portfolio. Even so, portfolio use did not become widespread until it became linked with the issue of assessment.

Authentic and Alternative Assessment

The broad acceptance of writing process and related approaches to learning and teaching inevitably clashed with a testing tradition rooted in *positivism*, the belief that knowledge could be analyzed into discrete elements and accurately sampled by multiple choice questions and that students could accurately be ordered and represented by the number of questions they could answer. Educators recognized that actually writing an essay during a test was much more valid than reacting to minute hypothetical writing problems. On the other hand, reliability was recognized to be lower because of the subjective nature of scoring the essay and the admission of uncontrolled variables such as familiarity with the assigned topic or experience with the chosen genre or rhetorical task. Nevertheless, the authenticity of having learners actually write prevailed, even as acceptable reliability was achieved through improvement in holistic scoring systems (Hamp-Lyons & Condon 2000; Herman, Gearhart, & Aschbacher 1996).

However, as authentic as direct writing tests were, they remained focused largely on a single writing *product* that said very little about *process*. In fact they probably discouraged or prevented writers from engaging in the very processes they had been taught to use to produce good work. Assessment remained disconnected from writing process in the classroom (Tierney, Carter, & Desai 1991).

In the mid 1980s Elbow and Belanoff (1986) recognized that portfolios could make that connection by encouraging and reflecting good process, and the notion of *portfolio assessment* spread *like wildfire* (Hamp-Lyons & Condon 15). This kind of assessment not only enjoys high validity, but satisfies the common sense, and often ignored the notion that learning/teaching and testing should be guided by the same goals. One should test *what* and *how* one teaches. If portfolios are an ideal tool for engaging in writing process, they are also an ideal way to assess the learning of process.

However, the adoption or promotion of portfolio assessment by larger entities beyond the classroom, including districts, state offices of education, university admissions programs, university departments, and national associations, is seen by many as a cause for concern. The danger is that to the extent the portfolio is detached from the local learning context, process benefits are minimized, its inherent advantages are destroyed, validity suffers, and fair evaluation is hard to achieve. Portfolios then become just a "complex form of multiple-choice test" (Jordan & Purves 1996).

Learning Theory

The process writing/whole language movement resonates with similar developments in cognitive science and learning theory often referred to as *constructivism* (Glatthorn 1996; Hamp-Lyons & Condon 2000; Murphy & Camp 1996; Wile & Tierney 1996). In this view learning is active, subjective and personal, contextualized, social, and affective in nature and involves reflection, metacognition, and authentic application (Glatthorn 1996).

CONSIDER

Expand your conceptual knowledge. Learn about another definition of *constructivism* in Langner/Prokop in this book.

Educators in many fields recognized that portfolio learning could facilitate the features of a constructivist view of learning. Bond (1999) lists 16 subjects from agriculture to theater in which reports of portfolio use were found. Among them is second language learning, which will be discussed in greater depth below.

Teacher Education and Development

As educators in all disciplines realized the value of portfolio work for students, they also recognized its value for the teachers. Not only can they gain insight into what their learners are doing, but their own growth as teachers can be influenced in the preservice and inservice stages by portfolio use.

As was the case with writing, portfolios in teacher education are becoming standard procedure, as the process is being adopted by the highest policy makers in the field. For example, in 1997, Texas mandated a system of teacher evaluation that includes holistic sections which are *portfolio-like* (Bond 1999). More importantly, virtually all the major players in the accrediting of teacher education programs or the licensing of teachers in the US have adopted performance-based core standards for what teachers should know and be able to do. In each case, reflective performance is to be documented through (student) teacher portfolios that will serve as the basis for both individual licensing and the accreditation of the program.

The many stakeholders are represented primarily by a few leading organizations. The National Board for Professional Teaching Standards (NBPTS) promotes the voluntary certification of quality teachers (NBPTS, 2001). The Interstate New Teacher Assessment and Support Consortium (INTASC) is concerned with state supervision of the training, licensing, and development of teachers (INTASC 1995). The National Council for Accreditation of Teacher Education (NCATE) accredits teacher education programs (NCATE 2002). Either through INTASC, NCATE, or both, most teacher education institutions will be required in the next accreditation visit to demonstrate program quality through the portfolios their teaching candidates develop during their education (INTASC 1995).

CONSIDER

Check the interview with Lee Wilberschied for possible content of teacher portfolios.

As in writing, and for similar reasons, the rapid adoption of the portfolio for high-stakes assessment purposes causes concern for the welfare of the portfolio as a learning experience (Hammadou 1997).

Second Language Portfolios

There has been much less use of portfolios in second language education than in subjects such as language arts, social studies, math, and science (Bräuer 2000; Padilla, Aninao, & Sung 1996). Recently, however, increased attention has been manifest in all aspects of the literature, from conference papers to dissertations. Nevertheless, the depth of practice probably does not match the breadth of interest. Second language education should, in fact, be a leader among the disciplines because all the important currents of portfolio development converge at this point.

Most obvious is the connection with writing and language arts. The process orientation is now a standard component of discussions of second language writing pedagogy, but often without mention of portfolios. Whereas first language arts is more concerned with reading and writing goals, second language educators are concerned with all four modalities. While portfolios easily reflect reading and writing, the possibilities to link these modalities with listening and speaking in a true whole language approach are clearly worth developing.

Second language education has a well-developed tradition of attention to strategy use and metacognition that fits easily with the portfolio's ability to facilitate reflective practice and learner autonomy. Portfolios allow one to step back from experience through the passage of time, to reconnect with it through the documents, to gain new appreciation for learning, processes, and achievements from the current perspective, and therefore to plan future learning (Wade & Yarbrough 1996).

The arguments for active, constructivist learning and authentic performance assessment apply as much to second language learning as any other subject, but there are also unique aspects of language and language learning that benefit from the *collection*, *selection*, and *reflection* aspects of portfolio work.

Delett, Barnhardt, and Kevorkian (2001) mention four of these aspects: 1) the connection between language performance and purpose and context; 2) the trial-and-error developmental nature of proficiency; 3) the linkage between language performance and other complex mental skills; 4) and the dual nature of proficiency as a holistic, communicative tool and a set of discrete skills.

Portfolio work responds to each of these qualities of language. It encourages purposeful work and captures contextual factors. It accepts and documents the flaws of interlanguage as the natural state of learners. It recognizes the collaboration, editing, and revising, and final imperfections that are part of second language production. This facility is especially important for minority language speakers in other disciplines, who might otherwise be compared unfairly with majority language peers (Hamp-Lyons & Condon 2000). For most learners, a second language is not the end in itself, as one expects to know about other topics, but a means to communicate about those topics, a means of connecting with other disciplines and communities (National Standards in Foreign Language Education Project 1999). Portfolio work is ideally suited to collecting work of an interdisciplinary or content-based nature.

A national standard of describing communicative proficiency has been achieved in the *ACTFL Proficiency Guidelines* (American Council on the Teaching of Foreign Languages [ACTFL] 1986), but an associated assessment instrument exists only for speaking in the form of the Oral Proficiency Interview (OPI) (ACTFL 2002). There are at the moment no comparable instruments for second language writing, reading, or listening. Even the OPI is subject to many of the limitations of standardized, one-shot, proprietary testing formats. Portfolio assessment offers possibilities for assessment of all modalities in a single package reflecting multiple topics, purposes, and contexts.

Such rich information about proficiency is also of interest to the general public, particularly for employment purposes. A showcase portfolio can reflect not only general proficiency, but skills tailored to the specific application.

Language teachers in particular will soon be required to demonstrate their teaching proficiency, including proficiency with the language, through portfolios. Just how to do this has been unclear to some pre-service teachers (Fox 1999). The language part of the teacher portfolio would ideally be an independent module, a portfolio within a portfolio that could also stand alone as a model to the teacher's own learners or for other purposes, such as continuing education, career changes, or volunteerism.

CONSIDER

Summarize the arguments listed above in favor of portfolio practice in foreign/second language education. What reasons would convince you to start a teacher portfolio yourself?

Now that the second language teaching profession seems committed to portfolios for its teachers, more widespread use with learners is bound to follow. It is likely that second language teachers will encounter both the frustrations and successes that others have reported. As practice develops, lessons can be learned from those with earlier and longer experience regarding some apparently inherent portfolio problems.

The Problem with Portfolios

As much as portfolios make sense in a communicative approach to learning and classroom assessment, there are concerns about their adoption by the highest authorities in education for assessment of learners and programs with high-stakes outcomes, such as admissions, financial aid, graduation, licensing, accreditation and resource allocation. Many warn that the embrace of portfolios by the evaluation and accreditation industry may create difficulties for the portfolio movement because of the mismatch in goals, methods, and assumptions (Bräuer 2002; Calfee & Perfumo 1993; Callahan 1997; Jordan & Purves 1996; Lucas 1992; Murphy & Camp 1996; Tierney, Carter, & Desai 1991; Wile & Tierney 1996; Yancey & Weiser 1997).

The conflict between good teaching and centralized testing is not unique to portfolios and existed before their advent (Murphy & Camp 1996). When standardized assessments are used to drive teaching, the curriculum narrows, fragments, and reflects mainly preparation for the assessment; teacher authority is weakened; and teacher and learner are demotivated. This could also be the fate of mandated portfolio assessment (Bräuer 2002; Murphy & Camp 1996; Ponte 2001). Furthermore, the inherent conflicts with assessment can be further magnified by the unique qualities of the portfolio, which is itself subject to its own tensions.

Portfolios are by nature susceptible to tensions between learners and educators. The type and characteristics of a portfolio are determined by its purposes, and those purposes inevitably involve at least two stakeholders—the author (subject) and the audiences (object). In this fact lie the major paradoxes and perils of the portfolio. To the degree that each player brings a different purpose and point of view, the portfolio may be subjected to a tug-of-war of tensions that can adversely affect success.

These tensions often seem to align themselves along the same polarity as the author-audience tension, as shown in Figure 1. The author's needs tend to align with a process emphasis, local control, flexibility, and high contextualization. The more distant the audience, the greater the preference for standardized, inflexible, product-oriented portfolio designs. These polarities should properly be viewed as probabilities, rather than certainties, because the alignments can shift. For example, authors may naturally develop a showcase product portfolio for audiences of their own choosing. Similarly, prudent authorities can be respectful of essential portfolio processes. In fact, each tension arises from different circumstances and requires to some degree independent decisions, meriting their individual consideration.

DISCUSS

Writing to learn. How would you describe the problem with portfolios mentioned above with your own words?

Figure 1. Tensions in Portfolio Work

AUTHOR-FRIENDLY	ISSUE	AUDIENCE-FRIENDLY
Process	Purpose	Product
Author	Ownership	Audience
Flexible	Content	Fixed
Artifacts	Origins	Attestations
Interactive	Collaboration	Independent
Open	Evaluation	Closed
Local	Standards	External
Embedded	Contextualization	Isolated
Flexible	Theoretical Orientation	Fixed

Purpose

These tensions involve a variety of issues, but most are subsumed under the primary tension of purpose: Is the portfolio a process or a product? The process purpose is to enhance learning through the activities, choices, and reflection that engagement in the portfolio fosters. The product purpose is to represent the author's best achievement at a point in time, probably in support of decision making.

Ownership

The issue of ownership is deeper than who gets to keep it—author or audience—although the answer is telling. It is more concerned with who makes the decisions on the rest of the issues. It also speaks to the question of personal investment, which in turn often depends on how the portfolio is presented, motivated, modeled, used, and evaluated. Hammadou (1996) finds that self-assessment promotes ownership of the portfolio. Because an audience stakeholder—teacher, principal, district, state, or national organization—generally initiates or requires the portfolio, author motivation and ownership need special attention. But the issue of ownership is not a dichotomy. The teacher may share many interests with the author. All local stakeholders share to some degree the need to be part of the decision-making process.

Content

Perhaps the most obvious question is what will be in the portfolio. Authors want to express themselves. Teachers want the document to connect strongly to instruction in order to avoid extra work of questionable validity and to utilize good portfolio process as part of the curriculum. Both learners and teachers are concerned with the connection to grades. External audiences are likely to prescribe content narrowly in order to achieve the higher reliability of standardized tasks. Based on the experience of the University of Michigan entrance portfolio, Hamp-Lyons and Condon (2000) warn that external stakeholders cannot expect more than local stakeholders can deliver, or validity will suffer; that is, learners may be asked to do that for which they have not been prepared.

Origins

Part of the content decision involves the question of whether or not authors and teachers are allowed to include contextualized or subjective reflections and (self)assessments, or whether external, objective evidence is required. External evaluators may worry that the inclusion of contextual information will bias their judgment (Murphy & Camp 1996).

Collaboration

In a similar vein, audiences may be suspicious of documents produced with (sometimes unknown) levels of collaboration. This is particularly true for proficiencies such as writing, where current notions of good process welcome input from others at all stages from generating ideas through revision and editing to publication (Herman et al. 1996). The documentation of spoken language presents its own problems, especially when group work and conversation are involved (Padilla, Aninao, & Sung 1996).

Evaluation

Whoever is to evaluate the portfolio will need to be aware of the standards and how to interpret them. This is no easy matter. Portfolios have been suspect from the beginning because their assessment was initially found to have low reliability. However, where standards are clearly stated and multiple evaluators are adequately trained, reliability estimates have achieved acceptable levels (Hammadou 1997).

Evaluation, is of course, dependent on the purpose of the evaluator. Again, what is ideal for the audience may not be good for the author. Is it possible to have one portfolio serve both internal and external purposes? Some believe it is possible under specific conditions (Calfee & Freedman 1996; Hamp-Lyons & Condon 2000; Murphy & Camp 1996). Murphy and Camp feel that psychometrics must adapt to good portfolio practice rather than the reverse. Some think the differences are too extreme to be bridged (Cole 1988; Jordan & Purves 1996). Instead, Jordan and Purves suggest the metaphor of *hypertext,* in which the portfolio can have different readings based on different purposes and contexts, but only at the local level where context is available. However, higher nodes in the hypertextual process could aggregate samples of portfolios or aggregate assessments of portfolios at the class, school, district, or state level. While the portfolios themselves could not become part of a large-scale assessment, higher levels could validate or affirm the assessments of lower levels. Also, national organizations can support the theory and practice of portfolio work at the local level.

Standards

Evaluation requires standards and criteria, another source of tension. Many local stakeholders shy away from standards and grading and prefer qualitative feedback linked more with the learning process (Calfee & Perfumo 1996). Their mistrust and resentment of externally imposed assessments and standards was one of the reasons for portfolio use in the first place. Murphy and Camp (1996) urge that higher authorities not impose standards through assessment, but focus on the coherence of the whole system of teaching and assessment, implying the need for local involvement in the development of standards.

The late popularity of portfolio use in second languages has allowed time for general standards of individual proficiency and program content to be developed and accepted as a coherent system at least to the state and district level. They provide a common footing for standards that can be specific to different purposes, yet harmonious in their ultimate effect upon learning. These developments may smooth the progress of portfolios in second languages.

Contextualization

An important question related to evaluation and standards is the extent to which the context in which the portfolio was developed is allowed to appear in the portfolio itself or to be considered in evaluating the document. Contextual information in the portfolio includes process artifacts such as biographical and personal information, plans, drafts, logs and records, reflections and explanations by the author and others, and the developmental trail of artifacts over time. Contextual information about the portfolio ranges from simply *being there* and understanding the author as a whole person in a specific situation to more objective information such as how the portfolio was assigned and completed. The degree of contextualization indicates how connected portfolio work is with instruction and how helpful the process may be to the author.

Theoretical Orientation

Every stakeholder brings a set of assumptions, beliefs, and values to portfolio work, affecting all other decisions. Wise and Tierney (1996) represent the view that some beliefs, such as positivism and the whole production/efficiency/accountability model of schooling, are fundamentally incompatible with portfolio work. This tension is distinct from that of stakeholder role and purpose. Classroom teachers in their isolated classrooms are perhaps most likely of all to portray traditional notions of learning as inimical to portfolio work. That is why portfolio work, if initiated from above, must be introduced gradually in order to convince local teachers (Murphy & Camp 1996).

ACTION

In the light of what you read so far, specify the description of the problem with portfolios you drafted earlier. Explain three areas of tension that seem critical for portfolio practice.

Resolution of the Tensions

Having considered the tensions individually, we return to the point that each tension has opposite poles that share qualities and orientations with other tensions, in many cases represented by the primary paradox of author and audience. Parker Palmer (1998) believes that much that is wrong with education is the result of failure to honor the opposites in paradox. "Thinking the world together" (62), instead of apart, is the path to wholeness and good practice. At the political level, Hamp-Lyons and Condon (2000) suggest seven C's of bringing this to pass: shared community, criteria, and locus of control; responsiveness to the context (meaning the needs of each stakeholder); valuing consensus, care in all aspects of the process, and an emphasis on conversation. The need for balance and consideration of all stakeholders in portfolio development has been frequently noted.

The United States experience with portfolios is peaking as authorities increasingly require portfolios as policy. It has yet to be seen whether these large-scale portfolio projects will involve sufficient consideration of local processes and positions to preserve the best effects of portfolio work. In this regard it is helpful to consider the case of a large-scale portfolio project for language learners in Europe.

The European Language Portfolio

The European Language Portfolio (ELP) represents an attempt to promulgate from the international level a document aimed at influencing learning at the lowest level, that of the individual, but also to facilitate the assessment of learning across a wide variety of audiences. It required the decade-long development of new standards for describing language proficiency. Through its centralized structure, the Council of Europe (COE) has been able to bring the project through the first stages of implementation and evaluation fairly quickly. The ELP therefore offers a glimpse of a possible future for other large-scale portfolio projects and, in particular, a possible design for a common second language portfolio in other regions of the world.

Detailed information can be found in other chapters of this volume on the ELP (Peter Lenz) and the role of the Council of Europe (COE) in its development (Joe Sheils/Adrian Butler). For the reader's convenience, a brief introduction is presented here followed by a discussion of how the project addresses the portfolio paradoxes described earlier. This summary is based on COE documentation (Council for Cultural Cooperation Education Committee 2000) as exemplified by the Swiss prototype (Schneider, North, & Koch 2001).

The Document

The ELP is a portfolio format adopted by the COE for the primary purpose of communicating a second language user's proficiency and language experience to others. The portfolio consists of three sections:

- The *Language Passport* documents and summarizes language proficiency and language and cultural learning experiences.

- The *Language Biography* documents the author's language learning history and facilitates self-assessment and planning.
- The *Dossier* presents the author's work in second languages in written, audio, or video form.

Countries and institutions may create their own versions of the ELP suitable to local needs and age groups. The Council of Europe accredits these formats if they meet the overall purposes and policies of the COE. These purposes include:

- Social goals, such as mutual understanding among cultures and promotion of plurilingualism.
- Development of the individual as an independent, life-long, plurilingual learner.
- System goals, including coherence across programs and a clear description of language competence.

The standards stipulate in part that the ELP:

- Is the property of the learner.
- Values the full range of the learner's language and intercultural competence and experience, regardless of whether acquired within or outside formal education.
- Has both a pedagogic function to guide and support the learner and a reporting function to record proficiency in languages.
- Is based on the *Common European Framework of Reference for Languages* (CEF).
- Encourages learner self-assessment, teacher assessment, and assessment by educational authorities and examination bodies.
- Incorporates a minimum of common features which make it recognizable and comprehensible across Europe.

ACTION

Apply your knowledge. What type of portfolio would you consider the ELP to be? Remember the different kinds introduced at the beginning of this chapter.

Learning from the ELP

Although the ELP comes from a political, cultural and linguistic context that differs from the United States in obvious ways, the ELP is nonetheless subject to the same paradoxes as all portfolios. The way the ELP responds to each of them may be of interest to other cultures.

Purpose

The ELP serves both process and product purposes. The processes of good language learning through self-assessment, goal-setting, autonomous learning, extracurricular learning, and reflection are fostered by factors such as the self-assessment grid and checklist, the goal-setting page, the biographical statements, and the possibility to include developmental, collaborative, and revised work.

On the other hand, the ELP clearly presents a product. It incorporates best work, and provides for documentation of current proficiency through external certification and teacher assessment.

Ownership

The ELP is explicitly made the property of the author/learner. Ownership is reinforced through the autobiographical content and the metaphorical language of personal documents—passport, biography, dossier. On the other hand, the Council of Europe maintains *ownership* of the concept, design, and purpose through the accreditation procedure and the COE logo. The rights of ownership are exercised just enough to ensure that the document will be recognizable and interpretable by a wide international audience.

Origins

A range of documents from a variety of sources are encouraged. The author provides original, reflective, and evaluative pieces; the teacher participates in the checklist of skills; and external authorities provide attestations and certifications.

Collaboration

The index to the work in the dossier provides a code to identify solo or group authorship and whether work has been subjected to correction or revision, thus allowing for all combinations of good process.

Standards and Evaluation

The ELP does not provide standards for evaluating a learner's portfolio document in whole or in part. It is left to teachers, administrators, and employers to determine what a specific portfolio means to them. In other words, the ELP serves an informative rather than a normative function.

However, the CEF provides the standards for a clear description of the owner's language proficiency at various levels, analogous to the *ACTFL Proficiency Guidelines* (ACTFL 1986) in the US. The standards are to be useable by everyone from the owner to clients even outside of education. Because the same standards are intended to describe the goals of language courses and programs, they facilitate the movement of the owner between teachers, schools, and even countries.

Contextualization

The ELP is particularly strong in providing for contextualization of all artifacts through the content of certain documents, the interrelatedness of the documents, and information appended to some documents.

The *Language Learning Biography* and the *Statement of Linguistic and Intercultural Experiences* provide the personal context for the whole portfolio, allowing one to see why and how a learner has gained, applied, and perhaps lost, proficiency.

For diplomas and attestations in the *Language Passport*, authorities can communicate what these documents mean in terms of the CEF as well as how that equivalency was established, ranging from simple estimation of the faculty to statistically documented research. Examinations are further described in terms of their content, conditions, and other contextual information.

Attestations regarding enrichment experiences such as exchange programs provide for narrative comments from both the institution and the owner. The coding system in the dossier provides contextual information such as who participated in the work and whether or not it was edited.

Orientation

The ELP is clearly oriented to achieve certain purposes—plurilingualism, intercultural understanding, learner autonomy. It requires the use and understanding of the CEF, which implies a generally functional, communicative orientation to language learning and teaching. But the implications are broad and based on an appropriate level of consensus. Specific orientations to teaching or testing methodologies or techniques are not evident. On the contrary, there is room to document and describe *any* learning experience or assessment system, although establishing equivalency to the CEF is clearly preferred.

In summary, the ELP appears to have achieved commendable balance with the inherent tensions of the portfolio. It is a format conceived at the highest levels of the European system with primary attention to the needs of the individual rather than institutions. It appears to meet Jordan and Purves' (1996) belief that (inter)national organizations should support portfolio work for the sake of the individual learner.

Problems

Lenz (2000, this volume) and Schärer (2000) discuss some problems with the ELP that will be addressed as the project continues. It remains to be seen whether the concept can be applied in the variety of situations that comprise Europe and whether it will be as broadly accepted as is necessary to justify the effort.

In spite of the achievements of the project thus far, the ultimate success of the ELP depends on its local reception and implementation. Bräuer (2002) maintains that it is possible to see the ELP as a product to be slavishly copied or routinely completed without welcoming it into the everyday learning/teaching process.

He makes several suggestions to help schools promote process-oriented learning in connection with the ELP:

- Deemphasize institutional documentation.
- Emphasize process over product.
- Include provisional forms of work.
- Make sure tools for self-assessment are meaningful to individual learners.
- Encourage reflections and connections between private writing (journals) and public writing (project reports).
- Seek long-term engagement with portfolio processes.
- Provide interdisciplinary advisement on interdisciplinary portfolio work.
- Use the portfolio for alternative assessment and feedback (not just grade-giving).
- Use the portfolio for program evaluation and improvement.

Perhaps most importantly, Bräuer (2000, 2002), along with some US scholars (Campbell, Melenyzer, Nettles, & Wyman 2000; Hammadou 1997), suggests the necessity of multiple portfolios, some embedded deeply in the local learning process while preparing the learner to engage creatively and usefully in more standardized forms, such as the ELP. This suggestion may be the key to the portfolio paradox.

CONSIDER

Could you explain further, from your own experience as a student/teacher, the necessity of multiple portfolios for learners as an alternative to one rather centralized portfolio?

Conclusion

Widespread concern has been expressed for the future of portfolio work in the US, particularly as national institutions are poised to implement portfolios from the top. At worst, such an effort can result in a boilerplate product completely insulated from local learning and teaching practices, or in a product that becomes itself the limited end of learning. At best, a portfolio can encourage, rather than prescribe, long-term portfolio processes, and invite a context-rich representation of the learner. Even then, local practice may not follow.

In the spirit of communication and consultation that is so essential to portfolio development, educators everywhere can learn from the European experience with both process and product. As process, the ELP demonstrates how quickly even an international project under central direction can progress. But its provisional success is due, not to the Council of Europe's authority, but to its commitment to the highest, most readily accepted values rather than narrow, detailed prescriptions; to the clarity, transparency, and commonality of the assessment tools; to the flexibility and openness of the structure; the rich contextualization of the content; and above all, to the preeminence of the individual learner in the purpose and structure of the document.

As product, the ELP is the first attempt at a complete language proficiency credential for personal and public use. Its format should not be viewed as an exact blueprint for other nations and regions. The US, for example, would substitute the *Proficiency Guidelines* for the CEF. The ELP is much more an example of addressing the needs of learners in an increasingly multilingual and interconnected world. As similar projects appear in other regions, they may one day lead to a truly international and universally interpretable language credential.

References

American Council on the Teaching of Foreign Languages (ACTFL). *ACTFL Proficiency Guidelines*. Hastings-on-Hudson: ACTFL, 1986.

American Council on the Teaching of Foreign Languages (ACTFL) Online. "Proficiency Testing." 2002. <www.actfl.org>.

Barnhardt, S., J. Kevorkian, and J. Delett. *Portfolio Assessment in the Foreign Language Classroom*.Washington DC: National Capital Language Resource Center. ERIC Document Reproduction Service No. ED 448 602, 1998.

Bond, J. N., Jr. "The Use of Portfolios Among Inservice Foreign Language Teachers: An Exploratory Study." *Dissertation Abstracts International* 60(12), 4384A (1999): University Microfilms No. 9956797.

Bräuer, G. "Portfolio Learning." *Writing Across Languages*. Ed. Gerd Bräuer. Stamford: Ablex, 2000. 167-179.

Bräuer, G. *Reformen durch Portfolios*. 2002 <www.ph-freiburg.de/schreibzentrum/didaktik>.

Calfee, R. C. and S. W. Freedman. "Classroom Writing Portfolios: Old, New, Borrowed, Blue." *Writing Portfolios in the Classroom*. Ed. R. C. Calfee & P. Perfumo. Mahweh: Lawrence Erlbaum Associates, 1996. 3-26.

——. "A National Survey of Writing Portfolio Practice: What We Learned and What it Means." *Writing Portfolios in the Classroom*. Ed. R. C. Calfee & P. Perfumo. Mahweh: Lawrence Erlbaum Associates, 1996. 63-81.

——. "Student Portfolios: Opportunities for a Revolution in Assessment." *Journal of Reading* 36 (1993): 532-537.

Callahan, S. "Kentucky's State-Mandated Writing Portfolios and Teacher Accountability." *Situating Portfolios. Four Perspectives*. Ed. K. B. Yancey and I. Weiser. Logan: Utah State UP, 1997. 57-71.

Campbell, D. M., B. J. Melenyzer, D. H.Nettles, and R. M. Wyman Jr. *Portfolio and Performance Assessment in Teacher Education*. Needham Heights: Allyn & Bacon, 2000.

Cole, N. S. "A Realist's Appraisal of the Prospects for Unifying Instruction and Assessment." *Assessment in the Service of Learning: Proceedings of the 1987 ETS Invitational Conference*. Ed. E.E. Freeman. Princeton: Educational Testing Service, 1988. 103-117.

Council for Cultural Cooperation Education Committee. *European Language Portfolio. Principles and Guidelines*. 2000. <culture2.coe.int/portfolio>.

Delett, J. S., S. Barnhardt, and J. A. Kevorkian. "A framework for Portfolio Assessment in the Foreign Language Classroom." *Foreign Language Annals* 34 (2001): 559-568.

Elbow, P. and P. Belanoff. "Portfolios as a Substitute for Proficiency Examinations." *College Composition and Communication* 37 (1986): 336-339.

Emig, J. *The Composing Processes of Twelfth Graders*. Urbana: National Council of Teachers of English, 1971.

Fox, R. "This is Who I Am: The Role of the Professional Development Portfolio in Foreign and Second Language Pre-Service Teacher Education." *Dissertation Abstracts International*, 60(05), 1516A (1999): University Microfilms No. 9933323.

Glatthorn, A. A. *The Teacher's Portfolio*. Rockport: Pro>Active Publications, 1996.

Hammadou, J. "A blueprint for Teacher Portfolios: Concerns that Need to be Addressed When Embarking on Teacher Assessment via Portfolios." *The Coming of Age of the Profession*. Ed. J. Harper, M. G. Lively, and M. K. Williams. Boston: Heinle & Heinle, 1997. 291-305.

——. "Portfolio Design and the Decision Making Process in Teacher Education." *Foreign Language Teacher Education. Multiple Perspectives*. Ed. Z. Moore. Lanham: UP of America, 1996. 123-149.

Hamp-Lyons, L. & W. Condon. *Assessing the Portfolio: Principles for Practice, Theory, and Research*. Cresskill: Hampton, 2000.

Herman, J., M. Gearhart, and P. R. Aschbacher. "Portfolios for Classroom Assessment: Design and Implementation Issues." *Writing Portfolios in the Classroom*. Ed. R. C. Calfee and P. Perfumo. Mahweh: Lawrence Erlbaum Associates,1996. 27-59.

Interstate New Teacher Assessment and Support Consortium [INTASC]. *Next Steps: Moving Toward Performance-Based Licensing in Teaching*. Washington DC: INTASC, 1995.

Jordan, S. L. and A. C. Purves. "The Metaphor of the Portfolio and the Metaphors in Portfolios: The Relation of Classroom-Based to Large-Scale Assessment." *Writing Portfolios in the Classroom*. Ed. R. C. Calfee and P. Perfumo. Mahweh: Lawrence Erlbaum Associates, 1996. 179-202.

Lenz, P. *Piloting the Swiss Model of the European Language Portfolio, May 1999—June 2000. Evaluator's Final Report.* <www.sprachenportfolio.ch>

Lucas, C. "Introduction: Writing Portfolios—Changes and Challenges." *Portfolios in the Writing Classroom: An Introduction* (1-11). Ed. K. B. Yancey. Urbana: National Council of Teachers of English, 1992.

Murphy, S. and R. Camp. "Moving Toward Systemic Coherence: A Discussion of Conflicting Perspectives on Portfolio Assessment." *Writing Portfolios in the Classroom*. Ed. R.C. Calfee and P. Perfumo. Mahweh: Lawrence Erlbaum Associates, 1996. 103-148.

National Board for Professional Teaching Standards [NBPTS]. *NBPTS Guide to National Board Certification.* San Antonio: NBPTS, 2001.

National Council for Accreditation of Teacher Education [NCATE]. *Professional Standards for the Accreditation of Schools, Colleges, and Departments of Education.* Washington DC: NCATE, 2002.

National Standards in Foreign Language Education Project. *Standards for Foreign Language Learning in the 21st Century.* Yonkers: National Standards in Foreign Language Education Project, 1999.

Padilla, A. M., J. C. Aninao, and H. Sung. "Development and Implementation of Student Portfolios in Foreign Language Programs." *Foreign Language Annals* 29 (1996): 429-438.

Palmer, P. *The Courage to Teach.* San Francisco: Jossey-Bass, 1998.

Ponte, E. "Negotiating Portfolio Assessment in a Foreign Language Classroom." *Dissertation Abstracts International* 61(07), 2581A (2001): University Microfilms No. 9979770.

Schärer, R. *Final Report. European Language Portfolio. Pilot Project Phase 1998-2000.* <culture.coe.int/portfolio>.

Schneider, G., B. North, L. Koch. *European Language Portfolio for Young People and Adults.* Bern: Berner Lehrmittel- und Medienverlag, 2001.

Tierney, R. J., M. A. Carter, and L. E. Desai. *Portfolio Assessment in the Reading-Writing Classroom.* Norwood: Christopher-Gordon, 1991.

Wade, R. C. and D. B. Yarbrough. "Portfolios: A Tool for Reflective Thinking in Teacher Education?" *Teaching and Teacher Education* 12 (1996): 63-79.

Wise, J. M. and R. J. Tierney. "Tensions in Assessment: The Battle Over Portfolios, Curriculum, and Control." *Writing Portfolios in the Classroom*. Ed. R. C. Calfee and P. Perfumo. Mahweh: Lawrence Erlbaum Associates, 1996. 203-215.

Yancey, K. B. and I. Weiser. "Situating Portfolios. An introduction." *Situating Portfolios. Four Perspectives.* Ed. K. B. Yancey and I. Weiser. Logan: Utah State UP, 1997. 1-17.

The European Language Portfolio—A Tool for Comprehensive Assessment and the Promotion of Plurilingualism

Peter Lenz

What is the European Language Portfolio (ELP)

The European Language Portfolio is at the same time a concept and a series of concrete products for use in various contexts, based on that concept.

Generally speaking, the ELP fulfills two main functions in the field of language learning: it is simultaneously a companion to learning and an information tool. It provides ideas and hints and contains a number of instruments (worksheets and forms) which have two purposes:

- Motivate learners for (further) language learning and to facilitate their self-assessment and planning efforts
- Support learners in building up an informative documentation of their language proficiency and intercultural experiences

A learner's ELP is a (pre-)structured collection of various kinds of documents, for example, self-assessment sheets and profiles; diplomas; pieces of work; personal accounts of learning experiences; forms for the planning of language learning. Language portfolios are owned by the learners and can be used in various learning contexts and for various purposes, usually over a longer period of time. Learners can complete and update their portfolios continuously in order to document their plurilingualism, their skills and experiences in various languages, their language learning, their language and cultural contacts, for themselves or others, in a transparent and internationally comparable way.

A large degree of transparency and comparability in reporting language skills and qualifications is possible because all ELPs refer to a common system of reference levels of language proficiency. These *Common Reference Levels* are described in detail in the "Common European Framework of Reference for Languages (CEF)," also developed by the Council of Europe (Council of Europe 2001).[1]

The European Language Portfolio has many characteristics in common with other portfolio concepts; at the same time, it differs from them in some respects. Unlike *showcase* portfolios assembled by architects, artists or creative arts students in order to present themselves and their work, and unlike many existing pedagogic portfolios assembled for (more) authentic assessment[2] (for example, writing portfolios), the ELP has a fixed structure, and the (language) skills are presented in relation to a given reference system. Many pedagogic portfolios are part of a particular syllabus or course of study. The ELP, on the contrary, is designed to bridge gaps between educational sectors, school and work, school learning, and out-of-school learning, by making achievements and requirements transparent and comparable.

CONSIDER

Comparing the portfolio definition mentioned above and the definition provided by Randall Lund, what are the main similarities and differences between the European Language Portfolio and portfolios used so far in the US?

In some respects, the ELP is similar to other pedagogic portfolios:

- The user is involved in selecting portfolio contents
- Portfolios may provide evidence of progress and, at the same time, contain the results of summative assessments and illustrate the best work a learner is able to do
- Learner reflection on portfolio contents and learning processes complement the *evidence* and information given

The ELP is different from portfolios exclusively designed for the world of work, for career planning, or job applications through its limitation to language proficiency and intercultural competence and experience. Moreover, it is designed to be useful not only in view of professional life but also in the learning process inside or outside the school. Therefore, the ELP has a very large group of (potential) stakeholders.

Purpose and Functions of the European Language Portfolio

The motives for developing the ELP, as well as its aims and intended functions, are of three kinds: practical, political, pedagogic/psychological. These sources are described below.

Practical

When the idea to create a *Language Passport* or a *Learner's Passport* was first discussed among some Swiss foreign language experts in 1989/1990, the main motive was to create an instrument that is suitable for reporting in a transparent way allowing comparisons, a learner's language proficiency as stated by qualifications, diplomas, and more informal evidence. One of the main reasons this need for transparency and comparability emerged was the federalist school system in Switzerland, which makes comparisons between learners' actual language skills just on the basis of the titles of their qualifications virtually impossible. A similar lack of coherence was diagnosed in the field of adult education and private language schools. Also, the need was felt to have a document that facilitates the reporting of language skills acquired informally outside school.

Political

The ELP was adopted by the Council of Europe[3] as a project that deserves major support because it appeared as a tool with great potential to contribute to the aims defined by the Council of Europe's language and cultural policy, i.e. "to promote awareness of a European cultural identity and to develop mutual understanding among people of different cultures" (as stated in the introduction to the standardized Language Passport contained in many ELPs for adults). Within this general framework, the ELP has, in particular, the following goals:

- To facilitate mobility within Europe by reporting the owner's language skills in a transparent and comparable manner.
- To promote plurilingualism and the dialogue between cultures.
- To preserve and to strengthen cultural and linguistic diversity.
- To develop the learner's ability to learn autonomously, in particular to assess his/her own language competence and progress and to plan his/her further learning.
- To encourage the life-long learning of languages (cf. *Principles and Guidelines* in Schneider & Lenz 2001, Appendix C).

There are political motives that go beyond language policy: the Council of Europe supports attempts to strengthen learner autonomy because of its concern with democratic citizenship: autonomous personalities form the basis of democratic societies.[4]

NOTE

For more information about the Council of Europe and foreign language policy in this organization, read the interview with Joe Sheils and Adrian Butler.

Pedagogic/Psychological

Even in the seventies and eighties, experts involved in Council of Europe language projects explored approaches to autonomous language learning because of its supposed effectiveness (cf. Oskarsson 1977; 1978; 1984). Meanwhile, learner autonomy and learner-centeredness have become widely accepted pedagogic principles and goals (see for example APA 1997), thus, the learner-owned European Language Portfolio fits well into one of the most influential recent trends in pedagogic psychology.

NOTE

To learn more about learner autonomy in language education, read chapters by Langner & Prokop and Wolff.

As has been outlined above, every ELP is, at the same time, a learning companion and an information tool. Therefore, its parts and instruments are designed to implement a pedagogic function and a documentation and reporting function. These functions can be concretized as follows:[5]

The Pedagogic Function

Language Portfolios may cover quite a broad range of pedagogic objectives, aiming either at better knowledge of languages and cultures or at more personal competence of the individuals as learners.

ELPs enhance the motivation of the learners to:

- Improve their ability to communicate in different languages.
- Learn additional languages.
- Seek new intercultural experiences.

ELPs incite and help learners to:

- Reflect on their objectives, ways of learning, and success in language learning.
- Plan their learning.
- Self-assess progress made.
- Learn in a self-directed way.

ELPs encourage learners to enhance their plurilingual and intercultural experience, for example through:

- Contacts and visits
- Reading
- Use of the media
- Projects

CONSIDER

Connect with your own language learning. What pedagogical focus would you choose for your own language portfolio?

In principle, all ELPs implement all these functions to some extent. The actual pedagogic focus of a concrete ELP, however, is strongly influenced by the institutional context and the target group(s) the ELP is intended for. For example, studying abroad must play an important role in an ELP for Western European university students.

The Documentation and Reporting Function

The European Language Portfolio aims to document its holder's plurilingual language proficiency and experiences with other languages and cultures in a comprehensive, informative, transparent and reliable way. The instruments contained in the ELP help learners to take stock of the levels of competence they have reached in their learning of one or several foreign languages in order to enable them to inform others in a detailed and internationally comparable way.

There are many occasions to present an up-to-date Language Portfolio, for example a transfer to another school, moving on to a higher educational sector, the beginning of a language course, a meeting with a career advisor, or an application for a new job. In these cases the ELP is addressed to persons who have a role in decisions that are important for the owner of the Language Portfolio. However, a learner may also be interested in having such documentation for him/herself.

Educational institutions, public agencies and companies; teachers and personnel officers who receive (elements from) an ELP from a learner may be particularly interested in:

- The results of relevant and reliable summative assessment.
- Diplomas and certificates.
- Other *evidence*, such as: up-to-date information based on self-assessment, attestations/descriptions of bilingual education, schooling in a language other than L1, participation in student exchange programs, practical training in other language regions, attestations/descriptions of regular private contacts with speakers of other languages, professional correspondence in other languages, information on objectives, curricula, representative examples, such as selected written texts, audio and video recordings of oral productions.

A wide range of *evidence* is important because successful language learning cannot always be *proven* by means of examinations or diplomas. For example,

- A learner may improve his/her language skills considerably through stays abroad *after* receiving a diploma; language proficiency may also deteriorate over the years because a language is not used frequently enough.
- Some aspects such as intercultural competence are rarely tested through examinations. For some languages no standardized examinations or certificates exist (as is often the case with languages of immigrants and their children).

In order to be informative and reliable, all information must be documented in a transparent way:

- It should be clear and possible to verify who (person/institution) is responsible for a statement and who would confirm its truthfulness.
- It should be related to a reference system such as the *Common Reference Levels* in the CEF wherever possible.
- A common language of description should be used.

Depending on the kind of use that is made of the ELP, the focus shifts from one element or function of the ELP to another:

- Central concerns from a pedagogic and methodological perspective are: learning processes, formative assessment, learning incentives, and learning occasions.
- Central concerns from the point of view of documentation and reporting are: results and products of learning; summative assessment; transparency and comparability of the information provided.

CONSIDER

Connect with your own language learning/teaching. Decide what evidence of your own learning progression you would include in your portfolio. Become aware of general differences among portfolio user groups, review the content of the ELP for elementary students in the materials section.

An ELP version for one specific target group, for example elementary school pupils or adult professionals, may put more emphasis on one of the two basic functions and provide more instruments to implement this function than another ELP version for a different target group. However, both functions must be implemented to some degree in every ELP.

Users and Their Uses of an ELP

As may have become clear from the above, not only language learners may benefit from a Language Portfolio but also teachers, schools, firms and agencies. The following overview[6] summarizes the various uses different stakeholders may make of an ELP for adult learners.

The European Language Portfolio helps *learners* to:

- Assess and describe their language proficiency.
- Situate their language proficiency in relation to the *Common Reference Levels* of the Council of Europe.
- Document and reflect on their language learning inside and outside

school, and on their intercultural experiences.
- Inform anyone concerned about their proficiency in different languages, for example when changing schools, starting a language course, participating in an exchange program, or applying for a job.
- Set personal language learning objectives and plan further learning.

The European Language Portfolio helps *teachers, schools, and other training institutions* to:

- Recognize the needs and motivation of learners and help them to set learning goals and put together programs.
- Obtain information about the learners' previous language learning experiences inside and outside school.
- Assess and document performance in a differentiated way.
- Situate final certificates and qualifications in relation to the *Common Reference Levels*.
- Describe their language programs and produce attestations of language learning experiences.

The European Language Portfolio helps *firms, agencies, and employers* to:

- Obtain a differentiated picture of the language proficiency of their employees or job applicants and make better use of their language abilities.
- Specify their employees' attainment targets and plan in-house and external training programs.
- Prepare certifications of the use of foreign languages in the workplace and periods of professional development in other language areas.

CONSIDER

Reconsider your own learner biography. Imagine you had a language portfolio, what could you have used it for (or could use it for)?

Parts and Elements

One of the distinguishing features of the European Language Portfolio compared to other portfolios is its fixed structure. According to the principles outlined by the Council of Europe, every ELP must have the following three parts (Schneider & Lenz 2001, Appendix C): a *Language Passport,* a *Language Biography,* and a *Dossier*. Each of these parts contributes in specific ways to the two basic functions of the ELP (pedagogic and documentation/reporting).

- The *Language Passport* shows at a glance the current level of language proficiency in different languages and summarizes the language learning and intercultural experiences the owner of the ELP has made.
- The *Language Biography* documents the owner's personal language learning history and his/her intercultural experiences. It also contains instruments for the self-assessment of language skills and the reflection and planning of further learning.
- The *Dossier* assembles pieces of personal work of various kinds which illustrate for different languages what the owner of the ELP has done,

what s/he is able to do, and what progress s/he made.
The Dossier part of the ELP is mainly intended as a dossier for presentation purposes (*showcase*). Ideally, the Dossier builds upon *working dossiers* established in everyday language learning and language use (cf. Kohonen 2000).

Each of the three parts is implemented in quite different ways in the various existing ELPs. Naturally, the age group of the learners an ELP is made for plays the most important role. The abilities, interests and needs of 9 year-old pupils are very different from those of active members of the workforce. When looking at the existing ELPs, the differences immediately become obvious: there are ELPs for elementary school children consisting of a single game board (plus an individualized Dossier) while other ELPs, for older learners, are ring binders containing roughly a hundred pages. Chapter 5 of Schneider & Lenz (2001) gives an impression of the great variety that existed even at the beginning of the implementation phase (end of the year 2000).

In the following section, the Swiss *ELP for Young People and Adults* is presented in some detail. It is intended for learners aged 15 and older.

Example: The Three Parts of the ELP as Implemented in the Swiss "ELP for Young People and Adults"

The Swiss ELP version for young people and adults is physically a ring binder. It contains a folder for each of the three parts, plus an appendix with assessment instruments, worksheets and forms to be used in connection with the three parts. The center-piece of each folder is a fold-out page providing detailed explanations, hints and suggestions. In the following, the contents of the Swiss *ELP for Young People and Adults* are listed and described in detail.

Part 1: Language Passport

This Swiss version of the ELP uses the standardized European Language Passport, a booklet in A5 format. It is included in nearly identical form in various other European Language Portfolios for adults. Depending on the language region an ELP is intended for, the standard texts and rubrics are translated into other languages. Either English or French, or both, are used in every version. In the Swiss version, French, English, German and Italian are present while Romansh, the fourth official language of Switzerland, will be added in the second edition. English was included as the most important international language although it is not an official language of this country.

The standardized Language Passport has the following sections:

- *Profile of Language Skills*: grids that can be used to enter the results of self-assessment for up to six languages. Language proficiency is assessed with respect to the five *macro skills* or *language activities* of Listening, Reading, Spoken interaction, Spoken production, and Writing. Thereby, six levels are distinguished: A1 and A2 (*Beginning User*), B1 and B2 (*Independent User*), and C1 and C2 (*Proficient User*).

Figure 1. Specimen entry in the Language Passport, *Profile of Language Skills* section. The entries for each of the five language activities are based on self-assessment. Six different levels of language proficiency are distinguished.

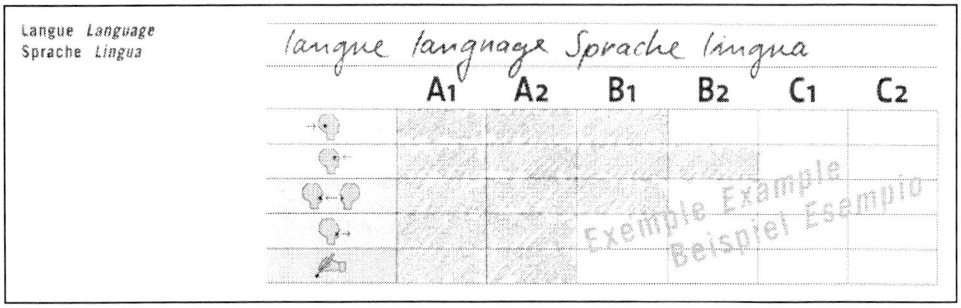

- *Summary of Language Learning and Intercultural Experiences:* two double pages allow for entries that quantify previous language learning experiences, language use for different purposes, and intercultural contacts within or outside regions where a particular language is commonly spoken.
- *Certificates and Diplomas:* a table for entries on language certificates and diplomas (with a language component) obtained. Space is provided to indicate the proficiency levels (A1-C2) at which the various certificates and diplomas (or the degrees attained) are located. Exams are normally assigned to their respective levels by the examination boards or institutions that offer these exams.

The Language Passport booklet also contains the *Self-Assessment Grid* (cf. Appendix), usually in two or more languages. It is mainly intended to help readers of the Passport to understand very quickly what the indications of levels in the *Profile of Language Skills* and in the overview of certificates and diplomas mean in terms of actual language proficiency.

The appendix to the Swiss *ELP for Young People and Adults* contains three different types of (photocopiable) instruments which support the use of the Language Passport section. Instruments that facilitate the self-assessment of language proficiency:

- *Self-Assessment Grid:* the grid reprinted in the Passport is provided as a master copy in the appendix. The *Self-Assessment Grid* is used as a point of departure whenever language proficiency is assessed by a learner, teacher, etc.
- The following may serve as an example of such a descriptor. It describes an aspect of Listening at level B1 (or *Threshold level*): *I can understand the main points of clear standard speech on familiar matters regularly encountered in work, school, leisure, etc.*
- *Self-Assessment Checklists:* compared to the *Grid*, the checklists contain more, and more detailed, descriptions of language proficiency, and are therefore suited to back up or correct estimates made with the help

of the *Self-Assessment Grid*. The checklists can also be used for formative assessment and planning (see also *Part 2: Language Biography*.)

Instruments that may be used to describe language exams and to position them within the system of six levels:

- *Examination Description:* a form that helps schools and examination boards to describe the relevant features of an exam in a transparent way: type of exam, parts, type(s) of interaction.
- *Global Scale:* a one-dimensional scale integrating the descriptions for each of the five language activities in one comprehensive description for each level from A1 to C2. Schools and examination boards are encouraged to use the *Global Scale* in a first attempt at attributing their exams to specific levels.

Forms for attestations (or certifications) that certify language learning experiences:

- Attestation of participation in an exchange programme.
- Attestation of participation in bilingual teaching/immersion teaching.
- Attestation of a language learning stay in a region where the language is spoken.
- Attestation of playing host to a foreign-language-speaking guest from a partner school, institution or family.
- Attestation of participation in a sustained correspondence with a foreign-language-speaking pen-friend.

These kinds of attestation are intended as complements or substitutes for diplomas or formal certificates. Learners will ask for them if the institutions involved do not provide some similar form of attestation spontaneously.

CONSIDER

Imagine yourself as a portfolio user. Come up with a list of documents for your language passport and develop your own profile of language skills. For further reference to help you to reply to this and the following two tasks (language biography, dossier) check the main ELP web site (see materials section for address).

Part 2: Language Biography

- *Personal Language Learning Biography:* a worksheet which encourages learners to provide a chronological overview of their language learning and intercultural experiences. Learners may choose to give an overview of their plurilingual and pluricultural development as a whole, or decide to write up a language learning biography per language learned.
- *Self-Assessment Checklists:* the detailed descriptions of language proficiency provided in these checklists may not only be used for self-assessment and assessment by others at a certain point in time; they may also be used to guide through the learning process, to identify and to set goals, and to assess one's learning progressively. The language proficiency descriptors may be complemented according to a learner's specific needs, for example, in the field of language learning for specific purposes.
- *Information About Important Linguistic and Intercultural Experiences:* a worksheet that encourages learners to describe important experiences

in more depth, such as contacts with speakers of other languages, learning about the cultural background of other languages, readings, and project work.

- *Information About Foreign Language Teaching in Schools and Language Courses:* an instrument that helps to describe relevant aspects of course-based language teaching and learning. It is mainly intended for the hands of teachers, language schools, and other educational institutions.
- *My Objectives:* a worksheet that helps to formulate objectives and to make plans for language learning. In an environment of guided self-study, this sheet may take on the shape of a learning contract.

ACTION

Based on the aspects mentioned above, draft your own biography as a language learner.

Part 3: Dossier

List of Pieces of Work in the Dossier: this list helps to present personal pieces of work in a systematic way. A coding system is suggested to indicate whether an element present in the Dossier is a piece of individual work or group work; typical work or a top achievement; a result of spontaneous production or the result of correction and redrafting, and whether it represents an earlier or the current stage of development.

CONSIDER

What personal pieces of work would you include in your dossier? Why? Come up with substantial reasons in regard to the main functions your language portfolio is supposed to cover.

The Core Elements

Among the various elements contained in the *ELP for Young People and Adults* presented above, the *Self-assessment Grid, the Self-assessment checklists* and the *Global Scale* have a special status as they are directly based on descriptions of communicative language proficiency used in the *Common European Framework of Reference* to define and illustrate the *Common Reference Levels* (Council of Europe 2001, chapters 3-5, esp. 3.2-3.4).

Most of these descriptions describe, in easily understandable language, relevant communication tasks language users are typically able to perform at various levels; other descriptors deal with qualitative aspects of the language produced or with communication strategies.

Scientific foundations

The descriptions (or descriptors) were originally developed for the CEF and the ELP in a Swiss National Science Foundation (SNF) project lead by G. Schneider and B. North (North & Schneider 1998; Schneider & North 1999; 2000a; 2000b; North 2000; Schneider 2001). In that project, empirical research involving 290 teachers and 2700 learners of all ages and from all educational sectors in different language regions in Switzerland was used to find out which of a large collection of descriptions of communicative language skills are commonly found relevant and are consistently assigned to specific levels. The project involved the following steps:

Collecting Descriptors of Communicative Language Proficiency

More than 40 existing scales of language proficiency which had been created within an action-oriented approach to language proficiency were collected, analyzed, and broken down to the level of simple descriptors. Other descriptors were created and added in order to fill systematic gaps.

Qualitative Validation of the Descriptors

Teachers' discussions of video-taped spoken learner productions were recorded and analyzed in order to find out whether teachers' categories and meta-language were appropriately represented in the collection of descriptors. Groups of teachers sorted sets of descriptors according to categories and levels. In addition, they noted down which descriptors they thought were relevant/irrelevant, clear/unclear, and suitable/unsuitable for learner self-assessment.

Collection of Quantitative Data

Teachers assessed some of their learners using partly different sets of those descriptors that had emerged from the qualitative validation phase. Every teacher also assessed a set of learner performances on a video-tape (one set for each target language: English, German, French) using descriptors from the workshops. Some learners also completed self-assessment questionnaires; others were asked to take external examinations in order to have some external control.

Statistical Analysis

The Rasch statistics package FACETS was used to calculate a difficulty value for each descriptor. Descriptors which were used consistently across educational sectors were retained while unstable descriptors were eliminated.

Interpretation

The validated (relevance and quality) and calibrated (level) descriptors were collected in a bank of descriptors. By means of a thorough analysis, 10 different levels of language proficiency could be identified.

Then, the best items from the bank of calibrated descriptors were used to create the scales and grids which describe the *Common Reference Levels* in the Common European Framework for Languages: *Global Scale* (CEF: Table 1); *Self-assessment Grid* (CEF: Table 2); *Qualitative aspects of spoken language use* (CEF: Table 3). In these practical applications the 10 levels previously identified were reduced to six broader level bands (A1, A2; B1, B2; C1, C2).

For the Swiss version of the European Language Portfolio many more of the descriptors available were used to establish the *Self-Assessment Checklists*.[7]

Arriving at that point in the SNF project was a major success. It was a tremendous contribution to one of the main aims set for the CEF and the ELP, namely to bring *transparency and coherence* into language learning (cf. Council of Europe 1992). Having an empirically sound and commonly understood system of descriptions of communicative language proficiency across education systems and borders does, in fact, facilitate talking about and comparing different learners' skills and qualifications, language requirements for examinations and jobs, etc.

Due to their origin and their specific properties, the instruments in the ELP that are based on the *Common Reference Levels* are often called *core elements*. However, they fulfill a *core* function even beyond these aspects:

- They link the different parts and functions of an ELP: the results of self-assessment are reported in the same terms as the results of assessment by others, no matter whether this assessment is based on judgement or testing. Individuals can use descriptions, at the same time, to plan the next steps in language learning and to assess whether the goals aimed at have been reached.
- The *Self-Assessment Grid* links the numerous existing ELP versions. It is one of the few elements common to virtually all European Language Portfolios – except some versions for young children where the level descriptions are adapted to the cognitive skills and the world of experience of the learners. The presence of the *Grid,* or an age-specific adaption thereof, in all *Language Passports* makes the different ELP models recognizable, acceptable, and comparable all over Europe as versions of basically the same instrument.

The *core elements* do not have the same importance in every ELP version or portfolio project. In Finland (cf. Kohonen 2000), for example, building up a Dossier, and learning from this process, is the main focus in most classrooms where the ELP is used. In Switzerland it became obvious during the official piloting of the ELP (1999-2000) that the *Self-Assessment Grid* and also the *Self-Assessment checklists* are perceived as the main instruments provided in the ELP. They were successfully used in a large majority of the classes involved, except where the learners were too young (under 14-15 years, depending on the academic level).

Many of the answers to the question *What is in your opinion the most positive aspect about the European Language Portfolio?* in a questionnaire that accompanied the piloting, illustrate the prominent position of the core elements in the Swiss project. The following points were frequently mentioned as particularly positive aspects:

- The approach taken by the ELP to describe the communicative language competence of the learners only in positive terms.
- The detailed description of communicative language competence.
- The common language of description.
- Relevant and understandable scales and checklists.
- The transparency provided by the descriptions and the six levels.
- The fact that communicative language competence becomes measurable and comparable.
- The checklists which can be used for self-assessment, assessment by others, and the planning of language courses.
- the development of pupils' ability to take responsibility through comparing and discussing self-assessment and teacher assessment (cf. Lenz 2000; Lenz & Schneider 2002).

Formulating and Adapting Descriptors

During the first phase of the SNF project, a large number of descriptions of language proficiency were extracted or collected from scales developed and used elsewhere, mainly in English-speaking countries. But many of these descriptions did not survive the empirical validation process that followed so that they had to be rephrased or eliminated. It was only in the course of the project that the characteristics emerged good descriptors should have:

Positiveness

Descriptors should be formulated using positive descriptions of what learners are able to do; negatively worded descriptions tend to be de-motivating and are less versatile.

It is often more difficult to formulate *positive* proficiency descriptors at low levels than to say what learners cannot do. But if proficiency descriptors are to serve also as objectives rather than just as instruments for screening candidates, then positive formulation is desirable.

Definiteness

Descriptors should describe concrete tasks and/or concrete degrees of skill in performing tasks:

- Descriptors should contain as little vagueness as possible.
- Distinctions between steps on a scale should not be dependent on replacing a qualifier like *some* or *a few* with *many* or *most*. This may result in gaps where meaningful, concrete distinctions cannot be made.

Clarity

Descriptors should be transparent—not *jargon-ridden*. They should be written in simple syntax; they should be comprehensible without special introductions and usable without previous training.

Brevity

Descriptors should be short, i.e. they should not span more than two or three lines (even in the case of adult users).

Independence

The interpretation of descriptors must not depend on other descriptors at the same level, or on descriptions of neighboring levels; they should allow for clear yes/no decisions (*Yes, I can do this*). (cf. Schneider & Lenz 47; Council of Europe 2001, Appendix A).

These characteristics of good descriptors should be kept in mind when institutions, teachers, groups of learners etc. formulate new descriptors that suit their specific needs. Adaptation and/or creation of new descriptors may be desirable for a variety of reasons and purposes:

- Descriptors are not adapted to a specific educational context well enough (e.g. links to an existing curriculum have to be established).
- Descriptors need to be rephrased for specific purposes (e.g. self-assessment, use on a rating scale, definition of objectives).
- Descriptions of skills necessary for specific domains of use need to be supplemented (work, study).
- Descriptors have to be made more easily comprehensible and better adapted to the world of experience of certain groups of users (e.g. young learners).
- Narrower level bands (e.g. B1 < B1.1 + B1.2) are needed so that progress can be seen more easily (a need that often arises in a school context when the descriptors are used for planning and formative assessment).

Whenever new descriptors are developed or significantly changed, it should be determined to what level each of the descriptors belongs and whether each of the descriptors is consistently attributed to the same level. This should be done using at least some kind of empirical or quasi-empirical method involving potential users of the descriptors who are not themselves involved in the development process (cf. Schneider & Lenz 48f; Council of Europe 2001, Appendix D).

Suggestions as to how existing scaled descriptors can be adapted or complemented successfully are made in the Guide for ELP Developers (Schneider & Lenz 43f).

As an example, the process which led to many of the descriptors for Writing and Extended reading in the Swiss *ELP for Young People and Adults*, is briefly outlined below.

When the SNF project was finished, not enough scaled descriptors were available. Therefore, an additional round of item creation was necessary. Financial and time constraints, however, called for a simplified procedure. The procedure chosen involved the following steps:

- A group of experienced teachers formulated descriptions (can do's) of relevant aspects of language proficiency in writing and extended reading basing themselves on uncalibrated descriptors from the original collection from the SNF project and on their competence in the field.
- Experts selected the most promising items for piloting, other items were rephrased, gaps were filled.
- The new descriptors were written onto strips of paper and then mixed with already calibrated descriptors from the SNF project (functioning as *anchors*). Sets of descriptors pertaining to the same categories were formed.
- Independent groups of teachers sorted the sets of descriptors according to levels of difficulty. They also noted down comments on problems they encountered or anticipated.

- Experts evaluated the results, then retained, rephrased, or discarded the descriptors.

The method used for the Swiss ELP can be adapted for similar purposes. It is important to note that any descriptor developing process should include some kind of empirical validation and involve individuals who are not seriously biased in their interpretation of the descriptors.

DISCUSS

If you read German, check out the descriptors for the Swiss ELP at its main web site. Let your peers know to what extent these descriptions would (not) work in the US.

Two Central Ideas: Promotion of Plurilingualism and Comprehensive Assessment

This chapter intends to highlight and illustrate two of the central ideas underlying the European Language Portfolio: the recognition and promotion of plurilingualism and a very broad understanding of assessment.

Plurilingualism

The ELP is based on the idea that individual plurilingualism is a common phenomenon which needs to get better visibility by means of an appropriate information tool. At the same time, the ELP as a companion to learning intends to motivate for plurilingualism and to facilitate (further) language learning. It will be shown in the following in what respects the idea of plurilingualism actually is represented in the ELP seen as an information tool (a), and seen as a companion to learning (b).

The ELP as an Information Tool

- The ELP as a whole is intended to provide a comprehensive and accurate overview of its owner's foreign-language proficiency, including skills in languages of origin or family languages, and the diversity and intensity of his/her language learning and intercultural experiences.
- It is a matter of principle that European Language Portfolios are open to entries on any language a person knows to some degree. There are no ELPs which are open for specific languages only. In some existing ELPs, primarily made for specific school contexts, space is provided for entries on certain predefined languages. But, at the same time, in any of these portfolios, space and instruments are also available for entries on languages acquired, as well as experiences, outside this primary context. Evidence is gathered informally since the pilot phase shows that children of immigrants, for example, actually use their ELPs to bring their richer language and intercultural backgrounds to the attention of the people around them, even if they had formerly avoided to do so.
- The standardized pan-European Language Passport booklet is designed in a way that the *plurilingual identity* of its holder stands in the foreground: the *Profile of Language Skills* and the *Summary of Language Learning and Intercultural Experiences* show at a glance entries concerning up to six different languages. In the table titled *Certificates and Diplomas,* entries are listed in chronological order, thus

CONSIDER

Expand your knowledge. For an introduction to multilingualism, see the chapter by Marx & Hufeisen.

illustrating the development of an individual's plurilingualism from the special angle of exams that have been passed.

- All language proficiency descriptors are chosen and formulated in such a way that they can be used for any modern language (cf. the descriptors in the *Self-assessment Grid* reproduced in the Appendix).

Even the descriptors in the rubric *Language Quality*, which are available in the *Self-assessment Checklists* of some ELPs, may be applied to various languages. The descriptors on language quality at level A2 from the Swiss *ELP for Young People and Adults* may serve as an example:

Language Quality
I can make myself understood using memorized phrases and single expressions.
I can link groups of words with simple connectors like *and*, *but*, and *because*.
I can use some simple structures correctly.
I have sufficient vocabulary for coping with simple everyday situations.

It is assumed that learners are able to translate the examples of simple connectors given in the second descriptor into the language they are presently assessing. A relatively small set of descriptors of this kind can actually help to make an estimate of a level. If a learner's stage of acquisition of a specific language were to be described and assessed in more detail, criteria relating to that specific language would have to be included.

The ELP as a companion to learning

Various instruments in the Language Biography stimulate and support conscious reflection of language learning and intercultural experiences. When learning experiences are reflected and evaluated, strategies and skills are developed that can be transferred to other language learning situations. The ability to assess language proficiency by means of descriptors as points of reference is one such transferable skill.

CONSIDER

See if you can find areas of transferable language and language learning skills in your school or in your own learning.

Whenever an ELP is widely introduced into a school environment, it may help to spread the idea among language teachers that they all work on the same learners' plurilingualism and transferable language and language-learning skills. This may be the case simply because teachers of different language subjects have to agree on procedures according to which the ELP is used with classes learning several languages if tedious repetition is to be minimized.

Comprehensive assessment

In portfolio pedagogy, the introduction of portfolios is often justified because of dissatisfaction with conventional assessment in which norm-oriented testing dominates. Portfolios are perceived as a means of *authentic* assessment which helps to "demonstrate the breadth and depth of students' capabilities" (Moya & O'Malley 14). The ELP shares this goal but uses a broader approach in order to reach it. Norm-oriented tests and *authentic* pieces of student work can both be accommodated within an ELP and would be considered as complementary pieces of information.

The European Language Portfolio is in its foundations an assessment instrument. It fulfills its two main functions (documentation/reporting and pedagogic functions) by means of a comprehensive view of assessment, which is comprehensive in several respects:

The Object of Assessment
Various aspects of communicative language proficiency as well as partial competencies are taken into account. Communicative language competence underlying language proficiency is seen as a complex phenomenon which includes language and intercultural aspects as well as *plurilingual* competence in itself.

The Time Frame
Assessment is more than a number of summative events at certain points in time; it is also a means of continuous (self-)observation of progress (formative assessment). Also, self-assessment is part of life-long learning, provided the learners have had the chance to practice the necessary skills.

The Assessors
Specialized institutions, testers, teachers, hosts, peers, and the learners themselves.

The Instruments of Assessment
Exams, tests, observation by peers or native speakers (based on descriptions of language proficiency), self-assessment tasks and checklists, dossiers containing learner products.

The Means of Feedback
Grades, diplomas, descriptions of competence and levels, progress reports—all stating explicitly the competencies and skills they refer to.

One constant behind this variety is a strong commitment to transparent, criterion-referenced assessment based on a coherent scale of communicative language proficiency. The *Reference Levels,* and the descriptors they consist of, make available a number of criteria which are easily understood and handled. Applying them facilitates efficient communication about partial language competencies, assessment instruments, results of assessment.

The ELP's approach to assessment of language and intercultural competence is more complete and more transparent. There is more coherence visible between assessments, and it is fairer towards learners—especially those who acquired some of their skills and knowledge outside the school context.

Implementing the ELP in Switzerland

In a way, the implementation of the European Language Portfolio in the Swiss context started even before the first draft of an ELP was finished towards the end of 1995. The relevant educational authorities and some private institutions supported the work towards an ELP from the beginning, if only modestly at first, because they were interested in having a Language Portfolio that they could introduce into their systems. Teachers got involved in the descriptor development process in 1994/95 within the SNF research project partially described above. Many of these teachers have been active in disseminating the different ELP versions and the ideas behind it ever since.

The following paragraphs are intended to provide a selective overview of the development and implementation process which has taken place since the beginning of the 1990s.

> In 1991 the Swiss authorities hosted an intergovernmental symposium entitled "Transparency and Coherence in Language Learning in Europe: objectives, evaluation, certification" in Rüschlikon (cf. Council of Europe 1992). There it was decided to develop "a comprehensive, coherent and transparent framework for the description of language proficiency" (Council of Europe 39). A working party was established "to consider possible forms and functions of a *European Language Portfolio* to be issued under its aegis and held by individuals, in which they may record their cumulative experience and qualifications in modern languages" (Council of Europe 40). Even at the conference, the idea was put in motion to carry through a national research project in order to develop a reference system describing language proficiency and possibly other aspects of language users' competencies, and then, on that basis, to develop Language Portfolio prototypes.
>
> Towards the end of 1993 the Swiss National Science Foundation project,[8] co-funded by several public and private institutions, was launched. In the years that followed, 290 teachers of English, German and French (as foreign languages) from different educational sectors and language regions were involved. In that process they became acquainted with the idea of describing language proficiency from an action-oriented perspective, and with descriptor-based (criterion-referenced) assessment and self-assessment procedures. On the basis of their varied experiences in the field of foreign language teaching, they helped to develop a comprehensive common view of language learners' growing language abilities.
>
> In 1996 all participants received the first draft of the Swiss ELP model. Just like the published 2001 version, this photocopied draft was already available in the four language versions German, French, Italian, English, and contained preliminary versions of most

elements, including the *Global Scale,* the *Self-assessment Grid,* and the *checklists*. The teachers were asked to use this draft version with their classes and to give written feedback. Most feedback received was related to these descriptor-based self-assessment instruments which seemed to be of main interest, which is not surprising considering the fact that all these teachers had contributed to their development.

At the Fribourg Conference which concluded the SNF project in September 1996, many of the teachers involved were present to discuss a slightly improved draft version of the ELP and to take the process even a bit further: workshops were carried through in which the newly assembled *Oral Assessment Grid* (now included in the CEF as Table 3: *Qualitative Aspects of Spoken Language Use*) was used to rate the same video recordings of learner productions (and interactions) that had been used during the SNF project in order to develop and scale the descriptors of qualitative aspects of oral language proficiency. The results were very encouraging: the descriptors the *Oral Assessment Grid* consists of were found (very) useful and a large majority of the teachers generally reached the same ratings after only short discussions with their colleagues, necessary mainly in the beginning. The ratings reached on the basis of the new *Grid* used in these workshops also confirmed the initial ratings that had been determined by the *Rasch* statistics program *FACETS,* then based on different draft sets of descriptors. This positive outcome meant, among other things, that the video recordings in combination with the *Oral Assessment Grid* could be used in future rater training workshops. In fact, this training package has been used at numerous occasions since and has been a convincing promoter of criterion-referenced assessment—and through this, also of the Language Portfolio, which, in many people's perceptions, was otherwise (too) closely associated with self-assessment.

A grammar school teacher of French who regularly teaches introductory workshops, has used the *Oral Assessment Grid* to demonstrate quite convincingly to his fellow teachers how criterion-referenced assessment can be linked to the numerical grading system that is common in Switzerland and, at the same time, how they can *anchor* the grades they use in relation to transparent performance criteria (Hodel 2000). Such concrete contributions are very important if the Language Portfolio is to be fully embedded in daily practice.

In the mid-nineties, a group of language experts elaborated a proposition for a global concept of language learning and education on behalf of the Swiss central educational authority (EDK/CDIP) in order to meet the growing language needs and to co-ordinate cantonal (state) initiatives. The *Common Reference Levels* developed in the SNF project and presented in *Draft 1* of the Common European Framework of Reference (Council of Europe 1996) and the European Language Portfolio were important elements of this proposition (EDK/CDIP 1998). The *Common Reference Levels* were used to define the desired educational outcomes for the main foreign languages learned during compulsory schooling. The ELP was presented as an assessment instrument comprehensive enough to support and document language learning and intercultural experiences in a multitude of possible circumstances such as immersion programs, exchange programs, out-of-school learning, early language learning, language awareness classes, modular and partial language learning, and, last but certainly not least, regular foreign-language classes.

ACTION

Check the Common Reference Levels (self-assessment grid) and compare them with the ACTFL Proficiency Guidelines <www.actfl.org>.

These propositions made by experts have not been adopted officially, to date, but this is mainly due to the fact that the political process has not come to an end. The developments are clearly going in that direction. Meanwhile, the approach taken has been adopted for several important curriculum or syllabus projects in different contexts in Switzerland: mainly for professional schools and colleges but also for compulsory schooling in certain regions and cantons. It seems that whenever new curricula, syllabi, examinations, textbooks, and sometimes even course programs, are developed in the field of modern languages, the *Common Reference Levels* and the European Language Portfolio cannot be ignored.

Based on the first experiences made with European Language Portfolios in Switzerland, France, Germany, and Britain, the Council of Europe decided at its Conference in April 1997 to further pursue the Common European Framework and the ELP projects (Council of Europe 1997). This was an important signal for the Swiss ELP authors to proceed. They now prepared a print version that could be piloted within a Europe-wide pilot scheme. With official support, they organized the first of a series of ELP seminars (Ascona, January 1998) in order to help disseminate the ELP throughout Europe. It was clear very early that in the long run, the ELP could only meet its purpose if it were recognized fairly rapidly throughout Europe. Therefore, implementation in Switzerland has always included dissemination across the borders.

In Switzerland, the official pilot phase started in April 1999 and ended in July 2000. The ELP was used in approximately 470 classes at the upper and lower secondary levels and in higher and adult education in 19 out of 26 Swiss cantons. About half of these classes were based in the canton Ticino where the pilot version of the ELP was directly recommended for implementation. The pilot project was evaluated by means of questionnaires, group discussions and telephone interviews. Over a hundred teachers and many of their learners gave extensive feedback. The detailed evaluator's report on the piloting is available in English on the Internet (cf. Lenz 2000b). The official piloting was helpful in many respects (cf. Lenz 2000c):

- The relevance of the central aims and purposes of the ELP was underscored by the users. However, it became also quite clear during the piloting that the ELP can only be credible as a useful instrument claiming to have international currency if very wide dissemination inside and outside Switzerland actually were to take place quite quickly, and if the ELP were to manage to become known also in the world of work. Without the advantages of mobility, the ELP does not seem to have sufficient appeal to some of the learners and teachers so that they would not be willing to invest the time and effort it takes to have a decent Portfolio.
- The practical usefulness of the core elements was confirmed. *Self-Assessment Grid* and *checklists*, in particular, were widely used with success. Feedback in general was very positive although many critical remarks concerning details were made. These remarks were tremendously helpful in preparing the final version.
- Mostly critical but helpful feedback was given concerning the physical appearance of the pilot version: heavy ring-binder, pages filled with texts in small print, etc. Based on this feedback, the graphical design could be significantly improved.
- Useful information concerning measures and materials that should accompany the implementation of the ELP was gained. Teachers particularly stressed the fact that an ELP needed to be embedded into its environment, i.e. the relation between syllabi, textbooks, grades, exams, and the ELP had to be established, and additional rating scales and tests needed to be made available.
- A significant number of pilot teachers gained enough experience to be ready to disseminate the ELP in their environment and even beyond.
- A network of contact persons working as administrators in the educational system was established.
- The presence of the ELP and its central ideas was marked so that proponents of related innovations could not subsequently choose to overlook the ELP (and the CEF).
- Facts and arguments were gathered on behalf of those who were willing to suggest and defend the introduction of the ELP on the regional, local and school level.

In view of the variety of positive effects that reach far beyond the ELP itself, it can be recommended to any ELP project group to engage in large-scale piloting within the environment their ELP is intended to be used.

After the piloting was over, the right to produce the final version of the ELP was sold to a textbook publisher. Most recommendations that emerged from the piloting were put into practice. The single most important improvement was probably an improved version of the Language Passport booklet already contained in the pilot version. This second edition had been agreed on by the Council of Europe and ELP developers from different countries as the future standard European Language Passport, now used in most ELPs for adults. The fact that this Language Passport has the same *look and feel* all over Europe tremendously increases the chance that ELPs from different countries are recognized as basically the same document. In recognition of the pioneer role the authors played throughout the nineties, the Swiss ELP for Young People and Adults was accredited as the first European Language Portfolio (number 1.2000) by the European Validation Committee, which had been newly set up by the Council of Europe.[9]

The European Language Portfolio became the most important Swiss project for the European Year of Languages (2001). It was officially launched on 1st March 2001 accompanied by a declaration co-signed by the Swiss Conference of Cantonal Ministers of Education (CDIP/EDK) and a significant number of partners from the public and private sectors including unions and the employers' association (<http://www.languageportfolio.ch> [> Background > Documentation]).

Still during the piloting, politicians in two cantons (Ticino and Jura) had decided to introduce the ELP on a compulsory basis in certain sectors of their educational system.

In order to support and co-ordinate the further implementation of the ELP, the CDIP/EDK set up a steering group consisting of representatives from all regions, plus two experts. In a first phase, the group established contacts with every canton because the cantons are responsible for most parts of the educational system(s) in federalist Switzerland. Within the first year after the launch, the ELP was introduced to only a small number of classes. But in-service training related to the ELP was in great demand, and the introduction of the ELP was considered in many environments.

Although it was recommended in the declaration to introduce the ELP during the last year of compulsory schooling (9th grade) so that the ELP, being an information tool, could help to smoothen the passage from one educational sector to the next, the cantons do not seem to be willing to do so. This seems to be the case partly for financial reasons: as long as the pupils are within the compulsory school system, cantons or communities would have to pay for the ELPs; afterwards, the students have to buy their school material themselves.

Some schools at the upper secondary level have introduced or intend to introduce the ELP; in other schools, the teachers use instruments from the ELP in their teaching but do not introduce their learners to the use and uses of the ELP as a whole. Still other schools are waiting for more official decisions and support.

In adult education, the *Reference Levels* seem to be quite well known. One important language course provider (Migros Club Schools) has fully embedded the use of the ELP in their most recent textbooks. But even they leave it up to the individual learners whether they actually wish to buy and use the ELP.

As far as information is available, most employers tend to wait for their employees or job applicants to bring their ELPs with them, and do not take an active role in gathering information. But there are exceptions, mainly in the public and semi-public sectors. Notable examples are the federal administration and the Swiss Federal Railroads which both operate in a multilingual environment.

Overall, it is very hard to make predictions concerning future sales of the ELP. So far, it is obvious that the great impact the ELP has had in various environments has not led to widespread use of the ELP. But when a Swiss region or a single large canton decides to introduce the ELP on a large scale, the situation changes completely.

In spring of 2002 the development of two Swiss ELP models for younger learners has started. Between 2002 and 2004, two ELPs are produced: one for pupils up to the 5th grade and another one for pupils from the 5th to the 9th grade.

At the kick-off event in January 2002, the language experts and teachers present agreed that particularly the following aspects should be treated and/or promoted in the new ELPs:

- Multilingualism that is a reality in many classrooms.
- Due recognition of (skills in) immigrant languages.
- Awareness of the variety and the functioning of languages in general.
- Reflection of different cultures and contacts with other cultures.
- Development of transferable language learning skills based on reflection.
- Reflection of foreign-language use and the development of communication strategies.

- Development of autonomous learning and, in particular, self-assessment.
- Bringing school language learning closer to the parents.

In 2002 a 3-year project entitled *Development of Instruments for the Assessment of Foreign Language Skills* started. Instruments for self- and teacher assessment of French and English are to be produced on the basis of the Common European Framework of Reference for Languages. The following products will emerge from the project:

- A bank of language proficiency descriptors suitable for learners aged 11 to 15, adapted from the bank of descriptors developed in the SNF project.
- Based on the descriptor bank: grids and checklists suitable for self-assessment; these instruments will also be used in the ELPs for younger learners being developed simultaneously.
- Based on the descriptor bank: a series of validated and partially calibrated tasks testing learners' performance (including rating scales for Speaking and Writing); other instruments allowing to test learners' linguistic resources (grammar, vocabulary).
- Sample test papers that allow for diagnosing learners' level of proficiency in listening, reading, speaking, and writing.
- Assessed and commented sample performances for Writing and Speaking.
- Training material to introduce teachers to the use of the assessment instruments produced.

CONSIDER

How would you implement portfolios in your foreing or second language classroom? Ideas on adapting aspects of the ELP may be found in the materials section of this volume.

Tests related to the *Common Reference Levels* have been in great demand since the early days of the ELP. The particular challenge in this project will be to gauge descriptors and test tasks to the experiences and the specific interests and competencies of the young learners they are intended for.

Some Characteristics of the ELP—A Brief Overview

(This chapter is based on Schneider 17-19)

1 The *learner is the owner* of the ELP (cf. *Principles and Guidelines*). S/he decides what information and documents s/he wants to insert, keep, remove or re-arrange for specific occasions.

2 The ELP illustrates its owner's *plurilingualism*. Every ELP is open to all languages someone may learn.

3 The ELP documents and promotes both: communicative foreign-language proficiency and intercultural experiences.

4 The ELP is used *across the curriculum*. It is not only relevant for the foreign-language subjects but also for other subjects as far as they contribute to the development of plurilingualism and enhance the

learner's intercultural competence, for example, through immersion teaching, reflection on language (*language awareness*) or stays in other language regions.

5 The ELP takes into account *language learning inside and outside school*; therefore, it also documents language knowledge and intercultural experiences of migrants and their children.

6 For the ELP *different forms of language learning are important*: language learning in schools and courses (e.g. regular foreign language classes, bilingual teaching, exchanges), as well as informal learning (e.g. private contacts, travel, practical/professional training abroad).

7 The ELP refers to *self-assessment and assessment by others*. Both forms of assessment are linked to the *Common Reference Levels* defined by the Council of Europe.

8 The ELP contains instruments or forms for *summative and formative assessment* and helps to declare their status in a transparent way.

9 The ELP may contain *formal and informal documents*, for example diplomas and report cards, progress reports written by teachers or learners. Information on school-leaving certificates is validated by the issuing institutions. Information on schools and language courses attended are confirmed by these institutions. The ELP does not replace certificates and grades; by linking them to a common reference system, they are *translated* into a language that is commonly understood so that they can be compared.

10 The ELP shows the *actual stage of language proficiency*, as well as a learner's *development*. The documentation on the actual stage of proficiency and the paths which led there, is updated whenever the need arises (information or planning purposes).

11 The ELP documents *products and processes*. A selection can be made from the collected products (Dossier) and the written reports and reflections (Biography) whenever the ELP is to be presented to others.

12 The ELP helps to *facilitate transitions between school sectors*. It accompanies a learner from one sector to the next and serves as an instrument of information and co-ordination for the institutions and persons involved.

13 The ELP *over-arches institutions*. The development of plurilingualism often starts before or outside school and goes on when formal education is finished. An appropriate version of the ELP can accompany a learner even after school and can support and document life-long learning. It does not make sense to use more than one Language Portfolio at any given point in time, for example, one ELP for every institution a learner has to do with. ELPs issued by one institution should be recognized by other institutions.

14 The ELP exists in *age-specific versions*. With respect to the considerable development an individual goes through from childhood to adulthood, and in view of the varying needs that arise at different points in time,

the Council of Europe suggests to develop different types of ELP for three age groups: an *ELP, Stage 1* for very young learners up to 10-12 years; an *ELP, Stage 2* for use during the remaining years of obligatory schooling; an *ELP, Stage 3* for young people and adults (from 15/16 years upward), whenever possible to be introduced still during compulsory schooling. Sucessive ELPs should be designed not only to suit the typical needs of pupils of one sector, but also to ensure the transition between neighboring educational sectors. Informing new schools and teachers, or employers and vocational trainers, is a model application of the ELP.

15 The ELP is at the same time a *learning companion* and an *information tool*.

16 An ELP has *many users*. The users of an ELP vary in a learner's life-long history of language learning and language use. The European Language Portfolio helps learners to document and reflect upon their language learning and intercultural experiences, and to inform others on a regular basis or for specific occasions, such as the beginning of a new school or language course, an exchange program or a job application. The ELP helps teachers, schools, and other educational institutions to get to know learners' previous knowledge and their needs and motives in order to agree with them on objectives, set up learning programs, and to assess their achievements in a differentiated way. The ELP helps companies, agencies, and other employers to get a comprehensive and differentiated picture of the language proficiency and intercultural competencies of employees or job applicants so that they can make better use of the available resources and offer more efficient on-the-job training.

ACTION

Challenge yourself as an expert on educational policy. In your opinion, what are the reasons for/against and adoption of the ELP concept for US foreign language education? Do you think the implementation of language portfolios could become part of the New Visions task force on curriculum, instruction, articulation, and assessment?

17 The ELP is *European*. It exists in various language versions. Normally, the learners use an ELP written in their first or main local language. The descriptions of levels are normally available in several languages, especially those which are directly related to the *Common Reference Levels* (online: *http://culture.coe.int/portfolio* [> Levels]). The European Language Portfolio exists in a number of versions which take into account the specific conditions of the contexts they are intended for. At the same time, all ELPs have some fundamental properties in common: they share the fundamental objectives defined by the Council of Europe; they have passed accreditation and carry the Council of Europe logo; they serve the double function of an information tool and a companion to learning; they have a fixed structure consisting of the three parts *Language Passport*, *Language Biography*, and *Dossier*. Finally, the descriptions of language proficiency used are related to the *Common Reference Levels* defined in the Common European Framework of Reference for Languages (Council of Europe 2001).

Notes

1. The *Self-Assessment Grid* in the Appendix provides a concise overview of this system of 6 levels. The *Common European Framework* is available from Cambridge University Press, and as a PDF file from the Council of Europe web site (<http://culture.coe.int/lang> Language Policy Division).
2. See Randall Lund's contribution to this volume and, for example, Paulson, Paulson & Meyer 1991.
3. The Council of Europe is an intergovernmental organization with 44 member states; 48 states have signed the Cultural Convention. Its permanent headquarters are located in Strasbourg, France. The Council of Europe's primary goal is to promote the unity of the continent and to ensure the respect for the fundamental values democracy, human rights, and the rule of law.
4. The interview with Joe Sheils in this volume provides more information on the Council of Europe's involvement in the European Language Portfolio project.
5. Cf. Schneider & Lenz 2001, pp. 3-5. This overview applies in particular to ELP models for learners beyond childhood.
6. Cf. Schneider et al. (2001), first fold-out.
7. For detailed information on the relationship between the *Common European Framework for Languages*, the SNF project, and the development of a Swiss model of the European Language Portfolio see Lenz & Schneider 2002.
8. Its full title was: Evaluation und Selbstevaluation der Fremdsprachenkompetenz an Schnittstellen des schweizerischen Bildungssystems. Transparente und kohärente Beschreibungen fremdsprachlicher Kompetenzen als Evaluations-, Informations- und Planungsinstrumente. (English translation by P.L.: Assessment and self-assessment of foreign-language proficiency at cross-over points of the Swiss educational systems. Transparent and coherent descriptions of foreign-language competencies as instruments for assessment, information and planning)
9. The role of the Council of Europe is not further explained in this article. The Council of Europe Web site provides an interesting collection of downloadable documents, including the *Common European Framework of Reference for Languages*, guides for teachers and ELP developers, studies, translations of the core elements, plus an overview of all ELPs validated to date, including links to the corresponding web sites.

References

APA/American Psychological Association's Board of Educational. *Learner-Centred Psychological Principles: A Framework for School Redesign and Reform*. 1997 <http: //www.apa.org/ed/lcp.html>.

Babylonia. Sondernummer in Zusammenarbeit mit dem Europarat: European Language Portfolio - Portfolio européen des langues - Europäisches Sprachenportfolio - Portfolio europeo delle lingue - Portfolio europeic da las linguas. 1999/1.

Babylonia. European Language Portfolio II - Das europäische Sprachenportfolio II - Il Portfolio europeo delle lingue II - Le Portfolio européen des langues II - Il Portfolio europeic da las linguas II. 2000/4.

Conseil de l'Europe. *Un Cadre européen commun de référence pour les langues: apprendre, enseigner, évaluer*. Paris: Didier. 2001 <http://culture.coe.int/portfolio> [>Documentation]>.

Council of Europe. "Transparency and Coherence in Language Learning in Europe: Objectives, Assessment and Certification." *Symposium held in Rüschlikon, 10 - 16 Nov. 1991*. Ed. Brian North. Strasbourg: Council for Cultural Co-operation, 1992.

Council of Europe. *Common European Framework of Reference for Language Learning and*

Teaching. Draft 1 of a Framework Proposal. Strasbourg: Council of Europe, 1996.
Council of Europe. *Language Learning for a New Europe. Report of the Final Conference of the Project 'Language Learning for European Citizenship', Strasbourg, 15-18 April 1997.* Strasbourg: Council for Cultural Co-operation (= Language Learning for European Citizenship CC-LANG (97) 7), 1997.
Council of Europe. *Common European Framework of Reference for Languages: Learning, Teaching, Assessment.* Cambridge: CUP, 2001. <http://culture.coe.int/portfolio> [>Documentation]>.
Council of Europe. *Common European Framework of Reference for Languages: Learning, Teaching, Assessment - Case Studies.* Ed. J. Charles Alderson. Strasbourg: Council of Europe, 2002.
EDK/CDIP ed. *Welche Sprachen sollen die Schülerinnen und Schüler der Schweiz während der obligatorischen Schulzeit lernen? Bericht einer von der Kommission für allgemeine Bildung eingsetzien Expertengruppe "Gesamsprachenkonzept."* Ed. EDK/CDIP. Bern: EDK, 1998. <http://www.romsem.unibas.ch/sprachenkonzept/>.
Europarat. *Gemeinsamer europäischer Referenzrahmen für Sprachen: lernen, lehren, beurteilen.* Berlin: Langenscheidt, 2001. <http://www.goethe.de/z/50/commeuro>.
Hodel, Hans-Peter. "Kohärenz und Transparenz im Benoten der mündlichen Kommunikation." *Babylonia* 4 (2000): 41-43.
Kohonen, Viljo. "Exploring the Educational Possibilities of the *Dossier*." *Enhancing the Pedagogical Aspects of the European Language Portfolio (ESP)* (2000): 5-30. <http://culture.coe.int/portfolio> [>Documentation]>.
Lenz, Peter. "Erfahrungen mit dem Europäischen Sprachenportfolio in der Schweiz." *Babylonia* 1 (2000a): 23-28.
Lenz, Peter. *Piloting the Swiss Model of the European Language Portfolio, May 1999 - June 2000.* (Evaluation report on behalf of the Swiss CDIP and the Council of Europe), 2000b: 53. <http://www.languageportfolio.ch> [> ELP Background > Piloting]>.
Lenz, Peter. "Der Beitrag von Erprobungen zur Portfolio-Entwicklung." *Babylonia* 4 (2000a): 32-34.
Lenz, Peter, and Günther Schneider. "Developing the Swiss Model of the European Language Portfolio." *Council of Europe* Ed. J. C. Alderson, 2002: 68-86. <http://culture.coe.int/portfolio> [>Documentation]>.
Little, David, and Radka Perclová. *The European Language Portfolio. Guide for Teachers and Teacher Trainers.* Strasbourg: Council of Europe, 2001a. <http://culture.coe.int/portfolio> [>Documentation]>.
Little, David, and Radka Perclová. *Le Portfolio Européen des Langues: Guide à l'usage des enseignants et des formateurs d'enseignants.* Strasbourg: Conseil de l'Europe, 2001b. <http://culture.coe.int/portfolio> [>Documentation]>.
Little, D. "The European Language Portfolio: Structure, Origins, Implementation and Challenges." *Language Teaching* 35.3 (2002): 182-189.
Moya, Sharon S. and Michael J. O'Malley. "A Portfolio Assessment Model for ESL." *The Journal of Educational Issues of Language Minority Students* 13 (1994): 13-36. <http: //www.ncbe.gwu.edu/miscpubs/jeilms/vol13/portfo13.htm>.
North, Brian. *The Development of a Common Framework Scale of Language Proficiency.* New York: Peter Lang, 2000.
North, Brian, and Günther Schneider. "Scaling Descriptors for Language Proficiency Scales." *Language Testing* 15.2 (1998): 217-262.
Oskarsson, Mats. *Self-Assessment in Foreign Language Learning.* Strasbourg: Council of Europe, 1977.

Oskarsson, Mats. *Approaches to Self-Assessment in Foreign Language Learning*. Strasbourg: Council of Europe, 1978.

Oskarsson, Mats. *Self-Assessment of Foreign Language Skills: A Survey of Research and Development Work*. Strasbourg: Council of Europe, 1984.

Paulson, Paulson, and Meyer. "What Makes a Portfolio a Portfolio?" *Student Portfolios. A Collection of Articles*. Ed. Robin Fogarty. Arlington Heights: 1996. 83-87.

Schärer, Rolf. *Final Report. European Language Portfolio. Pilot Project Phase 1998-2000*. Strasbourg: Council of Europe, 2000. DGIV/EDU/LANG (2000) 31 rev. <http://culture.coe.int/portfolio> [>Documentation]>.

Schneider, Günther. *Wozu ein Sprachenportfolio? Funktionen und Merkmale des Europäischen Sprachenportfolios (Schweizer Version)*. 1999 <http://www.languageportfolio.ch> [> Background > Documentation]>.

Schneider, Günther. "Kompetenzbeschreibungen für das *Europäische Sprachenportfolio*." *Fremdsprachen lehren und lernen (FLuL)* 30 (2001): 193-214.

Schneider, Günther, and Peter Lenz. *European Language Portfolio. Guide for Developers*. Strasbourg: Council of Europe, 2001. <http://culture.coe.int/portfolio> [> Documentation]>.

Schneider, Günther, and Brian North. *"In anderen Sprachen kann ich ..." - Skalen zur Beschreibung, Beurteilung und Selbsteinschätzung der fremdsprachlichen Kommunikationsfähigkeit. Umsetzungsbericht*. Bern: Nationales Forschungsprogramm 33 (NFP33), Schweizerische Koordinationsstelle für Bildungsforschung (SKBF), 1999. <http://www.languageportfolio.ch> [> ELP Background > Documentation]>.

Schneider, Günther, and Brian North. *"Dans d'autres langues je suis capable de ..." Echelles pour la description, l'évaluation et l'auto-évaluation des compétences en langues étrangères. Rapport de valorisation*. Bern: Programme national de recherche 33 (PNR33), Centre suisse de coordination pour la recherche en éducation (CSRE), 2000a. <http://www.languageportfolio.ch> [> ELP Background > Documentation]>.

Schneider, Günther, and Brian North. *Fremdsprachen können - was heisst das? Skalen zur Beschreibung, Beurteilung und Selbsteinschätzung der fremdsprachlichen Kommunikationsfähigkeit*. Chur/Zürich: Rüegger, 2000b.

Schneider, Günther, Brian North, Christoph Flügel, and Leo Koch, ed. *European Language Portfolio. Swiss Version*. Bern: Swiss Conference of Cantonal Ministers of Education, 1999. <http://www.languageportfolio.ch> [> ELP Background > Piloting]>.

Schneider, Günther, Brian North, and Leo Koch, ed. *European Language Portfolio for Young People and Adults*. Bern: Swiss Conference of Cantonal Ministers of Education, Berner Lehrmittel- und Medienverlag, 2001. <http://www.languageportfolio.ch> [> ELP Model 15+]>.

Appendix
Self-Assessment Grid

		A1	A2	B1	B2	C1	C2
UNDERSTANDING	***Listening***	I can understand familiar words and very basic phrases concerning myself, my family and immediate concrete surroundings when people speak slowly and clearly	I can understand phrases and the highest frequency vocabulary to areas of most immediate personal relevance (e.g. very basic personal and family information, shopping, local area, employment). I can catch the main point in short, clear, simple messages and announcements.	I can understand the main points of clear standard speech on familiar matters regularly encountered in work, school, leisure, etc. I can understand the main point of many radio or TV programs on current affairs or topics of personal or professional interest when the delivery is relatively slow and clear.	I can understand extended speech and lectures and follow even complex lines of argument provided the topic is reasonably familiar. I can understand most TV news and current affairs programs. I can understand the majority of films in standard dialect.	I can understand extended speech even when it is not clearly structured and when relationships are ony implied and not signaled explicitly. I can understand television programs and films without too much effort.	I have no difficulty understanding any kind of spoken language, whether live or broadcast, even when delivered at fast native speed, provided I have some time to get familiar with the accent.
	Reading	I can understand familiar names, words, and very simple sentences. For example, on notices and poster or in catalogs.	I can read very short, simple texts. I can find specific, predictable information in simple everyday materials such as advertisements, prospectuses, menus, and timetables. I can understand short simple personal letters.	I can understand texts that consist mainly of high frequency everyday or job-related language. I can understand the description of events, feelings, and wishes in personal letters.	I can read articles and reports concerned with contemporary problems in which the writers adopt particular attitudes or viewpoints. I can understand contemporary literary prose.	I can understand long and complex factual and literary texts, appreciating distinctions of style. I can understand specialised articles and longer technical instructions, even when they do not relate to my field.	I can read with ease virtually all forms of the written language, including abstract, structurally or linguistically complex texts such as manuals, speacialized articles, and literary works.
SPEAKING	***Spoken Interaction***	I can interact in a simple way provided the other person is prepared to repeat or rephrase things at a slower rate of speech and help me formulate what I'm trying to say. I can ask and answer simple questions in areas of immediate need or on very familiar topics.	I can communicate in simple and routine tasks requiring a simple and direct exchange of information on familiar topics and activities. I can handle very short social exchanges, even though I can't usually understand enough to keep the conversation going myself.	I can deal with most situations likely to arise whilst travelling in an area where the language is spoken. I can enter unprepared into conversation on topics familiar, of personal interest, or pertinent to everyday life (e.g. family, hobbies, work, travel, and current events).	I can interact with a degree of fluency and spontaneity that makes regular interaction with native speakers quite possible. I can take an active part in disucssions in familiar contexts, accounting for and sustaining my views.	I can express myself fluently and spontaneously without much obvious searching for expressions. I can use language flexibly and effectively for social and professional purposes. I can formulate ideas and opinions with precision and relate my contribution skilfully to those of other speakers.	I can take part effortlessly in any conversation or discussion and have a good familiarity with idiomatic expressions and colloquialisms. I can express myself fluently and convey finer shades of meaning precisely. If I do have a problem I can backtrack and restructure around the difficulty so smoothly that other people are hardly aware of it.
	Spoken Production	I can use simple phrases and sentences to describe where I live and people I know.	I can use a series of phrases and sentences to describe in simple terms my family and other people, living conditions, my educational background and my present or most recent job.	I can connect phrases in a simple way in order to describe experiences and events, my dreams, hopes and ambitions. I can briefly give reasons and explanations for opinions and plans. I can narrate a story or relate the plot of a book or film and describe my reactions.	I can present clear, detailed descriptions on a wide range of subjects related to my field of interest. I can explain a viewpoint on a topical issue giving the advantages and disadvantages of various options.	I can present clear, detailed descriptions of complex subjects integrating sub-themes, developing particular points and rounding off with an appropriate conclusion.	I can present a clear, smoothly-flowing description or argument in a style appropriate to the context and with an effective logical structure which helps the recipient to notice and remember significant points.
WRITING	***Writing***	I can write a short, simple postcard, for example sending holiday greetings. I can fill in forms with personal details, for example entering my name, nationality and address on a hotel registration form.	I can write short, simple notes and messages. I can write a very simple personal letter, for example thanking someone for something.	I can write simple connected text on topics which are familiar or of personal interest. I can write personal letters describing experiences and impressions.	I can write clear, detailed text on a wide range of subjects related to my interests. I can write an essay or report, passing on information or giving reasons in support of or against a particular point of view. I can write letters highlighting the personal significance of events and experiences.	I can express myself in clear, well-structured text, expressing points of view at some length. I can write about complex subjects in a letter, an essay or a report, underlining what I consider to be the salient issues. I can select a style appropriate to the reader in mind.	I can write clear, smoothly-flowing text in an appropriate style. I can write complex letters, reports or articles which present a case with an effective logical structure which helps the recipient to notice and remember significant points. I can write summaries and reviews of professional or literary works.

In Conversation with Johanna Schwarz About Portfolios

Gerd Bräuer

As we can read in this volume in regard to several key topics, foreign language educators on both sides of the Atlantic can profit a lot from each others' expertise. This seems true especially for the subject of portfolios.

During the 1970s and 1980s in the context of process writing research, US writing pedagogues such as Donald H. Graves and Donald Murray (for primary and secondary education), and Peter Elbow and Pat Belanoff (for higher education) started to use portfolios to help students reflect on their development as writers. During the 1990s, these curricular consequences, emerging out of a growing understanding of writing as a mode of learning (Janet Emig), also brought portfolios into foreign and second language instruction.

When I started offering teacher training on portfolios in Europe in the second half of the 1990s, I profited greatly from the work of my American colleagues. Also in the 1990s, under the leadership of the Council of Europe, the European Language Portfolio (ELP) was developed (see Sheil/Butler and Lenz in this book). As Lund's chapter in this volume indicates, the European portfolio model now seems to be back to the place of its original roots. Still, as has also been true of the US portfolio ideas I took to European teacher training workshops, it is hard to imagine that the ELP will be applied to US foreign language classrooms without adaptation.

In a conversation with Johanna Schwarz, a high school teacher from Innsbruck (Austria), who was among the first using portfolios in her country, we discussed some of these institutional differences between language education in the US and Europe, and the consequences for use of portfolios on both sides of the Atlantic.

Gerd Bräuer (GB)
Johanna, in 1998 you participated in CUNY's MA program on Language and Literacy where you encountered, as you said elsewhere, a different approach to teaching and learning that eventually turned into a new paradigm for your own career as an educator. What changes in your personal beliefs were inspired through your study of US process writing theories, the whole language approach, and methods of reflective teaching?

Johanna Schwarz (JS)
It soon became clear to me how error-focused and skills-based our teaching of English as a foreign language was. This was particularly true for the teaching of writing,

and, in fact this is still common practice. One of the deeply rooted beliefs in my educational setting is that learners need to be taught about isolated parts before they can be encouraged to write whole texts. Moreover, avoiding errors is of highest priority among both learners and teachers, and the idea of multi-draft writing and revision is widely unknown and hardly ever practiced. As a result, assessment schemes in language classrooms are mostly deficit oriented, or, in other words, a grammatically accurate piece equals a good grade. So learning about the approaches of whole language, process oriented writing, and reflective teaching introduced me to a completely new world...a world which I was more than willing to embrace because I have long been dissatisfied with this deficit oriented approach to language learning. "If I only could learn with my students and didn't have to assess them" was among the most frequent thoughts in my daily practice. The option to postpone issues of accuracy to a later stage in the writing process made immediate sense to me but demanded an intensive unlearning process for me, my students, and their parents.

What kind of practice is this if a teacher doesn't mark and correct every miscue in a text or oral utterance of a student? How will they ever use the language accurately if they are not corrected by the teacher? How can a teacher neglect errors in a reading log or early drafts of texts and trust in the fact that those errors are going to disappear sooner or later? These are some of the main questions that haunted me in my early days and are today uttered regularly in teacher training seminars when I present the portfolio approach.

The following anecdote perhaps relates a bit how I first introduced this new paradigm. I had been assigned to a new school and was working with a group of beginners in English. English was their third foreign language, in addition to French and Latin. We met four times a week for 50 minute periods and were supplied with a text book I had not chosen and which did not meet any of the students' needs. On the very first day in this classroom I asked them to come to the board and write down all the English words they already knew. Chairs and desks banged and rumbled, and bags and books flew as the whole group rushed to the board fighting to fill it with English terms that ranged from *mountain bike* to *pop groups* to *fuck*. I then told them to use the words on the board to write their first English text and encouraged them to use German words to make up for any lack of English vocabulary. As I suggested using drawings and symbols, my students' faces filled with amazement, skepticism, resistance, and shock. How could they be expected to write an English text in their first English lesson? Later that day I cursed my spontaneity since I had planned to apply what I had experienced in the MA program gradually and cautiously. My students were obviously left with similarly mixed feelings as the following reflection sample shows:

> It was an absolutely new Unterricht (form of teaching). I thought, "She is crazy." How should we learn English. I didn't accept the teacher. We had too many possibilities and freedoms. (E.)

Asking the learners for written reflections on how they experienced each lesson became a key strategy that I applied in the classroom. Through this process, I was able to learn the needs of the students and plan my lessons accordingly. This proved to be an important survival strategy in those early days when I was trying out a new approach, working in a new school, and using an outdated textbook. Although I found my learners extremely hesitant and resistant to writing reflections at the beginning, they did eventually come around. It does take a while for learners to realize that writing is a meaningful learning strategy that can help them organize their thinking and aid their development as autonomous learners.

The above example is just one of many I experienced when I started to implement these new approaches in a traditional Austrian educational setting. In this process, ideas, worries, needs, or interests uttered in my students' reflections became essential signposts along the way.

(GB)
You mentioned earlier that it was the change in your personal teaching approach, toward a more process-oriented work and student-centered classroom, which primarily made you also revise the way you understood assessment and evaluation for student performance. What was it that you had in mind when you first asked your students to prepare a portfolio?

(JS)
"Well, great! We revise our texts in the lessons, but when it comes to tests, we are assessed on a first draft!" This statement by one of my students made me radically change my attitude towards standardized testing. How could I still use a test mode that negatively assessed students' first drafts according to the number of errors they made, when in the lessons I told them to neglect errors in early drafts, work on their writing intentions, as well as revise their pieces up to five times? Fixing the grammar was really the last step in this process.

The portfolio model of which I had heard and read about during the MA program proved the way out. Here we, the students and I, could integrate all the different elements that had proved essential in the process: multiple draft writing; student centered interests and needs; choice, ownership, and time for the learners, a mutual link between teaching, learning, and assessing.

As mentioned above I was searching for an appropriate form of assessment able to adequately measure the potential of student work that I saw when implementing these new approaches. I also felt a growing need to encourage student self assessment and forms of peer assessment because I wanted them to become autonomous learners, rather than always looking to me, their teacher, for answers.

While I longed to share the responsibility for teaching, learning and assessing with my students, one memorable experience in my early days forced me to re-examine this plan. There was one girl in the class who performed particularly poorly on standardized tests. At the end of her first term, I took the first steps towards portfolios. I asked the students to select their best text, and in a reflective letter to a reader (some wrote to a friend, some to a parent, most to me) to describe the changes they observed in the various drafts of this text, as well as refer to their individual growth as writers. I gave them written guidelines, both in English and German, about what to refer to in those letters, leaving it up to them whether to use German, English or *Denglish*, a mixture of English and German. Here I followed a suggestion by Freeman/Freeman (1992) who stressed the supportive function of the mother tongue in acquiring the target language.

All the students, except that girl, wrote their letters in German! The fact that the weakest learner in the group (as assessed through standardized testing) had obviously made the biggest step in learning, by writing the entire letter in English, shattered my whole belief in my contemporary assessment scheme. From then on I consistently experimented with portfolios and looked for different sources of learning. Whereas before, I had only considered my notes, my observations, and test results, now there were the students' ideas, expectations, and self-assessment, all of which incredibly enriched our classroom.

(GB)
Could you please briefly explain the basic scheme of how you use portfolios in your language classrooms today?

(JS)
In order to implement my new assessment scheme, I applied for an educational experiment to allow me to replace three out of five standardized tests by portfolios. Now the students take one test per term and compile one portfolio. This format allows enough time for process-oriented work and offers a fair reduction of test-dates so as not to hinder portfolio work. As far as the portfolios are concerned there are three major elements that form the rough frame for my learners to present their work:

- Conscious and careful selection of work (texts, notes, tests, reflections).
- Critical reflection of those samples of work and their learning process.
- Self-assessment.

The minimum requirements for the portfolios include one critically reflected sample of work from the following frame: reading, writing, topic-based work, language use and oral work. This frame covers all dimensions of teaching English as a foreign language, including the four skills. Usually, the learners include more than just the minimum or add some extra work as well. Basically this rough scheme has proved to be so effective that I have applied it in a considerable number of other learning groups: young learners in a cross-curricular classroom; adolescents in their mother tongue; adult learners in teacher training. Even if the predefined sections differ in the various groups, the three elements (a-c) have worked well in all of them.

(GB)
Following up on what you just described: What did you have to change over time in order to adapt your original portfolio approach to the specific cultural context of your school?

(JS)
When I began experimenting with portfolios, it was as an extra classroom activity, for which the learners earned credits for class participation. Because portfolios motivate students to produce more good work than any other assessment tools, I soon found myself looking at up to 30 pages, rather than the two page essays of standardized tests. Not only was the work more extensive, it was of higher quality, showing amazing intensity, effort, and creativity. In the beginning, every term's portfolios caused modifications of my basic guidelines. What I learned in students' reflections about effectiveness of strategies, successful and unsuccessful strategies, and individual needs or obstacles to learning, all greatly influenced my lesson planning. As a result, the learners became my most important teachers in this process. A process of unlearning *teacher-centeredness*. Due to the amount of work that portfolios generated, as well as the fact that I saw a conflict between portfolios and standardized tests, I soon realized that I needed to make a choice. This was the main reason that I applied for the educational experiment through the National Educational Board.

That I gained the official authorization to reduce the number of standardized tests for the sake of portfolios is still one of my biggest successes. The approval of my educational experiment offered time, space, and energy to move my classroom towards a degree of learner-centeredness that I had never known before. Suddenly we had enough time to dive into a process of work which was not interrupted by standardized testing. Individual notions could be investigated more intensively; slowly but consistently the equation: *positive grade = end of learning* disappeared in my learners' heads to make room for a learning behavior that included extra-school language activities, as well as books read and films seen in the holidays. Suddenly learning English occurred outside of the classroom too. It is likely that there had been learning going on outside the classroom (perhaps even more than within!), but I had not seen it nor had ever imagined that it would make so much sense to invite it into the classroom. I saw practical non-readers in the classroom devour guitar magazines in English, or mutes in group activities turn to conversationalists when among young people from all over the world on the ski slopes.

Because of the success of portfolios, I found it difficult to not treat tests as merely an appendix to them. In the beginning, I mainly used them after portfolio deadlines to focus on problem areas which I had observed in the portfolios. Now I integrate them fully into the context of the class. Following the suggestion to make tests occasions of learning, I now have the learners take a standardized test very early in the term, so that the texts they produce can be revised, and eventually turned into potential samples for their portfolios.

Despite all the positive outcomes of my educational experiment, some difficulties did emerge. Since the portfolios replaced standardized tests, I felt a deeper responsibility to justify both within (the students and me) and outside the classroom (parents, colleagues, and administrators) that the learners' achievements were as reliable, objective, and valid as possible.

Currently I use transparent criteria which are both given to and negotiated with the learners in advance, an assessment sheet, as well as a personal letter as feedback on their portfolios, to assess performance. Sometimes I feel we lose the spirit of portfolios due to the fact that grades continue to be used so pervasively. Since I am the only teacher to experiment with portfolios, students often experience two conflicting systems. While I am encouraging them to develop into autonomous, self-reflective learners, many of my colleagues expect them to spit out facts and figures. This clash between a teacher-centered majority and our student-centered island often results in harsh discussions and debates about basic requirements.

(GB)
Among the pioneers of European portfolio work it is rather well-known that if you teach process-oriented (and use portfolios) but your colleagues don't (and focus primarily on products/tests), you will often have a hard time explaining to students, parents, and school administrators the reasons for the portfolio approach in your class. How did you respond to questions, doubts, fears, and perhaps forms of open resistance?

(JS)
The majority of students were easily won over in the beginning because two to three tests were replaced by portfolios. To most this seemed like a fair deal. However, as soon as they realized that compiling their portfolios meant a lot of hard work, critical voices were heard more often. Interestingly enough, most developed into highly motivated learners, whose own expectations about their own performance were soon higher than mine would have ever dared to become. Many became so critical of their work that we had to develop strategies to prevent them from exhausting themselves. I needed to stress that portfolios are dynamic and that they needed only to document a status-quo of their learning, and not aim at perfection. Matthew's comment best expresses the general sentiment: "Portfolios don't mean paradise on earth, but they offer the best way to learn English I know of."

An immediate doubt the students uttered when I first introduced the idea of portfolios was: "How do you know you are assessing my work and not that of a private tutor?" My response to this was: "Don't fake growth which is not there. In case you needed someone else's help or used private coaching be up front about it. If a parent or boyfriend helped you with your work, tell the reader so." This is exactly what they did, and soon I was amazed to see most of them refuse extra help because of their strong desire to hand in original work. Any student was proud to say: "This time my mom did not help me!"

Interestingly enough, the gifted students and successful test writers were the most resistant to the portfolio project. While the weaker students immediately saw that unlike regular test results, portfolios may guarantee their survival in class, the brighter ones needed a much longer time to realize what portfolios meant for them. They eventually did realize that learning was not about being measured against the average student in a class, but more about fully exploiting their own potential. "What do you want? I read more books than anybody else in this class!" was one furious comment by John. I left him thoughtful by pointing out that he should consider a different question: "What is the next level for you in reading and writing? What could you try next?" My role had changed dramatically from instructor to facilitator and coach, a role that in the beginning I had found difficult to fulfill.

I needed to inform parents, colleagues, and school administrators in order to be given permission to carry out this educational experiment. When I started doing this in 1999, I could neither offer perfect portfolios from former students to look at, nor give a very clear idea of how to carry this out in detail. Nevertheless, the concept was convincing to most of them. Parents joined their children in their consent to the project; if their children believed in the potential of portfolios, who were they to doubt it? Although they heard complaints about the hard work portfolios meant, all of them also acknowledged the pride their children felt after completing their portfolios: "I had never seen such pride in a product from school!" Most Austrian parents are dissatisfied with the stress brought on by tests, so they were grateful for something different. When I handed out a questionnaire on what they observed with regard to their children's learning behavior towards portfolios, the majority stated an increase in independent study skills and visible improvement in the range of vocabulary and style. Most named regular practice of revision as the main reason for this growth. Those parents whose children positively advocated for the portfolio project were similarly positive about it; the ones whose kids were more skeptical nevertheless stated that portfolios make more sense than tests, because they show a range of achievement rather than a single-shot-result. One concern many parents had was that of time management. As a result of this feedback, I worked intensively on developing adequate techniques to deal with this issue.

All in all, the parents were widely supportive of the project. However, many did ask the question: "Will they be prepared for real life and its stresses if they can decide when and how often to revise their work?!" In practice, I have found this not to be an issue. Rather, I have never seen students work so hard to meet deadlines. In addition, because many had poor time management skills, and they had to develop a range of strategies to cope with the stress of meeting deadlines.

In order to implement the portfolio model, I needed a two-thirds vote in favor among the students, parents and colleagues of the class. The head teacher and many other colleagues, as well as the headmaster, were very supportive of the model, so I had no problem in gaining enough votes. The most negative sentiments were expressed by my colleagues from the English department in our school. One of them harshly expressed what perhaps others also thought, "What's so new about this? I don't call it a portfolio, but I've worked like this for ages! Haven't we all?" I vividly remember how speechless I was at this statement, but in the end, this negativity could not stop the project. In fact, the portfolio idea has spread throughout our school. As mentioned above, another colleague is about to implement the model next year, and I have started with a new group this year. I feel that overall there is fair acceptance within the school. Moreover, I was publicly thanked by a colleague in a staff meeting for initiating this project last autumn. This educational experiment now is also part of our school profile, and is advertised in the leaflets that go to future students and parents. Currently, about 20 colleagues are involved in developing a type of cross-curricular portfolio, which goes beyond language learning, but this is another challenging story!

(GB)

Knowing how to respond to questions, doubts, and fears is one necessary skill for someone pioneering a new idea. In addition, school development theory says (see Dubs) it is also important to rally for that new idea within your institution, include other people in what you are doing, get them interested so that they will eventually take on personal responsibility and also themselves network for the idea. How did you make allies among your colleagues for your alternative way of teaching in general and the use of portfolios specifically?

(JS)

Well, first of all, I convinced two colleagues to attend the MA program in New York. This helped a lot because it put us on common ground since we believed in the same teaching and learning principles. One of those colleagues now is about to implement my portfolio model in a bilingual class. I repeatedly presented the model to small groups of colleagues, and in this way, the idea spread. A lot more important than talking about it however, was actually showing the portfolios. This convinced many doubtful minds and moved people to consider that there might be something to it. During the school year 1999/2000 I became involved in a national committee for developing an Austrian model for the European Language Portfolio. Although I have never fully moved to this European model in my own work, presenting this particular model did make sense to some. In fact, three colleagues are currently piloting a model of the ELP in junior high classes. The clear descriptors and levels of competence in the European Framework appeal to many language teachers. Another important issue is that the climate at our school is basically very supportive of new things, and our headmaster fosters any activity that will improve the quality of learning and teaching. Even if there are still colleagues who watch these changes suspiciously, open resistance is on the decline. Moreover, we are lucky to have many staff members who are experts in various fields; so applying elements of the approaches I so strongly believe in was natural to those who themselves had learned to appreciate similar approaches: suggestopedia, Gestalt pedagogy, open learning, or inquiry based learning. In fact, a couple of colleagues, apart from the MA people, have tried already to integrate elements of draft-writing, peer-response, or reflective teaching in their practice.

One of the obstacles in starting a portfolio system lies in the simple fact that portfolio work is, as US portfolio pioneers Pat Belanoff and Marcia Dickson once said, messy, not easily scored, and time consuming. We now know that portfolio work needs a certain quality of collaboration and, therefore, should be made part of school development: A writing/reading center for cross-disciplinary work (Bräuer 2003), for example, can be of great help to:

- Initiate collaboration and bring together the potential of different teachers.
- Help teachers develop concepts of portfolio work for their individual classes that foster cross-disciplinary learning.
- Help reflect and assess the quality of the classroom-based portfolio systems and, over a longer period of time, shape a school-wide portfolio system.
- Coordinate the evaluation of portfolios in teams of teachers and outside experts.

(GB)
In what way could an extra-curricular entity, as the writing/reading center mentioned above, help to foster such collaboration in the future?

(JS)
In my portfolio practice of the last six years, I have found how effectively some of my learners act as editors and writing tutors for their peers. This knowledge and expertise could be well transferred to a writing center. What if students 'taught' teachers how to write reflections? What if older students responded to the Netfolios/Portfolios of younger ones? What if there was a group of teachers/students who could be contacted as experts on reflective writing and compiling a portfolio? Currently, we are a team of three people (the school librarian, the portfolio colleague and I) who are attempting to set up such a center for our school. Since our building is about to be renovated, it would make a lot of sense to integrate this into the new building. Next, we will participate in a EU-wide Comenius project on the implementation of writing/reading centers in European educational institutions.

As just indicated, portfolio work needs to be made visible to other teachers so that it can gain recognition within a school, not least of all because of the specific values of reflective practice for cross-curricular education. At the same time it is also important for the students to experience its value for motivational and other reasons. Writing/reading centers can be of specific help for students to:

- Support them in their portfolio work as a resource center for independent learning (see Langer & Prokop in this volume).
- Initiate student-run portfolio workshops.
- Provide peer feedback (especially for the writing of portfolio instructions and resumés) done by tutors trained in the writing/reading center.

(GB)
Two questions in regard to establishing an extra-curricular entity for portfolio work: First: How do you direct portfolio work beyond your own classroom so that students from different disciplines, as well as different levels of instruction, can collaborate?

(JS)

Responding to suggestions in the literature (Kent 1996; Winter 2001), my plans included options for my students to present portfolios to a wider public than just that of our group. In June 2002, the first portfolio presentation took place in our school: I invited experts from Innsbruck University (Univ. Prof. Dr. Franz Kroath; Tanja Westfal-Greiter, MA, FHS-MCi) to host the meeting, with other local stall members also participating. The students were very nervous, but afterwards they were extremely proud and satisfied about the positive feedback they received. As a result, this is going to be a regular feature in my portfolio classes.

Regarding cross-disciplinary portfolios, we started right from the beginning to exchange portfolios between different classes. The procedure is as follows: Class A invites class B for their portfolio presentations; they all bring their portfolios, if available, and if students in one class are newcomers in portfolio work, they are encouraged to examine the work displayed and give spontaneous feedback on post-its. In the first round, students try to look at three to four different portfolios and give spontaneous feedback. Next, they join for a group discussion in which they either exchange opinions or answer the visitors' questions. As a follow-up they write feedback letters to one single portfolio and then have a look at the feedback on their own portfolios. These circles have led to important insights into different ways of documenting work, as well as motivating newcomers to start their own projects. In general, the generation of new ideas on how to compile one's own portfolio is considerably high. This exchange of portfolios is an important strategy to spread the idea of portfolio both for students and teachers; the latter are stimulated too if they see how clearly even the young learners reflect on the appropriateness of work in such a collection.

(GB)

Second, where, in a traditional school setting, do you see a physical/structural place for a writing/reading center, which could develop and grow over time especially through portfolio work?

(JS)

In my opinion, the ideal physical place is to combine a writing/reading center with the library, which in most schools, is already an established institution. So winning the librarian over is the first thing to do! Most of our learners are effective writers, as compared to secondary modern schools (Hauptschule) or vocational schools, so many teachers may feel that it is not necessary to have a reading and writing center. Only if portfolio work is of some importance already in a school setting will there be enough interest to instruct learners and teachers alike in practicing reflective writing. I know that this kind of writing is the only one which is not immediately associated with language teachers only. Writing across the curriculum is still no big deal in our setting so that there would be immediate positive response to such a venture. However, intensive cross-disciplinary learning will definitely call for such strategies and institutions. If learners autonomously explore subject matter and present it to other groups, it will become essential to develop/find adequate forms of documentation in portfolios, for instance. The physical place needs to be somewhere at a central position in a school, ideally linked to the library. In our case, we hope that there will be an extra room affiliated with the library when the whole building is remodeled. However, it will also be necessary that the writing/reading center can become a concept in people's minds that will be brought to life in the school community. It could be a space in which learners, teachers, and parents work together in a new way. For example, we had a read-aloud around Christmas; it was amazing how many students and teachers attended, as well as offered to read aloud. Another example was bringing in a group of elderly folks from Innsbruck to meet and read to children who were working on a cross-curricular project on *The Young and the Old*.

(GB)
As your own case suggests, having to fight for support from administration as an individual teacher can delay the application of new ideas and concepts tremendously. Top-down decisions such as the ones that led to the development and implementation of the European Language Portfolio sometimes help to push through new ideas and concepts. Nevertheless, as we all know from school development theory, this doesn't mean at all that the new concept will become accepted by others. A well-known tactic of those not wanting to participate is to remain passive and hope the initiative will eventually die off. How can these colleagues, who are often simply stifled by their own fear of change in their professional practice, be reached and integrated in portfolio work that will, hopefully, soon be experienced by themselves as advantageous?

(JS)
The optimist in me says they just need time to experience the potential of portfolios. Portfolios will speak for themselves through the freedom given to the learners to present work that is important to them, through learner reflections, and through learner motivation to tell the story of their learning in their own way. Easing legislative requirements which teachers view as limiting also significantly aids the process. Another important issue is offering intensive in-service-training for teachers. This training should not only include *how-to* guidelines, but should also aim at initiating a different attitude towards teaching and learning. Teachers should be presented with a philosophy that offers ownership, time and choice for learners, rather than only *tell and do*.

However, I agree with Donald Graves (Sunstein & Graves 2) who warns that the use of portfolios in top-down large-scale-assessment may easily come to standardization for the sake of comparability of achievements, standardization which portfolios initially wanted to fight. So one needs to be careful to keep the spirit of portfolios alive and not turn them into something resembling tests wearing a different hat. I cannot draw on large-scale-studies, but my personal experience is that as soon as the teacher-defined requirements become too tight, or are not perceived as negotiated between teachers and students, portfolios are immediately considered merely to be a teacher's task. This shrinks learner motivation as well as potential. As a result, I firmly believe there needs to be a delicate balance between enthusiastic bottom-up experience, both by teachers and learners, as well as top-down help in creating appropriate learning environments.

(GB)
Why did you, instead of using the ELP, develop your own portfolio model?

(JS)
Well, first of all, I was well on my way with my own model before I learned about the European Language Portfolio. In fact, I was about to apply for my school experiment when I heard about a seminar on the ELP (without knowing any details), which I immediately attended. The seminar was chaired by Rolf Schärer from Switzerland, one of the main proponents of the Swiss ELP model. In the school year 1999/2000 I even became involved in a national committee working on developing an Austrian model for the European Language Portfolio. Even if I have never fully converted to this European model in my own work, there are many appealing elements. First of all, teachers and students who have been working with it report similar findings of its potential. Moreover, its key intentions are about the same as the ones in my model: ownership of the learner; life-long learning; process-orientation (learning biography). Additive to my model would be the multi-cultural and plurilingual aspects, which I also greatly approve of. Furthermore, I strongly advocate the European Framework, which offers both clear descriptors and levels of competence.

So why do I still keep my own portfolio model? Perhaps one reason is that since I have invested so much time, energy, thinking, and work in my model that I find it particularly hard to give this up. Another far more important reason is that in fact I have feared too strict a standardization for a long time when looking at the tick-off forms (self-assessment, can-do-statements) of the ELP. Those tick-off forms too closely resembled the tests I had worked so hard to abandon, and I longed a lot more for open forms of reflections. I saw my worst fears justified in the fact that the only Austrian model available and then on the market, initiated by teachers from a vocational school, so much resembled the test mode. I eventually stopped participating in the committee since I wanted to concentrate on further developing my personal model, rather than making up an Austrian one. Nevertheless, I have introduced the idea of the ELP in my classes and eventually used the forms in order to assess various activities. I offer the forms to my students but do not regularly work with them. I also used the background information on the ELP as a justification for my portfolio model during a Matura exam in my early portfolio days.

Eventually, we developed an open self-assessment form based on the can-do-sheets from the ELP (thanks to Rosie Öhler, a dear friend and teacher at PÄDAK Stams, a regional teacher training college, who first introduced the idea to me). In this form the learners list their own learning goals in the can-do/have-done/mode when compiling their portfolios. I'd say that the main reason why I only occasionally refer to the ELP is the fact that my portfolio model is a learning-portfolio, whose reporting function is mainly to the learner herself, as well as the teacher, and maybe a wider public including family and friends or other teachers. When I participated in a conference in Bielefeld (Germany) in February of 2003 and presented the portfolio model, there was a strong advocate for basing portfolio work on the European Framework. Now this makes perfect sense, and as far as I know, there is a group working on basing the new English curriculum for high school exactly on this. When participating in an EU-Comenius project in Finland in March of 2003, I learned about similar trends. However, modifying the portfolio model and extending its use apart from language learning still seems more alluring to me personally than working on a predefined file.

(GB)
One important aspect for including new ideas and concepts into teaching is to experience them yourself. The newly founded University of Education in Zürich (Switzerland) has made portfolio work an integral part of teacher training, both within individual course work and for final examination. At the University of Education in Freiburg (Germany), pieces of reflective writing are required in order to be admitted to what is called a project exam. I am rather hopeful that students who themselves experienced the many advantages of portfolio work will also initiate portfolios into their future practice as educators. Nevertheless, the danger of letting go of a new idea brought in by a new colleague because of discouraging feedback by older teachers is well-known in school development. What needs to be done—by the new teacher herself, other colleagues, and school administrators—in order to help incoming teachers to unfold the new ideas they bring with them from college?

(JS)
Well, one thing might be to hire *them* and fire colleagues who don't seem to be willing to participate. I know that this is rough, but sometimes I just get tired of waiting for people to join.

The trends you describe above are being realized at Innsbruck University as well. I am currently involved in implementing portfolios in course as well as exam design at the Institute for School Development and Teacher Research (ILS). I fully agree with you that those student teachers who have positively experienced the potential of portfolios themselves will definitely implement them in their professional practice. Why does everyone have to work with this instrument? Since teachers need to be grounded in a constructivist approach to learning and teaching, some delicacy is needed here in order to avoid an abuse of this instrument.

Sometimes, top-down decisions to implement new ideas are done very swiftly and are put into practice by educators who themselves have not yet moved out of old notions. Something similar must have happened in Innsbruck, since one colleague once said in a team meeting at the university, "Portfolios are an emotive word already." This tells me that top-down implementation sometimes harms more than it helps. The more I work with portfolios, the more I'm convinced that a teacher who at heart is unwilling to let go of control in his classrooms should not work with portfolios. So I recommend the spreading of portfolios only if they correlate with an appropriate approach to teaching and learning.

Post-Reading Questions

1. *The articles in this part of the book have described the main features of portfolio work in foreign and second language education. Write in free form about the potential of the portfolio method for your own future language training. If you think portfolios would foster your own language learning, what are the next steps to put this idea into practice for yourself? What and where are possible resources to support this effort?*

2. *What format (process or showcase portfolio) do you prefer? Why? Outline the main features of a language portfolio you would like to use (or have been using already).*

3. *Portfolios can also be a powerful tool for reflection in professional development. If you are already a teacher, or will be one in the near future, outline a format that would fit the needs of a specific area of your professional practice, such as class preparation, daily teaching practice, or commenting on students' writing. Think about the format (process of showcase), and outline the main structure (parts) of your portfolio.*

4. *The practice of using portfolios in first language education in US secondary schools has steadily declined since 2000. This is primarily due to an increasing call for accountability and a growing interest in standardized tests among school administrators. What arguments can you think of to show the one-sidedness of standardized tests as the dominating assessment procedure, and the need to balance it with other forms of assessment? In what way could portfolios be a significant addition?*

5. *Assume you have started teaching in a school that stopped using portfolios a few years ago. What could you do in order to awaken new interest in portfolio work in the field of foreign and second language teaching? Outline both the strategies and steps you would need to take in order to accomplish this. Focus on using portfolios in your own classroom, on 'marketing' your successes, and on making allies for the future. Remember, one effective way to make allies is to team teach!*

Chapter 4
Research

In the fourth part of this book the authors consider the question of how to better understand foreign and second language acquisition. They see research, in regard to answering this question, as the key to the further development of curriculum, instruction, and assessment, as described in the second and third part of this book. Four actions that practitioners can undertake to better see the value of research in our profession are to:

- Become aware of what the theoretical discourse of a topic consists of.
- Learn what research methods are available.
- Realize what each of us can do through the daily classroom routine to participate in the research discourse.
- Understand what the impact of research can be on the quality of education.

Pre-Reading Questions

1. *Try to remember when you first recognized languages other than your mother tongue. Visualize the concrete situation: What happened and how did you respond?*

2. *When and how did you learn your first foreign language? Describe the process in as many details as possible. For example: Did you learn it at home or in school? What kind of support did you receive from your family? What do you remember about the teacher's methods (etc.)? When you are done, scan your list and ask yourself: Did each of these circumstances influence my learning positively or negatively? How?*

3. *Based on your own experience, make a list of circumstances that you consider as important to successfully learn a foreign language. How do you think language acquisition works within the framework of what you are suggesting?*

4. *Think back to learning your second foreign language. What happened to the quality of the foreign language you had learned before?*

5. *What strategies have you developed over time to keep the different languages separate so that they do not interfere with each other?*

6. *Have you experienced situations when your knowledge of one language helped you learn or use another language? If so, try to explain what happened. Be as specific as possible.*

7. *What strategies do you use to keep your foreign language(s) up to date? In your opinion what else could help maintain your knowledge?*

Introduction to the New Visions Initiative: Research

Sharon Wilkinson

The pursuit of a deeper and more complete understanding of second/foreign language (L2) acquisition has long been the driving force behind research in our field and, along with it, the desire to maximize our pedagogical efforts to bring about language learning. However, in contrast to other domains such as medicine or engineering, where an overarching agenda often guides the questions that are investigated, L2 acquisition researchers have typically worked in isolation from one another, selecting their research topics based on their own context and interests. Moreover, the disconnect between those involved in L2 research and those focused on L2 teaching has been fairly stark, further fortifying the perceived barriers between post-secondary and K-12 environments. Participants in the New Visions initiative, having identified research as a focal area for discussions about foreign language teaching and learning in the 21st Century, have grappled with these and other problems related to (1) the efficiency of our efforts and the scope of their impact, and (2) the expansion of what *counts* as research and who is included in the research community. This introductory chapter outlines the evolution of the discussion in each of these areas since the first New Visions conference in 1999.[1]

DISCUSS

Currently there exists a disconnect between those involved in L2 research and those focused on teaching. Why do you think this is the case? Discuss strategies to narrow this gap.

Efficiency and Impact

Of primary concern at the New Visions meetings in 1999 and 2000 was the fact that there is currently no systematic organization of L2 acquisition research. New Visions participants felt strongly that it is time for our field to take stock of what we already know and to increase our inventory by locating and analyzing data that already exist but have been abandoned. Once we have our knowledge base more centralized, our profession would then be in a position to identify logical directions for further inquiry, as well as new avenues of research.

In preliminary discussions, participants cautioned that such an agenda should not be used to constrain research activities or to prevent individual investigators from pursuing different avenues of empirical interest. However, by identifying certain key questions, we may be able to maximize our impact in crucial areas by encouraging greater attention to these issues. Those participants who strongly favored a formalized agenda felt that it would also help our profession become more visible to decision-makers outside of our field and could increase our chances of gaining grant support for our work. Naturally, the identification of key research questions—whether or not they are formalized as an agenda—involves power-laden decisions. New Visions participants emphasized that provisions must be made in the process for encouraging a wide variety of research approaches in both quantitative and qualitative paradigms, so as to avoid unnecessarily limiting future findings by *a priori* choices.

In addition to inventorying current research and identifying future directions, the idea of creating a national clearinghouse for foreign language research was proposed as a route to improving the access to and dissemination of findings. Such a clearinghouse would develop and maintain a searchable data base, so that anyone wanting to find out what has already been done in a particular area could locate all the necessary information in one place. Even though creating such an infrastructure would be an enormous logistic and financial undertaking, the benefits in terms of increased productivity would likely be significant.

Regardless of the form they take though, efforts to consolidate our current knowledge and to organize our pursuit of additional knowledge have the potential of also broadening our vision of research and expanding the professional constituencies who engage in and with L2 inquiry. Key questions that represent the needs and interests of our profession at large would necessarily include queries of particular interest to K-12 practitioners, for example. Likewise, an organizational system of current findings could facilitate greater inclusion by making research findings easily accessible to all members of our profession, as well as to those in other fields. These issues of inclusion and expansion also pervaded the New Visions discussions, giving rise to a number of additional ideas for change.

Inclusion and Expansion

What *counts* as research and who *counts* as a researcher are largely shaped by current reward structures in the educational system. At large research universities and at increasing numbers of smaller undergraduate institutions, faculty are required to conduct original research in order to meet institutional standards for tenure and promotion—the infamous *publish or perish* edict. Some institutions also tie individuals' salary increases to research performance, further bolstering the motivation to remain active in this domain. Traditionally, certain types of research have been seen as more rigorous and worthwhile by the committees and administrators who make tenure, promotion, and salary adjustment decisions, strongly influencing the questions researchers choose to investigate and the methods they use to do so. Likewise, the emphasis on quantity of publications has prompted many researchers to favor comparatively less time-intensive methods of investigation, further limiting the questions that receive attention.

While many post-secondary faculty are pushed to conduct and disseminate certain types of research and are rewarded for their successes, no such incentives are provided to K-12 and community college professionals. To the contrary, spending time on research can actually backfire for these teachers, making it even more difficult for them to fulfill their classroom obligations. Just finding the time to read professional literature can seem like an impossibility for many at the K-12 level who are overwhelmed by large class sizes and multiple preparations. If what they do read ultimately lacks apparent relevance to their professional experience (because those who conduct the research are not rewarded for investigating topics of interest to their K-12 colleagues), the motivation to prioritize research consumption is further diminished, and the feeling of alienation is intensified.

New Visions participants recognized the need for systemic changes in the reward structures for both K-12 and post-secondary professionals; however, they also felt that realizing such changes would represent a formidable challenge—one that would, at best, occur very slowly over several generations. In the shorter term, several smaller-scope actions were proposed. To help expand the vision of research, participants suggested that we survey stakeholders both within and outside of our profession to find out which lines of inquiry they find most intriguing or useful.

DISCUSS

Discuss with your colleagues the lines of inquiry that would be the most intriguing or useful for the day to day challenges you face in the classroom.

Recognizing that refereed journals often play a defining role in what counts as research, discussants also felt that there was a need for approach-specific criteria by which to judge the quality of a particular study. Currently, having a single set of standards that is particularly useful for one research approach but less applicable to others may be unnecessarily reducing the amount of work that is conducted and/or disseminated in certain areas.

DISCUSS

Discuss how to integrate a research component into both foreign language teacher preparation programs and ongoing professional development. What types of activities would be the most useful? How could you present research in a *teacher friendly* way?

To enhance the creation of an inclusive research community, New Visions participants felt that we must focus on both pre-service and in-service professionals. They suggested incorporating a research component into pre-service teacher development curricula, as well as offering more teacher-friendly in-service opportunities for increasing familiarity with research methods and findings.

Also vital to inclusion and expansion, organized collaboration and mentoring efforts, through academic alliances, via technology, across disciplines, and so forth, would facilitate mutually supportive and beneficial interaction among teachers at post-secondary, K-12, pre-service, and graduate levels, enhancing the impact of our collective work. A research community that is diverse and that capitalizes on its diversity, while maintaining high standards, will ultimately be in the best position to design and carry out useful research and to reach the greatest number of people with its findings.

Current Directions

Following the discussions of the 1999 and 2000 meetings, New Visions in Action, comprised of four task forces, was founded in 2001 to further the work on the ideas proposed. The Research Task Force has been charged with catalyzing changes that would enhance efficiency, impact, expansion, and inclusion in L2 inquiry.

NOTE

The word *research* comes from the French word *rechercher* (to seek out or to search again in a thorough manner).

It is perhaps fitting then that one of its first tasks has been to help conduct some research with the goal of taking stock of what we believe and what we already do. Specifically, the Research group has been involved in the design, implementation, and analysis of a national on-line survey that is intended to help shape the efforts of the three other task forces (Teacher Recruitment and Retention; Professional Development; and Curriculum, Instruction, Articulation, and Assessment). Additionally, to consolidate our knowledge and encourage wider interest in L2 research, the Research Task Force plans to propose special issues and on-going feature sections of professional journals devoted to *state-of-the-art* articles on topics of particular interest to the field. These summaries would not only organize current findings, but would also draw practical implications from this knowledge and suggest directions for future research. Addressing inclusion, expansion, and impact, the Task Force further seeks to promote school-based action research with K-12 teachers. In this vein, the Chair and another member of the Research Task Force collaborated with the National K-12 Foreign Language Resource Center at Iowa State University to sponsor a one-week Action Research Institute in the summer of 2002, during which ten language education professionals developed their own investigations to be carried out during the following academic year with on-going mentoring. Follow-up with these institute participants is slated for the summer of 2003, at which time dissemination of their findings will be a primary focus.

NOTE

Action research is a powerful tool that can help you develop as a professional. Though only briefly touched on in this introduction, the chapter in this volume entitled *The New Visions Task Force on Research: Promoting Action Research*, provides a much more in-depth discussion of this topic.

Similar institutes have also been conducted statewide in New Jersey and Texas. At the post-secondary level, the Research Task Force plans to become active in mentoring and supporting doctoral students and new faculty who are beginning a research program. Finally, it intends to expand the research community by working to make research an integral component of both foreign language teacher preparation programs and on-going professional development opportunities. Through all of these efforts, it is hoped that more people (both within and outside our profession) will become active in creating and using research, that our knowledge base will be enriched by that greater participation, and that our field will move forward with an ever-increasing understanding of issues related to foreign language teaching and learning.

Notes

1. Although I was a participant in the research discussions at the 1999 and 2000 conferences and am currently a member of the New Visions in Action Research Task Force, I am indebted to the New Visions web site <http://www.educ.iastate.edu/ new visions> for helping me collect and organize the information contained here.

Interview with Sharon Wilkinson

Svenja Dahlmanns

Svenja Dahlmanns (SD)
In your introduction, you stated that an overarching agenda could help to reveal directions for the unification of sometimes isolated research work. Nevertheless, this agenda should not limit research options, but offer an orientation regarding the most important research questions in the field. What are the key research topics identified by the New Visions Initiative?

Sharon Wilkinson (SW)
I mentioned the idea of an overarching research agenda because it was identified by participants at the various New Visions meetings as a top priority (as determined by a process of weighted voting). However, saying that we want a research agenda (or that we think we need a research agenda) is the easy part. Actually establishing one is a whole different ball game! By its very nature, an agenda prioritizes certain research questions—and by extension, the research methods best suited to exploring those questions—and devalues others. There has been a strong minority voice in the Research Task Force discussions that opposes the idea of an agenda on the grounds that it will limit, in a handicapping way, the types of questions we choose to investigate. Others argue that, while we may choose not to have an overt, stated agenda, we cannot escape the fact that we already have an implied agenda driven by our graduate course offerings (which determine the research interests and expertise of future professionals), by the preferences and expertise of the journal article reviewers (who control the types of research that are ultimately published), etc. This group feels that an overt agenda is preferable to the covert one, since the process of openly planning an agenda might actually result in a less limited scope of inquiry by recognizing the usefulness of some questions and research methods that may be undervalued by the current system. Some Task Force members also argue that a formalized agenda could help our political visibility as a profession, increasing our chances of obtaining competitive grant funding, for example. Others, who have already participated in such discussions with other professional organizations, are pessimistic about the likelihood of reaching sufficient consensus to ever produce an agenda, despite our best intentions. As you can see, there are many points of view on the feasibility and desirability of establishing an agenda in the first place—and we haven't even begun to discuss its content!

It is important to mention here that there has been a recent change in Research Task Force Chairs and with it, a shift in perspectives on the agenda issue. Currently, an idea is being pursued to convene a summit of representatives of the research community (broadly conceived) to discuss priorities and directions—a first step toward an agenda. It is too early, however, to know what the outcome of such conversations will be.

SD

You described the planning of a national clearinghouse including a searchable database for the collection and distribution of the various research results in the field of L2 education. This seems to be an important step toward the necessary inventory of knowledge, as you stated in your introduction. What advantages do you imagine for your own work when you think about the option of a database in L2 acquisition research?

SW

I think the word *planning* here is a bit premature. As in the case of the agenda, the idea for a searchable database came about as part of the New Visions' *wish list* and was heartily seconded by a number of people in the weighted voting process of prioritization. Once we moved into the implementation discussion, however, it became clear that feasibility would present a problem. More recently, following the Research Task Force session at ACTFL in November 2002, several of us stood in the hallway and continued to brainstorm this idea of a database. One person pointed out that it seemed unnecessary, since ERIC already provided such a service (although even that resource seems to be in some jeopardy of late, given the current budgetary climate). Another suggested that a discipline-specific database might allow for a more user-friendly format, which might, in turn, help expand the foreign language education research community to include professionals who might not currently access ERIC. In order to find out what would indeed be *user-friendly*, it was suggested that non-researchers could be asked to help with the design.

ACTION

Try to use ERIC to find additional material for your study or teaching. If there would be a specifically designed research database, what should be different from ERIC? For more information about ERIC see the material section in this volume.

As for the impact of such a database on my own research, it's hard to say for sure, since it is still such a nebulous idea. I imagine that it would simply facilitate the job of inventorying work on a particular topic, making it faster to locate bibliographic information and helping to ensure that all relevant sources have been accounted for. Sounds rather idealized, though, doesn't it?

SD

A searchable database can make research available for everyone. What needs to be done to actually bridge the gap between research and classroom practice? How can teaching and learning benefit from research, when it seems already challenging for many teachers to keep up with research published in professional journals?

ACTION

What is holding you back from using publications about research more frequently? Interview your instructors or colleagues about how often they access research data in order to enhance their teaching.

SW

This question focuses on the *teacher end* of the disconnect, namely, that many teachers are out of touch with research, database or no database. Perhaps what needs to be done to bridge this part of the gap is to find out why. Is it an issue of time? Lack of incentives? Seeming irrelevance of the research? Challenges to finding and accessing the research? A combination of these factors? Other factors? (Some of these answers may point to the *research end* of the disconnect, as well.) Once we know the stumbling blocks we can begin to address them.

I can't help but think that one issue may be simply that the professional culture of teaching has not traditionally prioritized remaining current with research in the way that other professions with licensure standards have. In the medical field, for example, it is not necessary for all doctors to conduct research themselves; however, it is expected that all doctors keep up with the latest developments in their field. Likewise, lawyers and accountants must remain current with developments in the law. Teachers, on the other hand, are not required to keep abreast of current educational research in order to remain certified (although some choose to do so on their own). Professional development credits can be earned in ways that do not involve accessing research. Of course, if teachers were required to keep up with professional literature, then time and money would need to be adequate for them to do so. And if they are going to benefit from what they access, it would need to be applicable to their situation. Currently, relatively little research involves K-12 student-participants, and the transferability of research done with college students to the K-12 environment is questionable.

CONSIDER

What would have to be changed in your immediate teaching/learning environment to make it possible for you to access publications about research more often?

That said, I really do believe that more effective instruction happens in classrooms where the teacher has a vision that is broader than the pedagogical events that take place within his/her own four walls. Research has the potential to broaden that vision and, as such, can be a powerful and positive influence on teaching. It is worth our while to address the gap between teaching and research.

SD

A powerful database can help keep the state of knowledge up to date. This, on the other hand, can also mean a confrontation with an overwhelming amount of information, maybe too complex to be dealt with individually. In what way could research results be evaluated, summarized, and reflected so that tendencies would become visible also for teachers not being involved in research themselves?

SW

Maybe this is where the idea of teacher input in the design of a database could be the most helpful. The invention of the internet makes it possible for non-computer-science experts to design and maintain a web-based database, but it would involve a sizable investment of time, finances, and human resources to make it work. I can't imagine such a database coming to fruition in the foreseeable future.

ACTION

Make a list of aspects you would want to see being covered in a research database. What information about language acquisition and pedagogy would help you improve the quality of your professional work?

SD

You stated that the current academic reward system becomes a crucial motivation for individual effort in research. What impact does this *publish or perish* mentality have on the quality of research? What could be done to provide real incentives for researchers?

SW

Certainly, the research that is conducted and disseminated in our field is of varying quality. Whether the weaker publications are a result of pressure that post-secondary faculty may feel to add lines to their CV is not sure. Perhaps the need to publish also pushes some researchers to strive for excellence in order to ensure that their work will appear in print. To be sure, *publish or perish* is already a *real*, albeit extrinsic, incentive. If by *real* you mean *intrinsic*, then I'm not sure I have an answer to the question. By definition, one cannot provide intrinsic motivation to someone else. The *publish or perish* issue is not one that can easily be changed, since it is entrenched in an established institutional culture, which is much larger than just the foreign language teaching profession.

Whether it falls under the category of *incentives* or not, I do believe that we could improve both the quality and the quantity of research through a more established system of mentoring. Success breeds success, and newer researchers are more likely to be successful if they are able to work with an experienced mentor. Mentoring is built into doctoral programs in the form of dissertation advisors, but there is no equivalent system for pre-tenure faculty (who are most vulnerable to the *publish or perish* syndrome).

SD

You mentioned that L2 research needs to be in touch with the practitioners of the field in order to realize what research topics are actually relevant for classroom work. To what degree is it important that teachers themselves become researchers, as seen in English composition over the past three decades? And what do teachers need to know in order to become successful teachers-as-researchers?

SW

Some would say that empowering teachers to become researchers is the key to making research relevant to practitioners. There are certainly a number of success stories that support this view. The most common way that teachers become involved is through classroom-based action research, which is usually qualitative in nature. The challenge, as I see it, is to make sure that these projects adhere to the same standards for trustworthiness and credibility that any well designed qualitative investigation would. There is a danger that a teacher, who attends a 6-hour workshop on action research, will feel empowered enough to launch his or her own study without sufficient training and support. It is all too easy to draw faulty conclusions from faulty data and never realize the problem. Conducting solid research takes a lot of preparation and guided practice. I think it would be irresponsible to suggest that any teacher can successfully conduct action research without providing a substantial support mechanism to ensure the usefulness of the investigation.

CONSIDER

Think about ways you could find a mentor among university faculty to help you conduct your own classroom-based action research successfully.

That said, I think that both teachers and research mentors could benefit enormously from collaboration on teacher action-research projects. There is nothing like personal involvement for increasing the relevance of research, and the communication among colleagues working at K-12 and post-secondary levels could help to bridge a number of gaps, not just the one between research and practice.

SD
In the summer of 2002 the National K-12 Foreign Language Resource Center at Iowa State University sponsored a one-week Action Research Institute, where teachers developed their own research projects to be carried out during the following academic year. You mentioned that these teachers are being mentored. Assuming this mentorship is being done by college or university faculty, what motivation would these people have for such a service instead of investing their time into their own research?

SW
In this particular case, I believe that the faculty mentor(s) are actually conducting research on the experiences of these teachers as they become researchers, so this service is also research. Some senior faculty are also motivated to mentor others because they are committed to shaping the next generation of researchers and because they find the successes of their protégés personally rewarding. But you are right: mentoring is not currently part of the post-secondary reward structure.

SD
Many issues of classroom work are not just related to L2 education, but also to other subjects across the curriculum. Is there any large-scale collaboration in L2 research with other disciplines?

SW
Not to my knowledge, although I know that there are researchers from the larger field of education who collaborate with specialists in L2 acquisition on a smaller scale.

SD
In what way is international research on language learning available and considered in the US? What is the current perspective in the US on international research collaboration in the field of foreign and second language education?

SW
I'm not sure how representative my perspective is on this topic, but my sense is that researchers may access particular studies conducted outside of the US as they relate to a topic of interest but that, in general, the focus is on research that is widely disseminated in the US. My impression is that we are largely unaware of the research conducted in Europe or Asia, for example, unless it is published in journals that are common here. Certainly some areas of work (such as the research on speech acts, for example) enjoy a well established collaboration and communication among international colleagues, but such connections seem to be the exception rather than the norm.

In Conversation with Amy Snyder Ohta About Vygotsky's Zone of Proximal Development

Gerd Bräuer

Introduction

Looking at research and literature on learning and instruction, and at preferred topics for conferences and teacher training seminars, there seems to be an increasing interest in what Lev Vygotsky in 1978 first described as the *zone of proximal development* (ZPD).

In *Mind in Society: The Development of Higher Psychological Processes* (1978) Vygotsky defines the term as "the distance between the actual developmental level as determined by independent problem solving and the level of potential development as determined through problem solving under adult guidance or in collaboration with more capable peers" (86).

In other words, researchers and educators have become more interested in the difference between the actual and the possible level of performance of a learner. Some key questions related to this topic are: What is needed in terms of social interaction, in order to make education more effective? How can teachers and peers help a student to push her/his individual limits?

Amy Snyder Ohta, Associate Professor in the Department of Asian Languages and Literature at the University of Washington in Seattle, has done extensive research on the phenomenon of the ZPD in the realm of foreign language acquisition (Ohta 1995, 1997, 1999, 2000, 2001a, 2002b, 2002c, in press). Her focus has been to explore the concept in both its theoretical *and* practical potential for the field of foreign language education, particularly its role within social interaction in the process of language learning and instruction. In her book, *Second Language Acquisition in the Classroom: Learning Japanese* (Lawrence Erlbaum Associates 2001), she explores the role of the ZPD in language learning. Through a longitudinal study she investigated the classroom interaction of learners of Japanese: their acquisition of interactional style in the target language, the role of private speech and corrective feedback, assisted performance in interactive learning tasks, and the influence of the students' use of the native language on their language learning process.

The purpose of this conversation with Amy Snyder Ohta is to shed some light on the phenomenon of the ZPD and on how our current knowledge of the ZPD can be applied towards more effective practices in foreign language education.

Personal Motivation

Gerd Bräuer (GB)

Amy, what initially motivated you to start researching Vygotsky and his concept of the ZPD (I am assuming this was during your doctorate)? How did you find out about the ZPD and what prompted you to decide to make it a central part, not only of your dissertation, but also of your research and teaching?

Amy Snyder Ohta (ASO)

Actually, my interest in the ZPD emerged quite a bit after I finished my dissertation and had moved on to other studies. My dissertation was a study of teacher-talk in Japanese classrooms. I collected data by using a central microphone for the class, and one for the teacher. There was a lot of group work (mostly in pairs) in the classes where I collected my data, and during group work there was nothing recorded that was useful for analysis—just a roar! My dissertation explored questions of pragmatic development of the learners, but all I could look at was how learners responded to the teacher in teacher-fronted portions of the class. I decided that for future work I would need to get lots of tape recorders and microphones so I could mike the students and see what was happening in those groups. First I began looking at the pragmatics of learner language (Ohta 1997, 1999). That made me start moving toward thinking about the ZPD. What really got the ball rolling faster was getting involved with a research group led by Jim Lantolf whose members were all interested in applications of Vygotsky to L2 learning. At annual research meetings I learned from my colleagues and was exposed to a lot of interesting ideas that I followed up in reading and in my own research. The real clincher in terms of using the ZPD in my analyses, though, was that I found the ZPD everywhere in my data. Students in the classes where I collected data were consistently presented with developmentally appropriate challenges that they were guided to tackle through pair work tasks. I think that the pedagogical emphasis of the program where I collected data on the use of pair and group work for learning new structures and vocabulary made my data a rich resource for investigating the ZPD in classroom foreign language learning.

(GB)

Have the factors that contributed to your initial motivation to deal with issues of the ZPD in research, teacher training, and in your own L2 classrooms changed since you started your work in the field of applied linguistics? If so, how?

How has your own understanding of foreign language acquisition and your own classroom practice changed through your work with the ZPD?

(ASO)

My interest in the ZPD as a way of getting a handle on classroom foreign language learning has remained constant. If it has changed at all over time, I'd say that I'm becoming more and more aware of how the ZPD applies to a broader range of learning situations than I initially thought it did.

In terms of my own understanding of second language acquisition (SLA), I have come to believe (though I think this is the first place that I'm talking about this) that some people seek out developmentally appropriate challenges more than others, and therefore find themselves *in the zone*, so to speak, more often than others. In my longitudinal data, there were big differences in how different students handled interaction with their peers, whether they sought to minimize tasks or whether they milked them to get as much as they could out of them. Those with the latter approach found themselves in the ZPD much more often.

As a language teacher and teacher trainer, my understanding of the ZPD has transformed both my teaching and how I mentor new teachers. I design my language teaching around the particular challenges I want students to be able to grapple with, building backwards from those in designing lessons. And, in teacher training, I work to help my trainees realize that class isn't just a chunk of time you have to fill up, but is an opportunity to maximize the L2 development of students in a meaningful way by designing developmentally appropriate challenges for them, and mentoring students through those challenges by answering their questions and providing good guidance.

Defining the Zone of Proximal Development (ZPD)

(GB)
Vygotsky's definition suggests the *zone of proximal development* is located between the learner's developmental level and his/her level of potential development. How can teachers recognize/define these levels in their daily classroom practice?

(ASO)
To me, this is quite simple. What can students do on their own? What kinds of utterances can they formulate with ease? What kinds of situations can they face with little difficulty? If we design classroom tasks around these, students will learn very little. In fact, when I attend conferences I occasionally attend a presentation where the researcher says there weren't any ZPDs in the data and questions the veracity of the ZPD. When I ask whether the task was challenging enough that students really needed to work with another person, the researcher is either flummoxed by the question or says the task was similar to things students were asked to do individually or admits that it was easy for them.

So, finding a developmentally appropriate challenge is key. But there is another thing that is important; that is providing the needed support. I think that there is a tendency in foreign language teaching in the US today for teachers to take a sort of non-interventionist approach to group work. They present the task and send students on their way, but during the process of the group work they don't want to interfere in any way. Many language teachers in the States are trained to do this—to stay on the sidelines during group work. But the teacher's *interference* is exactly what the ZPD tells us students need. They need developmentally appropriate support. Students are wonderful at providing that for each other, but they can't always do so, and need the teacher's helping hand and expertise along the way. In my data, students benefited tremendously from teacher intervention during pair and group tasks, and from direct teacher answers to student questions. In contrast, in classes where the teacher stayed at the front of the room and left students to their own devices, there was much more of a tendency for students to get bogged down in an unproductive sort of way.

(GB)
James Moffett, one of the most important curriculum developers in English during the last thirty years, has applied Vygotsky's notion of interpersonal and intrapersonal knowledge acquisition to the field of writing pedagogy. He sees the development of a child's writing as fostered through an interplay of what he calls interior and vocal dialogue (47). In this regard, he argues for "more realistic communication, dramas in which the student can practice being a first and second person (in writing—G.B) with better motivation..." He suggests letting the student write "for the class group, which is the nearest thing to a contemporary world-at-large; accustomizing him (the student—G.B.) to having his themes read and discussed workshop fashion...It is amazing how so-called writing problems clear up when the student really cares, when he is realistically put into the drama of somebody with something to say to somebody else" (12).

What is your opinion on what seems to be a *catch twenty-two* between the ZPD and learner motivation? To what extent is learner motivation initially needed in order to make use of the zone of proximal development, and how much influence can the emergence of the ZPD have on individual learning motivation?

(ASO)
L2 researchers working with Vygotskian and neo-Vygotskian thought might ask *What is motivation?* While most applied linguists probably think of motivation as something inside the head, for those who think about language learning in a more sociocultural way there is a tendency to consider motivation as activity. When one looks at motivation that way, then it is clear that without it learning is difficult—activity is necessary for learning, whether that activity is mental (like the interior dialogue you referred to) or interpersonal. I believe that the emergence of the ZPD has the effect of heightening involvement in the activity at hand. Seeing results, especially the result of being able to do something one could not do before, has a powerful effect, in my opinion.

Adapting the Concept of ZPD to L2 Education

(GB)
You have long been working on the ZPD phenomenon in the area of foreign language acquisition and, among other accomplishments, have adapted Vygotsky's original definition of the ZPD. You did so in an article in 1995 and in your own book in 2001. How is your definition different from what Vygotsky suggested, and what influenced these adjustments? In addition, please comment on the longitudinal study of learners

of Japanese which your book was based on. What did you find out about the impact of social interaction on individual zones of proximal development?

(ASO)

Rather than being a different definition, I think these tweakings of Vygotsky's definition help us to see better how his idea of learning as resulting from assisted performance applies to foreign language learning. Vygotsky was thinking of children when he wrote about the ZPD. He considered the providers of assistance to be more capable peers or adults. In my research (as in research in other learning contexts besides foreign language), I have found that true peers are effective helpers. And, I have been considering how other sorts of assistance can also support learning. In addition, I use linguistic criteria to investigate development since what I am looking at is language learning. I see ZPDs emerging through a microgenetic analysis of learner discourse, where Vygotsky and his students looked at children's behavior.

(GB)

Vygotsky (1987) argues for a kind of instruction in the classroom that challenges the actual stage of development of the learner. According to Vygotsky, this challenge "impels or wakens a whole series of functions that are in a stage of maturation lying in the zone of proximal development" (212). What happens when instruction moves ahead of the current developmental stage of the foreign language student?

(ASO)

Language learning! Language learners have many things they can't quite do, or are on the brink of becoming able to do, or that they need a bit more help or practice with. By moving beyond established abilities to these things that are lying in wait, we can help students to move ahead. If we just stick with what is already developed, we can't expect much progress. Vygotsky considered the ZPD as the place where higher mental functions develop. For example, in talking about his general genetic law of cultural development he mentions things like *logical memory* and *voluntary attention* as examples of functions which develop between people prior to becoming mental functions (Vygotsky 163). Foreign language learners already have well developed higher mental functions in the L1, but need to learn to develop cognition in a different language. And all of the functions needed to do that mature over time, moving from being things that a learner can only do with assistance to things that the learner can do independently. Well designed instruction moves ahead of students' developed abilities, leading students to develop further through, for example, peer activities and homework that combine developmentally appropriate challenges with support.

(GB)

Why should foreign language teachers become acquainted with the phenomenon of the ZPD?

(ASO)
The ZPD helps to understand how to use instruction to lead development forward, and prompts deeper thinking on how to maximize pair or group work to benefit student learning. I think that an understanding of the ZPD also helps teachers to have a deeper understanding of the role of instruction and of how teaching materials—whether those used in class or for home use—can be designed to support learner development.

(GB)
In your opinion, what do teachers need to know about the theoretical framework of the ZPD mentioned above, in order to foster the emergence of the *zone of proximal development* for individual students in a class?

(ASO)
To be honest, I think that for teachers what is most important isn't the theory, but is the balance between developmentally appropriate challenges and support that occurs in good teaching practice.

Practical Implications for Foreign Language Teachers

(GB)
In addition to the theoretical background mentioned above, what practical implications does the *zone of proximal development* have for foreign language professionals? In other words, how can teachers appropriately challenge and support students with regard to developmental levels?

(ASO)
The practical implications of the ZPD, in my opinion, come down to the importance of task design and implementation in foreign language teaching. Task design shapes what it is that students do in the classroom. For language acquisition to occur, students need opportunities to interact in the language—tasks are critical in providing a place for students to do that. But students (even well motivated college students!) won't necessarily interact in the L2 if they don't need to do it in order to complete the task. So well designed tasks promote L2 interaction. And tasks can also be designed to focus students on a particular area of weakness where the teacher knows growth is needed. Support is also an important part of the ZPD. Teachers need to be ready to provide appropriate support, whether, for example, via information on the blackboard, a helping hand at the right time, or differential information provided to different pair or group members. I think task design is so important that I devoted most of a chapter to talking about this topic (Ohta 2001, Chapter 6).

(GB)
We all know about learner diversity, differences in personal backgrounds, actual levels of development and intellectual potential. How can teachers stimulate the ZPD, (as just mentioned in your last answer), and still meet individual differences in the classroom?

(ASO)

One thing I've found that works well at the college level is to let students work with self-formed pairs or groups. Students tend to pair up with students who have a similar level of engagement in the course, and complementary L2 backgrounds. This allows the interaction in pairs and groups to be tailored to each student's level. Also, at the college level I've found it is important for teachers to directly answer questions that emerge from group work, and not to re-direct student questions back to the students for them to try to answer. The college students in my data only asked questions when they already had been unsuccessful in finding a solution themselves.

(GB)

In your previous work you have shown how dyadic and small group work can trigger individual zones of proximal development. Could you please summarize how this emergence of the ZPD happens, and what context needs to be provided by the teacher in order to make it happen?

(ASO)

The teacher needs to provide a well-designed task that presents a developmentally appropriate challenge to students and which is designed such that the L2 must be used in order to do the task. Interview tasks and mini-conversation types of tasks work well. The ZPD emerges as students enable each other to do what they cannot do as individuals, pitching in and helping one another by chiming in, prompting, waiting, and a variety of other strategies. The teacher needs to make the task clear to students by doing a demonstration or providing an explanation, and needs to include provision for support.

(GB)

Direct assistance through teacher or peers is not always available. To what extent can learning materials alone bridge the gap between actual and potential levels of development? Are there any necessary *ingredients* for ZPD-appropriate learning materials?

(ASO)

Learning materials can go far in providing support—for example, they can list words or expressions that might be useful for a task, show a grammatical pattern that the teacher knows is going to present difficulty, or guide students in doing dictionary work. I know that grammar-oriented teaching these days has been panned by a number of L2 researchers, but grammar-oriented teaching is absolutely necessary when students are being taught languages radically different from the students' first language. Grammar provides important tools for linguistic expression and I don't think teachers should be shy about pointing students towards tools useful for the task at hand. That means that grammar explanations and reference materials provide useful support that can help ZPDs to emerge. And some people may think that the ZPD can only be applied to small group learning situations where a teacher or peer can interact face-to-face. I don't think that's true. I've found an understanding of the ZPD helps me to design and deliver lectures in the linguistics classes I teach. I ask myself how my lecture can assist students in moving from where they are to another level of thinking about language or linguistics or culture. The ZPD helps me to conceptualize the interactional space created between me as lecturer and my students as they mentally interact with me in that space.

(GB)

As Newman and Holzman (1993) point out, Vygotsky's notion of the ZPD is not primarily concerned with the acquisition of skills or content knowledge, but with the cognitive development of the learner when being challenged by tasks and/or instruction. What does this obvious focus on the learning process mean for teachers in regard to classroom work, especially assessment and evaluation?

(ASO)

Here I have to say, "Yes, but..." You're right that Vygotsky's concern was cognitive development. BUT, as a foreign language professional my concern is cognitive development in the L2. Our L2 learners need to use new linguistic tools to think and to communicate, and our job is to help them to do that. That involves developing skills and content knowledge. With development in these areas, cognitive development also occurs. We cannot separate *cognitive development* from *skill acquisition* and *content knowledge*. Each new task students are able to perform pushes cognitive development forward as they learn new L2 skills and learn more about the L2 and target culture.

Practical Implications for Foreign Language Teaching Methodology

(GB)

From my own teaching experience, I find the project method in foreign language classes, as practiced by Dierk Hoffmann and others in this volume, can be an effective way of setting challenges and appropriate forms of assistance. Within a project group, students divide the main task into smaller units. By working on his/her personal unit, each participant provides a unique perspective on the main problem to be solved, and along the way receives feedback from other team members.

(ASO)

I haven't done any research on project work, but in my opinion it can certainly be useful if projects are designed with students developed abilities and developing skills in mind. The danger with project work for foreign language teaching that I've seen is the tendency to assign projects (or for students to try to tackle projects) that are so far beyond the students' L2 ability that they end up using the L1 to do most of the project. So, with project work, as with any other sort of teaching material, teachers need to be sensitive to students developmental levels, assist them in choosing projects that have an appropriate level of challenge, and provide an appropriate level of support to students to help them to meet those challenges.

(GB)
In your research on students in Japanese foreign language classes you observed learners pool their knowledge, and in this way challenge themselves to overcome their actual level of development.

Do you agree that assistance in learning doesn't necessarily have to come from *more capable peers* or from the teacher, as found in Vygotsky's the ZPD definition, but can also have its root in what Donato (1994) calls *collective scaffolding*? What goes on when pairs of learners accomplish tasks that neither of the partners could have done alone?

(ASO)
Absolutely, but it goes beyond collective scaffolding, which involves students contributing different bits of knowledge based on students' differential knowledge or their different levels of L2 ability. Assistance also emerges from the fact that the very process of interaction necessitates different interactional roles (*speaker* and *listener*): Listeners have cognitive resources available that speakers, who are occupied with speaking, do not. Listeners are capable, therefore, of accessing information and using it to help their speaking partner. And, when the listener becomes speaker, the partner then can help in return! I talk about this process quite a bit in the chapter in my book on the ZPD (Ohta 2001, Chapter 3).

(GB)
I mentioned earlier the work of James Moffett. He supplied arguments for the productive intertwining of personal writing and the writing for an audience. In this dance between the private and the socialized functions of writing, Janet Emig (1983) sees a specific *mode of learning* that has further been developed for peer feedback in writing conferences (see Gillespie & Lerner 2000). Here it seems it is the *lack of understanding* that helps the ZPD to emerge; the reader who doesn't understand what has been written. By asking the writer what he or she wanted to say, the reader seems to provide that bit of help, which is sometimes necessary in learning processes to finally internalize knowledge and make it usable. I would say that this approach to peer work (Gillespie calls it minimalist tutoring) is making perfect use of the ZPD. What is your own experience with the effectiveness of peer work for learning processes?

(ASO)
I think peers can do a lot of language learning together. I don't have any experience with peer tutoring in foreign language teaching—rather, my experience is with seeing what happens when peers work together doing interactive tasks in the foreign language being learned. And, I've seen good things happen there! For example, learners prompt each other, chime in with needed vocabulary, and wait for each other to produce utterances (with more patience than any teacher I've ever seen). And they ask the teacher for help not only for themselves, when they need it, but on behalf of their partners. In my research, I see again and again how students who say very little in front of the teacher will use a lot of language with their peers, and become more accurate and develop more complex utterances while doing that.

(GB)
Do you agree that modes of reflective practice, such as learning logs and portfolios, can help the learner keep track of the changes within his/her own *zone of proximal development*, by documenting what has been worked with, learned, maybe not yet understood? In what way, can reflective practice also help construct this dialogue between inner and socialized speech and, as such, become a seismograph for cognitive development?

(ASO)
This is an interesting idea. My research has all been with learners of fairly low proficiency. I'd be interested in seeing how this could be applied in that sort of setting. Most of the work I'm familiar with on the topic of reflective practice relates to students with stronger language proficiency. In terms of my own research, I can't really say anything about how these methods impact language learning. Theoretically, it makes good sense that learning occurs through interpersonal and intrapersonal dialogue. For language acquisition we call this sort of thing hypothesis testing. Students try out their linguistic hunches on the social stage, and then reflect upon the results of that.

(GB)
In this book, reflective practice is an important focus. Indeed, aspects of critical inquiry run through most parts of foreign language education being discussed here. How do you see the use of teaching logs, as well as professional portfolios, as instruments to detect and use zones of proximal development in the classroom? What consequences do you see of this for pre and in-service training of foreign language teachers?

(ASO)
I think that for pre- and in-service teachers to apply the ZPD, they need to learn about it and then design tasks for their classes, whatever the subject, that will work to push students ahead with the subject matter. With foreign language learning, I've found that if the teacher's goal is to help students interact in the L2, tasks must be organized to require this. And tasks must be meaningful and interesting from the students' points of view. That doesn't mean that all tasks have to be communicative; if students need to learn some new grammar, there's nothing wrong, in my opinion, with having students do drills together, moving toward communicative practice. (And teacher-led drills can also provide students with needed support). While I know that many of my colleagues in second language teaching work to avoid grammar-focused practice, with English speaking learners of Japanese, we need to do mechanical and communicative drills before getting to genuine communicative practice, since students don't get any real support from their first language in learning Japanese. I have done most of my learning about the ZPD by looking at what really happens in classrooms when students do L2 tasks together. I think that teachers can learn a lot by circulating in their classrooms during peer interaction to see what's happening, or by having a student or two wear a microphone so that they can listen in later. Through this pro-

cess, teachers can learn what works and what doesn't for their particular students. One thing great about being a teacher is how much we can learn while teaching that improves our ability to respond to student needs and improve instruction.

References

Donato, R. "Collective Scaffolding in Second Language Learning." *Vygotskian Approaches to Second Language Research*. Ed. J. P. Lantolf and G. Appel. Norwood: Ablex, 1994. 33-56.

Emig, J. *The Web of Meaning: Essays on Writing, Teaching, Learning, and Thinking*. Portsmouth: Heinemann, 1983.

Gillespie, P., and N. Lerner. *Peer Tutoring*. Boston: Allyn and Bacon, 2000.

Moffett, J. *Teaching the Universe of Discourse* . Portsmouth: Heinemann, 1983.

Newman, F., and L. Holzman. *Lev Vygotsky: Revolutionary Scientist*. New York: Routledge, 1993.

Ohta, Amy Snyder, and Tomoko Nakaone. "When Students Ask Language-Related Questions: Student Questions and Their Answers in Teacher-Fronted and Group Work Classroom Interaction."

Ohta, Amy Snyder. "Japanese Second Language Acquisition in the Classroom: What the Voices of Teachers and Students Tell us About the Process of Learning Japanese." *Advances in Japanese Pedagogy*. Ed. Hiroshi Nara. Columbus: National Foreign Language Center, Ohio State University, 2002.

——. *Second Language Acquisition Processes in the Classroom: Learning Japanese*. Mahwah: Lawrence Erlbaum Associates, 2001a.

——. "From Acknowledgment to Alignment: A Longitudinal Study of the Development of Expression of Alignment by Classroom Learners of Japanese." *Pragmatics in Language Teaching*. Ed. G. Kasper and K. Rose. Cambridge: Cambridge UP, 2001b.

——. "Re-thinking Interaction in SLA: Developmentally Appropriate Assistance in the Zone of Proximal Development and the Acquisition of L2 Grammar." *Sociocultural Theory and Second Language Learning*. Ed. J. P. Lantolf. Oxford: Oxford UP, 2001c. 51-78.

——. "Re-thinking Recasts: A Learner-Centered Examination of Corrective Feedback in the Japanese Language Classroom." *The Construction of Second and Foreign Language Learning through Classroom Interaction*. Ed. J. K. Hall and L. Verplaeste. Mahwah: Lawrence Erlbaum Associates, 2000. 47-71.

——. "Interactional Routines and the Socialization of Interactional Style in Adult Learners of Japanese." *Journal of Pragmatics 31* (1999): 1493-1512.

——. "The Development of Pragmatic Competence in Learner-Learner Interaction." *Pragmatics and Language Learning*. Ed. L. Bouton. Vol. 8. Urbana-Champaign: University of Illinois, 1997. 223-242.

——. "Applying Sociocultural Theory to an Analysis of Learner Discourse: Learner-Learner Collaborative Interaction in the Zone of Proximal Development." *Issues in Applied Linguistics* 6.2 (1995): 93-121.

——. "Socializing the Expression of Affect: An Overview of Affective Particle Use in the Japanese as a Foreign Language Classroom." *Issues in Applied Linguistics* 5.2 (1994): 303-326.

——. "Evidentiality and Politeness in Japanese." *Issues in Applied Linguistics* 2.2 (1991): 211-238.

Vygotsky, L. S. "The Genesis of Higher Mental Functions." *The Concept of Activity in Soviet Psychology* Ed. J.V. Wertsch. Armonk: Sharpe, 1981. 147-188.

——. "Thinking and Speech." *The Collected Works of L. S. Vygotsky*. Ed. Robert W. Rieber and Aaron S. Carton. Vol. 1. New York: Plenum Press, 1987.
——. *Mind in Society: The Development of Higher Psychological Processes*. Cambridge: Harvard UP, 1978.

Promoting Action Research

Lee Wilberschied

Introduction

It takes time to integrate the goals and values of New Visions into one's daily practice and operation. Yet that integration will be what makes the visions into realities. Recently, I did a less than adequate task of integrating these goals when talking with an enrolling student. A teacher returning to the university for courses for further credentials, she felt powerless to initiate changes in policy regarding language learners in her district. "How can I convince them [the administrators] that what they are doing is ineffective?" she asked. We both knew from previous experience that, despite our construction of reports containing results of meticulous research, practitioners in some systems often fail to convince boards or administrations that certain policies are inappropriate. I did, however, answer this colleague unhesitatingly, "Data. Research. But data that is specific to the district, consistently repeated, and systematically documented and interpreted." She thanked me and left to fill out her application forms.

By simply naming the tool and not discussing it, I had stopped too early in my beginning description of action research and thus missed an opportunity to ignite the interest of one more educator. Mine was a glib response, which, during this my own reflection, may have been appropriate for the context, since time was then limited. In order to be true to my own reflective practice, I will contact this colleague with some ideas on how she might undertake action research independently or in collaboration, either with me or with other teachers in our courses.

This authentic vignette illustrates two of perhaps the greater challenges for promulgators of the New Visions: integrating the theory with our own daily practice, and engendering the courage to politicize action research. Action research is a righteous tool for empowering one's own classroom practice, but it requires courage to teach it well and to practice it as a political tool. A third question must inquire how the results of the research will help to build formal theory.

DISCUSS

It is always a challenge to integrate theory with daily practice. Discuss ways of integrating the theory of action research into a daily classroom routine.

Burns (1999) noted that action research, as originally proposed by Kurt Lewin, was intended to be collaborative because group action encouraged empowerment and emancipation for the participants. Implicit in this description are the questions: "Empowerment for what? Emancipation from what?" Individual teachers may empower their own pedagogy and may have been researching intuitively in this manner for many years, but as van Lier (1996) observed, problem-solving is a component of action research but does not equate with it.

To go beyond one's classroom into collaborative inquiry is another stage of growth in this research methodology. To politicize one's action research is yet another possible outgrowth. Van Lier (1996) warned that one may begin an action research process in order to deal with what seems to be a limited problem lacking further implication. It may, however, impel the researcher to move from the technical to the critical realm and perhaps beyond, into issues of educational policy and infrastructure. He conceptualized action research as residing at the interstices of two dichotomies that are mediated by research—one between practice and theory, and one between the technical and the critical. The aim of both this volume and the New Visions task force is to bridge such dichotomies, to facilitate, as van Lier asserted, the existence of theory/practice and improvement/knowledge as "an organic unity in teacher research" (220).

Definitions of Action Research

Action research by practitioners entered language teacher education as a way to reduce the perceived gulf between research and practice (Freeman 1998) and to promote teachers' reasoning and reflection on their work in the classroom (Freeman & Richards 1996; Richards & Lockhart 1994). Action research requires teachers to systematize what they do naturally in classroom teaching situations when faced with a problem or dilemma: Ask relevant questions; devise a plan; collect, analyze, and take conclusions from the data; determine and implement an appropriate course of action; evaluate the results; and resume the cycle. It is a critical, reflective process (Burns 1999; Freeman 1998; Wallace 1998).

NOTE

Action research can help you build on your strengths and identify your weaknesses as a professional educator.

Allwright and Bailey (1991) contrasted action research to experimental research and to naturalistic inquiry. Experimental research implies high control over variables along with intervention; naturalistic inquiry most commonly lacks control and intervention. Action research, however, does presume intervention, but with a low degree of control, because the procedure is often one of taking an action and observing systematically the consequences. This approach requires participatory research, self-reflection, and collaboration (41-44).

Bailey, Curtis, and Nunan (2001) noted that such participatory research is carried out by stakeholders who are perhaps in the best position to develop solutions, improvements, and insights. This type of research differs from experimental research in which the investigator remains distanced from the subjects or clients. As Osborn (2000) noted, "Action researchers, among others, abandon the pretense of neutrality, choosing instead to focus on research results that are trustworthy" (122).

That is, the research must have credibility, and must be communicated in such a manner that the audience can also apply it and validate the findings. Thus, classroom action research incorporates a number of repeated, cyclical steps (Bailey, Curtis, & Nunan 2001; van Lier 1996; Wallace 1998). The aspects of the cycle (initial definition of a problem, preliminary inquiry, reflection, hypothesis, planning, intervention, observation, data collection, data analysis/reflection, revision of intervention, and so on) often are not clear-cut. Bailey, Curtis, and Nunan (2001) pointed out that it is sometimes impossible to distinguish one phase of the process from the one preceding or following it. For instance, reflection would ideally occur at all stages, and the preliminary inquiry may actually be continual.

The purpose and practice of action research move along a continuum, from individual research carried out for individual, professional purposes, to collaborative research across disciplines for improvement of praxis, to politicized research for support for change in consciousness and improvement of infrastructure and delivery of services. Osborn (2000) advocated such support through dialogue at professional conferences in presentations of teachers' action research. He said that in order for such research to bridge gaps between theory and practice, the classroom culture must frame and engender that research. He further advocated what he conceptualizes as *critical action research*, because it would be a tool for language educators at their level and in their environment. He discussed the notion that cultural power often implies economic and political power, and this reality should drive the focus of critical action research. The focus, he recommended, should be on three areas—the implicit or explicit (and thus economic and political) struggles within language program and practice; the illustration of cultural struggle for students; and how "praxis can challenge consent in the hegemonic relationships" supporting the struggles (122).

Illustrating the Benefits and Constraints

Burns (1999) discussed several advantages for teachers who conduct action research engaging closely with their own practice: self-awareness and personal insight; better understanding of the institutional climate; ability to contribute to institutional solutions; and acting with the authority of professional *knowers* rather than as the recipients (14-18). Further benefits would include a decreasing sense of isolation and enrichment of content and delivery.

Bailey, Curtis, and Nunan (2001) discussed five difficulties that teachers might face in attempting to carry out their research:

DISCUSS

Choose two of the five difficulties listed here by the author. Discuss possible strategies to address these issues.

- Administrative withholding of time or support to do the research, or lack of recognition for the accomplishment.
- Administrative undermining of the project.
- Criticism or subversion from peers.
- Detraction from or interference with teaching duties.
- Lack of technical skills to implement research.

This last impediment may be intensified by further constraints extended by the system's privacy regulations or the Internal Review Boards of institutions at which the teachers are studying (Wilberschied, Bauer, Jenkins, &Varghese, in review). Additionally, because there are varying notions regarding the generalizability of the results of such research (see, for instance, Wallace 1998; Bailey, Curtis, & Nunan 2001), the value of the research may be perceived as limited strictly to the teacher. Gebhard and Oprandy (1999) noted that action research itself may become a constraint if the individual chooses to focus solely on problem-solving, rather than increasing awareness through the exploration of many aspects of teaching.

Related to the first difficulty are disparities in role perception that may create a glass ceiling for the practitioner in his/her role as researcher. Osborn said:

> Classroom management issues may play a larger role in the maintenance of grammar syllabi than realized, since grammar lends itself well to worksheets and seatwork. Though grammar may not be the most beneficial in terms of language learning, it does assist the teachers in their roles as behavior managers. This role is increasingly the one teachers are pressured to take. (121-122)

Showing the Potential of Wide-Scale Training in Action Research—Increased Collaboration, Interdisciplinarity, and Professionalism

Research in professional development has called for systemic reform (Little 1993). It is necessary to view professional development as a way to improve the specific skills of teachers and personnel while improving the conditions in their particular environment. McLaughlin and Oberman (1996) asserted that teachers must work together to form a community of practice. Nevertheless, many professional development programs have only limited success because they adopt a top-down approach through once-only workshops that impart information (Clair 1998). They are often unsuccessful because programs are often instigated in contexts characterized by a lack of problem solving, networking, support, collegiality, and lack of mentoring (Little 1993). In addition, recent emphasis on accountability may promote teachers' sense of powerlessness and lack of efficacy as they are increasingly required to respond to top-down mandates for standardized testing (Benveniste 1985, cited in Clair 1998).

CONSIDER

Reflect on your own professional development experiences. How do you judge whether they are successful?

Yet the Draft of *Program Standards for Foreign Language Teacher Preparation* (ACTFL 2001), need not fall into the category of such mandates. Creation of standards could be viewed as a top-down tactic, an attempt to legislate change that could be met with adherence to the letter of, rather than the spirit of, the law. A contrasting view is that teacher education programs may implement such standards while molding further generations of teachers who are creators of knowledge rather than consumers of knowledge, and who will teach their students from a similar perspective. In that regard, several standards and specific items indicate that promoting action research is a means to meet and/or enhance several of the standards items. Several examples follow. The Standard and required are first indicated; then, a brief discussion of the relevance of action research follows.

2 C Integrating Other Disciplines in Instruction:

> *Planning for cross-disciplinary instruction*: Candidates collaborate with colleagues to connect language and other subject areas and locate authentic resources appropriate to age, grade level, program goals, and interests of their students.
>
> *Dispositions for integrating other subject areas into language instruction*: Candidates integrate subject-area content, locate authentic resources, and are willing to learn new content with students.

In teacher education or in professional development, this integration would provide the opportunity for collaborative action research among colleagues who teach different languages or different content areas in the same school. Just as importantly, it would encourage collaboration among colleagues in other schools in the same district or state, and in other states and/or countries.

4 B Integrating Standards in Instruction:

> Candidates integrate the *Standards for Foreign Language Learning* into language instruction.
>
> *Connections to other subject areas:* Candidates plan and design opportunities for their students to learn about other subject areas in the foreign language. They may collaborate with colleagues from other subject areas.
>
> *Connections to target-language communities:* Candidates provide opportunities for their students to connect to target-language communities through a variety of means such as technology and authentic materials.

The same opportunities as in 2C exist here. In addition, for this Standard and 2C, technological communities could be formed. Technology acts as a tool but also as a research focus, because it provides authentic material as well as many questions about the effective use of that tool, as an area for action research.

6A Engaging in Professional Development:

> Candidates engage in professional development opportunities that strengthen their own linguistic and cultural competence and promote reflection on practice.
>
> *Lifelong commitment to professional growth*: Candidates identify immediate professional development needs and a potential source of support.

> *Reflection as a critical tool for growth*: Candidates begin to frame their own reflection questions and show evidence of engaging in a reflective process to improve teaching and learning.

Pre-service and in-service action research projects help to refine professional development questions as well as to provide means for answering them and contributing to a greater body of knowledge, either in a small collaborative group or on a nationwide or international scale.

6 B Knowing the Value of Foreign Language Learning:

> Candidates know the value of foreign language learning to the overall success of all students and understand that they will need to become advocates with students, colleagues, and members of the community to promote the field.
>
> *The importance of building alliances for advocacy*: Candidates provide evidence of understanding the importance of building alliances to advocate for foreign language learning.
>
> Candidates use the results of empirical research to refine questions about their own action research in their advocacy.

Additional alliances with colleagues and community provide further resources and opportunities for research. Strengthening such alliances increases resources for advocacy. The *New Visions Research Issues* paper says: "research can be the catalyst that will bring the various cultures represented in our field together to build a community of inquiry composed of our many voices." This document also lists proposals for creating such a research community, including the establishment of "a national database of pre-K-16+ practitioners who are willing to participate in action-based research." In reality, such a database could be global, rather than national. Further proposed actions included increased emphasis on making research more readable for the average classroom teacher and enhancing the research activity of K-12 educators by several means, including the following:

- Providing preservice/inservice development in how to read and conduct action research.
- Rewarding K-12 teachers for reading about and engaging in action research.
- Establishing and publicizing action research guidelines.
- Asking K-12 teachers to establish research areas, issues and questions, to be completed by post-secondary faculty.

Both the *Draft of Program Standards for Foreign Language Teacher Preparation* as well as the goals of the *Research Strand of New Visions* make provisions for wider scale training in action research, and these measure will help to increase collaboration, interdisciplinarity, and professionalism.

Implications: Facilitating and Extending the Implementation of Action Research

Wilhelm (1997) described the initial resistance that typifies the reaction of many teachers (both pre-service and in-service) upon being introduced to unfamiliar paradigms. Van Lier (1996) said that classroom research is probably most difficult because of the energy, concentration, focus, time, and effort required of the teacher. From these descriptions and others (Wilberschied, Bauer, Jenkins, & Varghese, under review) it becomes clear that engendering action research must go beyond guidance, provision of venues, facilitation, and even rewards. In many cases, teacher educators and other language professionals will need to be courageous and persistent, to inspire passion for inquiry, or, at the very least, to provide credible substantiation that such research is vital for change in praxis, policy, and infrastructure. But how does that translate into practical, behavioral terms?

Impetus: Grassroots, Collaborative Implementation

Not everyone will agree or acknowledge that "to teach a second or foreign language is a political act" (Dr. M. Benedetti, personal communication, October 1998). Thus, not everyone will find action research a valuable tool in critical thought or as a basis for political action. The elegance of this type of research tool is in its versatility. However, if teacher educators are to make pre-service and in-service teachers aware of the potential of action research, we must be willing to put it forth in authentic ways, by modeling, collaborating, mentoring, and inspiring. Along with the other elements of the New Visions initiative, we will have to make this tool a part of our *modus operandi.* As van Lier (1996) proposed, action research is a manner of working rather than a project with a perceivable conclusion. This stance involves continuing to take personal and professional responsibility for reform. Each one of this will do this, to some degree, in a way that suits one's individuality. All of us, however, will continue to collaborate, which is the thrust of the New Visions initiative.

DISCUSS

Throughout this article the author argues that expanded collaboration is a key factor in facilitating the implementation of action research-based practice. Discuss *who* should be included in this collaborative effort and what each group brings to the table.

Both as individuals and collectively as we are able, we are undertaking or preparing to undertake some or many of the following actions.

- Introduce critical examination of issues in language learning at every stage of the professionalization process. This endeavor will go beyond articulation. It would require integration into curricula and instruction in pre-service and in-service instruction (Osborn 2000).
- Involve more classroom teacher colleagues in team-teaching or guest teaching or co-supervising action research projects in field or methods courses. In fact, graduates of previous courses could mentor current investigators. Osborn (2000) supported Goodlad's (1994) simultaneous renewal in regard to language education and a refocus of teacher education programs. He urged the formation of research teams in which both theorists and practitioners could begin to bridge the chasm between research and practice. He said that such teams would have to study language in the community as well as the "interrelationships

between language in US society and language education in the schools" (120).

- Combine action research projects with training in grant writing, in order to illustrate that research brings rewards.
- Seek funding for awards for outstanding action research and for exemplary collaboration at the local, state, national, and international levels.
- Promote and/or facilitate on-site teaching of professional development courses in action research, to alleviate the drain on energy and resources of classroom teachers. Distance learning arrangements are often helpful and even essential when working with non-local or international colleagues.
- Promote interdisciplinary, intercultural, bilingual, international projects to enlarge teachers' perspective. Such projects can also provide the context for collaborative action research (Benedetti & Wilberschied, in review).
- Provide opportunities for teachers to look outside of the classroom and into the community that houses that classroom, to examine the contexts in which they are teaching. Service learning assignments can introduce students to guided reflection and pave the way for action research.
- Promote action research as a partial requirement for tenure. Some local school systems require the completion of professional growth projects as a condition for earning tenure. Some systems require such projects every two years after tenure is awarded. Members of the administration supervise the project in some cases; in others, a peer mentor facilitates the process.

CONSIDER

Look at these many different ways in which we, both individually and/or collectively, can take action. Provide your own examples of taking action in regard to better foreign language education, and discuss whether they were successful.

Other endeavors will emerge, depending on the situation and the need, but the intent is to outline some of the ways in which teacher educators can promote the New Visions research initiative.

Conclusion—Contextualizing Action Research into Overall Research Goals

Post-secondary researchers will probably have to attain and go beyond the previously described recommendations of training and rewarding practitioners. Means of integrating the collaborative wisdom of pre-K-16+ will probably include the widespread valuing of action research by those who teach it and as well as those who implement it. In addition, the context for bridging any gaps in academic discourse between research and classroom practice will have to continue to expand globally.

Expanding the boundaries of collaboration to include varied levels and contexts has begun, more recently with the 2002 New Visions sponsored Summer Institute. This institute, held at the National Foreign Language Resource Center of Iowa State University, invited experienced and practicing teacher educators and practicing K-12 teachers to explore issues regarding action research, including the following:

- The nature, uses, and benefits of action research.
- The research tools; cross-disciplinary projects.
- Foreign language education projects.
- Identification of personal research questions and action plans.
- Formation of research teams that include both classroom teachers and teacher educators.

Thus, New Visions in Action carries promise, with continued effort focused on the stated goals, regular assessment of its efforts, and wide scale reporting of results. This mode of operation, with collaboration among levels, cultures, and contexts, provides a wide-scale demonstration of what it is like to implement action research as a practice rather than a project.

References

American Council on the Teaching of Foreign Languages (ACTFL). *Program Standards for Foreign Language Teacher Preparation*. (2002) <http://www.actfl.org>.

Allwright, D., and K. M. Bailey. *Focus on the Language Classroom: An Introduction to Classroom Research for Language Teachers*. New York: Cambridge, 1991.

Bailey, K. M., A. Curtis, and D. Nunan. *Pursuing Professional Development*. Boston: Heinle & Heinle, 2001.

Burns, A. *Collaborative Action Research for English Language Teachers*. New York: Cambridge UP, 1999.

Clair, N. "Teacher Study Groups: Persistent Questions in a Promising Approach." *TESOL Quarterly* 32 (1998): 465-492.

Freeman, D. *Doing Teacher Research: From Inquiry to Understanding*. Boston: Heinle & Heinle, 1998.

Freeman, D., and J. C. Richards. *Teacher Learning in Language Teaching*. New York: Teachers College Press, 1996.

Gebhard, J. G., and R. Oprandy. *Language Teaching Awareness: A Guide to Exploring Beliefs and Practices*. Cambridge: Cambridge UP, 1999.

Goodlad, J. I. Educational Renewal: Better Teachers, Better Schools. San Francisco: Jossey-Bass, 1994.

New Visions 2001-2004. 21 Nov. 2003 <http://www.educ.iastate.edu/newvisions/newsite/docarch/rtf.html>.

New Visions 2001-2004. 21 Nov. 2001 <http://www.educ.iastate.edu/newvisions/overview>.

Little, J.W. "Teachers' Professional Development in a Climate of Educational Reform." *Educational Evaluation and Policy Analysis* 15 (1993): 129-151.

McLaughlin, M.W., and I. Oberman, ed. *Teacher learning: New Policies and Practices*. New York: Teachers College Press, 1996.

Osborn, T. *Critical Reflection and the Foreign Language Classroom*. Westport: Bergin & Garvey, 2000.

Richards, J. C., and C. Lockhart. *Reflective Teaching in Second Language Classrooms*. New York: Cambridge UP, 1994.

Wallace, M. J. *Action Research for Language Teachers*. New York: Cambridge UP, 1998.

Wilberschied, L., L. Bauer, S. Jenkins, and M. Varghese. *Resisting Transformation: Learning from In-Service Teachers? Action Research?* (under review).

Wilhelm, K. H. "Sometimes Kicking and Screaming: Language Teachers-in-Training React to a Collaborative Learning Model." *Modern Language Journal* 81 (1997): 517-542.

van Lier, L. *Interaction in the Language Curriculum*. New York: Longman, 1996.

Multilingualism: Theory, Research Methods, and Didactics

Nicole Marx
Britta Hufeisen

Introduction

The term *SLA*, often first encountered in the final chapters of introductory linguistics textbooks or as the focus of more advanced linguistics courses, is primarily a North American term. In other areas of the world, *Applied Linguistics* is the preferred option to denote the study of the learning or acquisition of non-native languages. In their different usage, one can also ascertain the dominant foci of various research communities. SLA, or Second Language Acquisition, investigates the learning of a second (or foreign) language; more specifically, the term lends itself to the suggestion that the language in question is the *second* language, that is, the only language other than his or her mother tongue that a person speaks. Applied Linguistics, in contrast, is a more neutral term which does not immediately point to which language is being learned or acquired. It simply refers to the study of how people learn or acquire languages other than their first.

Both terms illustrate to a certain extent the contexts in which they are most widespread. In the United States, it is common that children learn only one foreign language in school (nowadays this is very often Spanish); even when more languages are offered in the school curriculum, they are optional courses. In Europe, in comparison, where different cultures and languages have lived in close contact with each other for hundreds of years, almost all schoolchildren learn at least two foreign languages in school, and many three or even more.

But even in the United States, the term SLA is somewhat of a misnomer, as it seems to exclude all language learners who have already had experience in learning a different language (why the learning of third or further foreign languages is different from that of a first foreign language will be discussed in the following section). Many students learn their L2, or second language, at school, in the course of the regular curriculum. But many other language learners cannot be lumped into a simple SLA or *L2-learner* category, as they are studying not their L2, but rather their *L3*—or L4, L5 or even L6. Children of immigrants, for example, often learn English as an L2 when they begin to attend school, having spoken only the heritage language at home. These children therefore begin to learn their third language, or L3, with the introduction of foreign language courses. University students, as well, have often had previous experience with other languages when they begin an introductory-level language course to fulfill a second language requirement at school. These and many other language learners find themselves in a different learning situation than that of their first Spanish or

ACTION

Interview someone who has learned a third or fourth language. How was it different from learning their first foreign language? If you have learned several languages yourself, *compare* your experience to that of other tertiary language learners.

French class in high school, and many of the learning and situational factors which played a role during the acquisition of their first foreign language are no longer applicable to the learning of the L3 or further languages.

Despite the geographical and historical closeness of Europe's languages, the belief that Second Language Acquisition might be different from Third Language Acquisition or Tertiary Language Learning (both referred to as TLA) is still relatively new. It was only in the 1970s that researchers began to question how learners of L3s, L4s or L5s might approach a new language differently than students learning the same language as their first foreign language (L2). Since this time, there has been heightened interest in a very common phenomenon worldwide, namely multilingualism, and in the learning and teaching of tertiary languages.

Although most of the research on TLA and language acquisition has to date been carried out in countries with a history of societal multilingualism, such as Finland, Israel or Switzerland, it is increasingly clear that the importance of this area needs to be recognized in all branches of Applied Linguistics. In North America, the specific characteristics of third language learning are demanding more attention due to the large number of language backgrounds from which students come, and the more recent push for internationalization in a global economy. Teachers may find themselves instructing ever-growing language minorities, children who are beginning to learn their L3 at a point where previously students were beginning their first foreign language. Instructors will therefore need to consider the theoretical and practical differences involved in these learning situations.

NOTE

Because the immigrant population in the US has grown dramatically over the past ten years, the issues around tertiary language acquisition are becoming increasingly relevant in this country. Example: Between 1900 and 2000, 60,000 new legal immigrants moved to Oregon—with 50% of these speaking little or no English. In addition, during this same time frame, the Hispanic population in the city of Portland increased by 160%.

This chapter will provide a short introduction to the field of tertiary language learning and multilingualism, discuss current models of multilingualism, projects and research methodology, and consider the teaching needs for tertiary languages.

Models of Multilingualism

Introduction

Research into multilingualism, still in its infancy following four decades of focus on second language acquisition and bilingualism, is an exciting area to be involved in. An understanding of TLA research is also absolutely crucial for our understanding of the processes of third language acquisition and tertiary language learning, and because so little is known about TLA, there is much room for new research and new projects in this field (see Section 3 in this chapter).

Empirical research alone, however, does not provide a complete picture of our knowledge of multilingual systems. The situation can be likened to the apples in the filling of a traditional American dessert—they taste great and without them, the apple pie wouldn't exist—but the pastry crust is what provides the structure and makes the dessert recognizable. In the following section, we focus not on the filling but rather on this crust, without which it would be difficult to accept that a separate *L3 pie* even exists. The crust here is made up of the models that have been proposed to explain the learning of third and further foreign languages and their interaction. They provide at least a temporary structure to help in our understanding of tri- and multilingualism—while at the same time expanding our knowledge of bilingual phenomena.

What Kinds of Models Exist?

The area of TLA has been developed and investigated by researchers and language teachers who grew into the fields of L3, trilingualism or multilingualism through work on bilingualism and second language acquisition. In fact, it is difficult to imagine future linguists specializing in trilingualism without a solid theoretical background in SLA and bilingualism studies. Because the applied linguistics research community has devoted much more energy to these latter fields, a large number of studies are available in the literature to account for bilingual language phenomena.

First a word about terminology: *hypotheses* about why certain multilingual phenomena are observed can lead to the development of a *model*, which is a simplified description that makes calculations or predictions. A model must go through a process of verification (or be shown to be false) before it can develop into a theory. It is estimated that over 40 separate theories exist in the area of SLA alone, and many more models have been developed and are still under construction (see Larsen-Freeman & Long 227).

Compared to the proliferation of bilingualism models, attempts to describe multilingualism and multilingual processes are fairly scarce. This is—quite obviously—due to the relatively short time period that we have been engaged in studying tri- and multilingual phenomena, and without a doubt they will increase in number in the coming years. In this paper, we would like to discuss those models which attempt to account for the acquisition and/or learning of further languages, models that have been developed and are continually being improved upon within this context (as opposed to bilingual models which claim to account for the learning of *all* foreign languages).

In this context, only the three currently more evolved models will be discussed, although others do exist. The models we will review here are Björn Hammarberg and Sarah Williams' *Language Switches Model;*[1] Britta Hufeisen's *Factor Model*, and finally Ulrike Jessner and Philip Herdina's *Dynamic Model of Multilingualism* (DMM). None of these models compete with or contradict each other; they simply describe different phenomena through different research perspectives.

Starting Points

Most discussions of models or theories focus on how they differ, and why. However, it can be much more fruitful to begin by considering which similarities the aforementioned models have—which assumptions all make, and what foci they have. In this way, we can concentrate on the generally accepted statements, thereby developing a basis for our understanding of multilingualism.

CONSIDER

In the following pages the authors will present three models for multilingual language acquisition. As you read, write down in a table the similarities and differences between them. Work in three steps: 1) underline the most important features of the model; 2) write down key words for each feature; 3) summarize at the end of each model introduction.

All three models agree that multilingualism is a natural state. Williams and Hammarberg (1998) stress that all humans are potentially polyglot by nature; Hufeisen (2000) shows that multilingualism, as opposed to mono- and bilingualism, is the worldwide norm; and Herdina and Jessner (2002) view bilingualism as a special subgroup of multilingualism. As well, all the authors assume that an adequate theory of language acquisition, language proficiency, and language use should be able to take multilingualism into account (thus within these frameworks, monolingualism and bilingualism are viewed as special cases).

All three models focus on the individual language learner (as opposed to societal multilingualism). They believe that languages converge at some level within an individual, and as a result all incorporate the phenomenon of interlanguage transference, which can be both positive (transfer) as well as negative (interference) in nature, into their models. Although only one of the models states this (Herdina & Jessner 2002) explicitly, all three assume that a person's competencies in his or her various languages are not normally at the same levels—that is, no multilingual will speak all of his or her languages with the same proficiency at all times. The category *balanced trilingualism* (and hence also *balanced bilingualism*) is therefore misleading, as all languages are not spoken to the same degree of fluency across all proficiencies (i.e. reading, social conversation, technical writing etc.; see Cook 1991).

The Factor and Language Switches models focus on language acquisition, especially in the beginning stages. The DMM, while accounting for language acquisition, looks beyond these first steps and discusses the development of language systems over time, considering both language acquisition and language attrition (see de Bot 1996).

After having discussed what the models have in common, we now turn to their respective areas of focus and discuss the main conclusions of each model briefly.

In Which Directions do the Three Models Go?

Each of the three models presented here have unique theoretical foundations and frameworks. While the Language Switches Model is based on Levelt's (1989) Speaking Model and de Bot's (1992) applications thereof, and therefore concentrates on speech production in a new foreign language, the Factor Model focuses on the different factors involved when learning a first, second, third and fourth language. The Dynamic Model of Multilingualism, in contrast, captures language changes in individuals over time and the interaction of different factors in the multilingual system.

Figure 1. Comparison of the foci of the three models.

Language Switches Model (Hammarberg/Williams)	Factor Model (Hufeisen)	DMM (Jessner/Herdina)
Speech production in a tertiary language.	Factors involved in first, second, and tertiary language acquisition and learning.	Language changes in individuals over time.

It must be briefly mentioned here that the terminology used in the models is not uniform. While the Factor Model and the DMM both use the term *L2* to denote the chronological second language of the learner, and *L3* for the third, the Language Switches Model refers to the target language as the *L3*, regardless of order of acquisition; all other previously learned foreign languages are termed *L2s*.

The Language Switches Model

It must be cautioned that Hammarberg does not yet view this model as a distinct entity, but rather as an extension of Levelt's (1989) Speaking Model and the applications of it made by de Bot (1992) and by Poulisse and Bongaerts (1994). However, this model is worth considering in the context of trilingualism and multilingualism research because it is a well-developed explanation for speech production in a tertiary language.

In his model of the monolingual speaker, Levelt proposes the three basic components of conceptualizer, formulator, and articulator. These components are all involved in the planning and production of (monolingual) speech. De Bot has applied these concepts to the bilingual speaker, allowing a part of the conceptualizer, formulator and articulator to be differentiated for the speaker's two languages. In this view, any given language may be *selected* (chosen as the language in which to speak), *active* (taking part in the current speech process) or *dormant* (stored in long-term memory, and not interacting in the speech process). Utterances are produced in parallel in the selected and active languages in all steps of formulation, but only those of the selected language are passed on to the articulator and in fact spoken (there are of course some exceptions to this general rule, such as the occurrence of code-switching in which words in the non-selected language are produced).

Hammarberg and Williams added to this model the concept of *role assignment* of the languages within an individual: languages which play a specific role during a given productive instance of the L3 are termed *supplier languages*. Most obviously, the L3 (target language) is the primary supplier in its production, and is thus termed the *internal supplier language*. This is the main language that is selected in the speech process. However, influence from other background languages in target language production is also possible, especially when a person is just beginning to learn his or her new foreign language.

What makes this model unique is the roles it assigns to the various languages involved in the speech process. After an extended study in which Williams' own speech production in a new language, Swedish, was studied (Williams was an English native speaker who had learned various languages and spent a number of years in Germany prior to moving to Sweden), the authors determined that her languages fulfilled different roles. Specifically, when a language switch was noticed—when another language *slipped in* to the production of Swedish—it tended to serve a certain purpose.

The authors noticed that the L1 of the learner was dominant in pragmatically functional language shifts. This means that it supported interaction between the speakers involved or the acquisition of words and other expressions; in other words, it displayed an instrumental role (and hence is termed the *instrumental language*). It was often used in metalinguistic comments, a strategy made possible because the interlocutor also spoke this language. Such shifts involved Williams asking questions like *what does x mean?* or trying to explain her thoughts to her conversation partner in English in an attempt to make herself clearer. However, more interesting was the fact that a different language tended to *slip in* to the production of the target language without Williams' intention while serving no pragmatic purpose in the statement, as happened with the slips into English (these switches were termed *WIPP—without identified pragmatic purpose*—slips). This was consistently another foreign language, German, and not the mother tongue.

The authors hypothesized that if a learner speaks other foreign languages, these may have a prominent role in his or her construction of new words as well as in attempts to cope with new articulatory patterns (i.e. pronunciation) in the L3. Therefore, an L2 may take the role of *default supplier*. In the view of de Bot, the target language may be selected, but another (often also foreign) language is also active, produced in parallel with the target language but, except for such language switches, not articulated. Only the language which has been assigned the role of default supplier will be regularly activated in parallel with the L3.

The authors found that there is a strong tendency for one language to predominate in the role of default supplier. The choice of whether the default supplier is the L1 or one of the L2s depends on four factors:

- *Typological Similarity* (how etymologically close are the two languages to another, i.e. are they both Romance languages? Germanic?).
- *Proficiency* (how well is the non-target language spoken?).
- *Recency* (how present is the non-target language in the mind of the speaker? has the speaker had much contact with the language recently?).
- *L2 Status* (the characteristic of foreignness, ascribed only to non-native languages).

So, for example, in Sarah Williams' case, although she also spoke French, Spanish and Italian, German was typologically closer to Swedish; her language proficiency was highest in English and German; these two languages had also been used more often and more recently; and only her foreign languages had L2 status. Therefore, German, which fulfilled these features to the greatest extent, was most likely to become the default supplier, the language involved in unintentional language switches. Hammarberg (2001) proposes possible reasons for the use of an L2 as the supplier language, these being: a different acquisition mechanism for foreign languages as opposed to the first language, and hence a reactivation of this mechanism in L3 acquisition; and a desire to suppress the L1 as being *non-foreign* and instead rely on an orientation towards a prior foreign language as a strategy when approaching the target language.

This role division between the background languages, such that the L1 dominates in an instrumental and another foreign language in a default supplier role, illustrates two different ways in which a speaker's languages can interact with each other. Their roles may also shift over time, with increased competence in the target language leading to a decreased reliance on various other languages.

NOTE

Do not forget to summarize the *Language Switches Model* based on your underlinings and notes in the page margins.

It must be mentioned that this model was based on the speech production of a single subject, who was a bit of a special case herself: she was herself a linguist, and her interlocutor also spoke English, German and Swedish. Other studies[2] are presently being carried out in an effort to reproduce these results, but it remains to be seen if the results pass the test of time.[3]

The Factor Model

Although the Language Switches Model may also be considered a developmental model in that it proposes a shift in language roles over the course of learning, the remaining two models to be discussed focus on these changes over time and over languages, and concentrate on the overall process of TLA as opposed to a specific competence. The Factor Model,[4] developed by Britta Hufeisen in Germany, explains why acquiring the first language is different from learning the second, and how new and different factors are involved when learning third and subsequent languages.

The basic premise of this model is that, as a person learns or acquires each new language, previously nonexistent factors come into play which influence how the new target language is learned or acquired.

1. During the acquisition of the mother tongue, factors assumed given include a general language acquisition capability (with which a child is born, such as universal grammar) and the learning environment in which the child is raised. Every (normal) child will acquire his or her first language effortlessly.
2. When this same child begins to learn its first foreign language (the case of children who are raised bilingually is not considered here)—often in school, these same factors are involved, although in a somewhat different form, e.g. the learning environment is now the language classroom. However, further factors also have an influence on how the second language is learned: the child now has acquired some general life experiences, and has acquired—often through other school subjects, but also through daily life—general learning experiences. She has also developed general learning strategies which assist her in the approach of new problems. As well, language learning motivation plays a role for the first time; if a child is not motivated to learn the second language, she probably won't; we can assume that this latter factor

plays no role during first language acquisition. Language acquisition aptitude is another, somewhat messy, factor (and is indeed still being debated in applied linguistic circles; see Baker 122f. for a brief summary of this issue, especially relating aptitude to general academic ability). Aptitude depends on both individual abilities as well as experience with learning foreign languages, and is assumed to remain relatively constant in a person. Finally, there is already a developed language system present in the mind of the learner—the L1—and this also exerts an influence on and serves as a basis for the learning of the foreign language. As Hufeisen (2000) illustrates:

Figure 2: Factors involved in the learning of an L2

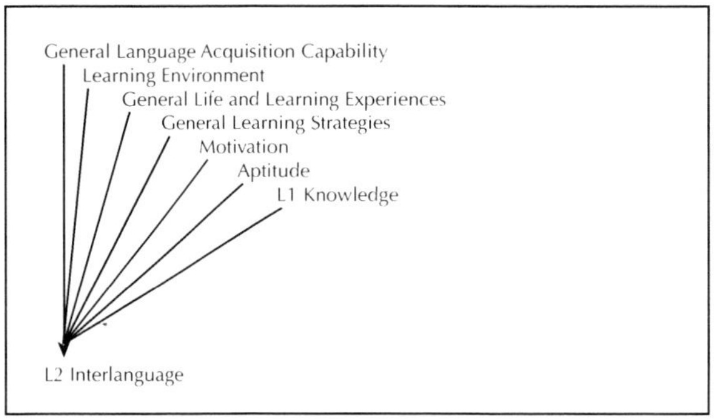

3. It was once assumed that factors involved in foreign language acquisition or learning remained similar after the learning of the L2—that the learning of a second language followed the same path as that of the third, fourth, and fifth languages. However, as Hufeisen outlines in her model, further factors come into play in the learning of a third language, and these have an important role during the acquisition process. For although the same factors are involved as during L2 acquisition, new ones have a major effect on how a learner approaches her second foreign language. These include foreign language learning experiences and strategies, which have developed during the learning of the first foreign language and which can assist a language learner significantly in her acquisition of the target language. As well, the student now knows how she should best approach the learning of a foreign language; she knows what type of learner she is. Finally, she has access to another (learner) language system, the L2 interlanguage, to which she can draw parallels with the target language, but which may also affect the production and reception of the target language in a manner not intended by the learner. The factors involved in learning an L3 now have been extended as shown in Figure 3:

Figure 3: Factors involved in the learning of an L3

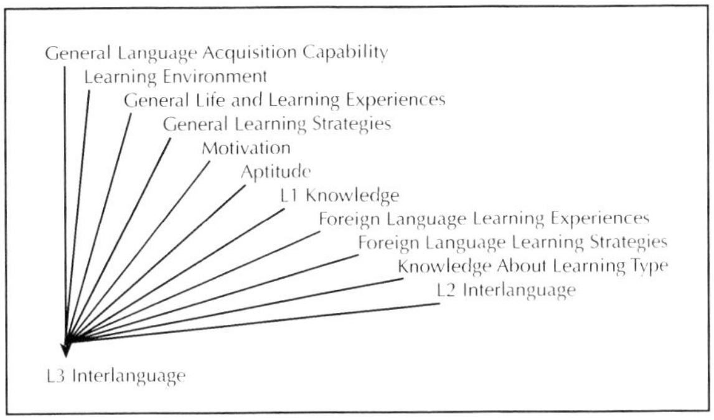

4. Learning further foreign languages—such as the L4, L5 or L6—is not as significantly different from learning an L3, as with each subsequent language, the only completely new factor involved is the previously learned language. Although language learning strategies will develop to a higher degree with each language (see for example Missler's 1999 work on learning strategies in multilinguals), they are no longer entirely new entities in the mind of the language learner.

The Factor Model therefore suggests major differences between not only the acquisition of the mother tongue and the learning of the first foreign language, but also proposes that the process of tertiary language learning is intrinsically different from that of second language learning. In this way, Hufeisen offers a developmental model of TLA that clearly reveals the importance of the distinction between second and third language learning. And while Williams & Hammarberg focus on the roles that previous languages play when a new language is being learned, Hufeisen shows why the learning of these new languages is more complex than that of first foreign language learning.

NOTE

Do not forget to summarize the Factor Model based on your underlinings and notes in the page margins.

The Dynamic Model of Multilingualism (DMM)

The DMM is—to quote its authors—a "psycholinguistic model which sees language change on an individual level as a function of time...a focus is placed on the variability and dynamism of the individual speaker system" (Herdina & Jessner 2).

This model is unique in that it attempts to incorporate and redefine the traditional distinctions of FLA, SLA and TLA within one wholistic model—*wholistic* because it tries to view the phenomena observed in language processes as a whole and not merely as its parts. As well, it is *holistic* in that it assumes that a multilingual system will have properties that its parts, i.e. individual language systems, cannot be shown to consist of. It also makes use of dynamic systems theory—which has been used to explain other biological systems—to explain language systems in individuals and the changes in these systems over time.

The DMM describes multilingual development. In contrast to the other models discussed, which consider the language systems in an individual as separate, Herdina and Jessner do not concentrate on each language as it is being learned or acquired, but strive to juxtapose each of an individual's languages to each other.

A key aspect of the DMM is that the language systems in a multilingual are seen as being in a state of constant flow, and that a learner will develop a language to the extent that it is perceived to be required for communicative needs. *Multilingual proficiency*—the term preferred by the authors to Cook's (1991) *multicompetence*—consists of dynamically interacting language subsystems which are always subject to variation, depending on different factors.

Language development in such dynamic systems is seen as showing six main characteristics.

1. The first is *non-linearity*. While other models of language learning might assume a constant increase in growth of a language system—using, for example, the metaphors of the straight line of language acquisition (whereby the learner shows a steady progression in the learning process) or of the ladder (whereby a language learner progresses in stages, continually climbing)—the DMM does not. Instead, it uses the sine curve metaphor to describe linguistic development. This metaphor is used to describe most biological systems, and according to the authors can also be useful when describing language acquisition and learning in the individual. Language acquisition, then, would follow a general course that looks like the following diagram (all graphs from Herdina/Jessner 2002):

Figure 4: Non-linearity of the Language System(s)

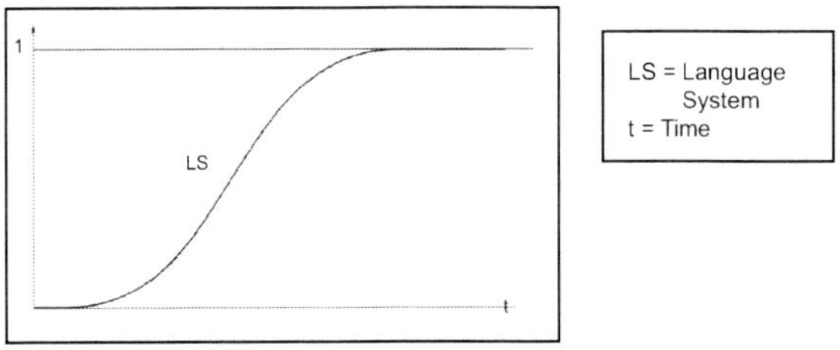

2. *Reversibility* is another characteristic. As the learner uses identical language resources for more than one language system, competition for these resources can lead to a reversal of the learning processes (language attrition), as shown in Figure 5. This can occur when the learner does not exert as much energy into maintaining the language as is required (consider the case of the university student who attends the required two semesters of foreign language courses and then seldom comes into contact with this language afterwards). The rate of decay of a language depends on factors such as the resources available to help maintain the language, pressure created by competing language systems, how long the language has been used, and the age of language acquisition.

Figure 5: Reversibility of Language Learning

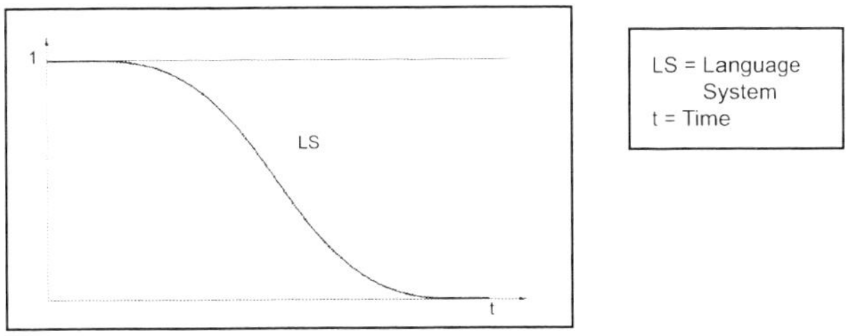

3. The *stability* of a language system depends on the degree of flexibility present in the maintenance effort of the learner; if the learner can adapt to environmental pressure by varying the amount of effort he invests into the language system, the stability of the system will increase (e.g. the same student decides to take evening courses to keep up the FL; or he finds a friend with whom he can practice the language). As well, stability can be affected by the number of languages available to a multilingual; the greater the number of languages a person speaks, the greater the amount of maintenance required and the more difficult it becomes for the person to find the necessary resources to maintain his languages. A person who speaks five languages will have to spend more cognitive energy maintaining these various systems than a person who speaks two languages.
4. Fourth, *interdependence* refers to the belief that the development of each individual language system within a multilingual depends to a large extent on the behavior of previous and subsequent systems. In this way, the overall system of languages in an individual is studied, and patterns in the entire multilingual system are determined.
5. A fifth characteristic is *complexity*. There is a complex relationship between personal factors which affect multilingual proficiency and result in the autodynamic nature of language systems within the multilingual (autodynamic because a change in one factor will influence the others and the level of proficiency). These factors are, in brief: multilanguage aptitude or metalinguistic abilities (which in this view is an emergent property of multilingual systems), the language acquisition process (which can be both positive and negative), motivation (the prime factor determining general language effort), perceived language competence (the greater it is, the less effort a learner is going to put into language acquisition), self-esteem, and finally anxiety. Changes in one factor will have effects on the entire system. The autodynamic nature of the system is displayed in Figure 6:

Figure 6: Complexity of the Language System(s)

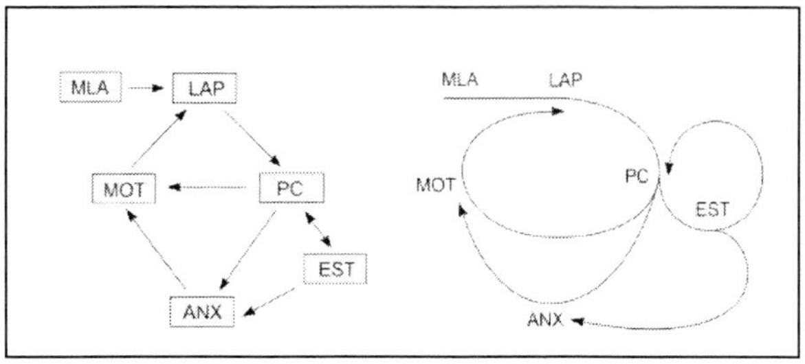

MLA = Multilingual Language Aptitude
LAP = Language Acquisition Process
MOT = Motivation
PC = Perceived Language Competence
EST = Self Esteem
ANX = Anxiety

6. Finally, *change of quality* may be compared to the factors of foreign language learning experiences and strategies as well as knowledge of one's own learning type, as explicated in Hufeisen's Factor Model. It also includes language management skills—how the multilingual balances communicative requirements with language resources—and language maintenance skills. This change of quality results from prior experience with the second language learning process, and is developed at a higher level in L3- than in L2-learners (see also Missler 1999).

There are two more aspects of the DMM that need to be mentioned. The first is the concept of *language maintenance* in multilinguals. Because most models deal with the acquisition of a foreign language but not with its maintenance or attrition after the period of active learning is finished, this consideration is often pushed to the back burner. However, if one goal of trilingualism and multilingualism research is to help students learn numerous foreign languages—and continue to be able to speak and understand them—then we must also consider the fact that languages need to be maintained, or they will attrite. Therefore, the DMM proposes a key factor in language systems called *language maintenance effort*. This suggests that one of the possible causes of inadequate or partial language learning is insufficient language maintenance—and this deficiency is far more obvious in multilinguals than it is in monolinguals (as multilinguals have many more languages to maintain and thus less time on average to devote to each language). Language maintenance, in turn, depends on language use and on language awareness: the more a language is used, the more it is maintained; and the more aware an individual is of her increasing deficiency in a particular language, the more likely she may invest effort in attempting to maintain the language. Because an increase in language knowledge will necessitate an increased level of language maintenance effort, a person's language maintenance factor will provide a natural limit to her acquisition efforts.

The second is the *M-factor* or *multilingualism factor*, which is a function of the interaction between language systems and is proposed to have a priming or catalytic effect in the learning of any language after the L1. It captures the difference between multilingual and monolingual systems; the multilingual system contains components that the monolingual one lacks, and even those components shared by both systems have a different significance within each system. For example, self-esteem can be seen as a fairly constant personality characteristic, but may still be higher when using one language than when using others.

Interestingly, the authors assume that although all humans are potentially multilingual, the individual speaker in isolation has a natural tendency towards monolingualism. This minimizes language maintenance effort because we are continuously trying to reduce the amount of energy we invest in our activities (i.e. an economical energy usage).

NOTE

Do not forget to summarize the Dynamic Model of Multilingualism based on your underlinings and notes in the page margins.

Summary: A Coherent View of Multilingualism?

Since only a brief discussion of these models can be offered in this chapter, the reader is referred to the bibliography for more information. However, it should now be apparent how all the models may contribute to our understanding of multilingualism and third language acquisition. As we have seen, each model deals with different aspects of multilingualism or has different focal points. Because of this, we can at present accept *all three* as valid models of multilingual phenomena; they do not contradict each other, but simply turn our attention to different aspects of language acquisition.

1. The Language Switches Model lays an emphasis on why language switches occur in a foreign language, and which roles the various languages play during the language learning process. This model allows us to understand better the interaction of languages in the mind of the learner.
2. The Factor Model, in turn, offers a comprehensible guideline to understanding which external and internal variables have an effect on language learning, and—most importantly—shows why learners of a second foreign language cannot be treated the same as those of a first foreign language. This model has, therefore, obvious consequences for curricular development.
3. The Dynamic Model of Multilingualism, finally, concentrates on the interaction of language systems and language changes over time in an individual. It helps us to understand the theoretical ebb and flow of language systems by explaining the factors which exert an influence on language acquisition and language attrition, and shows that language maintenance effort is one of the most important factors involved in retaining competencies in a foreign language. In this way, it too has consequences for the foreign language classroom.

DISCUSS

Discuss the implications the hypotheses of these three models have for curricular development. What would you do in order to put one of these models into your language classroom practice?

What is needed for the future are more empirical studies that can test the predictions made by these models. While all the models are based to some extent on empirical data (and indeed, the Language Switches Model was developed as a result of data gathered during a longitudinal study), more research is needed to prove or refute the hypotheses that the authors of these three models make. It remains to be seen if each of these models, in their present form, stands the test of time.

Methods of Multilingualism Research

CONSIDER

What areas of TLA would you like to see researched? Why? Read on to see what the authors think are some important considerations for future projects.

As stated at the beginning of this chapter, primary research is an exciting area to be involved in, and such research in the field of trilingualism becomes more interesting due to the fact that so little has been done in this area to date. In this section, we would like to review empirical data-gathering methods that have been applied in this field, as well as to explicate the research desiderata of the field. Because the area of TLA and multilingualism is still in its infancy in the linguistic community, new and further research is sorely needed to help uncover multilingual phenomena, support (or refute) the models which have been developed to explain multilingualism, and provide guidelines for teachers and curriculum developers who are being increasingly confronted with the special situation of TLA.

A look at previous research on multilingualism reveals an interesting fact: it does not follow the general tendencies of SLA research. This is most likely due to the fact that it began much later than research into foreign language acquisition per se; the first studies on the learning of third or further foreign languages were undertaken only in the 70s and 80s. In contrast to SLA research, interest in TLA actually began in the language classroom when teachers began to notice that their (tertiary) language students were producing errors from previous L2s. As well, its genesis is unusual. Consider the following situation: A researcher carries out an error analysis on the learning of German by Finnish schoolchildren. To her surprise, many of these students' production errors can be traced neither to the first language (Finnish) nor to developmental errors. Rather, they appear to correspond to correct elements in Swedish, the first foreign language of the children (i.e. Stedje 1976). Results showing that interlingual *errors* in a new foreign language not only originated from the mother tongue but could also be traced to other foreign languages known to the learner, led to the research field of *L3*.

Methods Employed to Date

Not surprisingly, until recently the most popular method of studying the learning of third and tertiary languages has been through error analysis. Generally, learner production data (either verbal or written) is investigated with the intention of determining sources of errors that were made. The main reason for this concentration can most likely be traced to the genesis of L3 research: much attention devoted to the study of learner errors arising from neither the L1 nor the target language. Error analyses are also practical: they are relatively simple and quick to carry out, and they can show in which linguistic areas and to what extent one language has an influence on another. However, they generally concentrate only on production data and can therefore say little about understanding or about the process of foreign language acquisition.

Approximately a third of all studies on the learning of a third language have been error analyses (whereby the first studies were almost exclusively so). In future, it will be important to balance out such concentration on the negative aspects (errors, incorrect interlingual transfer etc.) of language learning through studies on more positive results of having already learned a second or foreign language.

Similar to error analyses, language tests (either oral or, more commonly, written) are used to determine at what stage a language learner is, concentrating on right-or-wrong answers to reach conclusions. In the field of L3, such testing has been used to compare monolinguals and bilinguals in the school context, or determine transfer from one language to another. Another way in which this method has been used is to compare various didactical methods for learners of tertiary languages. Barbara Hinger (2001), for example, questioned whether an intensive course (with more classroom hours over a shorter time period) or an extensive one (a regular university language course) was more appropriate for Austrian learners of Spanish as a tertiary language. Such language tests are, like error analyses, generally easy to administer and allow for comparisons between different learner groups. They can also show at which stage a learner is at a given time and can therefore measure to some extent the progress of a learner over time.

A third methodological focus primarily in sociolinguistic research concentrates on the learner as opposed to the product of his or her language learning. This can involve, for example, interviews, learner questionnaires, think-aloud protocols or language learning diaries. Such data gathering can be structured (through set questions, such as on a questionnaire using a Likert-scale) or unstructured, whereby the learner can freely steer his or her comments. These may also be introspective (gathered during the learning task, such as in think-aloud protocols) or retrospective (gathered after the conclusion of a learning task). In the field of L3, learner-based methods have been used for different purposes, such as: to measure attitudes towards foreign languages or to foreign language learning; to question the interaction of languages in the mental lexicon of the learners; to question strategy use in language learning; or to tease apart correlations between different factors in the acquisition process. Bettina Missler (1999), for example, made use of both interviews as well as questionnaires in her study on the learning strategies, self-confidence and language learning attitudes of second, third and tertiary language learners. She found that tertiary language learners have more self-confidence, invest more effort into learning foreign languages, and are generally more positive about learning languages than students learning their first foreign language.

There are numerous benefits to using such learner-based methods. First, they provide information about the individual learning process, allowing for conclusions about ways in which learners approach the learning of the target language. More subjective data such as information about the usage of language learning strategies is inaccessible to traditional, psychometric research methods like error analysis. Learners may be questioned retrospectively as to why they made certain mistakes, comprehended texts in a certain way, etc. For example, language diaries have the advantage of illustrating the process of language learning, often daily, over an extended period of time, and allow for a longer period of consideration than questionnaires or interviews typically do. However, these methods are not without their disadvantages. Results obtained may not be reliable (will results be confirmed by those of another method?), due to the fact that learner testimonies must be interpreted by another person, the researcher. As well, learners are usually not as introspective as researchers find ideal; rather than the desired answer, "I understood this word through an analogy to the Latin xyz," learners will often reply to a researcher's question with, "I just knew it / guessed."

A further possibility for studying multilingualism and third language acquisition are through case studies of children growing up in families with three languages. Charlotte Hoffmann (1985) and Daniela Gatto (2000), amongst others, studied the simultaneous acquisition of three languages by their own children, drawing conclusions about the consequences of a trilingual upbringing. This method has the benefit of allowing the intensive study of a language learner over an extended period of time, and can therefore provide much data on individual progression in the acquisition of multiple languages.

A few discourse analytical studies have also been carried out in the study of tertiary language acquisition. Discourse analysis is still relatively new in the study of foreign language acquisition, and for this reason, it is still underrepresented in the field of L3. Such studies question how learners move towards mastery of language in interaction with other speakers of the language; speech acts are the focal point of research. In this area, Rita Franceschini (2000) has carried out a study in which store clerks in Basel (a German-speaking city in Switzerland) were approached by customers speaking Italian. The clerks, who had learned French in school but may not have acquired Italian, were observed in their attempts to communicate in this relatively unknown tertiary language.

Finally, diverse psycholinguistic experiments have been carried out in the area of L3. Some employ the method of think-aloud protocols to study thought processes during various tasks (such as translation), attempting to discover the links between different language systems in the minds of the subjects. Word association tests have also been used, for example to determine connotations of translation equivalents in the various languages of learners (Gabrys 2001). Other tasks such as word completion exercises or translations also have been used to probe into the multilingual mental lexicon. Ecke (2001), for example, studied TOT-states (*tip-of-the-tongue*) amongst learners asked to translate from the L1 and the L3 in his study of the organization of the trilingual mental lexicon, while Meissner (1997) studied the effects of knowing *primary lexemes* from other languages when reading texts in an unknown (but related to another known) language.

Two Further Considerations[5]

Through the preceding section, we have gained an overview of the various methods presently employed in the research of third language acquisition and tertiary language learning. Error analyses, language tests, learner-based methods such as interviews or diary studies, studies of childrens' multilingual acquisition, discourse analytical studies, and psycholinguistic research into the multilingual mental lexicon have served to expand our knowledge about language learning in many different areas of TLA. There are two further considerations concerning the preparation of studies into multilingualism which must be taken into account in future studies: whether research is cross-sectional or longitudinal; and whether it studies production or reception data.

NOTE

Research is an important source of information that can be used to develop guidelines for both curriculum development and instruction.

The first issue is whether research is cross-sectional (studying subjects at one specific period of time in the learning process) or longitudinal (whereby changes in the interlanguage are studied over a longer period of time). Perhaps not surprisingly, the majority of studies into multilingualism (comparable to studies on SLA) have been cross-sectional. This is most likely due to the large amount of time and energy required by longitudinal studies. As well, researchers are not guaranteed that the subjects with whom the experiment was begun will remain until its conclusion; learners might move away, lose interest, or be subject to time constraints.

Longitudinal studies are, however, imperative in such a research field as language acquisition, as they allow us to study the process (development and changes in a language system or systems) and not merely the product of language learning. One solution to the difficulties posed by such studies is quasi-longitudinal research, whereby learners of different, overlapping levels are studied over a certain period of time, but not to the extent of a *true* longitudinal study.

The second issue involves the study of language comprehension (listening and reading). Although this area is of utmost importance for the study of multilingual behavior, there has been little research performed, researchers having generally concentrated on learner production (writing and speaking). Only a few studies on reading (i.e. Lindemann 2000; Müller-Lancé 2002) or on listening comprehension in an L3 (i.e. Meissner & Burk 2001; Müller-Lancé 2002) have been carried out to date. These studies can reveal how previously learned foreign languages help students understand texts even in the beginning stages of L3 learning, allowing for a more motivating and faster-paced learning of the new target language.

One exciting new project that focuses on receptive competencies in *multiple* related languages and which developed partially through such research into language comprehension is *EuroCom* (European Comprehension). This undertaking, currently being carried out at different universities in Europe, aims to provide language learners with receptive competencies in up to six different (Romance) languages. By the end of the first one-semester course, students (who already speak at least one of the languages involved, either as an L1 or foreign language) should have achieved basic reading skills in French, Catalan, Spanish, Romanian, Italian and Portuguese (see Klein & Stegmann 2000). Such projects recognize the need for such receptive competencies in today's multicultural and multinational society, and similar endeavors are also in the planning stage for the Slavic and the Germanic languages.

Triangulation: Combination of Methods

Through the previous discussion it has become evident that numerous methods are available and have been used to study multilingualism, third language acquisition and tertiary language learning. One difficulty that arises pertains to the fact that each method has both advantages and disadvantages. A single method can reach conclusions which could gain considerably more reliability through collaborative results from other studies using different methods. For example, a study on the multilingual mental lexicon could involve word association exercises, translation tasks, listening and reading comprehension tests, as well as learner questionnaires on strategy use (i.e. Müller-Lancé 2002). Results obtained from the various aspects of the study can then be compared to those of other tasks. This technique is called triangulation: the use of more than one method in the comprehensive analysis and interpretation of data.

A disadvantage of this approach is that the researcher is faced with considerably more work in the collection and analysis of data—but the advantages are obvious. Triangulation increases the objectivity of a study, since the one-sidedness of a single method can be recognized and better avoided; as well, concurring results from different parts of the study can be seen as more reliable than those of a single method. Triangulation of data also allows for a more complete investigation into processes of language learning. For these reasons, future studies on TLA and multilingualism—as well as in other branches of applied linguistics—should seriously consider the use of multiple data-gathering methods.

Research Desiderata

Due to the fact that the area of *L3* is still far from being completely understood, there remain numerous open research desiderata in this field. Various methods have been applied in the research of multilingualism, but large gaps remain to be filled. Considerations for future projects might include:

- Research into positive results of multilingualism and TLA (transference) instead of merely errors (interference) is needed.
- Longitudinal studies can offer more information about processes involved in TLA.
- The study of language comprehension (reading and listening) is important, especially in today's global society where communication and understanding between different groups of peoples are becoming more important (i.e. the EuroCom project).
- Learner-oriented data such as learner questionnaires, introspection and retrospection, or think-aloud protocols become increasingly important in order to study learning processes as opposed to learning products.
- More experimental research needs to be undertaken.
- Individual phenomena such as the multilingual mental lexicon, language learning strategies, or phonological acquisition in an L3 should be considered.

- More interest needs to be directed towards metalinguistic awareness of learners for the purpose of drawing didactical conclusions.
- Studies of child trilingual acquisition should continue into the teenager years and beyond, when the language systems are further developed and when use and proficiency in them is more dependent on affective variables.
- Triangulated methods remain uncommon and must be used more often.

Teaching an L3

Teachers of a third or tertiary language are faced on the one hand with the difficulty of instructing students with widely varying language learning histories and knowledge: students have often learned different languages as the first foreign language, and sometimes also have first languages other than English. On the other hand, such teachers enjoy the benefits that students of L3s bring with them to the classroom: a broadened knowledge of the world, likely a more mature cognitive style, experience in learning foreign languages, and at least two languages with which comparisons to the target language can be made (as part of declarative knowledge). They also have previously developed language learning strategies (as part of procedural knowledge), and a heightened ability or aptitude to learn foreign languages due to this experience (cf. the *M-factor* in the Dynamic Model of Multilingualism, discussed previously).

For American teachers of foreign languages, of special interest are those students with first languages other than English, the language of wider communication, as well as older students who have already learned one foreign language at school. The conclusion to this chapter aims to familiarize teachers with the basic principles of multilingualism didactics: what characterizes the third language classroom and learner, and how the benefits of previous experience with foreign or second language learning can be exploited in order to optimize the classroom and learning situation.

TLA and Multilingualism in the Foreign Language Classroom

Many of the special characteristics of third and tertiary language learning have already been discussed in this chapter (see, for example, Hufeisen's model of the factors involved in L3-learning). These include the fact that a language learner approaching a second foreign language has already acquired experiences with learning a foreign language; he or she understands how it feels *not* to understand a strange text and is generally not as concerned about perfection as a student beginning to learn the L2. Such students also know how they learn best (do I learn more when I hear something, or read it? Do I need to move or combine movements with words in order to learn them? Is it important for me to write new vocabulary in order to remember them? How and where can I find opportunities to practice a language?), and they can draw on these experiences when they enter the L3-classroom.

As well, students learning their second (or subsequent) foreign language are generally older, in the United States often already adults, and they approach language learning in a different, more systematic and methodical way than do children. For this reason, adult learners can be entrusted with more self-sufficient learning; they can, for example, learn grammar or vocabulary at home, so that class time can be utilized for communicative exercises and further applications of what has been learned. They can (usually) motivate themselves to work outside of the classroom at learning a foreign language and might have different reasons for learning. The teacher of a tertiary language should ask students at the beginning of a course why they have chosen that specific language: for what purpose do they wish to use it? What are their goals for learning the foreign language? Once the reasons for participation in a course are known, the teacher can consider adapting her syllabus to accommodate or tailor the course best to the needs of her students. As well, making students themselves aware of their motivations for learning a new language can help them in retaining this motivation in the future.

In addition to these considerations, the classroom situation also has special characteristics that the teacher of an L3 cannot overlook. While the first foreign language is generally allotted considerable time in the curriculum, third language instruction must usually be faster-paced, covering more material in less time. Fortunately, this is possible through the greater maturity of the students; as well, their previous experience allows them to grasp concepts more quickly, and they understand how to approach the learning of a language. However, it is important that the L3-teacher consider and incorporate these benefits into her teaching, as students are often unaware of the many strategies and techniques that they have already used to learn the L2, as well as of the many linguistic (vocabulary, grammatical etc.) parallels that might exist between their first and second foreign languages.

Methodology of Tertiary Language Teaching

When planning the teaching of a third language, a first, most basic consideration is that no *new* methodology has been proposed. At present, most methodical and didactical considerations are based on the communicative method, which in Europe and North America has established itself as the most common in foreign language teaching. The basic principles for teaching third or further foreign languages can, however, be incorporated into most didactical situations. The method that is chosen in a foreign language classroom depends on the teacher, students, and context involved; planning for the teaching of an L3 should be integrated into this framework.

DISCUSS

Discuss how you would optimize the classroom and learning situation for students in your classes who may be learning a third language. Address the issues of both declarative and procedural knowledge.

There are two main guidelines for planning and instructing students of a second foreign language. These are, first, the consideration of *declarative knowledge* that students bring with them from various sources both outside and within the target language, and, second, the consideration of *procedural knowledge* that students have developed through their previous experience with foreign language learning (see Neuner & Hufeisen 2001, Part II, for a detailed discussion of these principles).

Declarative Knowledge: Knowledge *About*

The first factor involves the declarative knowledge that students bring with them to the L3-classroom. This can involve knowledge from different areas. At the most general level, students have knowledge of the world—customs, politics, history, language and so forth—which will affect how they approach a new language (not the least because this previous knowledge can affect their motivation to learn a new language).

On a linguistic level, the students will also have gathered a great deal of declarative knowledge. They might be able to draw on their vocabulary knowledge in other languages (including both the L1 and other foreign languages) to draw parallels to the L3, assisting them particularly in their understanding of L3 texts. Because languages have differing degrees of relatedness, certain languages will be of more help than others. For example, a student with Chinese as the first language and English as the L2 will, when learning German as an L3, often be able to use his knowledge of English vocabulary to understand German texts, as English and German have many parallels (they are both Germanic languages, and both share similar words in a variety of thematic areas such as health, computers, media, or business).[6] This might not be the case when the same student has learned Japanese as the L2 and then begins to learn German without having previously studied English.

Another area in which declarative knowledge can be helpful is grammar. Students know rules of sentence construction, and they understand that certain grammatical or morphological phenomena and patterns may not exist in the first language. A student with English as the L1 who has learned French in school will not be surprised that nouns are assigned gender in German, and can accept the relatively complex morphological system of German due to her prior experience with French. As well, at least at the beginning levels of learning, there are many parallels in the syntax systems of related languages which may be of great help when teaching or learning a tertiary language.

Further linguistic areas, such as phonology, orthography, or semantics, should not be neglected when considering what advantages a learner of an L3 might bring with him to the classroom. For example, an American student will probably have difficulties in pronouncing the German *ü* (either [*y*:] as in *früh*, or [*Y*] as in *Glück*); a comparison with the previously learned French *vous* [*y*:] might help alleviate this problem. However, further difficulties may also arise, such as in the pronunciation or spelling of cognates and homophones in different languages. A student who has already learned the English pronunciation of *hand* or the spelling of *house* might more easily make mistakes when encountering these words (*Hand, Haus*) in German. Teachers should be prepared to explain not only that the student has made an error, but also why she has produced it. Such interlingual interferences, especially when they stem from other foreign languages, are not serious, but should certainly be addressed. They can even become a game for students who might be asked to explain why these mistakes were made.

Even intercultural questions can be more understandable or more interesting to discuss when parallels are drawn to other languages and cultures. The differentiation between the German *du* and *Sie*, for example, is obvious even to English-speaking students when they have already encountered the French *tu* vs. *vous*, or the Spanish *tú* vs. *usted*. And discussions about norms of a target language culture can be greatly enriched by the inclusion of knowledge from other foreign cultures, allowing the students to share not just what they know of their own and the target language culture, but also of other areas of the world.

Students should always be encouraged to draw on parallels with other languages, not simply because this can make learning the new language easier, but also because the more entries in memory are connected with each other, the better these entries are retained. One responsibility of instructors is, from the first day of class, to point to *interlanguage* (between-language) similarities and help the students discover further comparisons themselves. In this way, students can become more self-sufficient in their learning and thus exert more control (and creativity) when learning a new language—and any further languages that they might endeavor to learn in the future.

Procedural Knowledge: Knowledge *How*

It is not merely declarative knowledge that students bring with them into the L3-classroom. In addition to this knowledge about the world and about specific languages that students learned or acquired and cultures that they have encountered, they also possess a large base of procedural knowledge about learning languages. Such knowledge includes both the experiences that students have already had with foreign language teaching methods in previous language classrooms, and the experiences they have with learning strategies and techniques. This prior experience has an effect on learning or teaching tertiary languages.

First, learners of a tertiary language generally have already taken part in foreign (or in the case of immigrants, second) language classes. They thus have experienced and become accustomed to specific methodologies which their previous teachers used, and their language learning styles are often influenced by these experiences. Students who, for example, learned their first foreign language through the grammar-translation approach will concentrate on the learning of grammatical categories and might assign more weight to the skills of reading and writing; communication (especially involving listening comprehension and speaking) will seem of less importance. A student who, on the other hand, has learned her L2 through the audiolingual or audiovisual method will concentrate more on listening and speaking. The much more recent communicative approach, with its emphasis on the integration of the partial competencies (reading, writing, listening and speaking) and concentration on creativity and communication, may be new to many learners. That is, younger students may adapt more easily to a language course and feel more positive about it than older learners who feel that the instructor is not *serious* enough and is *ignoring* vital exercises such as grammar drills.

A group of students who have learned their other foreign languages in different traditions (as sometimes occurs in university courses when mature students enter classrooms with younger high school graduates) can make the teacher's job more challenging, as each student has expectations about how the course will be conducted; some will demand more grammar tasks, others more communicative exercises. The

L3 teacher must be aware of such possible situations and develop strategies to help students succeed in whatever method the course is taught.

The second area of procedural knowledge which influences how learners approach an L2 stems from their experience with language learning strategies and techniques. Learners of a tertiary language have already developed, through their contact with the L2, various *shortcuts* which may assist them when learning a new language. Such strategies and techniques help learners in achieving their learning or communicative goals. These may include memory strategies (how can I remember this word?), social strategies (i.e. asking for clarification), simplification (reducing complicated statements to more straightforward ones which are easier to formulate) or general cognitive strategies (i.e. guessing the meaning of a word from its context). Other techniques might involve using a bilingual (or even monolingual) dictionary when an unknown word in the target language is encountered, or writing new vocabulary on index cards and reviewing these cards whenever possible.[7]

When working with concrete exercises and activities, L3 learners also have distinct advantages. Students have already encountered many of the exercise forms used in the language classroom, so lengthy explanations about cloze tests or translations become unnecessary. As well, such learners can generally define grammatical terminology (what is a verb? an adjective?) with less difficulty than students who have never learned a language other than their mother tongue, and can thus easily discuss new concepts and rules of language. Finally, they are also aware of which learning type(s) they are: do they learn better by reading something (visual learner), or by hearing it (audio learner)? Do they have to write new vocabulary to remember it, or do they prefer to visualize a picture to go with the word? Do they prefer to learn in a group or classroom, or alone with cassettes, language software or other self-study materials?

NOTE

Teaching students *how to learn* is one of the best ways to ensure success in your language classroom.

In conclusion, we would like to emphasize that one of the most important topics a language teacher can address in the classroom is that of *learning to learn*. Students learning a foreign language today will probably not stop with this language, but rather—at some point during their lifetimes—begin to study another. It is therefore essential that they understand how to approach a new language, become more efficient and develop strategies allowing for more self-sufficiency in their learning.

ACTION

Design an activity to encourage students to reflect on their learning processes and determine which are the most effective for themselves (i.e. focus on raising the students' awareness of their procedural and declarative knowledge). Remember what you have learned in part three of this volume about portfolios as a mode of reflective practice.

Classroom discussions of learning strategies, learning techniques and learning styles will assist students not only in the target language, giving them more control over their own learning and pace of acquisition, but also in the learning of future foreign languages. The instructor should discuss both aspects of prior knowledge that tertiary language learners possess: they should help students capitalize on their declarative knowledge, and they should raise awareness of procedural knowledge, i.e. previously utilized learning strategies and techniques, by encouraging students to reflect on their learning processes and to determine which are the most effective for themselves.

Notes

1. This title is by no means definitive and may also be termed *role-function model*, as debated during the Second International Conference on Third Language Acquisition and Trilingualism at Fryske Academy, Leeuwarden, 13-15 Sep. 2001.
2. For example, see Safont 2001; this study attempted to replicate Williams & Hammarberg's findings but could not ascertain that one particular language was predominant in WIPP switches; the characteristics of the learner group and learning situation, however, could explain why the proposed model was not supported in this case.
3. The reader is encouraged to reflect on his or her own experience when learning a new foreign language, and to observe his or her students who might be learning not simply their first, but perhaps their second or even third foreign language.
4. This model was first introduced in 1998 and has undergone various revisions since.
5. For further information on foreign language acquisition research, the reader is referred to the detailed summary presented by Larson-Freemann & Long (1997).
6. See for example Neuner and Hufeisen (2001), Part I.
7. For more information on learning strategies and techniques, the reader is referred to Chamot (1999).

References

Baker, Colin. *Foundations of Bilingual Education and Bilingualism*. 3rd ed. Clevedon: Multilingual Matters, 2001.

Chamot, Anna Uhl. *The Learning Strategies Handbook*. White Plains: Longman, 1999.

Cook, Vivian. "The Poverty-of-the-Stimulus Argument and Multicompetence." *Second Language Research* 7.2 (1991): 103-117.

De Bot, Kees. "A Bilingual Production Model: Levelt's *Speaking* Model Adapted." *Applied Linguistics* 13.1 (1992): 1-24.

De Bot, Kees. "Language Loss." *Kontaktlinguistik. Ein internationales Handbuch zeitgenössischer Forschung* Ed. H. Goebl et al. Vol. 1. Berlin: De Gruyter, 1996. 579-585.

Ecke, Peter. "Lexical Retrieval in a Third Language: Evidence from Errors and Tip-of-the-Tongue States." *Cross-Linguistic Influence in Third Language Acquisition: Psycholinguistic Perspectives*. Ed. Jasone Cenoz, Britta Hufeisen, and Ulrike Jessner. Clevedon: Multilingual Matters, 2001. 145-182.

Franceschini, Rita. "A Multilingual Network in the Re-Activation of Italian as the Third Language Among German Speakers: Evidence from Interactions." *Zeitschrift für interkulturellen Fremdsprachenunterricht* 5.1 (2000) <www.ualberta.ca/~german/ejournal/frances3.htm>.

Gabrys, Danuta. "A Cross-Cultural Aspect of the Interaction of Languages in the Mental Lexicon of Multilingual Learners." *Looking Beyond Second Language Acquisition. Studies in Tri and Multilingualism*. Ed. Jasone Cenoz, Britta Hefeisen, and Ulrike Jessner. Tübingen: Stauffenburg, 2001. 97-107.

Gatto, Daniela. "Language Proficiency and Narrative Proficiency of a Trilingual Child." *Tertiär- und Drittsprachen. Projekte und empirische Untersuchungen*. Ed. Sigrid Dentler, Britta Hufeisen, and Beate Lindemann. Tübingen: Stauffenburg, 2000. 117-142.

Groseva, Maria. "Dient das L2-System als ein Fremdsprachenlernmodel? [Does the L2 system serve as a foreign language acquisition model?]." *Tertiärsprachen. Theorien, Modelle, Methoden*. Ed. Britta Hufeisen and Beate Lindemann. Tübingen: Stauffenburg, 1998. 21-30.

Hammarberg, Björn. "Roles of L1 and L2 in L3 Production and Acquisition." *Cross-Linguistic Influence in Third Language Acquisition: Psycholinguistic Perspectives*. Ed. Jasone Cenoz, Britta Hufeisen, and Ulrike Jessner. Clevedon: Multilingual Matters, 2001. 30-64.

Herdina, Philip and Ulrike Jessner. *A Dynamic Model of Multilingualism. Perspectives of Change in Psycholinguistics*. Clevedon: Multilingual Matters, 2002.

Herdina, Philip and Ulrike Jessner. "The Dynamics of Third Language Acquisition." *English in Europe. The Acquisition of a Third Language*. Ed. Jasone Cenoz and Ulrike Jessner. Clevedon: Multilingual Matters, 2000. 84-98.

Hinger, Barbara. "An Intensive Multilingual Approach to Language Acquisition in School Context." *Looking Beyond Second Language Acquisition. Studies in Tri- and Multilingualism*. Ed. Jasone Cenoz, Britta Hufeisen, and Ulrike Jessner. Tübingen: Stauffenburg, 2001. 121-136.

Hoffmann, Charlotte. "Language Acquisition in Two Trilingual Children." *Journal of Multilingual and Multicultural Development* 6.6 (1985): 479-495.

Hufeisen, Britta. "A European Perspective: Tertiary Languages with a Focus on German as a Tertiary Language." *Handbook of Undergraduate Second Language Education*. Ed. Judith Rosenthal. Mahweh, New Jersey: Lawrence Erlbaum, 2000. 209-229.

Hufeisen, Britta. "L3—Stand der Forschung—was bleibt zu tun? [L3 State-of-the-Art: What Remains to be Done?]." *Tertiärsprachen. Theorien, Modelle, Methoden*. Ed. Britta Hufeisen and Beate Lindemann. Tübingen: Stauffenburg, 1998. 169-184.

Jessner, Ulrike. "Towards a Dynamic View of Multilingualism." *Language Choices: Conditions, Constraints and Consequences*. Ed. Martin Pütz. Amsterdam: Benjamins, 1997. 17-30.

Klein, Horst, and Tilbert Stegmann. *EuroComRom – Die sieben Siebe: Romanische Sprachen sofort lesen können. [EuroComRom – The Seven Sieves: Learning to Read Romance Languages.]* Aachen: Shaker, 2000.

Larsen-Freeman, Diane, and Michael Long. *An Introduction to Second Language Acquisition Research*. London: Longman, 1997.

Levelt, Willem. *Speaking. From Intention to Articulation*. Cambridge: MIT Press, 1989.

Lindemann, Beate. "Zum Einfluß der L1 und L2 bei der Rezeption von L3-Texten. [The Influence of the L1and L2 During the Reception of L3-Texts.]" *Zeitschrift für interkulturellen Fremdsprachenunterricht* 5.1 (2000) <www.ualberta.ca/~german/ejournal/lindem1.htm>.

Meissner, Franz-Joseph. "Philologiestudenten lesen in fremden romanischen Sprachen. Konsequenzen für die Mehrsprachigkeitsdidaktik aus einem empirischen Vergleich. [Philology Students Read in Unknown Romance Languages. Consequences for Multilingualism Didactics Through Empirical Comparison.]" *Interaktiver Fremdsprachenunterricht: Wege zu authentischer Kommunikation*. Ed. Franz-Joseph Meissner. Tübingen: Narr, 1997. 25-44.

Meissner, Franz-Joseph, and Heike Burk. "Hörverstehen in einer unbekannten romanischen Fremdsprache und methodische Implikationen für den Tertiärsprachenerwerb. [Listening Comprehension in an Unknown Romance Language and Methodological Implications for Tertiary Language Learning.]" *Zeitschrift für Fremdsprachenforschung* 12.1 (2001): 63-102.

Missler, Bettina. *Fremdsprachenlernerfahrungen und Lernstrategien. Eine empirische Untersuchung. [Foreign Language Research and Learning Strategies. An Empirical Study.]* Tübingen: Stauffenburg, 1999.

Müller-Lancé, Johannes. *Zugänge zum Wortschatz romanischer Sprachen. [Admission to the Vocabulary of Romance Languages.]* Tübingen: Stauffenburg, 2002.

Neuner, Gerhard and Britta Hufeisen. *Tertiärsprachen lehren und lernen. Beispiel: Deutsch nach Englisch. [Teaching and Learning Tertiary Languages. German After English.]* Draft Manuscript. München/Graz: Goethe Institut InterNationes and the European Centre for Modern Languages, 2001.

Poulisse, Nanda, and Theo Bongaerts. "First Language Use in Second Language Production." *Applied Linguistics* 15.1 (1994): 36-57.

Safont Jordà, Maria Pilar. "Unintentional and Intentional Codeswitching in Third Language Oral Production." *Language as a Tool. Immersion Research and Practices*. Ed. Siv Björklund. Proceedings of the University of Vaasa. Vaasa: University of Vaasa, 2001.

Stedje, Astrid. "Interferenz von Muttersprache und Zweitsprache auf eine dritte Sprache beim freien Sprachen—ein Vergleich. [Interference of the L1 and L2 on a Third Language During Speech—a Comparison.]" *Zielsprache Deutsch* 1 (1976): 15-21.

Williams, Sarah, and Björn Hammarberg. "Language Switches in L3 Production: Implications for a Polyglott Speaking Model." *Applied Linguistics* 19.3 (1998): 295-333.

Post-Reading Questions

1. *Look at your answers for pre-reading questions one and two. Using the information presented on language acquisition in the previous articles, further explain your first encounter with a foreign language.*

2. *Look at your answer for pre-reading question #3. After gaining additional knowledge about language acquisition, how would you now explain the process of language learning within the framework you suggested as being important for student success?*

3. In light of the previous question and answer, what are the circumstances for successful foreign language learning that you would strive for *as a teacher*? What would you change in your current teaching situation? Don't look only at curricular or methodological changes, but also consider the overall atmosphere of the school, and what it would take to challenge people's attitudes towards language learning.

4. *Attempt to more thoroughly explain the answer you gave in pre-reading question #4 around the collision of your first and second foreign languages.*

5. *Based on what you now know about language acquisition, revise your answers to pre-reading questions #5-7.*

6. *In your opinion, what areas of foreign language classroom practice should be further researched in order to increase the quality of language instruction?*

7. *How could you, as a pre- or in-service teacher, participate in this research?*

Chapter 5

Teacher Development and Recruitment

In this final section, the authors discuss the quality of teacher education in the US and Europe. They present new ways of teacher recruitment and development as the key to creating a lasting impact on people's attitude towards each other, other languages, and different cultures. This section also draws some conclusions about changes needed in the way we prepare our next generation of language educators, in order to assure that our new visions on the architecture of the profession, curriculum and instruction, articulation, assessment, and research become a reality.

Pre-Reading Questions

1. *Which one of your foreign language teachers has had the most significant impact on your language learning? How? What made him/her special?*

2. *What specific skills do you consider necessary to be an effective teacher? Try to assess what skills you already possess and how you make use of them.*

3. *Refine or expand your list from the above question to include the specific skills you think are necessary for a foreign language teacher to have.*

4. *What do you remember about the language proficiency of your former or current teachers? What impact, do you assume, does the quality of the teacher's language skills have on the learner?*

5. *Summarize what you have said so far in the other pre-, while-, and post-reading questions about the role of technology in language education. What should (future) teachers know about the use of technology?*

6. *Whether you are still a student or already a teacher, think about the support system that is necessary for you to grow as a person and as a professional. Describe this system and how you as an individual can best take advantage of it.*

Introduction to The New Visions Initiative: Recruitment and Retention

Lee Wilberschied

Introduction

Visions, for us, may be of little worth, if they are not accompanied by passion, focus, action, and sustainment. The New Visions initiative provides focus, cohesion, and effort at the national, or macro, level. Participation at this level will help to engender efforts at other levels—national, regional, state, and local. A reciprocal effort on the micro and middle levels will help to sustain synergy.

The Recruitment and Retention initiative is crucially interrelated with other elements of the New Visions effort. It is an integral part, which, if neglected or minimized, would seriously devitalize the other facets of New Visions. If we have an insufficient number of professionals in the future, the remainder of the issues will be moot, either because of lack of resources to work on them or because such a scenario would call for a change of vision.

The word *professionals* is important here because there will remain those who believe that, simply by virtue of being able to communicate in a second language, one is automatically able to teach it well. Thus, the argument proceeds, and we have many potential candidates for ready recruitment.

CONSIDER

Do you know people who hold this assumption? What arguments can you make to dispute this? For a more in depth discussion of the issue of teacher language proficiency see the chapter in this volume by Marjorie Hall Haley.

Such views discount the idea of professionalization and seem to ignore the need for support in order to retain educators. The need for publicity to help change these misperceptions is one that the current Task Force is addressing.

In May 2001, the Task Force refined and focused the goals that had been put forth in the previous two years' sessions. This phase of the initiative, called *New Visions in Action, 2001-2004*, has set out to do what it is named for—to implement the vision. Implementation for this phase focuses on three areas: publicizing successful models of recruitment and retention; expanding publicity for study of foreign language generally and for recruitment of *new and diverse members*; and creating materials to support and retain teachers already in practice.

ACTION

Explore this web site. Pull up one or more reports to see what is being done around the country in terms of teacher recruitment.

Publicizing Models of Recruitment

Current examples are described on the web site at <www.educ.iastate.edu/new_visions>. Initial reports from Alabama, Illinois, and California were posted, with others following.

On another front, sessions at ACTFL 2001 described statewide and district efforts. A panel of foreign language State Supervisors described the efforts of three states—Connecticut, Georgia, and North Carolina. One point discussed was the importance of easily accessible information for prospective teachers or for those returning to the field. In that vein, one state has updated its web site to make information easy to locate and people easy to reach.

In addition to making information easily accessible, these states are working on ways to fund course work, to adapt schedules in order to complete courses, to increase reciprocity arrangements with other states, and to extend temporary certification while candidates complete course work. One further attempt to facilitate certification or licensure is through development of web-based courses.

Of the other states not represented in these sessions, a few are implementing more drastic measures, such as Troops to Teachers, which facilitates the placement of discharged military personnel into the classroom. Some districts have sent recruiters overseas; they have returned with native speaker teachers along with content area teachers. These and other measures point to the dramatic need for support so that any new teacher will remain past the five-year stage at which many teachers resign.

Presenters of one ACTFL session were full-time FL mentors who support the well-being of beginning teachers professionally, emotionally, and socially, along with aiding long-term planning, classroom management, and time management. Presenters from Kentucky outlined that state's academy for foreign language teachers that incorporates mentoring, language immersion, leadership development, and networking.

Publicizing Languages and Careers

Current examples include a recruitment brochure that is downloadable at the web site of the National K-12 Foreign Language Resource Center at <www.educ.iastate.edu/new_visions>. Several states, such as Washington and Connecticut, have developed recruitment brochures.

This area of effort is crucial for the profession and, in a larger sense, the future of aspects of our society. In working to increase the perceived and material value of the study and use foreign languages and cultures, foreign language educators contribute to the well-being and vitality—perhaps even the survival—of citizens and nations.

Supporting and Affirming Educators

Current examples include support materials that can be viewed on the ACTFL web site at <www.actfl.org>. In addition, presentations at ACTFL conferences keep members up-to-date regarding research and best practices in mentoring. ACTFL's journal *Foreign Language Annals* also publishes articles on mentoring.

Some New Visions members' institutions have created or have contracted for some of the required professionalization and/or in-service courses to be delivered online or as distance education courses. These formats allow teachers and teacher candidates a more flexible schedule and perhaps even some cyber support. Some of these same institutions arrange for support sessions to prepare for Praxis exams and/or other exams required to gain credentials.

Some New Visions members of special interest groups (SIGs) work to support and retain new teachers. For instance, the Teachers of African-American Students SIG, in addition to its regular listserv messages, supports new teachers via E-mail. Annual sessions address strategies for optimal instruction.

In other institutions having New Visions members, there is mentor training, sometimes with the Pathwise model. Fostering and focusing effective mentoring skills will help to prepare designated and unofficial mentors who can help retain teachers competent in both content and delivery.

Going Beyond

The areas of focus described above show the attempt of the New Visions team to incorporate many of the needs identified by the teams of the beginning two years. The effort is cumulative and progressive, as well as laudable. Still there are two points that deserve to be emphasized—the need for additional effort to recruit and retain minority educators of foreign languages, and the need for efforts on the grass roots level, including taking personal responsibility in all ways that one can.

The Need for Minority Teachers

Each of us can sustain a focused effort to support, in particular, the recruitment and retention of minority teachers who will serve the increasingly diverse population of students in our schools. It is vital to promote recruitment of teachers who understand the needs and backgrounds of minority students, teachers to whom such students can relate, and who represent the overall composition of our society. Even if one does not live or teach in a particular area that reflects diversity, one can support scholarships and interest groups for minority students.

DISCUSS

The student population nationwide is becoming increasingly diverse. Discuss with a partner ways to make the field of foreign language teaching more attractive to minority educators.

In Ohio, for instance, the state foreign language association (OFLA), offers several scholarships—for high school students and for college students to attend the annual conference, and for teacher education students to study abroad. Encouraging our students, especially if those students are from minority populations, is one way to recruit and/or retain. In addition, state, regional, and national special interest groups (SIGs) for minority teachers might sponsor scholarships specifically geared to potential teacher candidates.

Grass Roots Parallel Efforts

To sustain efforts on the macro level, each of us as an individual at the micro level may make contributions toward recruitment and retention. One can establish, support, and mentor future teacher organizations. We can support local, regional, and statewide efforts to implement New Visions in Action.

We can all continue our own professionalization efforts in order to be good models and an inspiration for those we teach.

In addition, methodologies such as service learning can help to inspire an understanding of the relevance of content and the value and vitality of the teaching profession. Some service learning projects have matched potential teachers and teacher candidates with English Language Learners (ELLs) and have awakened a love of teaching and/or the recognition of one's aptitude for foreign language study and teaching. All of these contribute to and amplify the efforts put forth in New Visions. Matching one's individual efforts with membership in a state, regional, or national NV effort does intensify the initiative.

This envisioning is hard work. The New Visions initiative helps to prevent duplication of efforts, to assess and sustain ongoing efforts, to counteract the isolation of those in remote areas who wish to contribute, to maximize the activity, and to make the vision increasingly more manifest.

DISCUSS

Discuss with a partner two specific ways that you as an individual can be an inspiration to fellow teachers and thus positively contribute to both recruitment and retention efforts.

Interview with Lee Wilberschied

Svenja Dahlmanns

Svenja Dahlmanns (SD)

School development theory indicates that changes within institutional structures are most successful if there is an interplay between initiatives that work *top down* as well as *bottom up*. In your introduction you talk about a reciprocal effort on the micro and middle levels that will help sustain energy.

Lee Wilberschied (LW)

Initiatives are occurring at all levels concurrently but there are attempts to align efforts, and that helps somewhat. For example, a rough overview includes:

- The ACTFL National Standards for students. The bases for these actually go back to the 1980s, though the document is in its second edition as of 2000.
- The ACTFL/NCATE document (October, 2002) helps to set clear standards and guidelines for what teacher candidates must know and be able to do, as well as for dispositions (professional attitudes and behaviors that reflect such attitudes). Teacher education programs and departments of languages and literatures must demonstrate that preservice teachers receive the training required to meet these standards.
- State boards of education that require performance-based evidence from licensure candidates and continuing professional development from licensed teachers who wish to retain their credentials. One criterion for acceptability of such evidence is that it aligns with the above standards or with standards created by the state, which also align with the above standards. (For instance, Ohio's *Competency Model*, first introduced in 1995, is undergoing revision in order to align it more precisely with ACTFL *Standards*. Ohio state Consultants for Modern Languages are working with professionals (K-16+ educators, administrators, and community members from around the state) in a committee to complete the final revisions.
- Regional professional development committees often work with state boards of education, with local school districts, and with state chapters of professional associations (such as the *AATs*—American Association of Teachers of French, Japanese, German, Spanish, Portuguese, etc.) to align standards, define best practices, and increase professional development.
- The national board certification for teachers.
- The New Visions initiative weaves throughout these endeavors at many

levels. Individual educators may be involved in one or many of the strands, at the national, the state, or the local level, at one time.

A clear and concise discussion by Bronwyn Coltrane of the Center for Applied Linguistics appears in the *ERIC/CLL News Bulletin* Fall (2002): 6-8. More information about availability of that article appears at <www.cal.org/ericcll> or can be requested by calling (800) 276-9834.

(SD)
Who exactly do you see in this arena who will contribute to successful restructuring of our professional field? Where and how exactly did they learn to serve what you call a reciprocal effort between institutional and micro/middle levels of involvement?

(LW)
The simplest answer would be that professionals from the classroom K-16+ comprise much of the membership for this endeavor. Your question about where and how they learned to serve is crucial: they learned from mentoring, from personal awareness and concern, from dialogues with colleagues, from state professional associations, from concerned administrators.

(SD)
In practice, how much time are you and your colleagues estimating for the New Visions task force on recruitment and retention to have an impact on the profession?

(LW)
The New Visions documents and structure emerged over two to three years. The first part of the Initiative is set for a five year time period. Careful planning to achieve systemic change is realistic.

The membership receives annual progress updates at the ACTFL conference; this implies a yearly examination of the efforts. However, a year or so before the end of the cycle, it will be time to set the goals for the next period, including the possible addition, deletion, or revision of goals. Section leaders are in touch with each other throughout the year and at the ACTFL conference, so goal calibration is ongoing. This cyclical process, or ongoing evaluation and reform, will promote a systemic change, but it will not be sudden. The most obvious advantage is that this type of change engenders reform that is built on carefully reasoned and consensual thought, to provide a stable foundation that is capable of both adaptation and flexibility, as appropriate.

The Task Force has already made observable progress in the following ways:

- Developing a review of the literature regarding teacher recruitment and retention efforts in the nation.
- Establishing a national *teacher of the year* program for languages.
- Forming initiatives to develop a public relations campaign, to identify models for recruitment, and to provide strategies for retention.

Our profession is not isolated from society and its institutions, and some of the factors that impact our profession may not be easily predictable: catastrophes such as 9/11/2001 or wars in particular. Such circumstances might affect, for example, the number of those who want to enter the teaching field and to what extent they are supported. The infrastructure of the Task Force can unite the profession at such times and can be a means to initiate responsive measures.

(SD)
In Germany, the educational system differs from state to state; there are slightly varying school standards and rules, even in teacher education. This seems to make exchange, cooperation and reforms harder. Do you see cooperation on reforms between the micro (local), middle (state) and macro (national) level to be hindered by varying school standards from state to state?

(LW)
In a word, yes. However, at least two major initiatives are helping to create the delicate balance between independence/contextually-generated curricula and uniformity, which may imply rigidity or one-size-fits-all. These are the ACTFL Standards and the NCATE standards for teacher preparation.

Integrating the ACTFL Standards into my own instruction has made it easier to make adjustments and adaptations for revised or added sets of standards when they occur. The recently approved (October, 2002) and published NCATE standards provide extremely clear criteria. However, in many cases, the manner in which the criteria are met is not rigid.

DISCUSS

Read the chapter by Terry Osborn. Discuss how his position on working with standards differs from that of Sharon Wilkinson.

To be frank, however, there are articles that discuss the difficulties that you have described (For example, see Gibbs & Howley 2000). Hammadou Sullivan (2001) examined some of these issues as they pertain specifically to foreign language teacher education.

(SD)
What needs to be done to keep fulfilling the vision of the New Visions initiative and its different task forces successfully?

(LW)
We need to sustain and increase momentum. In order to do so, we will also have to increase the affiliate numbers, so many of us are working on the various initiatives and lending support. Frequent and inclusive communication among members would also help to keep us focused and motivated.

(SD)
Where do you see a need or a chance for the improvement of fulfilling the *Visions*?

(LW)

Grants that funded the first two sessions were not subsequently renewed, so contact and networking opportunities do not occur with such an inclusive and focused venue. Some of the leaders of the various initiatives do meet at least yearly on a smaller scale, but we could sustain momentum much better with yearly meetings that include all who participate in the *Visions* initiatives. Securing funding for that purpose does not seem likely now, despite the efforts of several dedicated leaders. Perhaps in the future the ACTFL conference could provide an alternative venue, if we were to acquire a block of time set aside for such a purpose, ideally before conference proceedings, so that we could focus on tasks and issues prior to devoting our attention to the conference itself.

(SD)

What is your personal vision for this rapidly changing field of foreign language education?

(LW)

I appreciate this last question. I am able to say that, to a great extent, my personal vision has become aligned with much of what is stated in the New Visions documents. In addition, however, my personal vision calls for a large investment in recruitment and retention of minority foreign language teachers, who will be resources for the institution of education and a strengthening for the life-blood of its members. Such teachers will be models and inspirations to their students and will enrich the thinking of educators and researchers who will be working to meet the needs of an increasingly multicultural student body.

(SD)

I think you will agree with me when I say that responsibility for substantial change in our profession needs to come from each individual member of this profession. Nevertheless, before each of us can pursue change, a clear definition of what exactly we are looking for is needed. New Visions works out a general profile of a professional Foreign Language teacher. What makes a teacher of a foreign language a professional? Would you suggest specific criteria for those who want to become more professional in Foreign Language teaching?

(LW)

Standard 6, Professionalism, of the ACTFL/NCATE document is available online at <www.actfl.org>. For the sake of clarity and brevity, here is an outline; the full document includes supporting explanations and descriptions of the range of fulfillment of each aspect:

6a. Engaging in Professional Development

- Awareness of the professional community.
- Life-long commitment to professional growth.

- Reflection as a critical tool for growth.
- Dispositions for seeking personal growth.

ACTION

Draft a personal list of professional criteria you do (or want to) strive for.

6b. Knowing the Value of Foreign Language Learning

- Developing of a rationale for foreign language learning.
- Accessing and employing data to support foreign language learning.
- The importance of building alliances for advocacy.
- Dispositions regarding the value of K-12 study.

That section concludes with a *Summary of Candidate Evidence* for that standard. The candidate needs not fulfill all elements in the summary but a sufficient combination of them. Some examples include the following:

- List of professional memberships and evidence of participating in them.
- Description of the professional activities in which the candidate has participated, and the benefits those activities have provided to the candidate.
- Professional development plan.
- Research questions that the candidate has at this point in her/his career.
- Philosophy statement that demonstrates advocacy of foreign language learning.

In addition to the above list, I believe that candidates as well as inservice teachers could also use the following as evidence of professionalism:

CONSIDER

See which requirements on both lists you already fulfill, and which still need some additional effort to be met.

- Community involvement with FL/SL populations at all stages of pre- and in-service teaching.
- Having a mentor and then, later, mentoring.
- Participating in recruitment and retention efforts to attract more foreign language educators.
- After the initial career stages, applying for National Board certification.

(SD)
In your introduction, you mention the overseas recruitment of native-speaker teachers to collaborate with content area teachers at US schools. This seems to be a specific effort to strengthen bilingual education. Have you yet seen any effects of this?

(LW)
There are two specific scenarios that may clarify this question. One is of communities which brought teachers from overseas to teach in the *content* areas, such as math and science. In most cases their native language was not English, or they spoke a dialect of English, and their customs were not familiar to the community. These individuals were not teaching a foreign language—but in some cases they were teaching in a foreign language or dialect.

In the second situation, native speakers of foreign languages were recruited from outside the country because communities had been unable to hire teachers for FL programs or for bilingual programs.

In both cases, many of the teachers had been educators in their native country. But, despite inservices to train them, their unfamiliarity with the US and local school culture presented difficulties for the teachers and for the communities (culture shock, for instance, on both sides).

(SD)
What do you think about the professional status of these native speakers, let's say, math teachers, in regard to their ability to teach foreign language learners?

(LW)
These teachers are often certified in their own country and therefore deserve the recognition that many states have granted, by granting a license or certificate on the basis of prior out-of-state licensure. Some of the teachers, however, came to their positions from other professions, much as those in the US who seek alternative licensure—with little theoretical or practical experience in education. These individuals are professionals in another sense, perhaps, but they need support throughout an induction period. In some states, the responsibility for that support and professionalization is left up to local committees or to individual school districts. There may be little uniformity, rigor, or content in such induction.

(SD)
In German Teacher Education, which takes four to five years, I observed a split between teachers who get trained for Elementary Schools and those who plan to work for Secondary Schools. The first group enjoys a training that has a strong emphasis on practical and pedagogical issues from the beginning. Also, they take part in several obligatory internships in school. The second group, especially those participants going towards jobs at high schools, is trained intensively in theoretical issues of their subject, but they do not enter a classroom until the end of their education. What is your opinion about this?

(LW)
I, too, have seen this in several programs, and it has a lot to do with concerns about preparing secondary teachers thoroughly in the content area. NCATE calls for several field experiences to help ensure that teacher candidates will have practice and insight into needs of learners. Both field experiences and course content for secondary school candidates do well when they integrate information regarding elementary school students and methods. Too often, candidates think that only little kids need to learn through concrete means. Those needs can be present in secondary students of foreign language also, and some programs may need to balance secondary teacher education programs a little more in order to promote the value of concretizing instruction without *teaching down* to older students.

Teacher educators might make mini-assignments for visits, observations, and interviews at the elementary and middle school levels in addition to the formal field experiences. Service learning is another fantastic way to get students involved. (See Boyle-Baise 2002, for example.)

Middle and secondary teachers can also help to offset this trend. They can begin their recruitment efforts in grades 6-12, with *Future Teacher* activities in which foreign language students work with elementary age students, perhaps even ESL students. Students of the foreign language could become active in tutoring, serving as teacher aides, giving performances, being ambassadors, and delivering mini-teaching sessions. By doing so, teachers can help change the belief or mind-set of some potential teachers that teaching at the secondary level must be totally abstract.

The ACTFL/NCATE Standards will be an enormous help. Standard 3 asks for candidates to "demonstrate an understanding of the physical, cognitive, emotional, and social development of K-12 students at all levels of instruction" (34). Standard 4 asks that candidates use and appropriately adapt authentic materials and instruction to integrate national and state standards into instruction. Such adaptation and integration will help candidates to focus on learner needs and age-appropriate delivery of instruction.

(SD)
In your introduction you say that publicity for the profession could help to avoid misperceptions about FL learning and the professional field of FL teaching. If I understand you correctly, most of the publicity has been gained through the Internet. What are the most effective media besides the Internet that help making the needs and opportunities of our profession transparent?

(LW)
I was actually thinking more of television, because so many students spend so many hours a week watching television. The website for the American Academy of Child and Adolescent Psychology gives us a clear picture of these numbers (See <http://www.aacap.org/publications/factsfam/tv.htm>.) as well as The Kaiser Family Foundation website at <www.kff.org> (*Kids and the Media at the New Millenium*). Their survey of more than 2000 K-12 students indicates that 64 percent of those children spent more than one hour a day watching TV versus 36 percent who used the computer for more than an hour.

CONSIDER

There are many views on the role of TV in language education. Look at the interview with Helene Zimmer-Loew in chapter one, and summarize her opinion on using TV for promoting language education.

In addition to considering the percentage of the *market* that each medium attracts, I believe that television has the capability to bombard the audience with repeated messages more powerfully than the Internet.

A colleague of mine in marketing once told me that we needed to *glamorize* foreign language in every way. Taken to the extreme, that would mean that we need to have role models in sports, contemporary music, fashion, and film who are bilingual or multilingual and who are willing to market that asset for us. The increasing Hispanic population in the US is giving us models, but such models are needed for world languages in addition to Spanish.

(SD)
In Germany, there are still many people who do not have access to a computer or the Internet. What measures are US Foreign Language educators taking to make sure that everyone can use the online offers of teacher development, recruitment, and retention you are mentioning?

(LW)
Pre-service teachers have the facilities of the institution, where computer labs are open long hours and staffed by aides.

Teachers who work in less affluent or rural districts may have to use public facilities in libraries or apply for government or corporation grants to help build the technology infrastructure of their institution or district.

Other avenues include distance learning, video training, and travelling workshops presented by consultants, corporations, or regional professional development centers.

The National Center for Education Statistics (US Department of Education) presents an in-depth picture of computer/Internet availability and use in *Teachers' Tools for the 21st Century: A Report on Teachers' Use of Technology. NCES 2000-102, by Smerdon, Cronen, Lanahan, Anderson, Iannotti, and Angeles. Washington, DC: 2000.* More information on the report and other publications can be accessed on their web page at <http://nces.ed.gov>.

(SD)
A second question in regard to the use of computers: what changes are necessary in the training of FL teachers to ensure they gain the technical skills they need to use the Internet with all its features in an appropriate, optimized way?

(LW)
NCATE requires teacher educators to demonstrate how we integrate the use of technology in our own instruction and how we integrate it into the assignments of the pre- and in-service teachers so that they can demonstrate their capability. State licensure programs often require successful completion of one or more courses in instructional technology, no matter what the area of specialization.

Consider

Read the chapter by Müller-Hartman & Schocker-v. Ditfurth to get a more detailed example of how language teacher training in using instructional technology is addressed in Europe.

(SD)
The third aspect regarding the important role of the Internet for communicating the idea of new visions: what gives you the confidence that FL teachers, even though they might have access to the Internet and possess the necessary skills, actually use the online resources to help develop professionalism? How will you measure the effect of the online teacher development and retention?

(LW)
Several universities in our state are in various stages of completion of program reports for NCATE. Teacher educators must show in what ways we have

- Incorporated technology into our own instruction (thus providing a model for teacher candidates).
- Trained teacher candidates to use technology.

For instance, Candidate Evidence for Standard 2 can include "projects/technology-enhanced presentations on literary or cultural topics" (21). One example of a Standard 4 criterion is for the candidate "to evaluate, select, and design materials...obtained through technology" (30).

The information required in the initial reports to NCATE is extensive, and it is extremely time-consuming to prepare statistics and descriptions. In the future, however, this information will be aggregated across time and institutions. That will give us measures of the number of candidates trained and in what manner.

Whether the teachers go on to use technology in their practice or in further professionalization is also part of the information that our institution is required to gather, through follow-up interviews of graduates. That is, we cannot enforce the use of technology, but we can monitor to see whether our training has been effective in engendering such use. If not, we are compelled, by virtue of our NCATE membership, to improve our teacher training until our graduates manifest such use. In addition, local and state professional and government organizations offer training, rewards, and/or requirements.

(SD)
Mrs. Wilberschied, in your essay, you mention that numerous teachers resign their jobs after reaching the five-year stage. In Europe, I read about a similar phenomenon known as *Burn Out Syndrome*. What are the specific major problems that make teachers leave?

(LW)
Low pay; lack of administrative support; isolation (or lack of mutual support by teachers); lack of public value of teachers; lack of safety for self and students; constant disruptions; demand for accountability; lack of materials and supplies brought on by lack of financial support from the community; lack of rigor; increasing demands for further recordkeeping; parent confrontations; bullying; and the gaping hole of need of the students or the district. In the broader context, one important factor is the glamor of other occupations—or their relative simplicity: teachers make 150 or more decisions during a 50 minute class. (See Cesarone 1999, for example.)

(SD)
We all know that teachers have a major influence on the individuals of the next generation. You stated in your text that foreign language education is crucial for the future, well-being, and even survival of our multicultural society. It seems that there

is more to it than just the knowledge of a different culture and language in order to make people able to live together peacefully. What other aspects do you see as important tasks of successful foreign language education in the future?

(LW)

We can't save the world, and one's being able to speak and understand a FL is still no guarantee that an individual has learned the ability to listen, in the psychological sense. All teachers, whether they teach FL or not, can work to model and teach the practice of authentic listening in L1 and all subsequently acquired languages.

We also work on changing thought, attitudes, and behavior of our students to enhance not merely their tolerance but more importantly their appreciation of cultural and linguistic differences.

We can exploit the cognitive changes that accompany FL study by consistently promoting critical thinking processes in and about the L2, the second culture (C2), and about L2/C2 learning. Such practices can begin with authentic communication at beginner levels and extend to critical analysis of world events or implications of L2 teaching policy in advanced language and pedagogy courses. Both van Lier and Osborn have inspirational discussions of such practices in their recent books.

Consider

See also Terry Osborn's chapter in this volume.

Preservice teachers would benefit from training in several areas of theory to a degree that they can integrate it with language instruction. Anthropology studies, for instance, promote depth of understanding in the phenomenon of culture, which the Standards have designated as an important element of instruction. Models such as Kluckhohn's[1] help to demonstrate the notion of culture as a spectrum of different ways of looking at the world and life, rather than one particular *culture as being right or wrong*. Exploration of identity theory could inspire teachers' discussions with their students, providing yet another area for authentic discussion in the L2 and about the study of the L2 on the personal, expanded, and global levels.

Other tasks include sustaining efforts, at least in the United States, to increase the number of P-8 FLES (foreign language teaching in elementary schools; see: the National Network for Early Language Learning at <http://nnell.org/>), immersion, and bilingual programs; keeping instruction current with a world that is changing more rapidly than it ever has, and continuing research, especially to show the varied and many benefits of FL study.

(SD)

You described various mentoring activities in aid of beginning teachers. How important in this regard is the role of reflective practice, such as teaching portfolios? In what specific way can teaching portfolios help colleagues with poor performance improve as language teachers?

(LW)

Mentoring, when the numerous variables that affect it are favorable, can be the most powerful tool for teacher development and retention. Reflective practice in the mentor/mentee relationship can occur with or without the existence of a portfolio.

The teaching portfolio is a tool or an instrument, but does not guarantee reflectivity, either in the product or in the practice. It is important to distinguish reflective practice as part of the portfolio—because other tools are also valid for showing that this practice is consistent in the teacher's behavior (for instance, teacher collaboratives, action research, or reflective dialogues with mentors). Reflectivity at its best can be complex and multidimensional; at its poorest, it can be *reportative*. Assignment of a portfolio will not guarantee that reflectivity will develop. In addition, we found that some teachers benefit more from dialogical or discursive reflection rather than written reflection (Dassier & Wilberschied 2000).

Another implication in your question concerns guidance in developing reflectivity. Gwyn-Paquette and Tochon (2002) point out that many preservice teachers needed guidance in developing reflective patterns. Such practices might be modelled in teacher education courses, and rubrics might provide a template. However, reflective conversation with a mentor teacher and even reflective dialogue journal writing with a mentor are powerful tools. Another model is peer coaching.

Another important aspect of your question concerns the function of a portfolio as an aid for improving poor performance. In such a situation, the process of the portfolio would have to be scaffolded in several ways:

- Facilitation in making clear the purpose and focus of the portfolio (to reflect professional growth, adoption of best practices, manifestation of desired dispositions).
- Providing opportunities to observe best practices (difficult in isolated areas but becoming easier with technological aids and distance learning).
- Change of beliefs. There has to be *awareness* on the part of the poorly performing teacher that desired results have not been met. The instrument on Dispositions that is coming into use will help to define and illustrate professional practice. However, individual teachers may need to discuss plans for change that meet their worldview and their needs.

We do need the willingness of one teacher or a team of teachers to work with the struggling educator. Mentors may be appointed, but there is no guarantee that there will be sufficient compatibility between mentor and mentee. There needs to be trust and collegiality; a sense of peers working together, not of the poorly-performing teacher being sent to an expert to be *worked on*, to be *fixed*. The models of mentoring are too numerous to discuss in a space as limited as this.

CONSIDER

You can find one example of mentoring in the chapter by David Jahner in this volume.

Notes

1. This method, developed by anthropologist Dr. Florence R. Kluckhohn, serves as a tool to facilitate examination of the underlying world views of cultures and identification of value orientations of cultural groups. This model has three main assumptions, the first of which is that all cultural groups must find some solution to common problems or

questions of existence: the inborn character of human nature, the relationship of humans to nature, the nature of time in human life, the important mode of human activity, and the relationship of individuals to those around them.

The other two assumptions are that the solutions to the above questions vary among a range of possible solutions and that societies prefer different solutions, even though all alternatives are potentially available to them. For a discussion and specific applications of the Model, please see Ortuño, M. M. (1991). "Cross-cultural awareness in the foreign language class: The Kluckhohn model," *The Modern Language Journal*, 75, 449-459.

References

Boyle-Baise, M. *Multicultural Service Learning: Educating Teachers in Diverse Communities.* New York: Columbia Teachers College Press, 2002.

Coltrane, B. "New Standards for Foreign Language Teaching: A Vision for the Future." *ERIC/CLL Newsbulletin* 26 (Fall 2002): 6-8.

Cesarone, B. "Stress, Burnout, and Changing Teacher Roles." *Childhood Education* 75 (1999): 317-318.

Dassier, J. L., and L. Wilberschied. "A Case Study of Reflection in Supervision: Does it Have Any Relationship to Interns' Reflectivity?" *SCOLT Dimension 2000: New Millennium, New Directions.* Valdosta: SCOLT Publications, Valdosta State University, 2000.

Gibbs, Tom, and Aimee Howley. "World-Class Standards and Local Pedagogies: Can We Do Both?" *ERIC Digest* Dec 2000 <http://mirror.eschina.bnu.edu.cn/Mirror1/accesseric/www.ael.org/eric/digests/edorc008.htm>.

Gwyn-Paquette, C., and F. Tochon. "The Role of Reflective Conversations and Feedback in Helping Preservice Teachers Learn to use Cooperative Activities in Their Second Language Classroom." *Modern Language Journal* 86 (2002): 204-226.

Ortuño, M. M. "Cross-Cultural Awareness in the Foreign Language Class: The Kluckhohn Model." *The Modern Language Journal* 75 (1991): 449-459.

Osborn, T. A. *Critical Reflection and the Foreign Language Classroom.* Westport: Bergin and Garvey, 2000.

Sullivan, J. H. "The Challenge of Foreign Language Teacher Preparation: Addressing State Teacher Standards." *Clearing House* 74 (2001): 305-307.

van Lier, L. *Interaction in the Language Curriculum: Awareness, Autonomy, and Authenticity.* London: Longman, 1996.

Technology-Enhanced Project Work in Pre-Service Language Teacher Education to Support Autonomous Student Teacher Learning

Andreas Müller-Hartmann
Marita Schocker-v. Ditfurth

The Context

We have been involved in developing and evaluating the effects of technology-supported learning environments for EFL student teachers for a number of years. There is a mutual concern we both have: in trying to align teacher education with teaching, we consider the core component of our curriculum to be the attitudes, knowledge, and the skills required to teach and learn a foreign language as a means of intercultural communication. Therefore the contents and procedures of teacher education should be derived from an analysis of the complex competencies foreign language teachers need to develop so that they will be able to organize, to support, and to evaluate language learning in the EFL classroom. We depart radically from what traditionally counts as the appropriate knowledge base of language teacher education in our context, which is linguistics, cultural studies, and literature studies (see Zydatiß 3-4).

CONSIDER

In your opinion, what constitutes the appropriate knowledge base for language teacher education programs? Or in other words, what would you find important for your own teacher training?

What are the consequences of this philosophy with regard to educating prospective EFL teachers who are expected to initiate autonomous and co-operative learning in classrooms?

Autonomy and Teacher Education

Numerous reports from foreign language classrooms during the past one and a half years have demonstrated that using technology in the language classroom to do research on the world wide web, to communicate with people all over the world, or to have learners publish their own texts for a world-wide audience, holds a promising potential to support autonomous learning (Fremdsprache Deutsch 1999). It is striking that the possibility to individualize learning goes along with a strengthening of social learning, because technology in the classroom does promote the use of project- or group-oriented ways of working: students don't just interact with learners all over the world in one-to-one settings; they also sit together in twos or in a small group in front of a computer and negotiate meanings. We therefore agree with Leni Dam who says that:

> Learner autonomy is characterized by a readiness to take charge of one's own learning in the service of one's needs and purposes. This entails a capacity and willingness to act independently and in cooperation with others, as a socially responsible person. An autonomous learner is an active participant in the social processes of learning, but also an active interpreter of new information in terms of what she/he already and uniquely knows. (505)

This changing role of students necessarily involves a changing role for teachers. This is why Seppo Tella (1996, 13) encourages teachers to join in this change process when he says that "... the teacher should be courageous enough to step aside, from the *sage on the stage* to the *guide on the side*." Other concepts used to try and label this new role of teachers are those of *coaches* or *facilitators*. One must be careful not to misunderstand this concept, though. It does *not* mean that teachers *disappear* from the stage, as is the case with Dieter Wolff when he says that "learning can only be minimally influenced by others, for example by teachers" (44).[1] This reminds us of the idea of *self instruction* (Little 1999, 30) where the teacher steps back and does not interfere with what his or her students do at all. If you believe in radical constructivists' views one gets the idea of a completely independent learner—completely independent of a teacher, of his or her peers, and of the curriculum. Little (1995) appropriately characterizes this approach as follows: "Total independence is not autonomy but autism" (178).

CONSIDER

Compare what you read here with what Langner & Prokop and Wolff have to say about the notion of learner autonomy embedded in a constructivist framework of education.

Learning is not just an individual and mental process of construction, but involves the social context in which learning takes place, and it involves fellow learners and the teacher. This learning environment in institutional language learning contexts—schools—is provided and structured by a teacher, ideally by way of a negotiated curriculum (Breen & Littlejohn 2000).

To be able to do this complex task appropriately, teachers not only need a sound target language competence, but they need also to know principles of coöperative ways of working, to negotiate purposes with their learners, and to guide and to support learners in their individual developments. Student teachers do not develop these competencies by studying linguistics or literature. If student teachers are to learn how to make use of the potential technology offers for autonomous learning in language teaching, teacher educators must put this purpose on their agenda. In other words, unless student teachers are not autonomous learners themselves, they will not be able to promote the corresponding processes with their learners in the language classroom. Therefore Little (1999) is right when he calls for models of teacher education which take account of this:

> ... we need models of teacher education that exploit the techniques of 'scaffolding' and 'appropriation' in the presentation and exploration of the theory and its practical implications, and set out explicitly to develop learners' (that is teachers') reflective analytical skills in planning, monitoring and evaluating their learning. (34)

And:

> What I am advocating…is that teacher education should be subject to the same processes of negotiation as are required for the promotion of learner autonomy in the language classroom. (180)

In the following, we would like to delineate how we try to meet these requirements in the courses we offer on teaching and learning foreign languages. How have we translated our claims in a learning environment for student teachers? And what changes have we introduced as a result of student-teacher feedback?

CONSIDER

Think of your own experiences in teacher education programs. Did (or does) the curriculum prepare you to be an autonomous learner? Give specific examples.

Principles of Computer-Supported Project Seminars for EFL Student Teachers

The availability of computer-supported learning in EFL classrooms offers the potential to provide a new quality of communicative and intercultural language learning (Byram 1997; Kramsch & Anderson 1999). In our EFL context, task-based E-mail projects between multinational classrooms offer a convincing and viable way to make use of the advantages technology offers, in that students use English as a means of international communication in the exchange of ideas with authentic audiences (Müller-Hartmann 1999; 2000). Therefore we believe that student teachers need to learn to create language learning environments which will allow them to *integrate* technology into their everyday work rather than just using it sporadically as an additive tool.

At the same time we support them in developing local understandings of teaching; that is why they learn to develop computer-related materials for a particular classroom, and to research the added value that technology offers for language acquisition in that classroom. To achieve both purposes, student teacher learning is based on three principles: research approach to learning, experiential learning, experimental learning.

Research Approach to Learning: Developing a Multi-Perspective View on the EFL Classroom (see Schocker-v. Ditfurth 2001)

Student teachers learn to develop a research approach to EFL learning to help them understand the complex dynamics that determine language learning in EFL classrooms. To do so, they learn to integrate the relevant perspectives on learning and teaching. These include three domains of knowledge: relevant published knowledge, student teachers' own perspectives on language learning (which, according to numerous learning-to-teach studies, affect their awareness and images of learning in classrooms and their dispositions to behave, regardless of whatever cognitive knowledge they may have encountered during teacher education), and the perspective of practice as represented by the experiences of teachers and their students who have been involved in multinational E-mail projects. We consider the inclusion of the perspective of practice to be crucial for various reasons. Research often is conducted in contexts outside language classrooms. But the appropriateness of tasks depends on the perceived value that teachers associate with them: "[S]chools are powerful places that create and sustain meanings and values...Therefore, it is misleading to see them merely as settings in which educational practices are implemented...Instead,...schools and classrooms function as frameworks of value and interpretation in which language teachers must learn to work effectively" (Freeman & Johnson 409). In accordance with Stenhouse, we believe that "the uniqueness of each classroom setting implies that any proposal...needs to be tested and verified and adapted by each teacher in his [or her] classroom" (Stenhouse 143).

Experiential Learning: Developing Action-Oriented Models for IT-Supported EFL Classrooms

Our seminars are organized to allow student teachers to work on projects, and to experience the very processes that they are to supposed to initiate with students in their prospective classrooms: within their project team, they choose a research question, they use Internet services to research, discuss, and publish the results of their project, they cooperate in virtual teams in which they exchange and discuss ideas with student teachers working on the same research question at different universities, they use English as their language of communication at all levels of the exchange, they evaluate selected aspects of the process and the product of their cooperation against mutually negotiated criteria; and, in doing all this, they experience the highlights and the drawbacks involved in coöperative learning. Thus, the seminars follow an approach to learning which is based on reflected experience, in that they integrate the experiences of students in classrooms and the experiences of student teachers at the university. In both of these learning environments, a teacher's role may no longer be adequately defined as a transmitter of knowledge to passive recipients. Instead, teachers need to offer expert guidance and support for students, to help them to cope with the multiple skills this learning environment involves. Teachers need to be positive role models from which students gradually learn. This concept of *teacher as model* must not be confused with the mechanical imitation of behavior, which characterized behaviorist-based teaching. Rather, it is understood in the sense of learning as *relational imitation* which Vygotsky expressed in his concept of the *zone of proximal development* (1978).

ACTION

Reread the interview with Amy S. Ohta, in chapter four of this volume, on Vygotsky's *zone of proximal development*.

Experimental Learning: Developing School Development Competencies Through Cooperation in Cross-Institutional Projects

The ability to develop a research approach to language classrooms implies that we overcome the traditional separation of school and university. This is particularly true of computer-mediated language learning, where the open structure of the medium may clash with the traditions of language teaching at schools: often lessons are textbook-based and follow a routine sequence of presentation, practice, and production. In computer-supported projects, teachers need what has come to be called *dynamic qualifications*, that is, competencies and values which are the basis for any innovation to be successful, such as "an appreciation of problems that one has identified during the process, student-orientation, process evaluation, an experiment attitude to practice,...and the ability to cope with controlled risks" (Krainer & Posch 25, TMS).

This is why student teachers cooperate in teams to develop materials for EFL classrooms, a process which involves intensive negotiation. Up to a point student teachers are proactive persons, change agents, who develop certain aspects of classroom language learning for a particular and clearly defined context.

DISCUSS

The authors present three principles on which student teacher learning is based. Summarize what these principles are and discuss to what extent they were/are present in your own educational experiences.

Let us now turn to the pedagogical implications of these principles. We will illustrate them, using two seminar types that we have developed as an example. As you will see, we have changed certain aspects as a result of student feedback.

Different Seminar Types

Seminar Type I - Internet Research Projects in Cultural Studies: Student Teachers as Direct Classroom Researchers

When we started our project three years ago, we defined student teachers' roles as direct classroom researchers. This seemed to be a viable way to achieve our purposes: teams of student-teachers developed and taught web-based cultural studies research projects in cooperation with EFL teachers and their classrooms. In the process of doing so they collected data to answer their research questions. These concerned different aspects of the added value the use of computer technology offers for language learning. At the end of the term, student-teachers presented their results at one of the participating universities, and they published their findings on a web site (For a detailed description of our experiences with this seminar type, see Legutke, Müller-Hartmann, & Schocker-v. Ditfurth 2001; Schocker-v. Ditfurth & Legutke 2002; for the project web site, see *References*).

CONSIDER

Reflect on what Sharon Wilkinson and Lee Wilberschied presented in their chapter 4 articles on research in schools, and how to prepare (future) teachers to conduct research.

This sort of seminar differs in several ways from the conventional seminars on teaching English as a foreign language. While the traditional arrangement of a graduate course as the central place for cooperative learning is maintained, it is extended to include activities in 5–7 school classrooms. Classroom teachers participate in a few key sessions of the university seminar, and at the same time they profit from the general development of the seminar via the Internet (E-mail and special conferences in *First Class*). Project work on the seminar level comprises four main phases:

Preparation of the School Projects

Teams of three to five student teachers design a project for a group of learners. It lasts three days, and it focuses on work with web-based materials. Student teachers research suitable web sites, develop tasks, and suggest procedures for the presentation and assessment of the projects.

Realization of the Project and Collection of Data in an EFL Classroom

During this phase the student teachers leave the university and carry out the projects. A team of students teachers works together with one teacher and her class. During the phase in the school, one student teacher takes care of one group of students. The school projects thus mirror the project approach in that they include preparation, research, presentation, and evaluation.

Evaluation of the Project and Presentation

After the school phase, student teachers return to the university where they evaluate their experiences in their respective groups. They analyze the data (e.g. teacher interviews, student questionnaires, observation protocols, and audio and video recordings). In the presence of all the partner teachers, the results are discussed at the end of the term in a public presentation.

Publication of Results

Finally, each group designs a web site on the topic of their project, taking into consideration the most important phases of the project plan, and they write a research report. This report will be made available to all the partner teachers. For an overview of selected projects go to: <http://www.vib-bw.de/tp7> (-> Unterrichtsprojekte).

Seminar Type II - Multinational Topic-Based E-mail Projects: Student teachers as Indirect Classroom Researchers

In contrast to the first seminar type, we no longer asked student teachers to both develop, teach *and* research the impact of school-based computer-projects (which would have been difficult anyway, given the unpredictable nature of E-mail exchange projects). Instead we, as course organizers (supported by a research assistant), developed computer-supported school-based projects in cooperation with teachers, and collected classroom data ourselves. Data included, for example, interviews with teachers, group discussions with students, project portfolios, and tasks and letters that students had exchanged in the course of their E-mail projects. When the projects had finished we put all of the classroom-based data onto *First Class,* our intranet server.

First Class serves two purposes in our seminars: it provides student teachers with the classroom-based *information* that allows them to get an idea of the processes an E-mail project triggered with students in a particular classroom, and to understand the perspectives of students and teachers involved in the projects, without having to go to classrooms in person to do their research. At the same time, *First Class* organizes *collaboration* between student teachers who study at three different universities but cooperate in virtual teams on different research question in so-called *conferences*.

A conference is an online-forum for user discussions, which serves as a mailbox common to a group of people. It is a kind of container for messages on a certain topic. Student teachers use these conferences as a forum for their collaborative and cross-institutional group work. Using this frame they deal with the virtual exploration of a research question over the course of a semester.

Examples of research questions which student teachers may choose from:

1. What is there to consider when you plan and organize an E-mail project that intends to promote intercultural learning? (Data: use teachers' letters and interviews; results of students' questionnaires).

2. Which qualities does a teacher need to have to be able to set up and sustain an E-mail project that promotes intercultural learning? (Data: use teachers' letters and interviews; results of students' questionnaires) .
3. Which task features are appropriate? How do they influence language and language learning in an EFL classroom? In what ways does language and language learning differ from learning in traditional classrooms? (Data: use students' letters, teachers' letters, teachers' interviews).
4. Was intercultural learning the outcome in the two projects? What was conducive to/ impeded intercultural learning? (Data: use text analysis of students' letters, teachers' interviews).
5. What kind of role does the literary text play in such projects? (You might want to consider aspects such as language help, language text difficulty, authenticity of input, cultural studies etc) (Data: use students' and teachers' letters, literary texts).

Let us now turn to the way student teachers involved in these seminars experienced their roles.

Autonomous Learning in EFL Teacher Education: How do Student Teachers Perceive Their Roles?

We will focus our seminar evaluation on aspects of autonomous learning and the development of the knowledge and the skills of teaching English as a means of intercultural communication as seen from student teachers' perspectives. Data collection involved a student teacher portfolio, a research diary for course organizers, a videotaped end-of-term group discussion, and various open-ended questionnaires at the beginning and in the process of the seminar.

We will present our findings in three steps:

- Recap features of autonomous learning as defined by published knowledge.
- Voices from student teachers.
- Our evaluation of student teachers' comments.

Coping with Autonomous Learning as a Complex Process: Easy to Say but Hard to Do

We subscribe to the notion of learner autonomy as defined by Leni Dam who has characterized it as

> ...a readiness to take charge of one's own learning in the service of one's needs and purposes. This entails a capacity *and* willingness to act independently *and* in cooperation with others, as a socially responsible person. [...as], an active participant in the social processes of learning [...and as] an active interpreter of new information in terms of what she/he already and uniquely knows. (505)

Responsibility for a group does not come about automatically. It depends on many factors:

One of the factors we identified is the student teachers' autobiography: Which learning routines have they developed both at school and university? Are student teachers used to working in autonomous learning environments? Which images of appropriate learning have they developed? What do they believe to be an appropriate way to demonstrate their progress?

> For the most part of the seminar we were supposed to work on our own. It was a good possibility to learn how to work independently, we had to organize ourselves. (...) I think some of the experiences we made in this seminar are really helpful for our later job as a teacher (student teacher, GI, E-mail, 12.07.2000).

> Individual initiative is what had been asked for. This failed with a group of four people already when we were trying to arrange for a date when we could all meet outside the seminar. This was a struggle at times. On the other hand, experiences like these also strengthen the group (student teacher, GI, portfolio, August 2000; TMS).

The extent of autonomous learning depends on the measures taken to promote social learning. We have intensified these measures in the course of our experiences. For example, we extended the first phase of getting to know each other, and we arranged the presentation phase at the end of the semester in form of a social event. This aspect has been emphasized by everybody involved as a positive feature and prerogative to ensure that a mutual responsibility for the project develops.

> I liked the idea of a meeting. From the very start I considered it to be very motivating that we would go to Freiburg together and present something; this way it doesn't all remain on a theoretical level, somehow (female student teacher, GI, group discussion, July 2000; TMS).

> I think this is a seminar which I will still remember in 20 years' time, since I will associate it with contact; the fact that you don't just deal with theories or read about methods and deal with literature, but that you also connect it with people and places, helps you remember it much more. Especially this meeting now, that was a very intensive experience. Although, in between, there was this feeling again and again: will we manage all of this, all that we have to do? And it was quite good to experience that you can work that intensively in such a short time and arrive at such good results (female student teacher, FR, group discussion, July 2000; TMS).

> I would have preferred to come here one day earlier—we would have got together comfortably, maybe we would have eaten to-

> gether, met each other, then we would have worked together for one day, would have done something at night…so that you also get to know each other apart from the coöperative work (everybody nodding in the group) (student teacher, SG, group discussion, July 2000; TMS).

The opportunity to develop autonomous learning also depends decisively on the institutional budgets and constraints. This is especially true for seminar type number two which presupposed seminars with students in different cultural contexts. Also, it would be ideal to offer seminars in parallel time slots, which will be possible only in few cases.

> It would be nice if the seminars took place at the same time. Then you would have the possibility to chat and clarify problems more quickly, and you wouldn't have to wait sometimes for a whole week (female student teacher, FR, portfolio, August 2000; TMS).

In contrast to traditional seminars in TEFL the seminar structure is extremely complex and student-teachers' workload much greater. Therefore the success of the seminar depends largely on the fact that student teachers understand the complex seminar structure, so that the additional work appears reasonable and will be accepted. If instructors fail to get this across, there will be a negative impact on motivation which will hinder the development of autonomous learning processes. Most of the workload is created through the project approach of the seminar, especially during the last third of the course, when the common product is being designed. This comes at a point when student teachers have to carry a higher workload because of the demands in other seminars. The strain of this intensive phase can be lessened somewhat, if student teachers negotiate the work plan with their partners early on. This presupposes a thorough understanding of the seminar's concept from the very beginning.

> I would like to emphasize the enormous amount of work involved in this. On the one hand, this is very motivating because you are involved in a process; but on the other hand, course organizers seem to believe that their seminar is the only one we need to work for (student teacher, GI, presentation, July 2000; TMS)

> The seminar structure is quite complex, you need a long time to understand it…in the beginning you can't picture anything concerning the research question and the presentation…then in between you lose your thread…(female student teacher, GI, group discussion, July 2000; TMS).

DISCUSS

Why is the promotion of social learning one of the key factors in the successful development of an autonomous learning environment? Discuss the advantages and disadvantages of focusing on social learning in the language learning classroom.

Expectations of Student Teachers Concerning Instructors' Work

The learning environment is structured by the university instructors in form of a *negotiated curriculum* (Breen & Littlejohn 2000). In practice, student-teachers experience the relationship of openness and monitoring of the learning processes through the instructors as a dilemma which the course organizers experience as well. This phenomenon has been documented elsewhere (Johnson 2000). The monitoring of the social group processes poses a special problem.

> On the one hand, I welcomed the open working atmosphere during which the instructor stayed in the background and took on a monitoring and guiding function. This offered us a lot of freedom, and also freedom for creative work, and a parallel control or better guidance could work in the background (via First class). On the other hand, there were also a few points where the frustration about communication that didn't take place in the groups subdued our motivation. Here a few discrete hints by the instructors would have possibly helped. In retrospect, I can now say that this still led to satisfying results without any outside influence; but if we had been students, perhaps we would have been frustrated and given in. There is a sharp edge between exerting one's influence and doing autonomous work supported by the instructor, since too much control, especially with university students, can easily have a negative effect (student-teacher, GI, portfolio, August 2000; TMS).

This quote shows that student teachers reflect on the differences between the specific situation of the university education of adult learners and the possible measures that might have to be taken in a classroom of younger learners. The following quotes illustrate that the student teachers have problems organizing the learning process (which is in stark opposition to the piecemeal transmission approach in other seminars) in such a way that they can develop a common product for the final presentation.

> Communication among the student groups should be improved regarding the presentation. But this is the task of the students and not that of the instructor. The instructors could point out this problem at the beginning, though, to facilitate a clear division of labor (female student teacher, FR. Portfolio, August 2000; TMS).

> All in all I really liked it, but at some points I also did feel quite alone...I don't know, whether you communicated about this or whether the purpose was to let things develop without control to see what would develop...but otherwise I was quite content, also because you could do what you wanted...I mean finally things did work out all right...Maybe you just need patience; that which is developing slowly needs time, and one really only connects concrete ideas over time... (student teacher, GI, group discussion, July 2000; TMS).

In general, the student teachers profess the surprise about the positive final result, and they express the wish for more transparency and selective intervention by the instructors.

From our experience a number of conclusions have to be drawn concerning the instructors' role. They are not just experts on the transmission of knowledge anymore, as is the case in traditional seminars. Three further functions have to be added. Increasingly they also are:

- Facilitators for linguistic *and* intercultural learning processes.
- Facilitators for social learning, i.e. they must be able to initiate, coach, and guide social learning processes.
- Experts for university teaching, i.e. the ability to apply project-oriented methods (e.g. suggesting methods of presentation).

Obviously they are still experts in their respective fields, offering support in the comprehension of texts. And they are also expert users of the target language, suggesting appropriate help to student teachers during the writing of their E-mails.

The extension of demands on instructors' competencies leads to an increase of the processes of negotiation during the learning process. That is why we have intensified measures of evaluation during the learning process (e.g. the introduction of regular feedback sessions at the beginning and end of a seminar, or the use of sheets for self-evaluation to reflect one's own role or contribution to the group work).

CONSIDER

Observe two or three language classes at your local school. Note the relationship of openness versus close monitoring of the learning process. Is the instructor following a *negotiated curriculum*? What needs to be changed?

The Development of Pedagogical Content Knowledge Concerning the Teaching Process

We attempt to respond to Little's (1995, 34) call for innovative teacher education models by trying to implement the three principles in our seminars which we mentioned above. In the remaining of this article, we try to further clarify each principle with the help of representative quotes from student teachers.

Action Research: Developing a Multi-Perspective View on the Foreign Language Classroom

Student teachers repeatedly say that they are unable to imagine alternative foreign language learning environments on the basis of the published knowledge they have read. Concepts need to be supplemented by images derived from practice. At the same time the student teachers' biographically formed ideas about the educational potential of the foreign language classroom that need to be taken into consideration as well.

> I couldn't really imagine what that is, an E-mail project, several classes in different places reading a young adult novel together, exchanging their personal views on that, how you do that, what you can learn doing that, and I was very surprised, astonished about all the things that were possible; I thought that was very interesting (student teacher, FR, group discussion; TMS).

> What I liked in retrospect was the fact that we worked in a twin-track kind of way, that is, we discussed an E-mail project, and at the same time we organized one. Because of that I was better able to understand students' concerns. I had the feeling that I really got something out of the seminar theory-wise, and at the same time I experienced the process myself (female student teacher, GI, group discussion; TMS).

Model Learning and Reflective Experiential Learning: Developing Experiential Knowledge

Here again it becomes clear that theoretical input needs to be reflected through participating in practice:

> I would especially like to praise the combination of theory and practice, which became clear only at second sight. On the one hand, we analyzed projects that had already been done at school and that way we pushed our own project ahead. It is exactly at that point (first-hand experience) that students' earlier problems, which we had analyzed theoretically, became obvious to me. This meta-level (E-mail project about E-mail projects) made insights possible into the difficulties of the exchange. We encountered communication problems which can also happen in students' E-mails (student teacher, GI, portfolio, August 2000; TMS).

> Just very clear, practically oriented, and you contribute yourself, you could do something yourself, experiencing that way what worked and what didn't. The other main seminars in TEFL don't offer this: you don't learn how to do something; I don't consider that very productive (student teacher, SG, group discussion; TMS).

> The seminar was very practically oriented; one of the few seminars at the close of which one can say that you have learned something that you can actually apply in school in the future. Because of the fact that we had to deal actively with different problems during our *Project About the Project*, quite a few things will be remembered which can help later with your own projects in school (female student teacher, GI, E-mail, 30.8.2000; TMS).

> You experienced at first hand the problems that can happen during an E-mail project (female student teacher, FR, questionnaire, July 2000; TMS).

> ...for once no general hot air/twaddle about TEFL, but experiencing how you can actually do it practically (student teacher, FR, questionnaire, July 2000; TMS).

> It is difficult to imagine this on an abstract level—an E-mail exchange for me was something quite abstract—you sit at the computer and you talk with somebody who is not present in that moment—you don't even talk, you type something into the computer...and if you only read about it, talk about it without experiencing it yourself, especially the difficulties; for example, when you ask a question which is very important for your further work, but which is not being answered, then you must ask the question again a week later... (student teacher, FR, group discussion, July 2000; TMS).

Experimental Learning: Developing Innovative Competencies in Cross-Institutional Cooperative Projects

Instead of subscribing to a deficit model of teacher education, our last principle refers to the idea of process-oriented teacher education which contributes to the development of professional growth. More often than not, student-teachers experience themselves at the university as people who are not taken seriously and who are not considered to be competent, let alone hold the potential for innovation. By involving them the way we do, we try to promote their creative potential. Thus, student-teachers have the opportunity to develop their innovative competency, guided by the instructors:

> The final presentation offered a challenge from the very beginning which included many aspects. You had to find concrete contents, send suggestions to your partners, make plans and think about forms of presentation. This was quite an incentive, and motivating in the group...Our presentation finally assumed acceptable forms. It was nice and surprising what you can achieve together. Finally, this working procedure offers one of the challenges of the modern information age [and the innovative cooperative development work among school staff—MS]. Working together with others/unknown people (possibly even via the Internet) will be expected from our students even more than from us (student teacher, GI, portfolio, August 2000; TMS).

> I think it is important that you take some time now during your studies to deal with things like these very intensively. I picture it as being quite problematic to create because then there are so many things to deal with, and if you haven't tried it out beforehand, you probably won't try it at all (female student teacher, FR, group discussion, July 2000; TMS).

DISCUSS

The authors stress that concepts need to be supplemented by images derived from practice. Discuss how you have applied the theories you learned in school to *real-life* practice. Give specific examples and discuss the impact on your professional development of this application.

Conclusion: Autonomous Learning in University-Based Teacher Education

Autonomous Learning in the Institution of the University

Student teachers concurred that in comparison to other TEFL seminars, the seminar involved a much higher workload. The reason is that the development of learning routines which are necessary for the successful management of autonomous learning processes needs to be experienced repeatedly. Without the support of such competencies from other seminars (especially those in pedagogy), the time factor will remain a topic:

> (T)he time constraints that are a major factor in shaping every programme of language teaching are likely to set strict limits on direct learner training. It seems likely that a continuous process of making learners aware of strategic possibilities is a safer bet in terms of both feasibility and likely effectiveness. (Little 1995, 177)

Despite these problems, student teachers stressed the need for more seminars of this kind to ensure the development of complex professional skills. The workload was caused primarily by the numerous working procedures which were new to the student-teachers. To give an example: out of 25 participants from the cooperating universities, only one student teacher had experienced autonomous learning processes in school. Approaches to process evaluation for organizing the autonomous group work was new for most of the participants, and they had to get accustomed to them. Also, instructors found themselves in a certain dilemma when guiding student teachers through such complex learning experiences, especially since the institutional structure of the university only offers a double lesson per week for these seminars. And excursions are only possible during vacation time. In the present institutional situation, a possible solution would be to give credit for the present seminar, plus one or two other TEFL seminars, (as an equivalent for the teaching practice). This should include at least one seminar in which student teachers work in a school setting.

Autonomous Teachers Need Autonomous Instructors

Student teachers' feedback highlights a clear rejection of TEFL seminars where knowledge is simply transmitted. From our perspective, the experience has contributed to our own learning in many ways: the mutual development of the seminar concept, the evaluation of the process by way of researchers' diaries and evaluation meetings, and the continuing development of the seminar concept. Like student teachers, we have participated in an experiment whose results were both surprising in a positive way and demonstrated some need for further development. We concur with Jorma Ollila, manager of the Finnish company Nokia, who, when asked what made his company so successful, replied: "Even in the most difficult of times we recognize our possibilities. We learn from crises and stick together. If somebody fails with his project he will not be fired or punished, since he has contributed to the mutual learning process" (*Die Zeit*). This sums up nicely the experiences of us, the instructors, who work in three different university contexts. Close cooperation facilitated the creation of a high-quality product in the form of this seminar. We exchanged our experiences on a regular basis to create an environment where we as instructors felt secure as well, despite the high amount of innovation involved. Finally the design and facilitation of learning environments as complex as these, which involve the selection of suitable texts and of research questions, ideas for presentations, and how to research them (e.g. the development of suitable instruments of evaluation and data analysis procedures), are being reduced to an acceptable degree through the instructors' co-operation.

CONSIDER

As you participate in your language teacher education program, take note of the information and complex skills that are necessary for the successful management of the autonomous learning process. In the long run this will result in a successful professional career.

Research Demands

We believe that the quality of teacher education at the university level will have to be researched in more detail so that we will gain empirical knowledge about the appropriate roles of prospective teachers and instructors in autonomous learning environments (Johnston 2000; Sandholtz, Ringstaff & Dwyer 1997; Tella 1991). The study of instructors' discourse strategies in such learning environments requires a qualitative research approach. Gremmo and Riley, for example, demand such an approach in the field of counselling:

> The first [area of research] is the analysis of the discourse of counselling...A better understanding of what counsellors and learners do and say together will help improve counselling techniques and the training of counsellors through the identification of those discourse strategies which really are appropriate to the negotiation of learning decisions and outcomes in asymmetric discourse. It would also hopefully enable researchers to study learners representations and beliefs about language and learning and to trace development in the training process itself as they are enclosed in the learners interpretative repertoires. (161)

The same is true of computer-based learning environments. Together with qualitatively researched data, such as open evaluation questionnaires, portfolios, and single and group interviews, a more detailed picture can be developed of the processes that take place in the classroom. During this investigation process, insights are being gained into monitoring of group processes. On the basis of this knowledge, instructors will finally be able to initiate and more effectively guide autonomous learning processes in complex learning environments.

Notes

1. We have translated quotes from German references and marked them TMS which stands for *Translation Müller & Schocker-v. Ditfurth*.

References

Breen, Michael, and Andrew Littlejohn. *Classroom Decision-Making. Negotiation and Process Syllabuses in Practice*. Cambridge: Cambridge UP, 2000.

Byram, Michael. *Teaching and Assessing Intercultural Communicative Competence*. Clevedon: Multilingual Matters, 1997.

Dam, Leni. "How Do We Recognize an Autonomous Classroom?" *Die Neueren Spra-chen* 93.5 (1994): 503-27.

Fremdsprache Deutsch. Neue Medien im Deutschunterricht 21.2 1999.
Der Fremdsprachliche Unterricht Englisch. Lernwelt Klassenzimmer: Internet, 35.49, 2001.
Der Fremdsprachliche Unterricht Französisch. Lernwelt Klassenzimmer: Internet, 34.43, 2001.
Dewe, Bernd, Wilfried Ferchhoff, and Frank-Olaf Radtke, ed. "Das, Professionswissen' von Pädagogen." *Erziehen als Profession. Zur Logik professionellen Handelns in pädagogischen Feldern*. Opladen: Leske & Budrich, 1992. 70-91.
Gremmo, Marie-José, and Philip Riley. "Autonomy, Self-Direction and Self Access in Language Teaching and Learning: The History of an Idea." *System* 23.2 (1995): 151-164.
Johnston, Bill. "Investigating Dialogue in Language Teacher Education: The Teacher Educator as Learner." *Teacher Education*. Ed. Karen Johnson. Alexandria: TESOL, 2000. 157–173.
Krainer, Konrad, and Peter Posch, Peter, ed. *Lehrerfortbildung zwischen Prozessen und Produkten. Hochschullehrgänge "Pädagogik und Fachdidaktik für LehrerInnen" (PFL): Konzepte, Erfahrungen und Reflexionen*. Bad Heilbrunn: Klinkhardt, 1996.
Kramsch, Claire, and Roger W. Andersen. "Teaching Text and Context Through Multimedia." *Language Learning & Technology* 2.2 (1999): 31-42.
Legutke, Michael, Andreas Müller-Hartmann, and Marita Schocker-v. Ditfurth. "Mediale Lernumgebungen im Schnittfeld von Lehrerausbildung und Lehrerfortbildung." *Fremdsprachenunterricht in medialen Lernumgebungen*. Ed. Helene Decke-Cornill and Maike Reichart-Wallrabenstein. Frankfurt: Peter Lang, (2002). 81-92.
Little, David. "Learning as Dialogue: The Dependence of Learner Autonomy on Teacher Autonomy." *System* 23.2 (1995): 175-181.
Little, David. "Autonomy in Second Language Learning: Some Theoretical Perspectives and Their Practical Implications." *Autonomes Fremdsprachenlernen*. Ed. Christoph Edelhoff and Ralf Weskamp. Ismaning: Hueber, 1999. 22-36.
Müller-Hartmann, Andreas. "Die Integration der neuen Medien in den schulischen Fremdsprachenunterricht: Interkulturelles Lernen und die Folgen in E-mail-Projekten." *Fremdsprachen Lehren und Lernen* 28 (1999): 58-79.
Müller-Hartmann, Andreas. "The Role of Tasks in Promoting Intercultural Learning in Electronic Learning Networks." *Language Learning & Technology* 4.2 (2000): 129-147. <http://llt.msu.edu>.
Müller-Hartmann, Andreas, and Marita Schocker-v. Ditfurth, ed. *Qualitative Forschung im Bereich Fremdsprachen lehren und lernen*. Tübingen: Narr, 2001.
Ollila, Jorma. "Die Welt im Handy. Wie man die Nummer Eins wird. *ZEIT*-Gespräch mit Nokia-Chef Jorma Ollila (Gesprächsführung Thomas Fischer mann und Matthias Naß)" *Die Zeit* 2 Jan. 2001.
Sandholtz, Judith Haymore, Cathy Ringstaff, David C. Dwyer. *Teaching with Technology. Creating Student-Centred Classrooms*. New York & London: Teachers College Press, 1997.
Schocker-v. Ditfurth, Marita. *Forschendes Lernen in der fremdsprachlichen Lehrer-bildung. Grundlagen, Erfahrungen, Perspektiven*. Tübingen: Narr, 2001.
Schocker-v. Ditfurth, Marita and Michael Legutke. "Visions of What is Possible or Lost in Complexity? How Student Teachers Experience Collaborative, Media-Enhanced Learning-to-Teach Environments." *English Language Teaching Journal* 56.2 (2002): 162-171.
Tella, Seppo. *Introducing International Communications Networks and Electronic Mail into FL Classrooms*. Helsinki: University of Helsinki, 1991.
Tella, Seppo. "Foreign Languages and Modern Technology: Harmony or Hell." *Telecollaboration in Foreign Language Learning. Proceedings of the Hawai'i Symposium*. Ed. Mark Warschauer. Honolulu: University of Hawai'i Press, 1996. 3-17.
Wolff, Dieter. "Zu den Beziehungen zwischen Theorie und Praxis in der Entwicklung von

Lernerautonomie." *Autonomes Fremdsprachenlernen*. Ed. Christoph Edelhoff and Ralf Weskamp. Ismaning: Hueber, 1999. 37-48.

Zydatiß, Wolfgang, ed. *Fremdsprachenlehrerausbildung – Reform oder Konkurs?* Berlin & München: Langenscheidt, 1998.

Web Sites

VIB Projekt, Pädagogische Hochschulen Freiburg & Schwäbisch Gmünd: <www.vib-bw.de/tp7>

VIB Projekt, Universität Gießen: <www.uni-giessen.de/~ga52>

Video

Schocker-v. Ditfurth, Marita. *No Dead Bodies, No Talking Heads. An Internet Research Project on Native Americans*. Pädagogische Hochschule Heidelberg (AVZ), Keplerstr. 87, 69120 Heidelberg, 1998.

E-mail: <avzhd@t-online.de>

Examining Language Proficiency of Teacher Candidates

Marjorie Hall Haley
Rebecca K. Fox

Introduction

The issues surrounding the study, the background of language proficiency testing in the US, and purpose of this project are described first in this article. The next section explains the research methodology including the instrument rubric, and the procedures for data collection and analyses used in this investigation. Finally, the authors provide a summary of results, a discussion of the findings, and a review of the implications of these outcomes.

Context

Goals 2000: Educate America (A Progress Report, 1996) elevated the status of foreign/second languages from a tangential subject to an integral component of the curriculum. The subsequent Standards movement that emerged from Goals 2000 emphasizes *Communication* as one of its five principle tenets. A rapidly changing student population, nationwide educational reform, and the development of National Standards for Foreign Language Learning are placing new demands on foreign language teachers (Peyton 1997). The present study is based on the creation, pilot, and subsequent implementation of a contextualized proficiency assessment tool used to determine the oral and written skills of foreign/second language teacher candidates preparing to teach at the pre-K through grade 12 level.

Issues Surrounding the Topic

Quite often, teacher licensure programs are at the graduate or post-baccalaureate level of study, rather than undergraduate programs housed jointly in departments of foreign languages. Admission requirements for graduate education programs do not always include assessment of written and oral language proficiency, and teacher candidates may not necessarily be required to take additional advanced course work in the target language prior to licensure. Numerous teacher candidates find themselves placed in student teaching assignments in which they are unprepared to teach middle to upper level language classes in meaningful communicative settings. Some candidates in our own institution find themselves in the described situation. The impact of this situation became most apparent when we were in schools supervising student teacher interns. Much to our dismay and surprise, we were sometimes sending into schools students whose language proficiency was questionable. Therefore, we undertook a research study whose aim was to assess language proficiency in order to see what the situation is in regard to language preparedness. The objectives of the study were to create, design, and implement an assessment tool that would evaluate teacher candidates' foreign/second language proficiency (specifically, oral and written skills in the target language). As a result of this study, the language assessment takes place prior to student teaching to better ensure teacher candidates' language preparedness for internship, and subsequent university recommendation for state licensure. The assessment is designed to take place during the fall and spring semesters of each academic year.

Review of Literature

Proficiency assessment, a process to gauge how well an individual speaks, writes, and comprehends a foreign/second language, consists of procedures that determine his/her ability to use a target language effectively for real authentic communication. This is an essential qualification for teachers facilitating learning in today's communicative classrooms (Lantolf & Frawley 1985, 1988; Linnell, Washburn, & Hoejke 1993). In a review of the forty year development of proficiency testing, it is important to note that the purpose of language rating has come full circle from its initial creation by the Foreign Service Institute where a language proficiency score played a key role in job selection, promotion, and job security (Hart-Gonzales 1994; Douglas & Selinker 1992; Bachman 1991; Davies 1990). Later, its adaptation for academic purposes by the American Council on the Teaching of Foreign Languages (ACTFL) and the Educational Testing Service (ETS) led to the development of an instrument for rating oral (Stansfield 1992) and written competencies of foreign/second language students.

The original purpose of the Interagency Language Roundtable (ILR) scale of oral proficiency developed at the Foreign Service Institute (Hart-Gonzales 1994) was to gauge whether the language proficiency of federal government and diplomatic personnel was adequate for the purposes of their missions. A viable rating scale needs to evaluate *authentic* language in communicative contexts of varied description (Bachman & Savignon 1986; Bachman 1988; Henning 1992; Hoejke & Linnell 1994). The scale should also remain practical enough so that raters can learn how to conduct and rate an oral proficiency interview according to the criteria of the scale, maintaining inter-rater reliability and test validity (Bachman 1990; Henning 1992). For this reason, we were strident about training raters, getting their input on modifying the instrument, and making certain that each candidate's performance was assessed by no fewer than three raters.

ACTION

Examine the ACTFL Oral Proficiency Interview (OPI). Consider the advantages and disadvantages of using it to assess teachers or teacher candidates.

Although the ACTFL Oral Proficiency Interview (OPI) <www.actfl.org> provides a tested procedure that meets the needs for student oral evaluation, there is no assessment available for rating teachers or teacher candidates (Bachman & Savignon 1986). At our university there are several factors that led us to developing our own instrument rather than using the OPI. First, we wanted an instrument that would assess language proficiency of graduate-level teacher candidates. Second, we were committed to providing assessment at no cost to our students. Finally, it was important to have an instrument that would allow raters to give specific feedback to candidates on areas of strengths and weaknesses.

In the US, legislation recommends proficiency-based foreign/second language curriculum, and as a result of legislation at the state (Virginia) level, there was an expressed need for specific language proficiency requirements for teachers already in the classroom. During the last decade, there has been considerable emphasis on the importance of assessing foreign/second language proficiency for teachers and teacher candidates seeking certification and job placement (Peyton 1997).

Investigation of The Topic: Purpose and Justification

The purpose of this study is to investigate the language proficiency of teacher licensure candidates in the foreign/second language teacher education program at George Mason University, to determine this aspect of preparedness for student teaching. Assessing foreign/second language teacher candidates is a challenge for any teacher education program. While teacher candidates often cannot be expected to evidence *native* proficiency in the target language, certainly a high level of language proficiency should be mandatory. Mistakes and errors in language usage may be immediately apparent during the internship and can result in poor teacher performance. Teacher candidates should only begin the teaching experience when they are confident that at least their language skills are of advanced proficiency. Having such an assessment at the beginning of their teacher education program allows students the opportunity to improve skills or re-examine their options prior to the internship. However, we must note that self confidence in one's own language skills cannot be created solely by positive test results.

CONSIDER

In your opinion should native proficiency be required for new language teachers? Why or why not?

The researchers decided to develop an assessment instrument to meet the specific needs at this university. Three considerations provided impetus for the decision for in-house assessment: 1) a university centered proficiency rating system would provide the foreign/second language program an additional opportunity to remain closely aligned with the Graduate School of Education's mission and goals, 2) a university created proficiency rating would enable the program to be more teacher and school division oriented by engaging master teachers from the local school divisions as raters, and 3) an internal system would provide opportunities for cross departmental articulation about curriculum and instruction between the Graduate School of Education and the professors from the Department of Modern and Classical Languages.

The George Mason University Language Proficiency Assessment

The George Mason University Language Proficiency Assessment (GMU-LPA) is designed to measure how well a foreign/second language teacher candidate speaks and writes in the target language. The assessment is conducted after program acceptance and prior to the student teaching internship semester. (Information about score requirements for internship follows.)

The GMU-LPA is comprised of two principle sections, each approximately one half hour in length: an oral interview and a writing sample. The speaking component consists of a tape-recorded face-to-face oral interview in the target language. Approximately 30 minutes in length, the oral interview portion consists of three segments, an opening free-response conversation (approximately 5-6 minutes), followed by guided open-ended questions (or scenarios) and a section of picture prompts eliciting a rich description of scenes or a short story (approximately 15 minutes), and a final time allocated for additional opportunity for clarification and closure (5-6 minutes). In both the free responses to questions or scenarios and to the picture prompts, the candidate is always provided a choice from a field of two or three possibilities, and may take up to two minutes to gather thoughts or to make notes. The order of the interview process is designed to put the candidate at ease to ensure the most authentic language sample possible. The half-hour time frame chosen for the interview, which is longer than many others researched, was chosen explicitly to allow enough time to capture sufficient natural language for an accurate sample, thus allowing time for authentic language patterns to emerge and be verified. The initial few minutes of the oral interview provides an opportunity for some informal opening questions. The candidate is asked to provide any information s/he would like to share about background, time in the country/ies in which the target language is spoken, or other details the candidate deems relevant. Usually this information includes such details as schooling, travel, time in country/ies, personal and professional goals. This is an important segment of the interview because it sets the tone for the remainder of the language sample.

The written section, also thirty minutes in length, asks the candidate to respond in writing to one of two broad-based questions. These questions seek open-ended responses and contextual, authentic language usage through creative expression of opinions. Evaluation is based on a candidate's ability to: 1) be comprehensible to educated native level speakers of the target language, 2) organize ideas effectively and logically, 3) use a level of language appropriate to the task and/or audience, and 4) communicate with a broad range of vocabulary and advanced expression without patterned grammatical errors. (See Language Proficiency Rubric and Scoring Guide, Appendix A.)

Since pilot phase implementation in the Fall of 1996, both quantitative and qualitative data have been collected. Updated picture prompts were implemented in 1999 (and again in 2001) to ensure confidentiality of test content. Because of the open-ended nature of the writing prompt, no change in prompts or questions has been deemed necessary. One significant change, however, has been implemented in the scoring of the oral proficiency interview. In the first two pilot studies, for reasons of availability and timing, the oral proficiency interview was first conducted face-to-face by a trained rater and audio taped. The tape was then sent to two additional trained raters for their scoring. As the interview scheduling process became more refined and convenient interview times were selected for both candidates and raters, opportunities for two to three simultaneous face-to-face interviews were possible. In the analysis of the data, we noticed greater score similarity in the rating of the simultaneous live interviews, whereas a larger range of scores was evident between the face-to-face vs. the taped scores. Interviews conducted with the two types of raters helped us to determine that the raters of the taped segments played and replayed the tapes for analysis. Speech patterns were examined closely on the tapes, as were the level, specificity, and variety of vocabulary used. Error patterns were carefully analyzed and specific recommendations made for the candidate. Although the real-time interviews did allow raters to capture error patterns and to feel confident about rendering a holistic rating of the candidate, it did not allow time for the same in-depth analysis conducted by the taped interviews. This caused us to look very carefully at our goals and objectives for the project. We believed that the program should decide to have either all taped interviews or all face-to-face, not a combination of both.

The researchers in charge ultimately decided that although the practice of analyzing taped interviews provided the opportunity for an excellent in-depth analysis of the speaker's oral language, there were several programmatic and research-based drawbacks to using taped interviews as the sole oral language proficiency rating. The programmatic decision was to conduct all face-to-face interviews for candidate rating. One major drawback to the all-taped interviews was the fact that, with a program seeking to meet the needs of individual candidates seeking entry into our program, we wanted the opportunity for a face-to-face component of the process. This would allow department members to learn of a candidate's ability in a more personal way than would be possible from a tape, and vice versa. Also, if we incorporated the face-to-face component of the interview process and combined it with an audio taped component, the resulting scores would show greater variation than those of interviews which were completely face-to-face or tape. We were not comfortable with such variation because, for program integrity, we sought reliable oral proficiency scores. Another problematic area was found in the timeliness of score receipt. We encountered difficulty in raters finding time for these in-depth analyses, and the time frame involved for the rating process became lengthier than desired for both timely program and candidate feedback. We have, therefore, now revised the system to conduct face-to-face oral interviews with two or more raters. These face-to-face interviews are still audio taped in case verification or questions arise, and for program reference, rater training, and archival purposes.

Methodologies

Prior to full implementation in the Fall of 1999, the researchers collected pilot data for two semesters. Students enrolled during the fall semester of 1996 in the foreign language methods course were the first group to be assessed. Students enrolled in the Spring semester of 1997 were also asked to participate in the study. Of these two semesters, the GMU-LPA was conducted with 16 of the methods class candidates from the Fall semester of 1996 and 10 from the Spring semester of 1997. The oral proficiency interviews were tape recorded for subsequent evaluation by no fewer than two additional trained raters. Interview question choices were standardized and ranged from novice use of the target language to probes seeking a more advanced level of language skill. The written language sample was also conducted with these two pilot groups.

The trained raters for both domains of the LPA were comprised of university professors from the Graduate School of Education, the Department of Modern and Classical Languages, and foreign/second language teachers from local school districts. Rater workshops were conducted prior to assessment administration to ensure score validity and rater reliability. The investigation considered the levels of oral and written proficiency based on a scale of 1-4 (4 = native or near native proficient and 1 = non-proficient, see Appendix A.)

Triangulation of language performance data served to validate findings and interpretations. University supervisors and cooperating teachers provided validation of language proficiency in the following ways: 1) observations made during the student teaching internship semester, which provided additional evidence of an intern's language performance and of the proficiency scores earned; 2) teacher candidate video tapes of teaching in the target language; 3) observation reports written by both the university supervisors and the cooperating teachers; and 4) teacher candidate and cooperating teacher reflective journals maintained during the 15-week internship. University supervisors maintained weekly contact with student interns and cooperating teachers. Their notes and memos served to provide evidence. Students maintained student teaching notebooks and make journal entries weekly, which they share with their university supervisor. These were also collected for analysis. Cooperating teachers also maintained written dialogues with student interns through Bi-Weekly Progress Reports, providing opportunities to comment on interns' in-class performance, which included use of the target language in the classroom.

DISCUSS

Discuss with a partner the pros and cons of implementing a written and oral language proficiency assessment in all language teacher training programs.

Since the GMU-LPA is conducted after acceptance into the licensure program and prior to the internship semester, the materials collected during the internship semester served to triangulate the LPA scores. Candidates gave their permission for the use in this study of all scores and relevant internship data.

During the two pilot semesters, data were collected to determine validity and reliability of the instrument. The results will be discussed in a subsequent section. The GMU-LPA is now an integral part of the teacher candidate licensure process. Students must obtain a score of three or more on both the oral and written components in order to be considered *proficient* and therefore be permitted to begin the internship semester. Specific recommendations are included in the reports to the students. If a student fails to pass either segment of the assessment, recommendations may include a semester or summer abroad, a program of residence in the target language, or advanced written or conversation courses at our university or elsewhere. Upon completion of recommended work, students may request another assessment, and the most recent score attained is the one remaining in the student's academic folder.

Although at first somewhat apprehensive about the potential test outcome and its impact on their program completion, candidates generally felt that the implementation of a written and oral language proficiency assessment was an important new program implementation. They were glad that the GMU-LPA was not an entrance requirement, but rather that it was used to help candidates see their strengths and potential weaknesses prior to entering the classroom for the internship semester. Students with a lower than desired score (less than a 3 earned on either the written or oral component) were allowed time for refinement or augmentation of skills before retaking the assessment. They found this to be empowering, saying that this opportunity for additional work in an area of weakness helped to provide additional confidence in their language ability prior to internship. Candidates who received high scores (e.g., a four in either one or both categories) were pleased that the school division receiving them for the internship knew about their high language skills level. Other candidates whose scores were lower than hoped were apprehensive about what this knowledge would do to their later seeking a full-time teaching position. However, with time spent in a target language setting and the results of retesting, most candidates were pleased with the results on both a personal and a professional level.

Findings

Analysis of the data suggests that the instrument is, for both the GMU Foreign/World Language Teacher Education Program and the school divisions served by the university, a strong indicator of the language proficiency of our teacher candidates. As a teacher education program working in partnership with surrounding school divisions, the Graduate School of Education is committed to sending to them the best-prepared candidates we can. It is also our commitment to provide our language teacher candidates with in-depth knowledge of best practices. We thus engage them in self-evaluation practices and critical reflection in an effort to foster commitment to ongoing professional development. Program candidates are able to provide to themselves, the university, and their potential school division employers concrete knowledge of their emergent teaching practice, which includes not only successful course work completion and evidence of content knowledge through GPA and program performance-based portfolios (Fox 1999), but evidence of language proficiency through scores attained in the GMU-LPA.

The LPA thus provides both program and candidates one of several ways to look at and ascertain candidates' preparedness for placement as full-time foreign/world language teachers. The LPA appears to be consistent with other measures of evaluating language proficiency. Compared with weekly reflective journals maintained by cooperating teachers and teacher candidates, the proficiency assessment data indicated similar areas of strengths and weaknesses. The findings included in this study should be considered preliminary rather than conclusive because the population samples were small, and random selection and assignment were not possible. On the other hand, although small, this data has proven powerful enough for our specific program purposes at this university, and it has been implemented as a formal program requirement. Data continues to be gathered each semester and is currently serving as formative evaluation data for continuing work with licensure candidates and school divisions. The feedback from school divisions has been positive. They believe they are better able to place candidates in internship situations that will best support their strengths and weaknesses than they were before information about candidate language proficiency was available to them. Likewise, our program is able to make recommendations about placement in target language immersion settings based on concrete language proficiency scores.

For this study, a total of 34 teacher licensure candidates at this university were assessed: two pilot semesters consisting respectively of 16 and 10 candidates, and two semesters of full program implementation, consisting respectively of 3 and 5 candidates. The sample sizes of each group thus range from 16 participants in the first pilot to 10 in the second, to 3 in the first implementation semester (semester three), and 5 in the second implementation semester (semester four) of this study. The numbers vary (and will always vary), depending on how many teacher licensure candidates at GMU are ready to be assessed each semester. Data in Table 1 displays the average scores for the oral and written assessments. The mean score for all candidates on the oral section is 3.35 with a standard deviation of .92. The mean score for all candidates on the written section is 3.26 with a standard deviation of .71. In general, these candidates were slightly more proficient in oral communication than in written communication. The greater oral proficiency score is due largely to the fact that our program has a large number of native Spanish speakers who grew up speaking Spanish in the home setting, whereas some candidates have had only minimal opportunity to be schooled in their first language. They have benefited from formal instruction in writing and grammar and have returned to retest, later achieving much higher scores. With the exception of the third semester of data, LPA scores fell in the low-3 range. Just over half of the candidates reached level 4 for oral proficiency, and less than half reached level 4 for written language skills.

Figure 1. Language Proficiency Scores

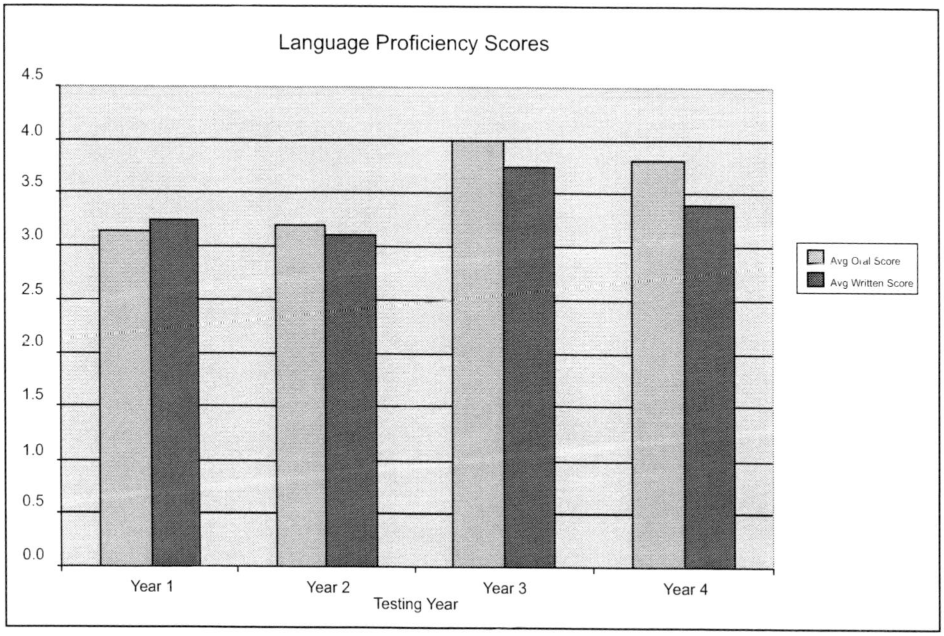

Those students who achieved a rating of 4 or high 3 were successful in their student teaching experiences. The successful achievement was ultimately born out in a candidate's internship grade of Satisfactory, which is documented by university supervisor observations and other required internship documentation, candidate journals and reflections, and feedback from the cooperating teacher. During the two pilot semesters, a policy was not yet in place with the university that would prohibit a candidate who had scores below a 3 in either domain from beginning the internship. (Formative evaluation of the study's results has enabled our program to now have a policy in place that requires a 3 in each domain in order to begin the internship.)

CONSIDER

Reflect on your own language proficiency skills. What are your strengths and/or problem areas? How can you best further develop or maintain your language skills throughout your professional career?

Those who scored a low 1 to low 3 experienced difficulty in student teaching even when teaching the lower levels of foreign/second language classes. One candidate who did poorly on the LPA decided herself to postpone her student teaching and spent time in France to improve her language proficiency. She experienced an extremely successful internship and has grown to become a teacher leader in the area of technology in the foreign/world language classroom. Two other candidates who received ratings lower than expected experienced many difficulties during the internship. One who needed greater oral proficiency later chose to spend time in a country where the target language was spoken, and another who had written evaluations of less than 3 decided to pursue more work in composition and grammar. Each of these latter two individuals is now experiencing success in the classroom setting. Two of the three who sought additional proficiency work retested and received scores greater than 3. Initially, some students complained that the LPA was just another hurdle, which slowed their progress toward completion of their teacher licensure program. However, they later commented on the value of the experience for raising their level of awareness of their own language skills.

We call for longitudinal research and ongoing data collection to confirm the validity of this assessment. Current findings do suggest that this approach taken by our department for determining teacher preparedness for the internship experience may be viable and reliable because it helps to ensure that only those candidates who are sufficiently prepared will begin their school-based internships.

Implications and Conclusion

There are some important implications to be drawn from these results. First, language proficiency assessment should be a critical component of the foreign/world language teacher preparation program at the university level. Particularly, our language proficiency assessment has served to inform our licensure program about the individual needs of incoming candidates. It has also served to inform our colleagues in Modern Languages about some of the particular needs of students who may be taking courses in their department. As a result, additional attention has been paid by Modern Language department members to help native language speakers work on the written domain of their language. Furthermore, our study suggests that the language proficiency assessment should be conducted early on in a teacher candidate's program and definitely prior to the student teaching internship.

This process is beneficial for teacher candidates because it gives them a current assessment of their own language proficiency. Many candidates come into our program after either being out of college for many years or having never been assessed in either domain of the language. The GMU-LPA gives them the opportunity to determine the strengths or problem areas and, based on that, to make decisions about further developing their language skills or considering other career or job options.

Today's world requires that our educational systems produce multilingual students. This can only be accomplished under the direction of proficient foreign/world/second language teachers. Universities and teacher education programs are remiss in their responsibilities if they continue to *pass* pre-service teachers along and out into school systems without first making certain that they are adequately trained and proficient in both the written and oral domains of the target language of their discipline.

America's classrooms need a teaching force with proficiency in multiple languages so that teachers can understand and help meet the needs of all learners (Phillips & Lafayette 1996; Hall Haley 2000). The challenge for the foreign/second language teaching profession is to focus its efforts on building a teaching force of proficient, caring, talented, and respectful teachers who possess the necessary skills for meeting the language acquisition and development needs of their students. These teachers must be well trained and proficient in the target language.

The development of the George Mason University Language Proficiency Assessment included two careful pilot studies. The instrument has been modified and is presently being used to determine language proficiency for all foreign/world/second language teacher candidates at GMU. The researchers believe that this instrument has provided a valuable service to the teacher candidates by allowing them an opportunity to demonstrate their proficiency and reinforcing their commitment to becoming effective foreign/second language teachers.

References

American Council on the Teaching of Foreign Languages (ACTFL). Oral Proficiency Interview. 15 Sep. 2002 <www.actfl.org>.

Bachman, L. "What Does Language Testing Have to Offer?" *TESOL Quarterly* 25.4 (1991): 671-704.

——. *Fundamental Considerations in Language Testing*. Oxford: Oxford UP, 1990.

——. "Problems in Examining the Validity of the ACTFL Oral Proficiency Interview." *Studies in Second Language Acquisition* 10 (1988): 149-164.

Bachman, L., and S. Savignon. "The Evaluation of Communicative Language Proficiency: A Critique of the ACTFL Oral Interview." *Modern Language Journal* 70 (1986): 380-390.

Davies, A. "Principals of Language Testing." Cambridge: Basil Blackwell, 1990.

Douglas, D., and L. Selinker. "Analyzing Oral Proficiency Test Performance in General and Specific Purpose Contexts." *System* 20.3 (1992): 317-328.

Fox, R. *This is Who I Am: The Role of the Professional Development Portfolio in Foreign and Second Language Pre-service Teacher Education.* Diss. George Mason University, 1999. Fairfax: UMI, 1999. 9933323.

Hall Haley, M. "Shaping the Future of Twenty-first Century Schools: Fulfilling the Need for Minority Teachers in Foreign Language Classrooms. In Reflecting on the past to shape the future." *ACTFL Foreign Language Education Series.* Ed. D. Birchbichler and R. Terry. Lincolnwood: National Textbook Co, 2000.

Hart-Gonzales, L. "Raters and Scales in Oral Proficiency Testing: The FSI Experience." Language Testing Research Colloquium. Washington: ERIC Document Reproduction Service, 1994. No. ED 380 983.

Henning, G. "The ACTFL Oral Proficiency Interview: Validity Evidence." *System* 20.3 (1992): 365-372.

Hoejke, B., and K. Linnell. "Authenticity in Language Testing: Evaluating Spoken Language Tests for International Teaching Assistants." *TESOL Quarterly* 28.1 (1994): 103-126.

Lantolf, J. P., and W. Frawley. "Proficiency: Understanding the Construct." *Studies in Second Language Acquisition* 10 (1988): 181-195.

——. "Oral Proficiency Testing: A Critical Analysis." *Modern Language Journal* 69 (1985): 337-345.

Linnell, K., G. Washburn, and B. Hoejke. "Making Performance Tests Reliable." TESOL Convention, Atlanta. Apr. 1993.

Minnesota Language Proficiency Assessments. University of Minnesota. <http://carla.acad.umn.edu/sla-links.html>.

Peyton, J. K. "Proficiency Development of Foreign Language Teachers." Center for Applied Linguistics. Washington: ERIC L & L Digest, 1997.

Phillips, J. K., and R. C. Lafayette. "Reactions to the Catalyst: Implications for Our New Professional Structure." *ACTFL Foreign Language Education Series. National Standards: A Catalyst for Reform.* Ed. R. Lafayette. Lincolnwood: National Textbook Co, 1996. 197-209.

Stansfield, C. W. ACTFL Speaking Proficiency Guidelines. *ERIC Digest* Sep. 1992. Washington: ERIC Clearinghouse on Languages and Linguistics, 1992. No. ED 347 852.

United States. Dept. of Education. *Goals 2000: A Progress Report, Fall 1996.* Washington: Educate America Act, 19996.

Appendix A

George Mason University
Graduate School of Education
Foreign/Second Language Teacher Candidate
Language Proficiency Rubric and Scoring Guidelines

Rating	Scoring Guidelines
4	Comprehends daily and school-related conversations; gives a complete and accurate/relevant response to all (or almost all) of a question. Is completely and easily comprehensible; may make errors but they rarely or never interfere with communication. Control of grammar consistently serves as an effective language teaching model (no errors in basic, high-frequency structures; no marked error patterns; frequent use of complex sentences when appropriate or required). Employs a broad, precise vocabulary adequate for almost all topics; uses idiomatic expressions with ease and appropriately in almost all situations. Has overall fluency: speech is occassionally (or only rarely) hesitant; may have slightly non-native pronunciation, with few or no phonological errors and no error patterns, but is always comprehensible; pronunciation and intonation appropriate and accurate.
3	Comprehends daily and school-related conversations; gives a mostly accurate/relevant response to most parts of a question. Is generally comprehensible; is likely to make errors and/or error patterns, but they do only occassionally interfere with communication. Control of grammar mostly serves as an effective language teaching model (few errors in basic, high-frequency structures; some error patterns in complex/low-frequency structures; some use of complex sentences and connectors with appropriate or required). Employs wide range of vocabulary adequate for most general topics, with word choice that is often idiomatic but occasionally awkward. Has considerable fluency: speech is sometimes hesitant. May have a markedly non-native pronunciation with some phonological errors and/or error patterns, but is nearly or always comprehensible; pronunciation and intonation do not interfere with communication.
2	Comprehends daily and school-related conversations; gives a somewhat accurate/relevant response to some parts of a question. Is somewhat comprehensible but may require the listener_s effort and interpretation of the intended meaning; produces errors and/or error patterns that may often interfere with communication. Has limited grammar control (demonstrates some major grammatical errors and/or error patterns in basic, high-frequency structures; no control of complex/low-frequency structures; little use of complex sentences and connectors when appropriate or required). Employs a daily-use vocabulary with word choice that is limited, often unidiomatic and awkward; may frequently confuse or grope for words. Has limited fluency, with halting speech and mostly short, simple sentences. Has a markedly non-native pronunciation with many phonological errors and/or error patterns, pronunciation and intonation sometimes obscuring tended meaning.
1	Comprehends daily and school-related conversations with marked effort; gives an incomplete and/or mostly inaccurate or irrelevant response to a question. Is generally incomprehensible, despite the listener_s effort to interpret the intended meaning; Produces errors and/or error patterns that very often interfere with communication. Has very little grammatical control (many serious errors and/or error patterns in many structures; little or no evidence of complex sentence structure or connectors when required. Employs limited daily vocabulary with some memorized phrases and fixed expressions, sometimes used inappropriately; typically confuses or gropes for words. Has virtually no fluency with fragmentary and halting speech, interrupted by pauses and repetitions; limited range of simple, fixed expressions and memorized phrases. Has markedly non-native pronunciation with many serious phonological errors and/or error patterns, pronunciation and intonation often obscure meaning and are sometimes incomprehensible.

*Scale reflects use of terminology, expressions, and basic guidelines from the ETS Praxis Speaking Section Scoring Guide for Productive Language Skills, (1995). The Praxis Series. Princeton: Educational Testing Service. (© Fox, 1996)

Corpus disciplinae? Toward a Critical Prognosis for Contemporary Language Teacher Preparation

Terry A. Osborn

Introduction

At the outset, I should clarify what I intend to discuss, lest someone accuse me à la Mark Twain of exaggerating the demise of United States foreign language teacher education. I do not claim that language teacher education has, or will, cease to exist. It certainly would not be too far-fetched to explore such a possibility, however, especially given an educational programming climate that relies on the same logic to make decisions as do the makers of leaf blowers, pet rocks, and reality television shows, namely what the market will bear. It is also possible to see the nation's preoccupation in all fields with standards and standardized tests to be a reincarnated *teacher-proof* attempt at engineering a curriculum. Nonetheless, I believe that language teaching, and thus language teacher education, will persevere. Yet I contend that a significant pathology continues to plague the profession, and suspect that the end of the matter could be death.

DISCUSS

What does the author mean by *teacher proof*? Discuss the implications of this suggestion.

Dead means, among other things, not having significance or relevance, being stagnant or unresponsive, lacking sensitivity, or having no resonance. It is in this sense that I suggest that contemporary language teacher education is on a collision course with reality that will likely result in its *death*. The convergence of developments in the field is resulting, I contend, in the exacerbation of divisions among components in the preparation of teachers and the realities within the language teaching field. Specifically, I will examine selected epistemological underpinnings that currently shape language teacher education practice, the limited role of critical reflection in foreign language teacher education, and the related dilemmas brought about by the standards movement(s) in the profession.

Henry Giroux (1997), in his landmark treatment of the *culture of positivism* in education, noted the far reaching effects of this form of rationality in the curriculum field:

> Guided by the search for reliability, consistency, and quantitative predictions, positivist educational practice excludes the role of values, feelings, and subjectively defined meanings in its paradigm. Normative criteria are dismissed either as forms of bias or are seen as subjective data that contribute little to the goals of schooling. Criticism of this sort is often couched in calls for more precise methods of pedagogy. (19)

Denzin (2001) pointed out a number of characteristics of the positivistic approach to education which can be illuminating in terms of our current approaches to language education. Drawing from these sources, I argue that contemporary language teacher education is based, in part, on the following assumptions:

- Language can be presented as an *objective* reality.
- The language user can meaningfully be separated from the language.
- Generalizations and observations regarding language teaching can be presented free from situational and temporal constraints.
- Learning to teach a language is a value-free (technicist) process.

DISCUSS

Based on your own experience, do these four assumptions make up the foundation of the teacher education program(s) your are familiar with? Discuss the similarities and differences between your personal experiences and the author's assumption.

Language can be Presented as an *Objective* Reality

Language, as a social phenomenon, is particularized. It is used in a multiplicity of individualized forms, known as ideolects. What we teach as the *language* is in fact a consensus form of similarities among numerous ideolects. There is no neutral and natural definition of *German* or *French* or any other language. Thus, teaching language by presenting it devoid of the social constellations that birthed it, including differential power relationships, is both inaccurate and a reflection of the *culture of positivism* within our own domain. The culture of positivism is explained by Henry Giroux (1997): "The central assumption by which the culture of positivism rationalizes its position on theory and knowledge is the notion of objectivity, the separation of values from knowledge and methodological inquiry alike" (11). Thus, in foreign language education we assume that we are transmitting a knowledge base (i.e., language) that is an objectively derived construct.

The Language user can Meaningfully be Separated from the Language

The second point follows the first in that having objectified the language by stripping it of the social context in its genesis, we reintroduce the social nature of language by *adding* the speakers of the language as part of the content. They are separated from the languages which they created and are viewed as a fragmentable sector of the language phenomenon.

Generalizations and Observations Regarding Language Teaching can be Presented Free from Situational and Temporal Constraints

Since language is, at its heart, a social activity, then it follows that language teaching is as well. *Methodology* courses which present principles of language teaching devoid of the myriad of social contexts in which language teaching takes place (even if also taught with a concurrent, but separate field experience or course in social and cultural aspects of teaching), thus perpetuate an illusion of *scientific* neutrality of theory.

Learning (Inquiry) to Teach a Language is a Value-Free (Technicist) Process

Language learning and language teaching become reified as value-free endeavors through the elements that have been presented above. Because the teacher preparation programs mask the value-laden decisions inherent in what constitutes language through the logic of positivistic discourse, the language teacher fails to grasp the most fundamental of assumptions necessary for theory-informed praxis—namely that the social context of language teaching is inseparable from its other aspects. As a result, reflection in praxis and particularly any form of critical reflection is at least stymied, and at worst, precluded.

Critical reflection in the foreign language classroom focuses on the ethical and moral dimensions of teaching and learning. In the case of United States foreign language classrooms, critical reflection would of necessity take into account that teaching languages is fundamentally a political activity. Thus, the context of the language teaching (including the school, the community, etc.) is intrinsic, and our values related to issues of language and cultural diversity are not separable in the process.

To be sure, language educators have addressed the role of contextualization in the classroom (see, for example, Shrum & Glisan 2000). This approach, however, focuses almost exclusively on the actual linguistic code itself being presented in context and not on language teaching as being a contextualized endeavor as well. As Kumaravadivelu (2001) explains in regard to a postmethod pedagogy:

> As a pedagogy of particularity, a postmethod pedagogy rejects the advocacy of a predetermined set of generic principles and procedures aimed at realizing a predetermined set of generic aims and objectives. Instead, it seeks to facilitate the advancement of a context-sensitive, location specific pedagogy that is based on a true understanding of local linguistic, sociocultural, and political particularities. (544)

In my earlier work, I referred to this shift in curricular emphasis as *macrocontextualization*:

> Macrocontextualization is the process of planning and implementing language instruction by incorporating the local political, economic, and cultural factors relating to linguistic diversity with the intent of developing students' skills in understanding the role that language plays in society. Beyond current goals of simply developing marginal skills in the language, students acquire an awareness of how language issues function in their society to both empower and discriminate against various segments of people. (Osborn 114)

DISCUSS

Discuss how you could integrate the process of macrocontexualization with, as the author defines it, the nation's preoccupation with national standards and standardized assessment. Where is the balance?

DISCUSS

Think about the social, political, cultural and historical context of your hometown. Discuss how each of these factors could specifically influence course design and day-to-day lesson planning.

When a foreign language teacher enters a classroom in New York City, the classroom processes and activities are fundamentally different than they are for a teacher who enters a classroom in Atlanta, Georgia. These differences are not attributable to the language as it has been objectified (after all, *Spanish* is still *Spanish*), nor does second language acquisition (SLA) theory change. The differences found among the many language classrooms around the country are not due merely to the differences in individual learners, but find their genesis in part within the social, political, cultural, and historical contexts of their locations. Languages in New York have a history, a political context, a cultural meaning, and a social value that differs from the Atlanta version of the same. Up until now, few language teacher education programs have prepared students for this reality.

The development of a postmethod pedagogy or macrocontextualization would include specificity in classroom application, and in such a case, what role can be played by reflection in the teacher education program?

Reflective practice has made significant inroads in teacher education (see Reagan, Case, & Brubacher 2002), as it has encouraged teachers to make sense of and pursue a reasoned, professional approach to theory and practice at multiple points in the educative process. It could be argued that such reflection already accommodates the need for a context-specific pedagogical approach by pointing students in the direction of mediating all of the factors involved in language education in their individualized contexts. Yet teacher educators report that reflection often loses its effectiveness at some point in the pre-service preparation, reflecting the view of Tochon (2002):

> Reflection has become our truth, because truth requires reflection. But can reflection be imposed from the outside and as part of overloaded curricula? Students prefer to cut and paste other people's reflections, to ape them, to script fake but extraordinary reflections rather than build their own modest truth, small, real personal truths that would attract no attention and only earn their authors mediocre grades. Thus, reflective curricula that form a part of teacher education paradoxically suck student teachers into lying. They're led to create reflective fictions of genius from whole cloth, because these will get them good grades…Having attained the status of a criterion of professionalism, reflection has produced a new generation of blackbelt teachers whose round-table discussions are driven by the wildest inspiration. (27)

CONSIDER

What role *can* reflection play in teacher education programs?

Reflective practice gets appropriated and reduced in an environment that accentuates a positivistic outlook on language teaching, in part because the premises driving such a curriculum tend to reject holistic models of truth for fragmentable, and thus controllable, elements. Yet critical reflection, with its emphasis on the moral and ethical dimensions of teaching, one rationally argues, should be able to incorporate insights into the teacher's knowledge base and allow for a particularized approach in the classroom, since it attempts to look at ethical and moral dimensions of schooling. Unfortunately, critical reflection cannot function effectively within the confines of our ideologically-constructed teacher education programs that are inundated with the logic of positivism applied to the endeavor of language education. Critical reflection becomes only a *proforma* exercise along the lines described by Tochon above because the *false consciousness from which teachers conceptualize the language teaching endeavor* is incompatible with the process of critical reflection.

As demographic changes are reflected in foreign language curricular offerings, and Spanish is offered by departments with greater frequency, the role of the social contexts of language teaching become more pronounced or at least more visible. Simply put, students in Spanish classes will have much more contact with native speakers of the language than we have seen in recent history. The social context of language teaching becomes of paramount importance in such an environment, since students leave the classroom (itself situated within a larger context) to enter their sociopolitical contexts with language knowledge that represents certain interests. For example, how many native speakers of Spanish have been told by well-meaning Spanish language learners that theirs is not the *real* Spanish? The development of standards in foreign language education, however, has not effectively anticipated these realities.

The standards movement has profound impact not only on curriculum redesign and the *Five C's* articulated by ACTFL and others. The standards movement is seen as controversial both by language educators and scholars in educational studies. Lange (1999), Welles (1998), and James (1998) explored in ACTFL issues papers the need for an ongoing dialogue in the profession in relation to the development, revision, and implementation of standards. Apple (1996) addresses the issue of national curricula from a broader perspective:

CONSIDER

Teachers in the field of ESL (English as a Second Language) have extensive experience dealing with this issue. Look to professionals in this field for examples of strategies used to address the relationship between sociopolitical contexts and language teaching.

> the major role of a national curriculum is in providing the framework within which national testing can function...while the proponents of a national curriculum may see it as a means to create social cohesion and to give all of us the capacity to improve our schools by measuring them against "objective" criteria, the effects will be the opposite. The criteria may seem objective; but the results will not be, given existing differences in resources and in class and race segregation. (32)

Apple concludes the thought by pointing out that national curricula become mechanisms for the political control of knowledge. Standards are evidence of a political movement based on underlying assumptions that reduce the nature of teaching to a technical, programmatic one.

Is there a role for standards to play in a redefined approach to teacher education? The answer is complicated in that if one speaks only of the existence of foreign language standards, they *can* be seen as an effective tool for curriculum, even including transformational curricula proffered by critical pedagogues. It is the implementation of standards which becomes problematic in terms of the social contexts. Standards hold underpinnings similar to the ones attributed to language teacher education programs above. The division of language into five *Cs* is certainly, as James (1998) puts it, a "gimmick" that is only authoritative under the logical parameters of positivism. From a macrocontextualized view of language education, such a gimmick borders on absurd in that it divides the indivisible. The significant danger, however, is that these divisions become codified and reified, and the nature of the standards for foreign language learning as a document requiring interaction among colleagues, students, and language teaching contexts to be optimally effective, despite any curricular weaving of the elements, is lost. We would simply need to constantly and critically engage the standards, revising them at local levels to a great extent. This process, however, would defeat the political agenda inherent in them.

From Prognosis to Postmortem?

How does the sum of these arguments lead me to conclude that a *death* is imminent? Fragmentable truth in the sense that it is assumed by epistemological constructs underlying teacher education programs and practices supports an environment in which teachers are seen as curriculum technicians. They implement presumably context-free pedagogical strategies in uniform (even if adjusted) ways in multifarious settings. Teacher education programs struggle to equip their students to work in increasingly diverse settings with an attention to the realities of social context and community multiculturalism; however, they find their efforts in vain. Students approach reflection as yet another one of many pro-forma hurdles toward earning the *credential* of the grade and the license to teach, at the same time they are saddled with a curriculum stemming from truth grounded in political motives of politically powerful segments of society. This should not be seen as a failing of the students, however, since the way organized knowledge is presented to them necessitates such an approach to reflective practice.

As a result, the teacher education program becomes largely a mechanism of credentialing and fails to offer teachers anything outside of technical skills, such as the administration of testing instruments or implementing a curricular plan, that the graduates will see as *relevant* to their world. There is no resonance to the sociocultural sensitivities teacher educators attempt to impart. The pre-service preparation takes on an appearance of being unresponsive and out of touch both with the needs of the teachers and the student body they will serve, and teachers are left with few tools they can utilize in analyzing or ameliorating the situation.

Confronting the Future

Now is not a time to rest upon our laurels as we make progress toward becoming one of the core curriculum elements and attempt to extend learning sequences. As a realist, I recognize that administrative structures that largely reflect the positivist influences described above are unlikely to undergo tremendous change in the near future. However, language teacher educators can work within existing structures to address the issues raised here, and minimally four prescriptions can result in an improvement of the condition.

Language Teacher Educators Should Facilitate Seeing Language Teaching as Inquiry, First and Foremost and Language Teacher Educators Should Facilitate Seeing the Language Speakers as Authorities, Both at Home and Abroad

If language teaching is seen as inquiry, then transmissionist models of language teaching are nonsensical. If language teaching is seen as facilitating group inquiry, then it cannot be easily reduced to technicist methods. Instead, it will by necessity shift toward assumptions of reality that are holistic. This transition is accomplished as the roles of language teacher and learner, formerly based in authoritarianism, are redefined as sharing joint authority (see Kanpol 1999). Similarly, native language speakers are not seen as resources or commodities, but also as *teachers* for the classroom of learners (teacher and students).

Language Professionals Should Diligently Guard Against Professional Organizations Making a Shift from Support Network to Regulator

The standards movement as it is currently manifested necessitates some entity serving as the evaluator of language classroom success. If ACTFL, the AATs (including AATF, AATG, AATSP, etc.), and similar professional organizations are tapped as the authorities to make such evaluations, then their relationship with the constituency of language educators changes considerably. The standards at that point no longer facilitate disciplinary dialogue, but become static documents serving as positivistic litmus tests for accountability. Is it the goal of the professional organizations who so collaboratively created foreign language standards to now regulate who may be a language teacher by testing their proficiency and then who may remain a teacher by creating standards against which to measure pedagogical success? How does such a relationship promise to alter the dynamics of professional dialogue?

Language Teacher Education Programs Should be Based in Emancipatory Frames

In essence, language teachers should be introduced to the political nature of all language teaching (see Osborn 2000; Reagan and Osborn 2002). The entire program of preparation, from introductory courses through student teaching, will have to be conceptualized and planned from the position of the language teachers' role as a cultural worker and mediator (see Bassey 1996).

Guidelines

- See language teaching as inquiry.
- See the language speakers as authorities, both at home and abroad.
- Guard against professional organizations shifting from support network to regulator.
- Base teacher education programs within an emancipatory framework.

CONSIDER

Give specific examples of how you, as an individual educator, can work within these guidelines to, as the author hopes, *result in an improvement of the condition.*

Mark Twain, of course, was no stranger to language learning, as his many witticisms regarding the German language demonstrate. His words also provide a fitting conclusion to this chapter as well. In a time when popular movements in the field threaten the best that teacher education can be, in part by reducing it to a mere caricature of its fullest potential, we are pressed upon to exhibit courage. And as Twain noted in *Eruption*, "It is curious—curious that physical courage should be so common in the world, and moral courage so rare." The price paid if we do not summon that courage will certainly be borne by the teachers of tomorrow.

Acknowledgement

My gratitude is extended to Gerd Bräuer, Steve Kercel, Timothy Reagan, Robert Terry, and Lee Wilberschied for their valuable insights and critiques. Shortcomings in the piece remain, of course, my own.

References

Apple, M. *Cultural Politics and Education.* New York: Teacher's College Press, 1996.

Bassey, M.O. "Teachers as Cultural Brokers in the Midst of Diversity." *Educational Foundations* 10.2 (1996): 37-52.

Denzin, N. K. *Interpretive Interactionism.* Thousand Oaks: Sage, 2001.

Giroux, H. A. *Pedagogy and the Politics of Hope: Theory, Culture and Schooling.* Boulder: Westview Press, 1997.

James, D. "The Impact on Higher Education of Standards for Foreign Language Learning: Preparing for the 21st Century." *ACTFL Newsletter* Fall 1998: 11-14.

Kanpol, B. *Critical Pedagogy: An Introduction.* Westport: Bergin & Garvey, 1999.

Kumaravadivelu, B. "Toward a Postmethod Pedagogy." *TESOL Quarterly* 35.4 (2001): 537-560.

Lange, D. "Response to Welles and James Article: ACTFL Newsletter Volume 10.1." *ACTFL Newsletter* Summer 1999: 9 11.

Osborn, T. A. "Critical Reflection and the Foreign Language Classroom." *Critical Studies in Education and Culture Series.* Ed. Henry A. Giroux. Westport: Bergin & Garvey, 2000.

Reagan, T., C. Case, and J. Brubacher. *Becoming a Reflective Educator: How to Build a Culture of Inquiry in the Schools.* 2nd ed. Thousand Oaks: Corwin, 2000.

Reagan, T., and T. A. Osborn. *The Foreign Language Educator in Society: Toward a Critical Pedagogy.* Mahwah: Lawrence Erlbaum Associates, 2002.

Shrum, J. L., and E.W. Glisan. *Teacher's Handbook: Contextualized Language Instruction.* 2nd ed. Boston: Heinle & Heinle, 2000.

Tochon, François V., ed. *The Foreign Self: Truth Telling as Educational Inquiry.* Madison: Atwood Publishing, 2002.

Welles, E. "Standards for Foreign Language Learning: Implications and Perceptions." *ACTFL Newsletter* Fall 1998: 7-9.

Support for New Language Teachers in Gwinnett County (GA) Public Schools

David J. Jahner

Introduction

If the foreign language profession is to realize its goal of extended sequences of language study from the elementary to the post-secondary level, it is critical for school systems to recruit, retain and support educators when they enter the profession. The definition of a *new* language teacher varies widely—some are first year recruits fresh out of college, others are beginning a second career, while still others are providing instruction in foreign language for the first time after teaching another subject area for many years. Each brings a unique set of skills, values and background to the foreign language classroom.

CONSIDER

Which type of *new* teacher are you?

Some professionals deliver quality instruction from the first day of school, while others will need more nurturing and assistance during their career. How does one provide sustained support for such a diverse group of people? This challenge is being faced by school systems throughout the United States, and the Gwinnett County Public School System in Georgia is no exception. Compounding the issue of retention is the critical shortage of language teachers. The University System of Georgia, comprising 34 institutions of higher education, produces fewer than fifty foreign language education candidates in a typical year—only twice the number hired by the Gwinnett County Public Schools alone annually. By blending support specifically designed for language teachers with programs that already exist at the local school and district level, Gwinnett is attempting to retain new language teachers in the face of the critical teacher shortage.

Traits of an Effective Staff Development Program

When designing a professional development program with the goal of retaining new language teachers, one needs to bear in mind the characteristics of a comprehensive staff development program. As Zepeda summarizes, the most effective professional development is highlighted by the following five traits: first, staff development is an ongoing part of the teacher's learning process throughout his/her career and should not consist of one-time events. Secondly, the program needs to engage all stakeholders, which will result in increased motivation and the establishment of a learning community. Thirdly, decisions about program development and change are based on the examination of data, rather than relying on instinct. Fourthly, staff development needs to be based on sound educational research and best practices, and fifthly, financial resources necessary to carry out the program need to be allocated (Zepeda 1999).

CONSIDER

What is effective professional development? It is ongoing; engages all stakeholders; bases staff development on research, not instinct; and has adequate funding.

Because of the diverse backgrounds and needs of teachers, no single staff development model works for all situations. Therefore, the staff developer needs to take into account the individual needs of the participants and the specific circumstances in which they work.

The program designed by the Gwinnett schools has taken Zepeda's tenets into account by examining how to design an integrated approach throughout the school year, as opposed to a one-time in-service; it attempts to cater to the expressed needs of the new educators. Follow-up surveys, discussions with previous participants, and surveys at various points in the school year serve to provide starting points for ongoing evaluation of the program. Finally, budget considerations are constantly taken into consideration.

Striking a balance between local school and district professional development is crucial in a district as large as Gwinnett County Public Schools, which has more than 123,000 students and 13,000 employees. Research indicates that the most successful school systems design their staff development programs on a variety of levels, including individualized professional development in areas of assessed need, as well as school level and district-wide professional development (Metzdorf 1989). District staff development is important because it shares the vision, mission, and goals of the entire organization,. but local school staff development is also crucial because that is where day-to-day instruction occurs. Without some centralized staff development, however, teachers and individual schools are more apt to fail to see and understand how their own school is a microcosm of a larger organization. Similarly, in a curriculum area such as foreign language education, teachers need to ensure proper articulation from one level to the next, and centralized professional development provides a means for accomplishing this objective. According to Ellis (1989), the most effective school district professional development programs are those that make the appropriate connection between individual, local school, and district level offerings. If such a structure exists in a district, the culture and environment focuses on teaching and learning, thereby resulting in continuous improvement. Therefore, the single greatest factor to successful school improvement, defined as increasing student achievement and learning, is professional development (Teacher Staff Development 2001). An effective staff development program directly influences how a teacher interacts with students on a daily basis, since the quality of the teacher-student relationship impacts achievement.

CONSIDER

Examine and evaluate your local staff development program according to Zepeda's traits. Do they apply to what you have experienced at the local level? In your experience, what connections have there been between individual, local, and district level opportunities?

Many of the characteristics of effective staff development programs have been integrated into standards established by numerous organizations in education. By using the standards developed by the National Board of Professional Teaching Standards for World Languages Other Than English (NBPTS 2002), ACTFL's *Draft of Program Standards for Foreign Language Teacher Education* (NCATE) (ACTFL 2002) and the National Staff Development Council's *Standards for Staff Development* (NSDC 2002) in addition to the works cited above as guidelines, school systems can have a direct impact on the success and retention of foreign language teachers.

Rationale for Supporting New Teachers

As anyone who has spent time in the classroom can attest, the job of a teacher can easily become overwhelming. Teachers make thousands of conscious and subconscious decisions every day, and the reality of teaching can take even the most well prepared educator by surprise. In an attempt to break down the myriad responsibilities of teaching so that educators can critically analyze their strengths and discover areas for improvement, Danielson (1996) has developed a framework that divides the role of teaching into four major areas. The four major areas (planning and preparation, the classroom environment, instruction, and professional responsibilities) are further divided into 22 components. Each component has a rubric in order for the practitioner to be able to evaluate his/her performance level and target areas for improvement. In a similar vein, Clement (1996) offers a schema for looking at the first year of teaching and honing in on a variety of topics, ranging from getting started at the beginning of the year, to parent communication, to management issues throughout the school year. Both Clement and Danielson advocate dividing the complex tasks of teaching into manageable chunks. By targeting specific areas and encouraging reflection and self-evaluation, the novice professional can develop habits that will help them become better teachers. Anything the profession does to help new teachers gain a better understanding of their strengths and weaknesses will likely enhance retention of teachers in the classroom.

Another critical component to the success of recruiting and retaining teachers is leadership. Whitaker, Whitaker, and Lumpa (2000) contend that leadership at all levels is directly related to the success of a school system. Therefore, leaders from the superintendent to curriculum coordinators to human resources officials to principals to department chairs all need to be focused on the task of seeking out and keeping highly qualified teachers. In the case of recruitment and retention, each of the aforementioned plays a vital role in communicating the direction and goals of the school system, establishing a commitment among all employees to make hiring and keeping teachers a priority, and anticipating the future needs and challenges of new professionals. For example, all persons involved in hiring foreign language teachers need to be aware of the district level support that exists.

School System Background

Establishing an environment of teaching and learning in the Gwinnett County Public Schools is an ever-evolving process, because the challenges the district faces are constantly changing. Gwinnett County Public Schools is the largest school system in Georgia, and is located in Northeast Metropolitan Atlanta. There are more than 123,000 students enrolled during the 2002-2003 school year, placing it among the 25 largest school systems in the United States, and the district is projected to grow at the rate of 6,000-7,000 students annually for the next several years. Currently, there are fourteen high schools, sixteen middle schools, and fifty-two elementary schools, with twenty additional school sites scheduled to open during the next three years.

CONSIDER

Gwinnett County Public Schools is one of the largest school systems in the United States. As you learn more about this professional development system, ask yourself what pieces of it could also be successful both in smaller districts, and in rural areas.

Accompanying the growth are challenges to meet the needs of the increasingly diverse student population, including those students who are Limited English Proficient (LEP).

The foreign language program currently has approximately 200 teachers, with the majority of the teachers serving at the middle and high school levels. All high schools offer at least four languages (French, German, Latin and Spanish), with Russian being offered at one high school. Spanish is by far the most popular language, with more than 13,000 high school students enrolled in Levels I – AP in the 2002-03 school year. French is the second most popular language with approximately 2,800 students, with German and Latin tied for third with roughly 1,400 students each. The middle school program consists of exploratory classes that last for nine weeks and provides an introduction to various languages, and level one study that prepares students for level two upon entering high school. The elementary schools have non-sequential FLEX (Foreign Language Exploratory) programs at nine sites and one sequential K-5 FLES site (Foreign Language in the Elementary School) with 30 minutes of daily instruction in Spanish. Funding for the FLES program is provided in part by a state grant.

Heightened awareness on the part of parents and students of the benefits of longer language study sequences, coupled with a burgeoning student population, has resulted in dramatic increases in high school enrollments in recent years. Although the state of Georgia requires only two years of language study to fulfill the requirements for a college-preparatory high school diploma, enrollment in Levels III and higher has increased by at least fifteen percent annually for the past three years. Hence, the need for language teachers stems both from total student population increase and growth in the number of advanced level classes.

Four years ago, Gwinnett created a full time position for a Foreign Language Coordinator to assist with ongoing development in curriculum, budget, professional development and growth of the program. Prior to this, the coordinator responsible for foreign languages also oversaw the English to Speakers of Other Languages (ESOL) program. Due to the explosive growth of the ESOL population, as well as the continued growth and plans for future expansion of the foreign language program, the original position was split.

Central to Gwinnett's assessment of individual, school, and district goals is the Results Based Evaluation System (RBES), which is based in large part on the work of Schmoker (1996). Schmoker contends that the most long-lasting improvements in student achievement need to be centered by setting measurable goals and examining results by using data. Hence, every classroom teacher develops annual goals and an action research plan tied to the Local School Plan for Improvement (LSPI), which is in turn directly connected to the district's vision, mission and strategic goals. The teacher's goal must be based on measurable data, such as student scores on pre- and post-tests, perception surveys, and performance levels on rubrics. For example, a foreign language teacher can state that her goal is to have eighty-five percent of her students performing at the *Meets Expectations* level on writing assessments (in the case of Gwinnett, *Meets Expectations* is equal to a *B*). Her goal is directly tied to the school's goal to integrate writing in all curriculum areas and the district's goals at having students perform at a high level on mandated state writing assessments. At the end of the school year, the teacher evaluates his/her success based on the data accumulated. The results from the district, school, and individual goals are used to inform professional development needs, strengths, and challenges regarding student achievement and next year's LSPI goals.

DISCUSS

In his chapter, Terry Osborn argues that the nation's pre-occupation with standards and standardized tests has led to a *teacher-proof* attempt at engineering curricula. Discuss how this view would influence the assessment process and subsequent goal setting and instructional practices of the teachers in Gwinnett County.

Aspects of New Teacher Support during the Fall Semester

In order to provide effective support for new teachers, one needs to be continually aware of the variety of obligations they face in their new roles. One must be cognizant of the delicate balance between being supportive yet not overbearing. Along with day-to-day lesson planning, grading papers and instruction, new teachers can easily feel overwhelmed by the other demands of education, including classroom management, serving on committees, keeping up with required paper work, and sponsoring clubs and other school organizations. Often, the new teacher receives a difficult teaching assignment with three, four, or five different preparations and does not have a traditional classroom to serve as a home base. Many first year teachers float between as many as five or six different classrooms, or are placed in portable units detached from the school building, making lesson planning even more demanding and exacerbating the stress and isolation felt by many beginning teachers.

DISCUSS

How can a new teacher balance these various obligations, and still remain focused on serving the students in the best way possible? Discuss some strategies you have for doing so.

Given the rigorous demands placed on new foreign language teachers, the professional development support in Gwinnett seeks to take advantage of opportunities that already exist in the school calendar.

The program for foreign language teachers new to Gwinnett commences the week prior to the beginning of their contract days. Two days prior to New Teacher Orientation (described below), a course titled *Introduction to the Foreign Language Program* is offered. The first day of the course features an overview of the Gwinnett County foreign language curriculum structure, provides a model lesson on the importance of using the target language from the first day of Level One, gives participants a calendar overview of professional and extracurricular events relevant to foreign language teachers and students, and focuses on establishing good management and organization from the onset. During the course's second day, participants are divided into language groups and receive language-specific information and overviews from veteran teachers in the district. The goals of the class are to establish a sense of community and network for the new teachers, to supply an overview of the expectations and curriculum of the school system, and to answer questions they may have regarding the beginning of the school year. Time is also allowed for the participants to work together to design lessons for the first several days of school. In addition to receiving a Staff Development Unit (SDU) for the course, participants also receive financial compensation for their time. Because of effective communication among department chairs, local school administrators, and the Human Resources Division, one-hundred percent of the new foreign language teachers participated in the current year's course.

Later the same week, all new hires to Gwinnett County Public Schools are invited to participate in a New Teacher Orientation. The success of this program is impressive: for the 2002-2003 school year, more than 1,300 new teachers voluntarily participated in this staff development opportunity. There are several reasons this class has been successful, not the least of which is that teachers receive a stipend for attending both days of the course. The financial compensation is possible because the event takes place outside regular contract time. Even veteran teachers (new to the district) are invited to participate in order to give them an overview of Gwinnett's curriculum and strategic vision, mission and goals, as well as an introduction to the RBES process described earlier. Another facet of the program is a block of time spent focused on individual curriculum areas. This opportunity enables subject area coordinators or other designated specialists to meet with new hires from across the school system at the same time. In the case of foreign language, time is provided to follow up on the course they took earlier in the week. Based on the feedback from this year's participants, the foreign language professionals felt like they had an advantage over their counterparts in other disciplines that did not receive specific curriculum-area staff development prior to New Teacher Orientation.

The week after New Teacher Orientation marks the beginning of contract days and pre-planning activities for the new school year. The majority of the week is devoted to programs at the local schools in order to disseminate information such as a review of any new policies or procedures specific to a school, student registration, etc. Time is built in the schedule, however, to provide three hours of district staff development for the various curriculum areas. This meeting is an opportunity to set the tone from a district perspective regarding the mission and goals of the foreign language program. For the new teachers, it further establishes the sense of belonging to the Gwinnett community of language professionals.

Program teachers have a second opportunity to gather again in mid-October, following the end of the first nine weeks of school. For the past several years, this meeting has been structured as a mini-conference. Teachers choose from a variety of one-hour breakout sessions, including topics such as language specific sessions, thematic units, best practices, and developing RBES goals and assessment. The sessions strive to build on the themes established at the August meeting, as well as on feedback gathered from program teachers. One session is devoted specifically to the new teachers. During the hour-long meeting, attendees receive a preview of the upcoming staff development course, *Survival Strategies for New Foreign Language Teachers*, along with some practical activity ideas. In addition, the teachers have an opportunity to talk with each other about their roles in a non-threatening environment. Between the *Introduction to the Foreign Language Program* class, New Teacher Orientation, the pre-planning week session, and the October system staff

CONSIDER

Contrast and compare Gwinnett, Georgia's 18-hour plan to the professional development programm in your local area. What are the biggest differences and what are the reasons for them?

development day, new language teachers have had at least eighteen contact hours of program-related professional development. All of these meetings are carved out of time already allotted in the school system calendar or prior to the beginning of the school year. Therefore, scheduling additional meeting times once the school year commences may not always be necessary when looking at ways to begin to support and network with new teachers.

In addition to the face-to-face meetings, the new teachers have a variety of other means to remain in contact with their peers from the beginning of the school year. By taking advantage of Gwinnett's technology infrastructure, the names of all new teachers are added to a variety of E-mail groups prior to the first day of school. The E-mail groups are designed to facilitate communication across languages and levels. For example, by typing *FLGerman* in the *To*: line of E-mail, one can reach all K-12 German teachers in the school system. Similar groups exist for French, Latin, all Spanish, Spanish III, and Spanish IV/V/AP teachers as well as all elementary, middle, and new program teachers. Hence, the new French/German/Latin/Spanish teacher has the opportunity to reach all of his/her colleagues concurrently if a question comes up or any assistance is needed. In addition, any web sites recently discovered, classroom activities and ideas, or upcoming community events can be readily shared through this communication channel.

During the first semester, the district coordinator also makes an effort to make as many site-visits as possible in order to observe the new teachers in action. However, in any given year there may be as many as thirty new foreign language program teachers in Gwinnett County. Even though it is often difficult to meet with all of them during the beginning of the year, every effort is made to help ensure they become an important and viable part of the program as soon as possible. Subsequent communication with the new teachers during the remainder of the school year is targeted to provide assistance in small, manageable chunks. The communication may be distributed to the entire cadre of new educators, or may be directed at an individual teacher. Topics range from ideas on how to become a more reflective teacher and sharing active learning ideas to practical information such as explaining upcoming summer staff development offerings and how to register for them. Hence, of all the district support pieces mentioned to this point, none takes any additional time from the new teacher's already full schedule.

Many schools also have specific mentoring programs to assist the new teachers. The district wide activities for teachers are intended to supplement what happens at the local school, since that is where the teacher spends the majority of his/her time. At nearly every school in Gwinnett, newly hired teachers are paired with mentors who help the new person find their way around the school, answer questions about day-to-day operations, and assist in whatever way possible to make the new colleague comfortable in their new surroundings. While most of the local school programs do not include classroom visits and observations at this point, it is critical for the new hire to have someone to answer questions and facilitate acclimation especially in regard to concrete classroom practice. Even veteran teachers need to become familiar with a school's culture when starting at a new building. Often, the mentors are from the same teaching discipline or have the same planning period so regular meetings can be scheduled. The importance of being comfortable with one's working environment should not be dismissed, since it can be correlated to worker productivity and effectiveness.

CONSIDER

Think back over your educational/teaching experiences. Was there someone who acted as your mentor? How did that person most help you?

Even though it is beneficial to have a person at the school to help learn the building's culture, efforts are underway to ensure a more comprehensive mentoring program that includes classroom observations, assistance with planning lessons, and other activities that have a direct impact on classroom instruction and assessment. An extensive mentoring program has now been implemented in two of Gwinnett's school clusters. (A cluster is a group of all schools that feed into one of the system's high schools.) Because of budgetary implications, the school board determines which clusters will receive the funds for the mentoring program. The program matches a veteran teacher with an incoming protégé, and the two engage in an intensive series of interviews, observations, and reflection. Mentors are trained during a fifty-hour course that takes place both during the summer vacation and during the school year. As part of the training, mentors practice observation skills and conferencing techniques. Whenever possible, pairs teaching the same subject area are matched, and the mentor/mentee meet at least once every three weeks. Because of its organization and specific rubrics, much of the theoretical basis for the program centers on Danielson's (1996) four domains of teaching. With a school system as large as Gwinnett, each local school has to assume a large part of the responsibility for supporting new teachers, and the mentoring program provides a framework for the local schools.

A Professional Development Course at the Beginning of the Spring Semester

In addition to the district workshops and mentoring programs at local schools, one of the most important aspects of the support program for new language teachers in Gwinnett is an annual staff development course that begins in January. The class is intended as a follow-up course to the support pieces that already exist. Once again, all teachers new to the foreign language program in the school system are invited to participate in the class, which is team taught by the coordinator and one of the district's master language teachers.

January is a perfect time to offer such a course for several reasons. Most importantly, new teachers are refreshed and ready for a new start after the winter holidays, according to research on new teacher's growth and development during the first year (California Department of Education 2001). Secondly, because one of the course objectives is to troubleshoot areas where the teachers may be having difficulties (e.g. classroom management, transitions between activities during lessons, etc.), the new teachers need to have some in-class time before they are ready to know what issues are important to them. Thirdly, the teachers have probably exhausted their activity ideas, and the course provides an opportunity for them to acquire some new strategies and to share ideas with their colleagues about what methods work with various types of students. Finally, it is important to offer teachers a non-threatening environment to discuss their challenges and successes.

Because it is difficult to take teachers out of the classroom for two days, the class is offered on two Saturdays. In Georgia, a course must meet for at least ten contact hours in order to award staff development credit, so each session lasts for five hours. In order to renew a teaching certificate, Georgia public school teachers also need to accumulate ten Staff Development Units (SDUs) every five years. Together with the one SDU each awarded for the Introduction to the Foreign Language Program class and New Teacher Orientation in August, participants in the course will have accumulated at least three SDUs during their first year in the school system. Having three SDUs at the end of their first year keeps them on track for renewing their teaching certificates and establishes the thought of not waiting until the last minute to take ten SDUs of course work.

Once again, because the course is offered during off-contract time, participants are awarded stipends upon successful completion of the course. It is critical to support new hires not only with activities and strategies to help ensure their success, but also to be able to reward them financially for making the effort to attend two Saturday workshops. Even though the stipend is not the sole reason teachers enroll in the course, it definitely offers an incentive.

One of the course objectives is to embed best practices and teaching methodologies in the delivery of instruction. Each segment of the class is developed so that participants experience the strategies firsthand. At the end of each segment, participants and the instructors discuss how the various activities are structured and how they can be implemented in a variety of classroom settings. For example, different strategies for getting participants to be assigned partners or groups are modeled as part of a particular activity. Other concepts include moving from teacher-centered to student-centered activities and exploring what types of instruction are more appropriate for different objectives. Therefore, the course provides teachers some of the concrete activities they like to learn when attending a workshop, but promotes reflection and discussion by talking about what they experienced in a particular activity. Course evaluations and follow-up conversations with participants indicate that participants are more cognizant of how they structure their lessons after taking the class.

Besides embedding teaching strategies in various segments of the course, the class also incorporates a variety of interactive learning activities and games at several points during both sessions. In addition to providing participants with personal experience of the activities, it is important to furnish the participants with written directions for the activities, and to leave time for them to reflect on the directions and ensure they can successfully take the idea back to their individual locations. Participants discuss implications for their classrooms and possible variations of the activities. Sharing ideas and activities, both those that are successful and those that are not, is an excellent way to promote personal and professional growth.

Another goal of the course is to help troubleshoot areas where participants perceive they are having difficulties. Based on personal experience, observation, and data collection, the workshop leaders have assembled topics that tend to be issues with new teachers. Each topic is then broken down into smaller points. For example, under the general topic of grading, a variety of issues are addressed. Teachers discuss how to make the best possible use of the time they spend grading. Different strategies for grading writing samples, keeping up with oral participation programs and grading notebooks are also featured. Similar discussions take place around the themes of make-up work, daily procedures like taking attendance and keeping up with E-mail, as well as documentation. With all these problematic areas, the workshop leaders facilitate the discussion and encourage participants to share ideas and strategies that work for them.

At the end of the first session, the new teachers are given an opportunity to write down any additional problematic areas they would like to address during the second session. The instructors then tailor parts of the second meeting to meet the specific needs of the group that may not have been met during the initial session.

One aspect of the second session focuses on strategies for planning lessons and thematic units, because one of the more difficult things for new teachers to realize is how each lesson is part of a larger unit, which in turn is part of a larger goal for the year. New teachers tend to be so focused on filling each lesson with a string of student-centered activities that the larger question of *Why am I doing this particular activity?* is often ignored. Hence, the goal of this segment is to help teachers think of ways to keep the overall goals of the year and unit in mind when planning each lesson. A variety of visual aids and discussion helps teachers see how it can be possible to use the textbook as a guide and resource rather than as a prescribed set of activities that needs to be completed under any circumstance. An ancillary objective is also to show how each teacher might have the same end result in mind, but may take different paths in reaching that goal. Showing multiple ways of putting together a series of lessons helps new teachers realize that there isn't a *cookbook recipe* method to the art of teaching.

After talking about individual lessons, the instructors walk the participants through planning a thematic unit. The two workshop leaders each present how a topic can be used at a variety of learning levels and how each segment of the thematic project relies on the other. Several participants have commented on how a segment of the course benefited them, and how the course has helped them plan their own thematic projects. For example, one teacher stated that she became much more aware of keeping the overall goal in mind with each activity during a unit. Others have said how looking at results from daily work, quizzes and tests helped them design better lesson plans.

In order to celebrate their attendance at the class, the end of the second session culminates with a *graduation* ceremony. Digital pictures of each person receiving his/her certificate of completion are taken, and the picture is sent as an attachment on the school system's E-mail network the following week. A group photo is also taken and sent to all the participating teachers for them to have as a lasting memory of the class. It is important for people to leave with smiles on their faces and with something tangible to show that their time was well spent. Subsequent follow-up surveys of the participants have shown the ceremony to be one of the enduring highlights of the course.

ACTION

Using Gwinnett's annual January staff development course as a model, work with others to design a one-day workshop for new teachers.

Evaluation and continuous improvement of the courses and support described above is important in order to meet the needs of future generations of teachers. Evaluation forms are filled out at various points during each course, and a follow-up survey is sent electronically several months afterward. Feedback has provided valuable suggestions for improvements, such as including written directions and outlines of the various activities presented. Providing each teacher with a list of participants and their school locations has led to groups of teachers meeting periodically. This networking is one of the greatest benefits of teaching a course for new language teachers hopefully will help meet the goal of keeping teachers in the profession for longer than one or two years.

Future Plans

There are also future aspirations for supporting new language teachers in Gwinnett County Public Schools. One of the long-range goals is to continue to blend support for language teachers at the system level with what occurs at each individual school. The district support must continue to evolve, just as local school mentoring programs and site observations continue to improve. For example, one school is encouraging all foreign language teachers (not just new teachers) to visit language teachers across the school system. Having a list of master teachers willing to be observed could facilitate these types of visits and ensure that teachers are seeing and learning from the best of the best. Such a list would also help to prevent a master teacher from having too many observations during a semester or year.

Based on feedback from participants in the courses, another goal is to expand the new language teacher course to include a class for teachers in their second and third years in the profession. The course does not need to be a traditional on-site course, but may include online professional development where teachers discuss various themes or topics throughout the course of the year using discussion threads or chat rooms. The virtual professional development course option frees teachers from many of the time restraints of a traditional course offering, and encourages the use of technology. It is still important, however, for teachers to meet face-to-face during the first year, so they can establish good interpersonal relationships with each other and achieve the comfort level necessary for professional sharing of information and ideas online.

NOTE

For a detailed discussion of action research, see Lee Wilberschield's article in chapter four of this volume.

A further aim of the courses is to better connect the classes to the goals of the Results Based Evaluation System and how to use action research to inform instruction. Although the courses mention using data to assist in planning lessons and units, the professionals new to Gwinnett could benefit from a clear overview of how the individual teacher's RBES relates to the school and district goals.

At this point, none of the support refers specifically to the language proficiency of the teachers. Programs, both in the United States and abroad, are in place at the state, regional and national levels, however, for the modern languages taught in Gwinnett County, and information regarding the opportunities is distributed throughout the year. One goal for the future is to increase participation in these activities.

Conclusion

Every effort is made in the professional development program for new Gwinnett County Public School language teachers to capitalize on providing the support they need to be successful, while making the best possible use of time. Part of the program's success can be attributed to balancing district level offerings that function in cooperation with efforts at the local school level. The first semester foreign language program meetings take advantage of time built in the school calendar and allow for mentoring programs at local schools to help the teacher become acclimated with local school and district culture. By contrast, the second semester focuses on bringing the group together for a staff development course that gives the new teachers time to network. Graduates from the course have commented on the positive experience of the class and how it helped them realize they are not alone in struggling with adapting to the daily life of an educator.

ACTION

Using the information presented in this article, list the three most important factors (in your opinion) in retaining foreign language teachers.

In Gwinnett, the evolving program of support for new teachers has taken into consideration Zepeda's (1999) qualities of effective professional development programs. By combining courses throughout the year, new professionals have the opportunity to meet and develop relationships that would not be possible at a single session. Information about the classes continues to be communicated with all stakeholders so no one is excluded; the courses will continue to be improved and refined, based on feedback from participants and the latest research from the profession. No additional sessions should be added until the financial resources necessary to execute them successfully are in place.

Recent developments in the foreign language profession have stated the goal of expanding language programs and offering ever-increasing sequences of study. The National Standards for Language Learning in the 21st Century (1996) focused the goals of the profession on teaching students "how, when and why to say what to whom," and the ACTFL Performance Guidelines for K-12 Learners (1998) put the Standards in a context of realistic proficiency goals. Similarly, the vision of many national, state, and local foreign language professional organizations is to offer students extended sequences of language study to produce citizens proficient in at least one language other than English. Increasing the quantity and quality of foreign language-teachers in every school system is necessary if the profession's long-term goals are to be realized. It is the responsibility of all language teachers and foreign language professionals to encourage and support the types of professional development opportunities that enable new teachers to feel supported and successful. Retaining teachers is the key if the vision for foreign language education in the United States is to become a reality.

References

American Council on the Teaching of Foreign Languages (ACTFL). *Standards for Foreign Language Learning: Preparing for the 21st Century*. Lawrence: Allen Press, 1996.

——. *ACTFL Performance Guidelines for K-12 Learners*. Yonkers: ACTFL, 1998.

——. *Draft of Program Standards for Foreign Language Teacher Preparation. (Proposed NCATE Standards)*. 15 Sep. 2002 <http://www.actfl.org>.

California Department of Education. *Beginning Teacher Support and Assessment*. (2001). 2 Jan. 2002 <http://www.btsa.ca.gov>.

Clement, M. "A Curriculum and Resources for Beginning Teacher Programs." *Kappa Delta Pi Record* 32.3 (1996): 87–90.

Danielson, C. *Enhancing Professional Practice: A Framework for Teaching*. Alexandria: Association for Supervision and Curriculum Development, 1996.

Ellis, S. "Putting it all Together: An Integrated Staff Development Program." *Staff Development: A Handbook of Effective Practices*. Ed. S. Caldwell Oxford: National Staff Development Council, 1989. 58-69.

Metzdorf, J. "District Level Staff Development." S. Caldwell, 14-24.

National Board of Professional Teaching Standards. "World Languages Other Than English Standards." 24 Sep. 2002 <http://www.nbpts.org/pdf/br_world_languages.pdf>.

National Staff Development Council. "NSDC Standards for Staff Development, Revised 2001." 24 Sep. 2002 <http://www.nsdc.org/educatorindex.htm>.

Schmoker, M. *Results: The Key to Continuous School Improvement*. Alexandria: Association for Supervision and Curriculum Development, 1996.

"Teacher Staff Development: A Strategy for School Improvement." *LAB Education Notes* 3.2 (2001): 1–2.

Whitaker, T., B. Whitaker, and D. Lumpa. *Motivating and Inspiring Teachers: The Educational Leader's Guide for Building Staff Morale*. Larchmont: Eye on Education, 2000.

Zepeda, S. *Staff Development: Practices that Promote Leadership in Learning Communities*. Larchmont: Eye on Education, 1999.

Post-Reading Questions

1. *As a (future) foreign language educator, what impact do you want to make in the lives of your students? What is it that you want to initiate in their learning?*

2. *Look at your list from pre-reading questions #2 and #3. Which of the skills listed do you want to develop further? How? Make an action plan for the next semester.*

3. *Several of the pre- and post-reading questions in the other parts of this book have asked you about your future engagement in your own language learning. Summarize your thoughts about how to maintain your current language skills, and to further develop them. Make an action plan for concrete short and long-term goals. Consider especially how language skills could be fostered while dealing with the challenges of a daily teaching load.*

4. *The use of technology in the language classroom is very complex. As an instructor you must master both the technical aspects, as well as content of what you are teaching. Identify areas of personal strengths and weaknesses in using technology, and come up with ways to share the first with others and deal with the latter by drawing upon help from colleagues.*

5. *Summarize what you consider key areas for your own growth as a person and as a professional. What specific forms of support do you imagine in each of the areas you have identified? Make an action plan for organizing and accessing this support.*

Instead of an Afterword

Editor's Note: Gerd Bräuer

Much has been said in this book about the state and the future of language education on both sides of the Atlantic. It became clear that, due to challenging differences in how languages are being taught in both places, much can be learned from each other and, in the times to come, much more can be found out *together* about the nature of language acquisition.

Nevertheless, all the good news in this book will not matter as much if the development of our schools goes by without close examination. What if the findings from second language research does not have the necessary impact on our daily classes? What if curriculum development fails to reach the learners' needs? What if teacher training does not acknowledge the reality of schools to the necessary degree?

We chose this contribution by the internationally known Swiss educator, Rolf Dubs, instead of an afterword to this book, because we believe that the development of *early individual* school needs to be on our minds if we want to strive for better foreign and second language education programs. The learning and teaching of foreign languages, as many authors in this volume noted, neither stops beyond the walls of our classrooms nor beyond the borders of our professional field. Successful language education needs healthy and thriving institutions.

This article about quality management in school development is written in German. If you are not able to read German at all, you will again rely on information from people who understand the language. Use the resources that worked for you while dealing with the other chapter written in German by Dieter Wolff.

If you have some knowledge about German, you can guide yourself through the chapter with the help of the extended summary and the additional material about quality management and school development listed above. Please share your insights with peers who are unable to read German.

Think about what specific information you want to provide to your peers. Obviously, it would be too time-consuming to provide a full translation. What are the major factors outlined in the article? Try to extract the provided summary even further. Come up with examples to illustrate your comprised summary. What aspects from other articles of this volume would you suggest to your peers in order to get a sense of the larger context of the ideas by Rolf Dubs?

Material on Quality Management and School Development (in English):

Mayer, D.P., Mullens, J.E., Moore, M.T. & Ralph, J. *Monotoring School Quality: An Indicators Report*. Washington: US Department of Education, 2000.

Association for Supervision and Curriculum Development
<www.ascd.org>

Create high performance public schools
<www.topschools.com>

Quality Management in School Development: A Model

Rolf Dubs
(summarized by Karen Sanders)

In recent years, quality management has become a household phrase. In the following article, the author presents a process-oriented (rather than product) model that addresses the issue of quality management in school development.

Introduction

For many years quality management (QM) has been a topic of discussion in education circles. Furthermore, some good work related to this topic has been accomplished. Unfortunately, today there exists a danger of this concept dying out. The reasons for this include:

- The inability of current models to clearly identify desired outcomes.
- The inability to meet instructors' expectations and the failure of the process, resulting from a lack of planning and leadership.
- The *burn-out* of participants, resulting from long-lasting projects that show no visible results/positive changes.
- The lack of commitment on the part of administrators of the general QM concept.
- The incredible difficulty of defining scientifically what *quality* in an educational setting means.

The goal of this article is to examine the following questions:

- What are the desired outcomes of having quality management in the schools?
- What challenges must be overcome for quality management to be effective?
- How should quality management look in education?
- What is the role of state school administrators in the process?

Quality Management: Goals and Terminology

Theoretical Foundation

When looking at QM today, there are two accepted paradigms that stand in contrast to one another. On the one hand is a *top-down* model, in which an outside institution imposes QM for various reasons not necessarily connected to the needs and culture of individual schools. On the other hand, is the *bottom-up* model, in which each individual school develops its own approach to QM. The first model is very product oriented, whereas the second is much more focused on the process.

Quality Management: A Developmental Model

The decision of which paradigm to follow will of course greatly impact the formation of a quality management model. (See figure 1 in Dubs' article)

Quality Management: The goal of QM is to develop and maintain high quality educational processes. This goal will only be met, when those responsible for creating the system understand that the process needs to evolve out of the needs of each individual institution.

A QM system is made up of both the organization, and the process and procedures. There are two ways to look at such a system. *Internal* quality management is defined as an individual school developing its own QM system. *External* quality management is defined as a third party developing the system for the individual school.

Evaluation: In the QM models there are two types of evaluation, self-evaluation and outside evaluation. In the first, school officials evaluate their own systems. For the second, an outside evaluator comes in to evaluate and give feedback.

All of the above concepts play a role in the development of a comprehensive QM model. The author suggests such a model consisting of the following three elements:

- Each individual school must initiate/implement an internally conceived QM model, including a self-evaluation piece.
- Outside state school administrators must conduct a comprehensive evaluation to determine if the self-evaluation has been properly done, and if the internally developed QM model is appropriate.
- In order to truly impact the educational system, outside administrators should also conduct a third-party evaluation of the QM model.

Using these three elements as a foundation, the author makes the following recommendations for those considering the development of a QM system (see figure 2):

- Use a bottom-up approach with a strong process orientation.
- Integrate an outside evaluation process into the overall QM system in order to ensure that all QM procedures are developed to the same high level.
- Use outside evaluators, not to do any sort of *quality order/ranking*,

but rather to evaluate the development and implementation of the overall system.

QM: A Definition
Developers analyze several factors, in all areas of the educational realm, during the building of any QM system. Using this analysis as a foundation, individual institutions/schools will then initiate action to improve quality in their chosen areas. At the same time, administrators at all levels will also be initiating steps to encourage quality improvement. This definition of QM is intended to be broad, and to include pedagogical, administrative, economic and all other areas, which influence a strong and high-quality educational system.

For the remainder of this article, the author has chosen to focus on *one* of the QM paradigms mentioned above, the *internal* model with a self-evaluation component.

Internal Quality Management with a Self-Evaluation Component: The Individual School

Assumptions
The author based his model on the following assumptions:

- It is best to use a step-by-step procedure that evaluates multiple areas in the schools, (such as climate, instructional quality, administrative structure etc.) one after the other. The author argues that in order to sucessfully use the internal QM model to achieve continuous program improvement, it is necessary to avoid complex evaluation models.
- QM should not be a static or an automatic process. Rather, it is important to build into the QM model variety; variety of focus areas in the schools, variety of evaluation tools and procedures, and variety in personnel.
- For process-oriented QM models, it is important to develop specific measures for further school development. Only then, when all who take part perceive the improvement in quality in the schools, will the model be effective. Such visible measures will also undoubtedly strengthen the belief in the importance of QM.

Internal Quality Management with a Self-Evaluation Component: A Model
The author introduces a QM model by outlining the six key steps (see figure 3):

Step 1: Select the areas to be evaluated.
Step 2: Set the expected level of quality.
Step 3: Select the methods and personnel that will be used.
Step 4: Complete data collection and/or document analysis.
Step 5: Analyze the results and make recommendations for school development.
Step 6: Plan and complete measures for future school development.

When deciding which areas to evaluate, it is important to choose carefully and to clearly define what good quality is, and what quality standards need to be met. Ideally, data collection tools and methods should be chosen and/or designed with each individual school in mind. Unfortunately, however, because of the enormous time commitment, and because many school personnel do not have extensive training in research methodology, most programs use tools designed by third parties (for example, scientific institutions).

Organization

Under the suggested model, a quality management project group is formed in the school. This group usually consists of instructors and representatives from both the administration (although usually not the principal) and the student body. The leader of the group is usually an instructor with special training in the area of quality management. In some cases, parents are also asked to participate. How participants are chosen does vary by school, however, in many cases a school administrator will appoint the committee chair and a couple of instructors. The remainder of the committee is then chosen using a voting process. In order for the evaluation process to be truly successful, it is essential that the work of this committee be shared regularly with the larger school community.

Quality in the Schools: The Problem

Describing the Quality of a School

As mentioned above it seems extremely difficult, if not impossible, to scientifically define the concept of *school quality*. Despite this reality, many have attempted to do so, but no one definition has yet been universally accepted. One of the most interesting attempts, has been by the US Department of Education (USDOE). After analyzing extensive empirical research, they developed indicators of program quality. The 13 indicators are grouped under the three areas of school environment, instructional staff and the classroom, and all play a part in learner success. The indicators are divided as follows (see figure 4):

> *School Environment*
> Leadership, School Objectives, School Community, Discipline, Intellectual Environment
>
> *Instructional Staff*
> Scientific capabilities, Education, Instructional experience, Professional Development
>
> *Classroom*
> Content of instruction, Pedagogy, Technology, Class Size

Although many agree that these indicators do have an impact on learner success, the extent of this influence remains controversial. Furthermore, some ask whether school quality should only be viewed from the perspective of student success, or, if there are other factors that are not addressed by the above model.

Since science has been unable to clearly answer the question, *what IS school quality?*, it is the responsibility of the educational community to step up and attempt to do so in a meaningful way. To successfully do this, schools need to individually consider the issue of quality as they develop their processes, procedures and long-term visions.

Building a QM concept in the Schools

As each project group develops its quality management concept, it must consider the following fundamental questions:

- Which areas should be evaluated and in what timeframe, and how should the information be collected?
- For each chosen area, how will quality be defined, which methods will be used and which measures in school development should be taken in response to poor quality?

QM planning should be done over at least a five-year period. Because of the length of such a project, it is important that the project group have a clearly defined plan, and that they are able to maintain their focus. During the five-year period different areas will be evaluated in different ways. One such example is (see figure 5):

Year	**Area**	**Process**
1	School Climate	Interview Instructors and Students
2	Parental Perceptions of the School	Interview the Parent Body
3	Instruction	Evaluation of Instruction by the Students
4	Leadership	Evaluation by the Staff
5	School Facilities	Student Projects

In choosing the areas to be evaluated, the project groups should consider the following:

- Each chosen area should have the potential to improve the overall quality of the school.
- For each chosen area *quality* should be clearly defined.
- Lobbying and manipulation should not be accepted practice.
- Never begin with an area that can be seen as threatening to the instructors (such as student evaluation of class instruction).

The author recommends, in the beginning phases of a QM project, to use already established evaluation tools and methods in order to allow one to focus on the most important task, that of clearly defining *quality*. He also outlines some technical considerations for QM implementation. For example, he suggests the following:

Area	*Desired Quality*	*Methodology*	*School Development*
Instruction	Positive Perceptions by the Students	Questionnaire Developed by the Students	In the Case of Negative Evaluation, In-house Trainings with the Faculty Should be Done

See table 6 in the original article for additional examples.

Administrative Challenges

In order to successfully implement a quality management model, and to avoid excessive resistance and/or burn out on the part of the faculty, it is very important that administrators at the highest levels establish a strong and effective QM concept. This entails providing support to the QM process by offering a balance between being the source of advice, and offering unbiased and useful feedback through the evaluation process.

Administrative bodies should also be responsible for providing sufficient and high quality professional development opportunities for those involved in quality management at the local level (see the original article for an example for QM in Austrian schools).

Qualitätsmanagement an Schulen
Bestandesaufnahme und ein Modell für Schulen

Rolf Dubs

Summary

Qualitätsmanagement ist zum Schlagwort geworden. Ob der vielen Begriffe und Modelle sind viele Lehrkräfte verunsichert. Im Beitrag werden Begriffe geklärt und darauf aufbauend ein Modell dargestellt, wie es in der Schweiz Eingang gefunden hat. Das Schwergewicht dieses Modells liegt auf der Prozessorientierung mit dem Ziel der Schulentwicklung. Gefordert sind auch die staatlichen Schulbehörden, die endlich konzeptionelle Vorgaben machen müssten.

Ausgangslage

Seit einigen Jahren gehört das Qualitätsmanagement (QM) zu den wichtigsten Diskussionsthemen in der Bildungspolitik, und an vielen Schulen wurde gute Pionierarbeit geleistet. Heute besteht aber die Gefahr, dass das Thema *totlaufen* könnte, was auf mehrere Gründe zurückzuführen ist: Erstens ist ob der vielen vorgeschlagenen

Modelle oft nicht mehr ganz klar, welchem Ziel das QM dienen soll. Zweitens ist das QM an vielen Schulen nicht zweckmässig konzipiert und schlecht geführt, so dass sich nicht die Erfolge einstellen, welche die Lehrkräfte erwarten. Drittens ist das QM an Schulen zeitaufwendig, so dass—vor allem bei schlechter Führung—die Ermüdungserscheinungen bei den Lehrpersonen sehr gross sind. Viertens tun sich die staatlichen Schulbehörden mit einer Gesamtkonzeption des QM (wer hat welche Aufgaben?) schwer. Und fünftens schliesslich ist es wissenschaftlich ausserordentlich schwierig, die Qualität einer Schule zu definieren. Deshalb müssen auch alle Modelle, die mehr oder weniger aus der Wirtschaft auf die Schule übertragen werden, scheitern. Qualitätsmanagement an Schulen ist etwas viel anspruchsvolleres als Qualitätsmanagement in Unternehmungen.

Ziel dieses Beitrages ist es, sich mit den folgenden Fragen auseinanderzusetzen: (1) Was ist mit dem QM an Schulen gewollt? (2) Welches sind die Anforderungen an ein wirksames QM an Schulen? (3) Wie kann das QM an einer Schule gestaltet werden? (4) Welche Aufgaben müssen die staatlichen Bildungsbehörden erfüllen?

Ziele und Begriffe des QM an Schulen

Paradigmatische Grundlagen

Paradigmatisch stehen sich heute zwei Ansätze gegenüber: Einerseits gibt es den zentralen Ansatz (top-down), bei welchem irgend welche Instanzen oder Institutionen das QM in den Schulen durchführen. Hier stehen Kontrolle und/oder Überwachung sowie Zertifizierung und/oder Akkreditierung im Vordergrund. In diesem Fall ist das QM stark produktorientiert. Andererseits wird ein dezentraler Ansatz (bottom-up) vertreten, bei welchem jede Schule ihr eigenes QM aufbaut und die Daten daraus den obern Instanzen zur Einsicht vorlegt. Bei diesem Ansatz steht die Prozessorientierung im Vordegrund, d.h. jede einzelne Schule versteht das QM als ständigen Prozess zur steten Verbesserung der Qualität einer Schule.

Modell zur Ausgestaltung des QM

Der Entscheid über das zu wählende Paradigma prägt die Ausgestaltung des QM-Konzeptes. Für schulpraktische Zwecke kann von der in Abbildung 1 dargestellten Gliederung ausgegangen werden.

Abbildung 1

Modell für die Ausgestaltung eines Qualitätsmanagement-Konzeptes

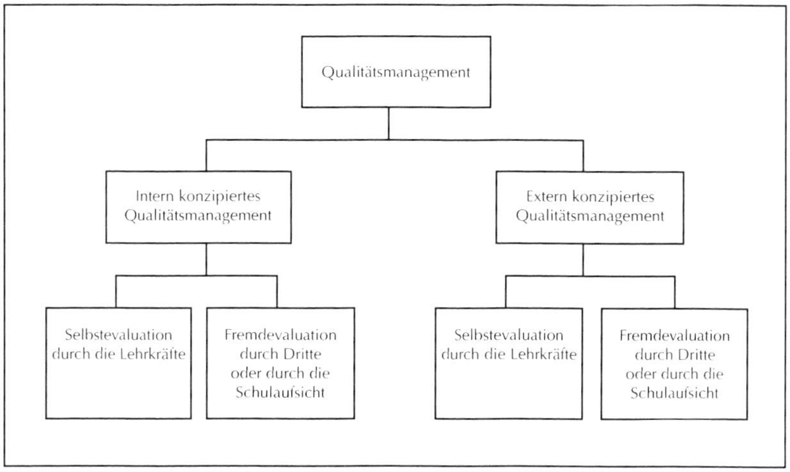

Das **Qualitätsmanagement** an Schulen umfasst systematisch eingesetzte Verfahren, mit denen ihre Qualität verbessert und gesichert wird. Sein Ziel ist also die Qualitätsentwicklung oder Qualitätssicherung, wobei diese beiden Begriffe die gleiche Bedeutung haben. Dieses Ziel wird nur erreicht, wenn die für das Qualitätsmanagement zuständige Instanz oder Institution die Verfahren so ausgestaltet, dass sie für die betroffene Schule zu einem Qualitätsinstrument für die Qualitätsentwicklung und -sicherung werden. Dazu sind die einzelnen Verfahren zu einem Qualitätsmanagement-Konzept auszubauen.

Das **Qualitätsmanagement-Konzept** beschreibt die Organisation und die einzusetzenden Verfahren in einer oder mehreren Schulen oder in einem Schulsystem für das Qualitätsmanagement. Dieses Konzept kann durch die einzelne Schule entwickelt werden. Dann liegt ein **intern konzipiertes Qualitätsmanagement** vor. Entwerfen Dritte das Konzept, so liegt ein **extern konzipiertes Qualitätsmanagement** vor.

Vom Qualitätsmanagement zu unterscheiden ist die Evaluation. **Evaluation** heisst Durchführung des Qualitätsmanagements. Sie kann erst erfolgen, wenn ein Qualitätsmanagement-Konzept vorliegt. Führen die Schulangehörigen die Evaluation in ihrer Schule selbst durch, so liegt eine **Selbstevaluation** vor. Wird sie Dritten übertragen, so handelt es sich um eine **Fremdevaluation** (vergleiche dazu Dubs 1998a und die dort zitierte Literatur).

Aufgrund dieses Modelles sowie der paradigmatischen Annahmen lässt sich das QM-Konzept aufbauen. Wir vertreten ein Konzept, das gemäss Tabelle 2 aus drei Elementen besteht.

Tabelle 2

Elemente einer umfassenden QM-Gesamtkonzeption

1. Element:	Jede einzelne *Schule* ist verpflichtet, ein *intern konzipiertes QM* mit einer *Selbstevaluation* einzuführen.
2. Element:	Eine staatliche *Schulaufsichtsbehörde* führt eine *Metaevaluation* durch, d.h. sie überprüft, ob das intern konzipierte QM einer jeden Schule zweckmässig aufgebaut ist, ob die Selbstevaluation richtig durchgeführt wird und ob bei ungenügenden Qualitäten zweckmässige Schulentwicklungsarbeiten geleistet werden.
3. Element:	Für Zwecke der Beeinflussung des Bildungssystems, der Systemsteuerung, der politischen Rechenschaftsablegung oder des Systemvergleichs ordnen die zuständigen *Bildungsbehörden* je nach Bedarf ein *externes QM mit Fremdevaluation* an.

Das hier vorgeschlagene QM-Gesamtkonzept will folgenden Anliegen Rechnung tragen:

(1) Es ist auf die Idee der teilautonomen Schule (Schule mit Gestaltungsfreiräumen) ausgerichtet, in welcher die selbstgesteuerte Schulentwicklung im Rahmen strategischer Zielvorgaben der staatlichen Behörden im Vordergrund steht (vergleiche dazu ausführlich Dubs 2001). Damit wird ein bottom-up-Ansatz mit einer starken Prozessorientierung (laufende Verbesserung der Schulqualität in jeder einzelnen Schule) angestrebt.

(2) Leider lehrt aber die Erfahrung, dass ein internes Qualitätsmanagement mit Selbstevaluation nicht an allen Schulen mit dem gleichen Verantwortungsbewusstsein umgesetzt wird. Deshalb bedarf es einer Metaevaluation durch die staatlichen Behörden, die aber entgegen der von Lehrerseite immer wieder gehörten Behauptung, nicht eine neue Form von kleinlicher Kontrolle darstellt, sondern im Sinne eines modernen Controllings nur überwacht, ob jede Schule ihr QM zweckmässig gestaltet und durchführt.

(3) Ergänzend zur Führung und Entwicklung des gesamten Bildungssystems ordnen die zuständigen Behörden je nach Bedarf ein extern konzipiertes QM mit Fremdevaluation an, das tendenziell produktorientiert ist. Dieses dritte Element sollte aber in erster Linie der Führung und Entwicklung des gesamten Schulsystems und nicht irgend welchen Zielen eines Rankings (Rangliste der *Güte* einer Schule) dienen, denn Ranglisten sind angesichts der Unbestimmtheit des Qualitätsbegriffes (siehe Abschnitt 4 dieses Beitrages) nicht nur unzuverlässig, sondern sie führen in der Öffentlichkeit oft zu unbedachten Reaktionen und lösen bei der Lehrerschaft Ängste aus, die für die Schule nicht förderlich sind.

Definition des QM
Das QM ist ein Teil des Bildungscontrollings, das in einem dynamischen Vergleich zwischen definierten Zielvorstellungen und der Realität besteht. Analysiert werden die wesentlichen (Einfluss-)Faktoren und die Ergebnisse in allen Bereichen des Bildungswesens. Auf der Grundlage dieses systematischen Vergleichs werden die einzelnen Schulen selbst Massnahmen zur Qualitätsverbesserung vornehmen. Zusätzlich werden die staatlichen Schulbehörden selbst Massnahmen zur Qualitätsverbesserung durchführen. Diese Definition ist sehr umfassend. Sie beinhaltet alles, was im ganzen Bildungssystem und in den einzelnen Schulen im Sinne eines Soll-Ist-Vergleiches erfassbar ist: Auf der einen Seite die pädagogischen Qualitäten, das eigentliche QM, und auf der anderen Seite die verwaltungstechnischen (Organisation und Führung der Schulverwaltung) und administrativen sowie die ökonomischen Aspekte wie Kosten-Nutzen-Analysen, Effizienzstudien usw.

Im Folgenden wird nur auf das intern konzipierte Qualitätsmanagement mit Selbstevaluation eingegangen und ein mögliches Modell für einzelne Schulen beschrieben.

Das intern konzipierte QM mit Selbstevaluation in einer einzelnen Schule

Voraussetzungen des Modells
Beim Aufbau des Modelles wird von folgenden Voraussetzungen ausgegangen:

(1) Im Hinblick auf die Prozessorientierung wird ein *Schritt-um-Schritt-Verfahren* empfohlen, bei welchem in einem zeitlichen Nacheinander einzelne Schulbereiche (z.B. Klima der Schule, Qualität des Unterrichtes, Ordnung im Schulhaus) evaluiert werden. Zu rechtfertigen ist dies mit der Idee der Schulentwicklung. Mit dem intern konzipierten QM wird also ein fortlaufender Qualitätsverbesserungsprozess angestrebt. Um eine zeitliche Überforderung der Lehrkräfte zu vermeiden, müssen sich die Qualitätsarbeiten fortlaufend auf einzelne Schulbereiche, die nacheinander evaluiert werden, beschränken. Es zeigt sich immer deutlicher, dass herkömmliche, alle Schulbereiche umfassende Systeme wie ISO und EFQM zu stark produktorientiert und—sicher in den ursprünglichen Formen—zu umfassend und damit zu komplex sind, die Gefahr zu einem Schematismus in sich tragen sowie wichtige pädagogische Aspekte nicht berücksichtigen. Deshalb tragen sie zur pädagogischen Qualitätsverbesserung der Schule nicht so viel bei, wie immer wieder behauptet wird (siehe auch Altrichter & Posch 1999; Tenberg 2001). Geeignet sein mögen sie für Qualitätsverbesserungen in der Schuladministration.

(2) Das QM darf nicht zu einem Ritual werden, d.h. es darf nicht so konzipiert sein, dass die gleichen Personen mit den gleichen Instrumenten in grosser Regelmässigkeit in gleichen Schulbereichen zur Beurteilung herbeigezogen werden. So zeigt sich immer deutlicher, wie Lehrkräftebeurteilungen, die am Ende eines jeden Jahres durch die Lernenden mit dem gleichen Beurteilungsbogen durchgeführt werden, nicht nachhaltig zur Qualitätsverbesserung beitragen, weil die Beurteilungen immer oberflächlicher werden. Deshalb ist das QM-Konzept so aufzubauen, dass immer

wieder andere Schulbereiche mit verschiedenartigen Verfahren und Instrumenten (Fragebogen, Dokumentenanalyse, Beobachtungsbogen usw.) durch verschiedene Personengruppen (Lehrkräfte, Eltern, Schülerinnen und Schüler, Lehrmeister) erfasst werden.

(3) Beim prozessorientierten QM ist nicht die Erfassung des Qualitätszustandes das Wesentliche, sondern das QM-Konzept muss Massnahmen der Schulentwicklung vorsehen, denn das QM macht nur Sinn, wenn alle Beteiligten Qualitätsverbesserungen in der Schule spüren, was auch das Vertrauen in die Notwendigkeit des QM unmittelbar verstärkt.

Ein Modell des intern konzipierten QM mit Selbstevaluation
Abbildung 3 zeigt das Modell (vergleiche dazu ausführlicher Dubs 1998a).

Abbildung 3

Modell des Ablaufes des intern konzipierten Qualitätsmanagements

1. Schritt:	Bestimmen des oder der Schulbereiche, die zu evaluieren sind
2. Schritt:	Festlegen der gewünschten Qualität
3. Schritt:	Bestimmen der Methoden, mit welchen die Qualität erhoben werden soll, sowie der Personengruppe, die bei der Qualitätserfassung anzusprechen ist, bzw. der Unterlagen oder Erscheinungen, die zu evaluieren sind
4. Schritt:	Durchführen der Datenerhebung bzw. der Dokumentenanalyse
5. Schritt:	Analysieren der Ergebnisse und Diagnose für die Schulentwicklung
6. Schritt:	Planen und Durchführen von Schulentwicklungsmassnahmen

Zunächst ist zu entscheiden, welcher oder welche Schulbereiche evaluiert werden sollen. Wesentlich ist dabei, dass wichtige Bereiche einbezogen werden (z.B. Bereiche mit Schwachstellen, Schulentwicklungsprozesse, wichtige Aspekte des Schullebens aufgrund des Leitbildes). Dann gilt es die Schulqualität (erwünschte Qualitätsziele oder Qualitätsstandards) festzulegen. Dies ist der wissenschaftlich kritische Aspekt, weil alles andere als Einigkeit darüber besteht, was eine gute Qualität ist (vergleiche dazu Thonhauser 1996). Deshalb müssen die Qualitätsverantwortlichen für die zu beurteilenden Schulbereiche selber bestimmen, welche Qualität erstrebenswert ist. Darauf wird in Abschnitt 4 dieses Beitrages näher eingegangen. Dann ist zu entscheiden, mit welchen Methoden die Qualität zu erheben ist (Fragebogen, Beobachtung, Dokumentenanalyse usw.). Im Idealfall erstellen die für das Qualitätsmanagement Verantwortlichen die dazu notwendigen Instrumente selbst, um sie auf die Eigenarten ihrer Schule auszurichten. Leider zeigt sich aber immer deutlicher, dass sich viele Schulen bei dieser Arbeit überfordert fühlen. Einerseits ist der Zeitaufwand sehr hoch, andererseits fehlt es an Kenntnissen der empirischen Sozialforschung. Deshalb werden Musterinstrumente gefordert, die von wissenschaftlichen Instituten oder von der Schulaufsicht zur Verfügung gestellt werden können. Anschliessend werden die Daten erhoben und ausgewertet, um darauf aufbauend Schulentwicklungsaufgaben (z.B. schulinterne Lehrerfortbildung) in Angriff zu nehmen.

Die Organisation des intern konzipierten QM mit Selbstevaluation
Das hier vorgeschlagene Modell lässt sich innerhalb einer Schule am zweckmässigsten mit einem Projektmanagement verwirklichen, d.h. in der Schule wird eine Projektgruppe *Qualitätsmanagement* eingesetzt, die alle Aufgaben des QM im Auftrag der Schulleitung erfüllt. Diese Projektgruppe setzt sich aus Lehrkräften, einer Vertretung aus der Schulleitung (nicht aber der Schulleiter selbst, der aus Gründen der Unabhängigkeit nie einer Projektgruppe angehören darf) und einer Vertretung der Schülerschaft zusammen. Geleitet wird sie von einer Lehrkraft, die sich in Fragen des QM speziell weitergebildet hat. Ob auch Eltern und an Berufsschulen Lehrmeister einbezogen werden, ist nach örtlichen Gegebenheiten zu entscheiden. Empfehlenswert ist es, Eltern und Lehrmeister dann beizuziehen, wenn ein Schulbereich evaluiert wird, zu dem sie etwas beizutragen haben. Die Wahl dieser Projektgruppe soll sich nach den örtlichen Gegebenheiten richten. Eine wirksame Lösung kann folgendermassen aussehen: Die Schulleitung bestimmt den Vorsitz sowie die Hälfte der Lehrkräfte, die andere Hälfte wird durch die Lehrerschaft gewählt. Eine umfassende Wahl durch die Lehrerschaft empfiehlt sich im Interesse der Wirksamkeit nicht. Die Schulleitung muss die Möglichkeit haben, solche Lehrpersonen in die Projektgruppe zu delegieren, welche die Fähigkeit haben, ein Projekt voranzutreiben. Rein demokratische Wahlen in einem Lehrkörper garantieren dies nicht.

Für den Erfolg des QM entscheidend ist die Transparenz der Arbeit der Projektgruppe. Deshalb sollte das Konzept des QM (360°-Methode, siehe Abschnitt 4) vom Lehrerkonvent beschlossen werden, und an den Lehrerkonventen sollte regelmässig über die Absichten und Arbeiten der Projektgruppe berichtet werden.

Das Problem der Schulqualität

Die Umschreibung der Schulqualität
Wie weiter oben angedeutet, ist die Wissenschaft nicht in der Lage, die Schulqualität

eindeutig zu beschreiben. Zwar werden immer wieder Versuche gemacht, die aber sowohl aus normativer als auch aus schulpraktischer und bildungspolitischer Sicht umstritten bleiben. Einen interessanten Versuch, der für die Praxis sehr anregend ist, hat das US Department of Education (Mayer, Mullens, Moore & Ralph 2000) unternommen. Es hat versucht, mit Hilfe einer Analyse empirischer Untersuchungen Indikatoren der Schulqualität abzuleiten, die eine genügende Validität haben, wobei sie drei Gruppen von Indikatoren nach Verlässlichkeit der Erfassung unterscheiden. Tabelle 4 gibt die gefundenen dreizehn Indikatoren wieder.

Tabelle 4

Indikatoren für die Schulqualität

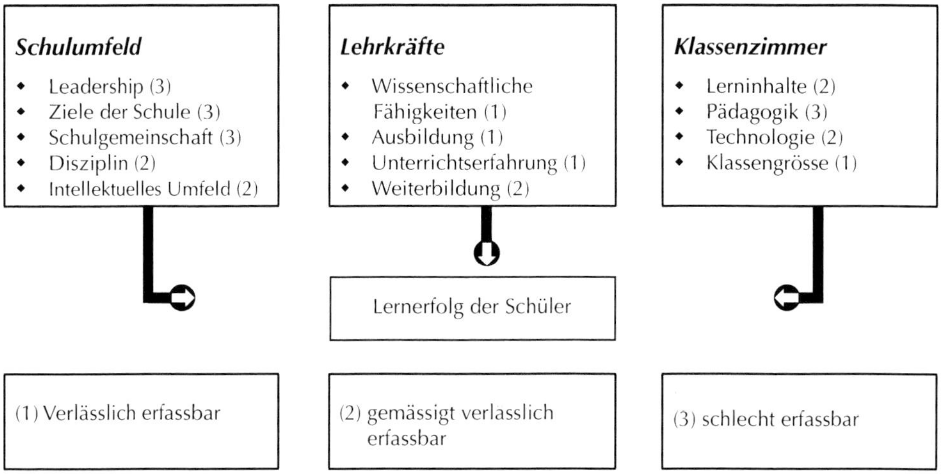

Obschon diese dreizehn Indikatoren empirisch recht gut abgesichert sind, bleiben sie diskutabel: Darf die Schulqualität nur aus der Sicht des Lernerfolges gesehen werden, oder gibt es weitere Faktoren, die in diesem Modell nicht angesprochen werden?

Nachdem die Wissenschaft das Problem der Schulqualität nicht zu lösen vermag, muss sich die Schulpraxis pragmatisch behelfen, indem für jeden Schulbereich, dessen Qualität zu überprüfen ist, die gewünschte Qualität durch die Schule selbst definiert wird. Am einfachsten ist dies, wenn die Schule über ein Leitbild verfügt, das nicht—wie dies leider häufig zu beobachten ist—aus pädagogischen Leerformeln besteht, sondern klare Zielvorstellungen beinhaltet, die der Schule ein bestimmtes Profil geben. Anders ausgedrückt sollten bei der Entwicklung des Leitbildes immer auch Qualitätsüberlegungen angestellt werden. Daraus ergibt sich, dass prozessorientiertes QM nicht aufgrund eines einheitlichen Qualitätsbegriffes in allen Schulen genau gleich aufgebaut werden, sondern jede Schule ihr Konzept nach ihrem Schulprofil und anhand ihrer Qualitätsvorstellung individuell aufbaut.

Das Vorgehen beim Aufbau des QM-Konzeptes in einer Schule
Wenn die Projektgruppe *Qualitätsmanagement* für ihre Schule das intern konzipierte QM entwickelt, muss sie sich mit zwei grundlegenden Fragen beschäftigen:

- Welche Schulbereiche sollen in welchem Zeitraum evaluiert werden, und wie sollen die Daten (Unterlagen) dafür gewonnen werden?
- Wie ist für den jeweiligen Schulbereich die Qualität zu definieren, welche Methoden sind anzuwenden, und welche Schulentwicklungsmassnahmen drängen sich bei Qualitätsmängeln auf?

Zu 1: Auszuwählen sind Schulbereiche, die gemäss Leitbild für eine Schule zur Profilierung besonders bedeutsam sind (z.B. eine Schule möchte Jugendliche aus andern Kulturkreisen oder aus untern sozialen Schichten besonders gut integrieren), welche als Schwachstellen in der Schule erkannt wurden (z.B. viele Mängel im Prüfungs- und Selektionssystem der Schule), welche für die gute Schule besonders bedeutsam sind (z.B. Indikatoren gemäss Tabelle 4) oder welche dem pädagogischen Ethos der Lehrkräfte entsprechend ein Anliegen sind (z.B. Ordnung und Disziplin in einer Schule).

Aufgrund der Erfahrung sollte das QM-Konzept für eine Zeitspanne von fünf Jahren geplant werden. Wird auf eine solche konzeptionelle Planung verzichtet und von Fall zu Fall über den zu evaluierenden Schulbereich entschieden, ist die Gefahr gross, dass das QM infolge Ziellosigkeit und Überlastung der Lehrkräfte *versandet*.

Das QM-Konzept lässt sich im Sinne der 360°-Methode darstellen, d.h. im Verlaufe der fünf Jahre sollten verschiedene Personenkreise unterschiedliche Schulbereiche evaluieren, wie dies Abbildung 5 zeigt.

Abbildung 5

QM-Konzept einer Schule

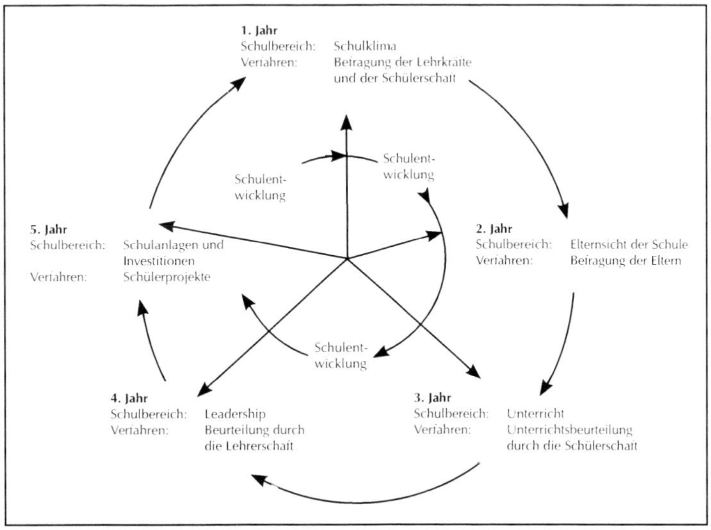

Bei der Auswahl der Schulbereiche sind die folgenden Anforderungen zu beachten:

(1) Sie müssen schulrelevant und geeignet sein, die Schulqualität zu verbessern (kein Ausweichen auf irrelevante Aspekte, die gute Ergebnisse garantieren). (2) Die Qualität muss in eindeutiger Weise erfassbar sein, um Grundsatzdebatten zu vermeiden. (3) Beeinflussungs- und Manipulationsmöglichkeiten müssen unmöglich sein. (4) Die Reihung ist so vorzunehmen, dass nicht mit solchen Schulbereichen begonnen wird, die bei den Lehrkräften Ängste auslösen (z.B. sollte nie mit einer Unterrichtsbeurteilung der Lehrkräfte durch die Schülerschaft gestartet werden, obschon sie aussagekräftig ist [vgl. Peterson 1995], weil sie zu viele Ängste auslöst und deshalb das ganze QM gefährden könnte).

Zu 2: Für die Überlegungen technischer Art empfiehlt es sich, die Gedankenfolge gemäss Tabelle 6 vorzunehmen. Die wichtigste Aufgabe ist die Definition der Qualität. In vielen Fällen wird man sich vorderhand mangels Vergleichsdaten auf *beste Ergebnisse,* die sich aus den Instrumenten ergeben, beschränken müssen. Denkbar ist es, den Fortschritt in der eigenen Schule durch wiederholte Anwendung eines Instrumentes zu erfassen. Zu empfehlen ist weiter, in der Anfangsphase auf vorhandene Instrumente zurückzugreifen, um die Arbeit zu erleichtern.

Tabelle 6

Technische Überlegungen zur Durchführung des QM

Schulbereich	*Erwünschte Qualität*	*Methode/Instrument*	*Schulentwicklung*
Schulklima	Qualitätswerte, die über den wissenschaftlich ermittelten Normwerten liegen	Klima-Instrument Bessoth (1997): durch Lehrerschaft und Schülerschaft bearbeitet	Im Falle schlechter Ergebnisse einen Massnahmenplan durch eine Projektgruppe entwickeln
Urteil über die Schule aus der Sicht der Eltern	gutes Urteil der Eltern	Fragebogen an die Eltern (Eigenentwicklung oder Dubs 1998a): durch Eltern beantwortet	Im Falle schlechter Ergebnisse Arbeitstagung der Lehrerschaft
Unterricht	hochstehender Unterricht aufgrund der gewählten Beurteilung	Eigenentwicklung eines Beurteilungsbogens: durch Schülerinnen und Schüler ausgefüllt	Lehrerfortbildung über Unterrichtsfragen
Leadership	hohe Werte im Beurteilungsbogen	Instrument Dubs (1998a): durch Lehrerschaft ausgefüllt	Workshop der Schulleitung
Schulanlagen und Investition	gutes Schülerurteil	Projekt-Arbeit ausgewählter Klassen im Deutschunterricht über „Unsere Schulanlagen und -einrichtungen"	Investitionsanträge an Behörden Schulinterne Verbesserungsmassnahmen

Die Anforderungen an die staatlichen Schulbehörden

Ob der vielen theoretischen Aussagen, den vorgelegten QM-Modellen und vieler Erfahrungen in einzelnen Schulen wird die Verunsicherung unter Lehrkräften immer grösser. Deshalb besteht die Gefahr, dass das QM, wie vieles andere in der Schule, totläuft. Vermieden werden kann diese Entwicklung nur, wenn die staatlichen Schulbehörden eine Gesamtkonzeption für das QM verbindlich festlegt. In Tabelle 2 ist eine solche Konzeption dargestellt. Für Österreich würde dies folgendes bedeuten:

1. Das Ministerium und die Landesschulräte legen die Gesamtkonzeption für alle Schulen verbindlich fest.

2. Die Aufgaben der Landesschulinspektoren sollten darauf ausgerichtet werden. Ihre traditionelle Rolle einer herkömmlichen Schulaufsicht entfällt (nachdem sie sie heute allein schon aus Zeitgründen ohnehin nicht mehr erfüllen können). Dafür erhalten sie zwei neue Aufgaben:

   Einerseits sollten sie den Schulen beim Aufbau des Qualitätsmanagements beratend zur Seite stehen, denn viele Schulen benötigen Unterstützung. Andererseits müssen sie die Metaevaluation durchführen, denn ein intern konzipiertes Qualitätsmanagement mit Selbstevaluation reicht in Erwartung aller Ermüdungserscheinungen und der damit zusammenhängenden Routinisierung bei den Lehrkräften nicht aus. Diese Controllingaufgabe der Schulinspektion ist auch aus staatspolitischen Gründen notwendig. Die Schulbehörden sind dem Volk gegenüber für eine positive Entwicklung des Schulsystems verantwortlich. Diese Verantwortung übernehmen sie, indem sie die Landesschulinspektoren mit dem gesamten Controlling im Schulwesen beauftragen. Controlling ist aber nicht kleinliche Kontrolle, sondern Controlling heisst Überprüfung der Zielerreichung (bei der Metaevaluation, ob das intern konzipierte Qualitätsmanagement zweckmässig gestaltet und durchgeführt wird, und ob aufgrund der Erkenntnisse geeignete Schulentwicklungsmassnahmen getroffen werden).

   Es wird nun immer wieder behauptet, es sei unzweckmässig, der Schulaufsicht diese Doppelaufgabe der Beratung und des Controllings zu übertragen. Es ist nicht auszuschliessen, dass es in Einzelfällen zu Problemen kommen kann. Dies dürfte vor allem dann der Fall sein, wenn die Schulaufsicht im traditionellen Sinn kontrolliert und ihre Aufgabe nicht als Controlling wahrnimmt. Deshalb müssen die Rahmenbedingungen für die Schulaufsicht im Schulrecht angepasst werden (Dubs 1998b). Übernimmt die Schulaufsicht auch die Beratungsfunktion, so kann sie zur Weiterentwicklung des Qualitätsmanagements beitragen, indem sie Nachbarschulen anleitet, um gewisse Qualitätskriterien gemeinsam zu erfassen und die Ergebnisse zu vergleichen, was einem Systemvergleich auf unterster Ebene entspricht.

3. Die Pädagogischen Institute sollten den Schulen Instrumente für das QM zur Verfügung halten und für längere Zeit Weiterbildungen im Bereich QM für Leiter und Mitglieder der Projektgruppen anbieten. Die Annahme, man könnte die

Schulen zur Einführung eines QM auffordern, ohne aber Weiterbildungsmöglich keiten anzubieten, hat sich längstens als nicht machbar erwiesen.

Ob sich das Qualitätsmanagement langfristig und in wirksamer Weise in den Schulen durchsetzt und sich zur Verbesserung der Schule auswirkt, ist meines Erachtens trotz der übermässig vielen Aktivitäten noch offen. Auf einen Nenner gebracht meine ich: Wenn die Schulbehörden nicht einen verbindlichen konzeptionellen Rahmen vorgeben, und die Rechtsordnung nicht angepasst wird, so besteht die Gefahr, dass auch das Qualitätsmanagement eine vorübergehende Episode in den vielen Bewegungen der Pädagogik bleibt. Deshalb kommt der Erziehungswissenschaft eine bedeutende Aufgabe in der Politikberatung zu.

Literaturhinweise

Altrichter, H. & Posch, P. „Aufbauprozesse der Qualitätsentwicklung im Schulwesen." *Wege zur Schulqualität*. Hrsg. H. Altrichter & P. Posch. Innsbruck: StudienVerlag, 1999. S. 193-247.

Bessoth, R. *Organisations-Klima-Instrument für Schweizer Schulen*. Aarau: Sauerländer, 1997.

Dubs, R. *Qualitätsmanagement für Schulen*. St. Gallen: Institut für Wirtschaftspädagogik, 1998a.

Dubs, R. „Recht und New Public Management im Schulwesen." *Verfassungsstaat vor neuen Herausforderungen*. Hrsg. Ehrenzeller et al. Der St. Gallen: Dike, 1998b. S. 389-413.

Dubs, R. „New Public Management im Schulwesen. Eine kritische Erfahrungsanalyse." Excellence durch Personal- und Organisationskompetenz. Hrsg. N. Thom & R.J. Zaugg. Bern: Haupt, 2001. S. 419-440.

Mayer, D.P., Mullens, J.E., Moore, M.T. & Ralph, J. *Monotoring School Quality: An Indicators Report*. Washington: US Department of Education, 2000.

Peterson, K.D. *Teacher Evaluation. A Comprehensive Guide to New Directions and Practices*. Thousand Oaks: Corwin, 1995.

Tenberg, R. „Problemanalyse in der wissenschaftlichen Begleitung eines Modellversuchs. Aus der Anfangsphase des Modellversuchs Qualitätsentwicklung in beruflichen Schulen (QUABS)." *ZBW* 97.1 (2001): 6-24.

Thonhauser, J. Neuere „Zugänge der Forschung zur Erfassung von Schulqualität." *Schulqualität. Entwicklungen, Befunde, Perspektiven*. Hrsg. W. Specht & J. Thonhauser. Innsbruck: StudienVerlag, 1996. S. 394-423.

Additional Materials

This section will introduce you to additional resources related to the topics of this volume. The websites listed below represent a rich sampling of Internet resources available to our profession.

Explore these websites on a regular basis. Note their foci, and specific ways in which they benefit you professionally. Identify to what extent these sites can help you by noting their strengths and weaknesses.

Develop your own search categories based on your areas of expertise. Use the Internet's significant resources to explore both the areas you already have knowledge about and to learn more about other areas.

Freiburg Writing Center
<www.ph-freiburg.de/schreibzentrum>

This site offers online support for writers in foreign and second languages (currently in English, French, German) on all levels of instruction. This page encourages autonomous learning, process writing, reflective practice such as peer tutoring and working with learning logs and portfolios. Foreign and second language teachers can find classroom materials and online support on pedagogical issues of L2 writing (e.g. design of writing tasks and writing projects, group writing, portfolio). The Freiburg Writing Center also organizes Internet-based, collaborative L2-writing instruction (team teaching) and research. Contact the center at <schreibzentrum@ph-freiburg.de>.

Council of Europe: Language Policy Division (Strasbourg)
<www.coe.int/T/E/Cultural_Co-operation/education> (see Languages)

The Council of Europe accords special importance to fostering the linguistic and cultural diversity of its member states. Its activities in the field of languages aims to promote plurilingualism and pluriculturalism among citizens in order to combat intolerance and xenophobia by improving communication and mutual understanding between individuals. (Homepage)

Further information on:

- Common European Framework of Reference for Languages (PDF File).
- European Language Portfolio.
- Policy Development.

European Centre for Modern Languages (Graz)
<www.ecml.at>

Within the framework of cultural co-operation and respecting the rich linguistic and cultural diversity in Europe, the center has at its mission:

- The implementation of language policies.
- The promotion of innovative approaches to the learning and teaching of foreign languages. (You can also find further information on teacher training on this site.)

European Language Portfolio (ELP)
<http://culture.coe.int/portfolio>

The ELP was developed and piloted by the Language Policy Division of the Council of Europe from 1998-2000. It was launched on a Pan-European level during the European Year of Languages as a tool to support the development of plurilingualism and pluriculturalism.

The Web site contains information about the standard form of the ELP, certified national and regional adaptations, as well as adaptations for different groups of learners (primary, secondary school, vocational training, and continuing education). The site also provides reflections on various national pilot studies.

Web Site of the Swiss European Language Portfolio Project
<www.languageportfolio.ch>

This web sites provides insight into adaptation and implementation of the ELP into the national foreign language curriculum of Switzerland. Information is in English, French, German, and Italian.

National Advisory Centre on Early Language Learning (NACELL)
<www.nacell.org.uk>

NACELL is a Department for Education and Skills (DfES) initiative to promote and develop the provision and quality of Modern Foreign Language learning in the primary sector. NACELL was set up in the CILT Resources Library in June 1999 as part of the Early Language Learning (ELL) initiative. The ELL initiative is being managed and coordinated by the Centre for Information on Language Teaching and Research (CILT) on behalf of the DfES.

The International Society for Language Studies (ISLS)
<http://isls.education.uconn.edu>

ISLS encourages and promotes critical discourse and research in language matters, broadly conceived, by the provision of a forum and the interchange of information through publications, and by the recruitment of active members who are from areas interested in critical language studies. We currently have members from Africa, Asia, Australia, Europe, North America, and South America.

Critical Inquiry in Language Studies (CISLS)
<http://isls.education.uconn.edu/cils.htm>

CILS is the peer-reviewed, quarterly journal of the International Society for Language Studies (ISLS). Language studies overlaps fields of applied linguistics, language policy, language planning, languages and literatures, education, anthropology, sociology, history, political science, psychology, and cultural studies. The primary purpose of the journal is to provide a forum for discussion of the research from emerging paradigms in the above mentioned fields and at the same time to bridge arbitrary disciplinary territories.

American Council on the Teaching of Foreign Languages (ACTFL)
<www.actfl.org>

ACTFL is the only national organization in the US dedicated to the improvement and expansion of the teaching and learning of all languages at all levels of instruction. ACTFL is an individual membership organization of more that 7,000 foreign language educators and administrators from elementary through graduate education, as well as government and industry. From the development of proficiency guidelines, to its leadership role in the creation of national standards, ACTFL focuses on issues that are critical to the growth of both the profession and the individual teacher.

This web site provides a wealth of information on the profession and of materials for foreign and second language classrooms. Under "Resources"/"Useful Links" you find the web sites of all current National Language Organizations, National Resource Centers, Regional and State Language Associations, as well as a link to the State Department of Education.

International Society for Technology in Education (ISTE)
<http://www.iste.org>

ISTE is a nonprofit professional organization with a worldwide membership of leaders and potential leaders in educational technology. This organization provides service to improve teaching and learning by advancing the effective use of technology in K–12 education and teacher education. Members receive information, networking opportunities, and guidance as they face the challenge of incorporating computers, the Internet, and other new technologies into their schools.

Home of the National Educational Technology Standards (NETS), the Center for Applied Research in Education Technology (CARET), and the National Educational Computing Conference (NECC), ISTE meets its mission through knowledge generation, professional development, and advocacy. ISTE also supports a worldwide network of Affiliates and Special Interest Groups (SIGs), and offers the latest information through periodicals and journals.

International Association for Language Learning Technology (IALLT)
<http://www.iall.net/>

Established in 1965, IALLT is a professional organization whose members provide leadership in the development, integration, evaluation, and management of instructional technology for the teaching and learning of language, literature, and culture. Its strong sense of community promotes the sharing of expertise in a variety of educational contexts.

The IALL Journal: published by IALL, International Association for Language Learning Technology
<http://www.iall.net/iallj.html>

ALSIC
<http://alsic.u-strasbg.fr>

This journal (ALSIC: Language Learning and Information and Communication Systems) aims at presenting and exchanging theoretical and practical work in fields related to its domain (didactics, applied linguistics, psycholinguistics, educational sciences, computational linguistics, computer science).

Language Learning and Technology Journal
<http://llt.msu.edu>

Language Learning & Technology is a refereed journal that has been publishing in the field since July 1997. The journal seeks to disseminate research to foreign and second language educators in the US and around the world on issues related to technology and language education.

Language Learning & Technology is sponsored and funded by the University of Hawai`i's National Foreign Language Resource Center (NFLRC) and the Michigan State University's Center for Language Education And Research (CLEAR), and is co-sponsored by Apprentissage des Langues et Systèmes d'Information et de Communication (ALSIC), the Australian Technology Enhanced Language Learning Consortium (ATELL), the Center for Applied Linguistics (CAL), the Computer Assisted Language Instruction Consortium (CALICO), the European Association for Computer Assisted Language Learning (EUROCALL), the International Association for Language Learning Technology (IALLT), and the University of Minnesota's Center for Advanced Research on Language Acquisition (CARLA).

Language Learning & Technology is published exclusively on the World Wide Web. In this way, the journal seeks to (a) reach a broad audience in a timely manner, (b) provide a multimedia format which can more fully illustrate the technologies under discussion, and (c) provide hypermedia links to related background information.

ON-CALL/CALL-EJ Online
<http://www.lerc.ritsumei.ac.jp/callej/index.html>

Australian Journal of Computers and Language Education, published by the University of Queensland, Australia. In January 1999 ON-CALL journal became available only Online and in May 1999 merged with CALL-EJ Online (Japan Association for Language Teaching).

ReCALL
<http://www.journals.cup.org>

The primary focus of *ReCALL* is the use of technologies for language learning and teaching, including all relevant aspects of research and development. Typical subjects for submissions include theoretical debate on language learning strategies and their influence on courseware design; practical applications at the developmental stage; evaluative studies of coursewares used in the teaching and learning process; exploitation and assessment of the potential of technological advances in the delivery of language learning materials; discussions of policy and strategy at institutional and discipline levels. *ReCALL* aims to appeal to researchers and practitioners in the area of computer-assisted and technology-enhanced language learning, normally but not exclusively operating in universities. It is also of interest to language teachers in secondary and tertiary education who may be considering the introduction of technologies into their teaching practice.

TELL&CALL
<http://www.e-lisa.at/magazine/tellcall>

Online journal on foreign language teaching: The journal of CALL-Austria contains articles in English and German.

Computer Assisted Language Instruction Consortium (CALICO)
<http://www.calico.org>

CALICO, the **C**omputer **A**ssisted **L**anguage **I**nstruction **Co**nsortium, is a professional organization that serves a membership involved in both education and technology. CALICO has an emphasis on modern language teaching and learning, but reaches out to all areas that employ the languages of the world to instruct and to learn. CALICO is a recognized international clearinghouse and leader in computer assisted learning and instruction. It is, by several years, the senior global association dedicated to CALL (Computer Assisted Language Learning).

German Online Distance Education Network (GOLDEN)
<http://golden.unl.edu>

GOLDEN is an interactive Online teacher development project that offers German teachers distance learning courses on Instructional Planning, Technologically Enhanced Language Instruction, Writing, Reading, Speaking, and Listening Pedagogy via the web. This asynchronous learning environment allows participants to work individually, in small groups and with instructors in the context of instruction for your German classroom.

TraiNDaF
<http://www.aatg.org/programs/profdev/index.html>

TraiNDaF is a joint program of the German government and AATG in cooperation with the Goethe-Institut Inter Nationes that aims to provide professional development for future leaders in the field of teaching of German. Application may be found at the above mentioned web site.

Kinder lernen Deutsch
<www.aatg.org/programs/KLD/>

KDL is a joint initiative of the German government and the Goethe-Institut to encourage early language learning (K-8) through program development grants (*Centers of Excellence*), support for inservice and preservice teacher education, development of teaching materials, and public relations/networking.

National Network for Early Language Learning (NNELL)
<www.nnell.org>

NNELL is an organization for educators involved in teaching foreign languages to children. The mission of the organization is to promote opportunities for all children to develop a high level of competence in at least one language in addition to their own. NNELL provides leadership, support, and service to those committed to early language learning and coordinates efforts to make language learning in programs of excellence a reality for all children. NNELL also publishes a journal (Learning Languages).

National Board for Professional Teaching Standards (NBPTS)
<www.nbpts.org>

The mission of the NBPTS is to advance the quality of teaching and learning by:

- Maintaining high and rigorous standards for what accomplished teachers should know and be able to do.
- Providing a national voluntary system certifying teachers who meet these standards.
- Advocating related education reforms to integrate National Board Certification in American education and to capitalize on the expertise of National Board Certified Teachers.

National Council for the Accreditation of Teacher Education (NCATE)
<www.ncate.org>

NCATE is the profession's mechanism to help establish high quality teacher preparation. Through the process of professional accreditation of schools, colleges, and departments of education, NCATE works to make a difference in the quality of teaching and teacher preparation today, tomorrow, and for the next century. NCATE's performance-based system of accreditation fosters competent classroom teachers and other educators who work to improve the education of all P–12 students. NCATE is a coalition of 33 specialty professional associations of teachers, teacher educators, content specialists, and local and state policy makers. All are committed to quality teaching, and together, the coalition represents over 3 million individuals. The US Department of Education and the Council for Higher Education Accreditation recognize NCATE as a professional accrediting body for teacher preparation.

Association for Supervision and Curriculum Development
<www.ascd.org>

ASCD is an international, nonprofit, nonpartisan organization that represents 160,000 educators from more than 135 countries and 66 affiliates. Members span the entire profession of educators—superintendents, supervisors, principals, teachers, professors of education, and school board members. ASCD addresses *all aspects of effective teaching and learning*—such as professional development, educational leadership, and capacity building. ASCD offers broad, multiple perspectives—across all education professions—in reporting key policies and practices.

Center for Applied Linguistics (CAL)
<www.cal.org>

CAL is a private, non-profit organization that uses the findings of linguistics and related sciences in identifying and addressing language-related problems. In response to these identified problems CAL becomes active in research, teacher education, analysis and dissemination of information, design and development of instructional materials, technical assistance, conference planning, program evaluation, and policy analysis. For example, in response to a growing number of early language programs CAL developed two language proficiency instruments, the Student Oral Proficiency Assessment (SOPA, grades 1-5) and Early Language Listening and Oral Proficiency Assessment (ELLOPA, grades Pre-K through grade 2).

ERIC Clearinghouse on Languages and Linguistics
<www.cal.org/ericcll/about.html>

ERIC/CLL is operated by the Center for Applied Linguistics (CAL) and provides a wide range of services and materials for language educators, most of them free of charge, including: Resource Guides Online, an Online Newsletter, Information Digests, a News Bulletin, a question-answering service <eric@cal.org>.

English as a Second Language Worldwide
<www.eslworldwide.com>

This premier job search web site helps recruit instructors across the globe, in all areas of language study.

WISP-Work Immersion Study Program
<www.cdsintl.org/wispintro.html>

This program provided an opportunity for community college students to gain practical work experience in their field, to improve German language skills and experience German culture firsthand from June through August 2003.

CDS International, Inc. (CDS), in cooperation with the American Association of Teachers of German (AATG) and the Goethe Institute, arranges for internships in a variety of business and technical fields. The three-month program starts with a one-month language course at a Goethe Institute in Germany, followed by a 2-month of paid internship with a German host company.

Teachers of English to Speakers of Other Languages (TESOL)
<www.tesol.org>

This global education association has approximately 14,000 members. TESOL has more than 90 worldwide affiliated organizations representing another 50,000 TESOL professionals. Its mission is to ensure excellence in English language teaching to speakers of other languages. TESOL values professionalism in language education; individual language rights; accessible, high quality education; collaboration in a global community; interaction of research and reflective practice for educational improvement; and respect for diversity and multiculturalism.

TESOL publishes three serials: a scholarly journal (*TESOL Quarterly*), a practical magazine (*TESOL Journal*), and a quarterly newspaper (*TESOL Matters*). TESOL also publishes and an electronic bulletin of employment opportunities (*Placement E-Bulletin*) and a newsletter of headlines and resource links related to the field (*TESOL Connections*). It also publishes books and materials on a wide range of theoretical and practical topics as well as professional papers and resources for newcomers. TESOL's annual convention, usually held in March in North America, attracts 7,000-10,000 participants. This weeklong event offers participants full-length papers, workshops, poster sessions, materials exchanges, plenary speakers, and other forms of professional stimuli and networking opportunities.

National Foreign Language Center
<www.nflc.org>

Since its founding in 1986, the **National Foreign Language Center** has served as the nation's principal institutional resource for strategic planning and drafting of policy for language in the United States. The centers' action agenda consists of developing a comprehensive understanding of the strategic impact of language and cross-cultural communication challenges on globalized institutions, organizations, and enterprises. It also provideds programming to clients in the public, private, and non-profit sectors, consultancies, and studies. The mission of the NFLC is to improve the capacity of the US to communicate in languages other than English. That missions is implement through intensive and innovative strategic planning and development with globalized institutions, organizations, and enterprises throughout the US.

Foreign Language Teach (FLTEACH)
FLTEACH is a LISTSERV founded in February 1994. It is housed at SUNY/Buffalo. The topic of the list is foreign language teaching methods including high school/college articulation, training of student teachers, curriculum, and the New York State syllabus. Students, teachers, and administrators interested in any aspect of foreign language teaching are invited to participate in the discussions. FLTEACH membership includes colleagues from across the US and around the world. It is hoped that this list will also be used to foster a community in which colleagues at all levels can share ideas, outlines, handouts and other teaching materials, syllabi and bibliographies.

To subscribe to FLTEACH: (1) send a message to: *listserv@listserv.acsu.buffalo.edu*, (2) in the message put only the following: Sub FLTEACH first name last name (3) Send the message just like that—add nothing else.

National Association for Bilingual Educators (NABE)
<www.nabe.org>

This is the only professional organization at the national level wholly devoted to representing both English language learners and bilingual education professionals. NABE represents over 5,000 educators and parents and has affiliate organizations in 28 states. As the name implies, the organization was established to advocate for bilingual education. Now, however, NABE advocates for a variety of programs that provide language support to English language learners through:

- Providing professional development opportunities for our members.
- Collaborating with other civil rights and education organizations to ensure that the needs of language minority students are met in every state.
- Lobbying Congress for adequate funding of all programs that serve English language learners.

Zeitschrift für interkulturellen Fremdsprachenunterricht (ZIF)
<http://www.ualberta.ca/~german/ejournal/ejournal.html>

ZIF is an online, German-language journal published triannually at the University of Alberta in Edmonton, Alberta, Canada. It concentrates on the didactics and methodology of teaching German as a foreign language, focusing especially on intercultural questions.

L3 Homepage
<http://www.spz.tu-darmstadt.de/projekt_L3/>

The *L3 Homepage* is maintained at the Technical University of Darmstadt, Germany, and aims to keep researchers interested in the area of multilingualism and tertiary language learning, informed about recent developments in the field, links to various projects, and upcoming conferences. The organizatino also maintains an extensive bibliography on publications that focus on multilingualism. A special section, the annotated bibliography, provides English summaries of German-language publications for researchers who cannot read German.

Foreign Language Resource Centers
<http://nflrc.msu.edu/>

The United States Department of Education has awarded grants to a small number of institutions for the purpose of establishing, strengthening, and operating national foreign language resource and training centers to improve the teaching and learning of foreign languages. Presently there are fourteen Title VI Language Resource Centers nationwide.

1 Center for Advanced Research on Language Acquisition (University of Minnesota): <http://carla.acad.umn.edu/>

2 Center for Advanced Language Proficiency Education and Research (The Pennsylvania State University): <http://calper.la.psu.edu/>

3 Center for Applied Second Language Studies (University of Oregon): <http://casls.uoregon.edu/>

4 Center for Language Education And Research (Michigan State University): <http://clear.msu.edu/>

5 Center for Languages of the Central Asian Region (Indiana University): <http://www.indiana.edu/~celcar/>

6 Language Acquisition Resource Center (San Diego State University): <http://larcnet.sdsu.edu/>

7 National African Languages Resource Center (University of Wisconsin): <http://african.lss.wisc.edu/nalrc/>

8 National Capital Language Resource Center (Georgetown University, Center for Applied Linguistics, and George Washington University): <http://www.nclrc.org/>

9 National East Asian Languages Resource Center (Ohio State University): <http://nealrc.osu.edu/firstpage.htm>

10 National Foreign Language Resource Center (University of Hawai'i): <http://www.nflrc.hawaii.edu/>

11 National K-12 Foreign Language Resource Center (Iowa State University): <http://www.educ.iastate.edu/nflrc/>

12 National Middle East Language Resource Center (Brigham Young University): <http://nmelrc.byu.edu/>

13 Slavic and East European Language Resource Center (Duke University and UNC - Chapel Hill): <http://seelrc.org/>

14 South Asia Language Resource Center (University of Chicago): <http://salrc.uchicago.edu/>

Meta-Sites Web Resources for German
<http://grow.aatg.org/vol_2-3/web_resources/resources_pages/meta.html>

Presents the links to major online resources for German.

Confédération Européenne des Centres de Langues de l'Enseignement Supérieur
[European Confederation of Language Centres in Higher Education]
<http://www.cercles.org>

Founded in Strasbourg in 1991, CercleS is a confederation of independent associations from 21 countries of Europe. It brings together some 250 language centers, departments, institutes, faculties, and schools in higher education, whose main responsibility is the teaching of language. Its members have several thousand academic, administrative, and technical staff, and some 250,000 students who learn a large number of the world's languages. CercleS is committed to the highest possible standards in language education and research. Information is available in English, French, and German.

Arbeitskreis der Sprachenzentren, Sprachlehrinstitute und Fremdspracheninstitute (AKS) [Association of language centres, language teaching institutes and institutes of foreign languages]
<http://www.ruhr-uni-bochum.de/aks/aks.html>

This is the only association in Germany which comprehensively represents the field of foreign language teaching in Higher Education. The AKS provides a forum for collaboration and the exchange of information and experience in language teaching for all the institutions and staff working in the fields of:

- Practical language teaching in Higher Education.
- Language teacher training and further education.
- Research in language teaching and language learning.

Information is available only in German.

DIALANG
<http://www.dialang.org>

DIALANG is a European project for the development of diagnostic language tests in 14 European languages. Tests are available on the Internet free of charge. The project is financially supported by the European Commission, Directorate General Education and Culture, under the SOCRATES Programme, LINGUA Action D.

DIALANG is:

- Computer-based and Internet-delivered.
- Offers separate tests for reading, writing, listening, grammatical structures, and vocabulary.
- Covers all levels from beginner to advanced.
- Asks users to assess their own level of proficiency before offering them tests in the area selected.
- Gives users feedback on their performance and tells them how they can improve their proficiency.

ELIAS
<http://www.elias-nc.org>

ELIAS is an international working group for the evaluation of computer software and Internet materials for language learning. The objective of the group is to develop criteria for the assessment of media-based language learning materials and to produce independent evaluations of software and of websites.

European Language Portfolio for Elementary Schools
<www.foxus.de/ps/sprachenportfolio/index.html>

The state of Hessen (Germany) is the first place where the European Language Portfolio (ELP) has been adapted for early language learners (English). The site contains an online version of the portfolio and hands-on information for teachers. Both can be downloaded.

Contributors

Theresa Austin

Theresa Austin, PhD., researches how languages and literacies are learned through schooling. She is concerned with analyzing bilingual socialization, academic literacies and curricular practices that afford students support to fully develop their multilingualism and multiculturalism. As a teacher educator, she has served as a consultant to the National Boards for Professionals in Teaching's projects to develop professional certifications in World Languages other than English, and designed bilingual teacher and student language proficiency assessments at several major universities in California, New York, Japan and Colombia. Dr. Austin is associate professor in the Bilingual/ ESL/Multicultural Program at the University of Massachusetts, Amherst. Her articles have been published in Foreign Language Annals, NABE Journal, Journal Asian Pacific Communication and various professional newsletters for researchers and teachers in language education.

Gerd Bräuer

Gerd Bräuer, Dr. phil., is Associate Professor of German Studies at Emory University. He taught German as a foreign language in Prague (Czech Republic), Eugene and Portland (Oregon). At the University of Oregon he held a post-doctoral fellowship sponsored by the Deutsche Forschungsgemeinschaft (DFG). He was (2001-03) DAAD Professor at the University of Education Freiburg (Germany). His major research interests are writing pedagogy, foreign and second language pedagogy, and institutional development in secondary and higher education. Most recent book publications include Pedagogy of Language Learning in Higher Education (2001), Body and Language: Intercultural Learning Through Drama (2002), and Teaching Academic Writing in Higher Education (co-ed., 2003).

Adrian Butler

Adrian Butler comes originally from the UK. He started his professional life as an English-language teacher in France and Spain, before joining the Council of Europe in Strasbourg, where he spent 25 years in a variety of functions. He was appointed Executive Director of the Council's European Centre for Modern Languages in Graz, Austria, in January 2003.

Christine M. Campbell

Christine M. Campbell is Dean, Middle East School I, the Defense Language Institute (DLI), Monterey, California where she manages a school with 115 faculty who teach Arabic and Hebrew to 550 students. She was Test Project Director, Division of Tests and Standards, DLI from 1987 to 1998 and Director of Test Development of the National Spanish Examinations of the American Association of the Teachers of Spanish and Portuguese, the latter a non-paid position in service to the profession, from 1993 to1998. She has published in the areas of language testing and learner variables, specifically, language anxiety, and has presented papers at ACTFL and AATSP conferences. Currently, she is co-author of the "In Other Professional Journals" column of The Modern Language Journal (MLJ). She is on the Editorial Boards of Applied Language Learning and Dialog on Language Instruction and has been a reviewer for the MLJ and Hispania.

Svenja Dahlmanns

Svenja Dahlmanns is currently studying to become a teacher at the University of Education in Freiburg, Germany. Her subjects are German and Arts. She is taking part in a special training program for counsellors at the University's Writing Center. Some of her interests are alternative assessment methods like portfolios and reflective practice in writing. She also did some pedagogical research on the "3journal", a trilingual student magazine from Germany, Switzerland and France.

Rolf Dubs

Rolf Dubs, born 1935, Professor emeritus at the University of St. Gallen (Switzerland). Former President of the same University. Specializations: School Management, Curriculum, Teaching and Learning Theory.

Rebecca K. Fox

Dr. Rebecca K. Fox is Acting Director of the Advanced Studies in Teaching and Learning Program and Assistant Professor of Education in the Graduate School of Education at George Mason University in Fairfax, Virginia, where she teaches in the Center for Language and Culture. In addition to field work with teacher candidates, some of the courses she teaches are: Bilingualism an dSecond Language Acquisition Research, Teaching Foreign Languages in the PK-12 Schools, and courses in research methodology. She has taught French at all grade levels from Kindergarten through 12th grade, and at the university. She has published articles and presented numerous workshops at regional, national, and international conferences on her research and scholarship in multilingual and multicultural education, critical reflective practice, and on the integration of technology into world/second language curriculum. Her current research focuses on technology in the service of language learning, and the role of the portfolio in the growth of critical reflective practice and as a performance based assessment tool in teacher education. She is the current chair of the Research SIG for the American Council on the Teaching off Foreign Languages.

Catherine C. Fraser

Catherine C. Fraser earned her PhD at the University of Connecticut and is currently Professor of German and Language Coordinator at Indiana University, Bloomington, where her prime responsibility is the training and supervision of graduate student instructors in a task-based program. Designing tasks that are motivating and at the appropriate level for learners requires a background in assessment research and practice and it is in this area that Fraser has focused much of her energy. She recently recertified as an Oral Proficiency Interviewer, served the Educational Testing Service and the College Board on the Test Development Committee and as a Reader, Question Leader and Chief Faculty Consultant of the Advanced Placement Program. She has also published in this field, in integrating technology into language teaching and learning, as well as in literature. In the latter field, a major interest has been in the relationship between the painting and writing of August Strindberg, resulting in several articles, a book and a one act play.

Marjorie Hall Haley

Marjorie Hall Haley, PhD, is tenured Associate Professor of Education in the Center for Language and Culture in the Graduate School of Education at George Mason University in Fairfax, Virginia. She is a former Spanish, French, German, and ESL teacher of 14 years. In her 16th year at GMU, she teaches Foreign/Second Language Methods, ESL and Bilingual methods, Teaching Reading and Writing in Foreign Language Classes, and Bilingualism/Second Language Acquisition Research. In 2002, GMU awarded her its Outstanding Faculty Award in Teaching. Her research and publication record is wide, including an upcoming co-authored book, Content-based Language Teaching and Learning: An Interactive Approach (Allyn & Bacon, 2003) as well as her work with the Spanish textbook series, Paso a Paso.

Dierk O. Hoffmann

Dierk O. Hoffmann, Dr. phil. (Universität Basel, Schweiz), is Professor of German at Colgate University, New York. Before coming to the States, he worked at an editing institute affiliated with the University in Basel and worked in a publishing company in Germany as editor and director of a new textbook series. His research interests are in second language acquisition (including Suggestopedia), textology, literature and art of the Turn of the Century, and use of technology in the Humanities. His publications include monographs on the Prague author Paul Leppin (a contemporary of the more famous Franz Kafka) (1973, 1982); the critical edition of the opera Der Rosenkavalier by Hofmannsthal/Strauss (1986); a German grammar and reader for Intermediate German (1989, 1990); several editions of prose and poetry by Leppin (1984, 1988, 1990, 2002); and computer programs (1989).

Britta Hufeisen

Britta Hufeisen, Dr. phil, is a Professor of Applied Linguistics and German as a Foreign Language at the Technical University of Darmstadt, Germany. She also spent three and a half years at the University of Alberta, Edmonton, Canada as an Assistant Professor in the Department of Germanic Languages and Literature. Her research interests include multiple language acquisition and FL-writing. She is co-editor of the online journal "Zeitschrift für interkulturellen Fremdsprachenunterricht". Most recent publications (with Jasone Cenoz and Ulrike Jessner) include Looking Beyond Second Language Acquisition. Studies in Tri- and Multilingualism (2001), Cross-Linguistic Influence in Third Language Acquisition. Psycholinguistic Perspectives (2001) and The Multilingual Lexicon (forthcoming).

David Jahner

David Jahner (M.Ed.) is the foreign language coordinator for the Gwinnett County (GA) Public Schools. He obtained his bachelor's degree in German and History in 1988 from Augustana College in Sioux Falls, SD, and Master's degree in Second Languages and Cultures Education from the University of Minnesota in 1992. Prior to his current position, David taught German for seven years at Brookwood High School in Gwinnett County, where he also served as department chair. He is an active member of the National Association of District Supervisors of Foreign Language, American Council on the Teaching of Foreign Languages, Association for Supervision and Curriculum Development, American Association of Teachers of German and serves on the Executive Board of the Foreign Language Association of Georgia.

Michael Langner

Michael Langner, Dr. phil., is University Lecturer (Lehr- und Forschungsrat / Maître d'Enseignement et de Recherche) at the bilingual University of Fribourg (Switzerland) and director of the self-access center for language learning (Mediathek). He was a research assistant of German Linguistics at the University of Geneva (Switzerland) and taught German as a foreign language for 14 years at the University of Fribourg (Switzerland). He is responsible for language policy of the University of Fribourg. His major research interests are bi-/multilingualism, evaluation of online-/offline-language materials (CD-ROMs and Internet), concepts of autonomy.

Betty Lou Leaver

Betty Lou Leaver (Ph.D., Pushkin Institute, Moscow) is Director of the Coalition of Distinguished Language Centers, Senior Consultant for Curriculum and Faculty Development at the American Councils for International Education, and an international educational consultant. She has been president of the American Global Studies Institute, dean of the Schools of Slavic and East European Languages at the Defense Language Institute, and Russian/Ukainian Language Training Supervisor at the Foreign Service Institute. She has more than 100 publications, most of them in the area of language pedagogy, particularly in the areas of content-based instruction, task-based instruction, faculty development, and attaining very high levels of proficiency.

Maria D. Lekic

Dr. Maria D. Lekic is associate professor of Russian at the University of Maryland (College Park) and director of curriculum and test development at the American Council of Teachers of Russian in Washington, D. C. (USA). Dr. Lekic has published extensively on the study and teaching of Russian as a foreign language and is co-author or editor of several widely-used American textbooks of Russian, including Russian: Stage One (Live from Moscow!), Russian: Stage Three (Focus on Discourse), "Peers," and "Ogonyok." She is the director of "RussNet," and principal methodological advisor of CenAsiaNet. Professor Lekic has also led the development of the Business Russian Language-Learning Modules project for RussNet and the high school to college articulation project for ACTR in cooperation with the College Board, the pilot for the first internet-based curriculum and examination program for Advanced Placement in Russian.

Peter Lenz

Peter Lenz is a lecturer of German as a Foreign Language at the Centre of Foreign Language Teaching and Research at the University of Fribourg, Switzerland. His teaching focuses on pre-service and in-service teacher training. He has been actively involved in the European Language Portfolio project at a European and national level since 1998. Presently, he develops performance-oriented assessment instruments for French and English on behalf of the Swiss public school system.

Randall J. Lund

Randall J. Lund is Assistant Professor of German at Brigham Young University, where he is responsible for German teacher education and supervision of first-year German instruction. He received a Ph.D. in Second Languages and Cultures Education at the University of Minnesota. His research interests include listening, the acquisition of grammar, and teacher education.

Nicole Marx

Nicole Marx teaches German as a Foreign Language and organizes the German language programme for international-oriented degree programmes at the Technical University of Darmstadt, Germany. Her principle research interests include multiple language acquisition and technology-enhanced language learning.

Peter Merrill

Peter Merrill received a masters in linguistics and a doctorate in Slavic Languages from UCLA in the early 1980s. While at the University of Maryland in the 1980s he worked on Russian aspect and cognitive approaches to linguistics. In 1989 he moved to Phillips Academy in Andover, Massachusetts, where he is currently chair of the Russian Department. In the 1990s, his work focused on Russian language pedagogy, during which time he co-authored a national curricular framework and the Russian section of the National Standards project. He is currently involved in the development of a pilot program for advanced Russian, aimed at the high-school-to-college articulation problem. From 1996-1999, he was vice president of the American Council of Teachers of Russian, and president from 2000-2003.

Andreas Müller-Hartmann

Andreas Müller-Hartmann is a professor of American Studies and TEFL at the University of Education in Heidelberg, Germany. He is involved in a number of research projects focussing on the use of new media in foreign language learning and teaching. Apart from the project outlined in his contribution to this book, he is about to finish an ethnographic post-doc study on the integration of telecommunication into the foreign language classroom. He is also developing and evaluating a distance-learning M.A. primary TEFL course.

Terry A. Osborn

Terry A. Osborn, Ph.D., is on the faculty in the Department of Curriculum and Instruction, Neag School of Education, University of Connecticut. Dr. Osborn is co-editor of Critical Inquiry in Language Studies: An International Journal (Lawrence Erlbaum Associates) and editor of the Praeger Publishers Contemporary Language Studies series. He has authored or edited five books, including Critical Reflection and the Foreign Language Classroom, winner of the 2001 American Educational Studies

Association Critics' Choice Award. Dr. Osborn serves on the Executive Board of the International Society for Language Studies, and his work has appeared in Educational Foundations, Educational Studies, Foreign Language Annals, Language Problems and Language Planning, Multicultural Education, School Arts, and NECTFL Review. Dr. Osborn's research interests include culture and literature in the foreign language classroom, critical pedagogy, and interdisciplinary pedagogy.

Manfred Prokop

Manfred Prokop is Professor of German (emeritus) at the University of Alberta in Edmonton, Alberta, Canada. His main areas of research interest have been the methodology of second language learning and teaching, with special emphasis on learning and teaching strategies, and the dynamics of German language maintenance in Canada. He is co-editor of the "Zeitschrift für Interkulturellen Fremdsprachenunterricht".

Karen Sanders

Karen Sanders received a masters degree in adult education from the University of Oregon and has taught ESL in Oregon, Minnesota, Germany, and Alaska. Her current postition is operations manager for the Adult Basic Skills division at Portland Community College. She authored several publications on foreign language instruction.

Marita Schocker- v. Ditfurth

Marita Schocker- v. Ditfurth is a professor of Applied Linguistics and TEFL at the University of Education in Freiburg, Germany. She is currently involved in various research projects on language teacher education. Apart from the project outlined in her article for this book, she has conducted a longitudinal, ethnographic post-doc study in which she researched the effects of a learning environment for EFL student teachers that integrates the practicum as a core component. She is also developing and evaluating a distance-learning M.A. primary TEFL course.

Johanna Schwarz

Johanna Schwarz has been experimenting with portfolios since 1996. Currently, she is teaching at the Akademische Gymnasium Innsbruck and lecturing at The Institute for Teacher Training and School Research (ILS) , as well as at the German Department at Innsbruck University. She has several publications and numerous teacher training seminars about portfolios on her records.

Joseph Sheils

Joseph Sheils is Head of the Department of Language Education and Policy within the Directorate for School, Out-of-School and Higher Education of the Council of Europe in Strasbourg. His current activities in Strasbourg are concerned in particular with the development of policies for plurilingualism through a global approach to language education involving all languages in the curriculum. In addition, his Division is responsible for the European Language Portfolio, guidelines for relating examinations to the widely used six level scale in the 'Common European Framework of Reference for Languages', assisting countries with reviews of national language education policies, and education policies for minorities. His Council of Europe publications include a handbook on language teaching methodology and a contribution to the 'Common European Framework of Reference for Languages'.

Amy Snyder Ohta

Amy Snyder Ohta is Associate Professor of Japanese at the University of Washington's Department of Asian Languages and Literatures where she teaches applied linguistics, Japanese linguistics, and Japanese language. Dr. Ohta received her doctorate in Applied Linguistics from UCLA. Her recent book, Second Language Acquisition in the Classroom: Learning Japanese, is published by Lawrence Erlbaum Associates. Dr. Ohta's research interests are in the areas of classroom language learning and bilingualism.

Lee Wilberschied

Lee Wilberschied (Ph.D., The Ohio State University) is an Assistant Professor of Foreign and Second Language Education at University of Cincinnati. She works extensively with preservice and in-service teachers. Her research interests are the recruitment and retention of minority foreign and second language teachers, service learning, and teacher thinking.

Sharon Wilkinson

Sharon Wilkinson is Associate Professor of French and Coordinator of the Basic French Program at West Virginia University. She has been an active member of the research group discussions at the New Visions meetings in 1999 and 2000 and currently serves on the New Visions in Action Research Task Force. Her own research interests center on using qualitative techniques to deepen our understanding of the study abroad experience as a context for the acquisition of conversational skills and cultural insights.

Dieter Wolff

Dieter Wolff, born 1939, Professor of Applied Psycholinguistics at the University of Wuppertal. Research interests: bilingual education, second language comprehension, New Technologies and language teaching, learner autonomy. Co-editor and board member of "Neusprachliche Mitteilungen", "CALL", "Applied Linguistics". Vice-president of AILA (Association Internationale de Linguistique Appliquée), former president of GAL (Gesellschaft für Angewandte Linguistik). More than 200 publications on foreign language learning and teaching.

Helene Zimmer-Loew

Helene Zimmer-Loew has served as executive director of the American Association of Teachers of German since 1985. She holds a B.A. in German from Connecticut College, M.S. in Education from St. John's University, and a M.A. in German from Middlebury College. She has been president and chair of various national foreign language organizations, is a frequent speaker at conferences and contributor to professional publications, and is a recipient of several teaching awards.